Aspects of Teaching and Learning in Secondary Schools

The Open University *Flexible*
Postgraduate Certificate of Education

The readers and the companion volumes in the *flexible* PGCE series are:

Aspects of Teaching and Learning in Secondary Schools: Perspectives on practice

Teaching, Learning and the Curriculum in Secondary Schools: A reader

Aspects of Teaching Secondary Mathematics: Perspectives on practice

Teaching Mathematics in Secondary Schools: A reader

Aspects of Teaching Secondary Science: Perspectives on practice

Teaching Science in Secondary Schools: A reader

Aspects of Teaching Secondary Modern Foreign Languages: Perspectives on practice

Teaching Modern Foreign Languages in Secondary Schools: A reader

Aspects of Teaching Secondary Geography: Perspectives on practice

Teaching Geography in Secondary Schools: A reader

Aspects of Teaching Secondary Design and Technology: Perspectives on practice

Teaching Design and Technology in Secondary Schools: A reader

Aspects of Teaching Secondary Music: Perspectives on practice

Teaching Music in Secondary Schools: A reader

All of these subjects are part of the Open University's initial teacher education course, the *flexible* PGCE, and constitute part of an integrated course designed to develop critical understanding. The set books, reflecting a wide range of perspectives, and discussing the complex issues that surround teaching and learning in the twenty-first century, will appeal to both beginning and experienced teachers, to mentors, tutors, advisers and other teacher educators.

If you would like to receive a *flexible* PGCE prospectus please write to the Course Reservations Centre at The Call Centre, The Open University, Milton Keynes MK7 6ZS. Other information about programmes of professional development in education is available from the same address.

Aspects of Teaching and Learning in Secondary Schools

Perspectives on practice

Hilary Bourdillon and Anne Storey

The Open University

London and New York

First published 2002
by RoutledgeFalmer
11 New Fetter Lane, London EC4P 4EE

Simultaneously published in the USA and Canada
by RoutledgeFalmer
29 West 35th Street, New York, NY 10001

RoutledgeFalmer is an imprint of the Taylor & Francis Group

© 2002 Compilation, original and editorial matter,
The Open University

Typeset in Bembo by Bookcraft Ltd, Stroud, Gloucestershire
Printed and bound in Great Britain by TJ International,
Padstow, Cornwall

British Library Cataloguing in Publication Data
A catalogue record for this book is available from the British Library

Library of Congress Cataloging in Publication Data
A catalog record has been requested

ISBN 0–415–26080–9

Contents

Figures

Readings

Abbreviations

AST	Advanced Skills Teacher
BECTa	British Educational Communications and Technology Agency
BTEC	Business and Technology Education Council
CPD	Continuing Professional Development
DfEE	Department for Education and Employment (now Department for Education and Skills, DfES)
ERA	Education Reform Act
GCE	General Certificate of Education
GCSE	General Certificate of Secondary Education
GTC	General Teaching Council
GNVQ	General National Vocational Qualification
ICT	Information and Communications Technology
LEA	Local Education Authority
NCC	National Curriculum Council
NCVQ	National Council for Vocational Qualifications
NQT	Newly qualified teacher
NRA	National Record of Achievement
NVQ	National Vocational Qualification
Ofsted	Office for Standards in Education
PSHE	Personal, Social and Health Education programme
QCA	Qualifications and Curriculum Authority
SCAA	School Curriculum and Assessment Authority
SEN	Special Educational Needs
SGTC	Scottish General Teaching Council
TTA	Teacher Training Agency

Sources

Chapter 1　Reading 1.1 reproduced by permission of Garibaldi School, Mansfield. Figure 1.3 from the *Times Educational Supplement*, 15 December 2000, reproduced by permission of the Times Supplements Ltd.

Chapter 2　Figure 2.2 reproduced by permission of Bartley Green Technology College, Birmingham. Figure 2.6 reproduced by permission of the Qualifications and Curriculum Authority.

Chapter 3　Reading 3.3 reproduced by permission of the Teacher Training Agency.

Chapter 4　Reading 4.1 from Moon, B. (ed), *A Guide to the National Curriculum,* (2001), reproduced by permission of Bob Moon. Reading 4.2 by permission of Whitecross School, Lydney and John Sheppard.

Chapter 5　Diagram describing differentiation by permission of the British Educational Communications and Technology Agency (BECTa) (formerly NCET).

Chapter 7　Readings 7.1 and Figures 7.3, 7.4 and 7.6 by permission of the British Educational Communications and Technology Agency (BECTa). Figure 7.2 from Nicholls, G., *Learning to Teach*, (1999) Kogan Page by permission of Kogan Page Publishers. Figure 7.7 adapted from Leask and Pachler (eds), *Learning to Teach ICT in the Secondary School*, (1999), RoutledgeFalmer, reproduced by permission of International Thompson Publishing Services.

Chapter 8　Figure 8.3, from Wragg, E.C., *Classroom Teaching Skills*, (1984), Routledge, reproduced by permission of International Thompson Publishing Services. Figure 8.4 reproduced by permission of Kelvin Hall School, Kingston upon Hull.

Chapter 9　Figure 9.1 reproduced by permission of the Qualifications and Curriculum Authority. Figure 9.3 reproduced by permission of the Centre for Assessment Studies, Graduate School of Education, University of Bristol.

Chapter 13　Figure 13.3 from Hopkins, Ainscow and West, *School Improvement in an Era of Change* (1994), by permission of Continuum International Publishing Group. Figure 13.4 reproduced by permission of the National Foundation for Educational Research

Chapter 14   Figure 14.1 reproduced by permission of Usha Devi, Deputy Head, Adderley Primary School, Birmingham. Reading 14.1 from Blandford, S., *Managing Professional Development in Schools* (2000) RoutledgeFalmer, reproduced by permission of International Thompson Publishing Services.

Acknowledgements

The authors would like to acknowledge colleagues who have contributed to the production of *Aspects of Teaching and Learning in Secondary Schools: Perspectives on practice*.

Bob Moon, Ann Neesom and John Butcher for contributions to the writing of Chapter 9. John Butcher for a contribution to the writing of Chapter 2. Michèle Deane, for a contribution to the writing of Chapter 5. John Bryson and Penny Lewis for ideas and discussion relating to Part 2 of the book.

OU PGCE beginning teachers 1999 and 2000 for their reflections and willingness to learn.

Foreword

The nature and form of initial teacher education and training are issues that lie at the heart of the teaching profession. They are inextricably linked to the standing and identity that society attributes to teachers and are seen as being one of the main planks in the push to raise standards in schools and to improve the quality of education in them. The initial teacher education curriculum therefore requires careful definition. How can it best contribute to the development of the range of skills, knowledge and understanding that makes up the complex, multi-faceted, multi-skilled and people-centred process of teaching?

There are, of course, external, government-defined requirements for initial teacher training courses. These specify, amongst other things, the length of time a student spends in school, the subject knowledge requirements beginning teachers are expected to demonstrate or the ICT skills that are needed. These requirements, however, do not in themselves constitute the initial training curriculum. They are only one of the many, if sometimes competing, components that make up the broad spectrum of a teacher's professional knowledge that underpin initial teacher education courses.

Certainly today's teachers need to be highly skilled in literacy, numeracy and ICT, in classroom methods and management. In addition, however, they also need to be well grounded in the critical dialogue of teaching. They need to be encouraged to be creative and innovative and to appreciate that teaching is a complex and problematic activity. This is a view of teaching that is shared with partner schools within the Open University Training Schools Network. As such it has informed the planning and development of the Open University's initial teacher training programme and the *flexible* PGCE.

All of the *flexible* PGCE courses have a series of connected and complementary readers. The *Teaching in Secondary Schools* series pulls together a range of new thinking about teaching and learning in particular subjects. Key debates and differing perspectives are presented, and evidence from research and practice is explored, inviting the reader to question the accepted orthodoxy, suggesting ways of enriching the present curriculum and offering new thoughts on classroom learning. These readers are accompanied by the series *Perspectives on practice*. Here, the focus is on the application of these developments to educational/subject policy and the classroom, and on the illustration of teaching skills, knowledge and understanding in a variety of school contexts. Both series include newly commissioned work.

This series from RoutledgeFalmer, in supporting the Open University's *flexible* PGCE, also includes two key texts that explore the wider educational background. These companion publications, *Teaching, Learning and the Curriculum in Secondary Schools: A reader* and *Aspects of Teaching and Learning in Secondary Schools: Perspectives on practice*, explore a contemporary view of developments in secondary education with the aim of providing analysis and insights for those participating in initial teacher training education courses.

Hilary Bourdillon – Director ITT Strategy
Steven Hutchinson – Director ITT Secondary
The Open University
September 2001

Introduction

The agenda of modernization in all phases of education, linked to a push for improved national standards of achievement from pupils, unfolded in *Teachers: meeting the challenge of change* (1998) and confirmed in subsequent documents and initiatives in the years since, has impacted in radical ways upon teachers and pupils in schools. New procedures, opportunities, evaluation processes, and a vast expansion of e-communication and information systems, have been put into place with rapidity and detail.

This period of exciting and extremely fast-paced change has seen new professional development openings for teachers at every level of experience. The continued expansion of curriculum development work in Key Stage 3, enhanced inclusion, core skills and citizenship dimensions of the secondary curriculum, and the restructuring of A level syllabuses and examination structures, have all demanded focused effort and development strategies from teachers trying to meet learning achievement targets alongside the wider needs of their pupils.

Beginning teachers, engaged in training and education in HE institutions or in schools themselves, are entering a quite different professional world from the one they would have encountered only a decade earlier. The standards and requirements of entry are testing and numerous. The personal and social skills demanded of them by pupils, parents, government agencies, and by employers, are exceptionally far-reaching.

The chapters of this book have been devised to inform and to raise issues and debates relating to the professional work life of beginning, and more experienced, teachers in secondary schools. It is intended to make a contribution to supporting, in practical ways, individuals seeking to engage with the debates about teaching and learning within the contexts which currently define and determine educational priorities and policy. Yet this is not simply a book which covers the latest initiatives. Given the current pace of educational change, that would be a somewhat redundant task. Rather, what we have aimed to distil in these chapters are the core skills, knowledge and understandings which have been developed by teachers and about which there is consensus and to set them alongside more enduring educational debates. Our chapters draw from research into teacher development, with the aim of encouraging the reader to connect the debates explored here with their own professional knowledge and to respond creatively to them.

Part 1, Contexts for teaching and learning, consists of four chapters and addresses issues relating to teachers' curriculum understanding, teachers' subject knowledge, and matters related to language and learning. Chapter 1 focuses on the changing national context of teaching and learning relating to England and Wales and is intended, as its title suggests, as an introduction to the nature and implications of the twenty-first century's challenge of change to teachers in these countries. This context of change also applies in general terms, however, to other areas of the UK. Although many of the details offered in this book relate to teachers in England and Wales (Scotland and Northern Ireland making separate provision), nevertheless, the key issues and challenges underpinning the detail are largely commonly owned.

Part 2, The practice of teaching and learning, is substantial and its eight chapters focus on central areas of a teacher's practice. Its core elements of planning, methodology, ICT-use, management, assessment, inclusion strategies, and wider role dimensions, are presented both as aspects to examine and ones to be implemented in classrooms and reviewed as one outcome, among many, of practice. This view of a teacher's 'practice' is predicated upon key assumptions: it is actively reflective; informed by research in the classroom; has at its heart the view of teacher as a leader-learner within a community of colleagues and pupils which seeks to do better, to do it humanely, and with a place for everyone.

Part 3, Developing as a professional, examines in two chapters issues and practical perspectives about a central endeavour of teachers, that of making a contribution to effective and improving schools. It explores, too, the career-long means available to teachers to do this: professional development.

The three sections in this book are linked to the idea that teaching is a complex intellectual and practical exercise. One of society's most valuable roles, that of educating its youth and thereby influencing its future, requires imagination, enquiry and, above all, the flexibility to learn from pupils and colleagues. Teaching is not something which can be developed unproblematically simply by working alongside experienced teachers in schools or responding to the basic requirements of government or regional directives. This is not to undermine the importance of these influences, since both certainly have an appropriate place, but rather it is to locate teacher development at the heart of an interconnnected web of influences and competing considerations. At the centre of this web is the day-to-day practice which happens in schools: the organization of the timetable, the length of the lessons, the layout of the classroom, the responses of pupils, the interactions between staff, and the links with the local community and beyond it. It is this practitioner knowledge, and its placement in relation to other compelling considerations which have an impact upon it, which we have attempted to articulate here. Our aim is to stimulate further discussion and practical exploration – that is, to put perspectives into informed practice.

Hilary Bourdillon and Anne Storey
Milton Keynes, September 2001

1 Contexts for teaching and learning

1 The changing national context of teaching and learning

Those who can, teach.
(TTA 2000/2001 advertising campaign)

Introduction

For the experienced classroom practitioner, few statements capture the new millennium's sea-change in attitude to teachers in schools by their assessors as much as the one that headlines this chapter on the changing national context of teaching and learning.

The three great Education Reform Acts of the twentieth century – in 1902, 1944 and 1988 – had a crucial and controversial impact on the structures and processes of teaching and learning in our schools. All were politically shaped and galvanized, and each was charged with a particular social vision. The details and procedures which accompanied them, to create the foundations for a national system of secondary education, for free secondary education, and for a national curriculum, respectively, provided the substance for each vision.

So, education, it might be argued, has not been short of visions. This though has not protected it from vacillating fortunes. Rather the reverse, since the creation of contesting visions has provided irresistible meat, particularly in the last decades of the twentieth century, for the manifestoes of multiple political parties anxious to be seen to be 'doing something' about education – and about society. Teachers, experienced or beginning, were undoubtedly hit hard during this period by political forces of both Left and Right in Britain. These opposing political forces both claimed educational terrain as a key arena for regular diagnosis, prescription and (initially) routine check-ups. The radical agendas of successive governments led to a ratcheting-up of what teachers were expected to be able to do in the classroom. This, allied to wider, social developments and demands impacting upon schools and teaching and learning processes, added to the professional obligations and role of teachers. During this period, the 'professionalism' of teachers, particularly in England, was caught up in an unsettling process of change, redefinition and dispute (Welch and Mahony 2000; Quicke 1998, 2000). This central debate continues and is an issue examined at different points in this book.

A new metaphor is appropriate here. Not a few teachers felt that they were, in effect, being de-professionalized (Hodkinson 1997; Golby 1998; Harris 1997), that they were not playing on a level pitch, that the goalposts were continually being moved, that new rules were created and withdrawn at will and that the referee was not neutral. No matter how hard they played, the outcome was predictable: they would lose. Too often, it was implied, if no longer given utterance: those who could would do something other than teaching for a career.

In the mid-1990s, for example, typical 'stories' even in the relatively temperate broadsheet newspapers were heavily critical in tone and language use, and 'Schools get their annual report: one in four must try much harder' and 'Blair leads "crusade" to oust bad teachers' represent this. These 1995 *Daily Telegraph* articles, sourced often by DfEE and by Ofsted reports, and mediated even more insistently particularly by the tabloid press at the time, overshadowed tangible and wide-ranging achievements in schools and did much to vitiate the sense of professional expertise owned by teachers. They nurtured, too, a prevalent view by media pundits that they could provide the solutions – if only teachers could be prevailed upon to work more intelligently/more critically/harder. A common view among many practitioners as a result of these sustained critical commentaries on their work was that teachers had become devalued in society.

So, contrast what is above with the sentiments and language of the statements below, publicly aired at the turn of the century, just five years on:

> teaching offers great intrinsic rewards, combining intellectual discipline with the chance to help shape lives. *But there are many other rewarding careers.*
> *We must meet the competition head-on* so that teaching recruits the high fliers it needs
>
> (DfEE 1999a, original emphasis)

and the progress report by the Chief Executive of the Teacher Training Association (TTA), expressing rising confidence about the issue of recruitment into teaching in that:

> in a buoyant economy and competitive recruitment market, [there has been] an eight per cent rise in recruitment to all teacher training routes compared with 1999/2000

which included details of:

> the launch of our recruitment campaign for 2001/02 applications, during which we are developing better tracking and *customer care* so that more high quality enquirers are converted into firm applications.
>
> (TTA 2001, emphasis added)

A great deal had happened in the few years that separated these differing responses to teachers, their value and their role.

During the two decades that preceded the headlines from 1995 referred to above, teaching, teachers and their educating institutions had become subject to increasingly formal checks on the processes and content of their work. It is an explanation of these most recent, telling changes of the late 1990s and an exploration of the opportunities available to teachers in post and others who are beginning teaching or considering teaching as one career within the range of options available, that will provide a key focus of this introductory chapter of *Aspects*.

Component parts of this exploration and explanation will be:

- further detail of the impact of change upon teachers in the last quarter of the twentieth century
- wider opportunities and rewards for teachers
- the changing nature of leadership in schools
- the role of the General Teaching Council in the professional lives of teachers.

The impact of change upon teachers in the final quarter of the twentieth century

The agenda of change

The DfEE statement in the introduction to this chapter, taken from its Fast Track literature, differed markedly from much that had gone before in the closing years of the century. They pointed to a recognition that teaching is (or ought to be, if it is not) demanding, potentially dynamic in its effect on children's lives, yet was but one of many challenging career paths available to able teachers. A stable, capable and confident teaching workforce needed to be recruited and retained. The process, it became increasingly evident, needed to be managed in an assertive and systematic way. It is no secret that recruitment and retention issues have to be assessed along with the demands and levels of remuneration tied to a career. Much of the new language needed and currently espoused by teachers' employers is a result of the same market-economy logic used to drive through many recent educational changes. It has its own sting: teachers who are multi-faceted, multi-skilled and people-aware, currently in post or being trained to take up posts, are valuable human resource assets in other career niches too. The much-vaunted and valued organizational capital of emotional intelligence, is possessed and practised daily by successful teachers. The language of blame, directed at teachers and evident in the headlines common in the 1980s and early 1990s, had been replaced in significant measure with other tones and arguments by a government which asked in 1997 and in 2001 to be judged particularly on what it managed to achieve in its educational reform agenda.

Moreover, on projections made in 2000, 50 per cent of the current teaching workforce, it was estimated, will have retired by 2010 (Storey 2000). Recruitment drives, even if they successfully meet their targets through bursaries and diverse training programmes, will not replace these lost numbers. Governments of any persuasion, then, are faced with a conundrum: the expectations of the electorate have been expanded in terms of what educational practice can do to raise achievement in schools; at the same time, the market-economy argument has percolated to beginning teachers and potential future teachers so that much more is required by them in terms of work environment, pay, prospects and overall competitive edge to persuade them to choose teaching as one of many other aggressively canvassed career options on offer in a buoyant employment sphere. It is interesting to note, in this connection,

Haydn's research which indicates that friendly colleagues and intellectual challenges are more important to sixth-formers considering a teaching career than a good starting salary. This finding clearly makes any one simple strategy targeted to the recruitment and retention issue a risk-taking one (*TES* 2000a).

The traditional characterization of a teacher then, held in idealistic moments by 'society', as a dogged purveyor of enduring principles, struggling to get by on poor pay but strengthened by a sense of vocation was, inevitably perhaps, overlaid with another template – one that showed a decisive action-taker, managing change, leading it and receiving realistic rewards appropriate to the marketplace. Latterly, principles and vision, a belief in the life-changing capacity of the teacher who makes a difference to children and their futures, has been added to what was criticized by teachers and their professional associations as an overly mechanistic approach to what teaching must be about, whether set in a national or global context. Arguably, a new realism that combined rigour, creativity and a moral dimension with benefits and career paths, and what happens in real classrooms with secondary pupils, became visible. The DfEE rationale for Fast Tracking, to guide competent classroom practitioners to speedy rewards and greater and faster responsibility for leading others in teaching, became a metaphor for change and new flexible routes during this period.

Fast-track details indicated some of the urgency of delivering the 1998 vision. Results, in terms of recruitment, retention, pupil progress, teaching and learning environments, the status and career opportunities of teachers, the life-chances of pupils, the kinds of leadership required for new (global) times and the career-long professional development of teachers, were all needed in place quickly, simply so as to compete with other markets. This meant meeting successfully the public agenda issues of national literacy and numeracy targets, ICT achievement, building on primary school gains in secondary schools, having creative, enquiring professionals working together in groups and sharing good practice, and expanded leadership groups to help to galvanise more change and to manage it productively. If 'our vision for teaching is of a modern, forward-looking profession determined to produce results' … 'for a world class education system' (Figure 1.1) then, clearly, much would rest upon how teachers interpreted the support, challenge and stimulation offered by their Fast-track (or other similar-variant) colleagues, the education and training opportunities available to themselves, ensuing benefits for their pupils, and realistic salaries. Beginning teachers can be heartened, though, that the less positive impacts of recent past history have receded. What is certain is that all political parties and governments will continue to see education as both an exciting challenge and a deeply worrying issue since it touches so many aspects of social, and therefore political, life.

Recent history and the changing nature of teaching

The post-Second World War working arrangement between teachers, other professionals and the state was mutually beneficial. The professions provided the means for the implementation of government policy in areas such as social welfare and they themselves were a source of expertise on which the state could draw to legitimate its power and its reforming policies. Allied with this post-war settlement

Fast-trackers have

- A strong commitment to and talent for teaching.
- Academic strength and subject knowledge.
- The ability to communicate, to inspire their pupils, and their colleagues.
- The ability to lead them.
- The ambition to make a lasting impact on their pupils, their schools and their communities.

Fast-trackers will be suitably rewarded and supported in their work

- The core of the fast track will run up to the performance threshold.
- They would be expected to cross the threshold within five years.
- To stay on the fast track, teachers will have to demonstrate that they are turning their exceptional potential into exceptional performance.
- Some teachers will decide that the fast track is not for them. Some will fall short of the rigorous standards demanded … .

After Fast-track

- An expectation of progress to Advanced Skills Teachers (AST) posts.
- Some fast-track teachers will not see teaching as a career for life. A recognition that some will want to move on to pursue other careers, in education or elsewhere.
- Some teachers will take time out from their teaching career to pursue other interests, and gain wider experiences, before returning to teaching.
- Some will move to the top of the profession, as headteachers or Advanced Skills Teachers, and then take their skills on to other highly skilled management or professional posts.
- Some will want to teach only for a limited time.

Cross-fertilisation

- Greater movement between the school system, the wider education service and the rest of society will strengthen links and encourage cross-fertilisation of ideas.
- This will help to raise the status of the teaching profession, and encourage high-quality graduates to enter teaching as a profession that widens – not restricts – their career horizons.

Figure 1.1 Fast-track rationale and details

Source: DfES wesbsite www.dfes.gov.uk

was the strengthening of the professional associations and the trade unions. For a time the state was content to negotiate on a collective basis with these representative bodies. At one point, indeed, in 1960, the Minister of State for Education was averring that 'of course Parliament would never attempt to dictate the curriculum, but from time to time, we could, with advantage, express views on what is taught in schools and in training colleges' (Whitty 1989). But this state of affairs was not to persist. The system came under challenge most notably and strongly with the Thatcher era (1979–90) and the application of 'the market' to ever-increasing segments of former state bureaucracies.

With the strong mandate that followed the defeat of Callaghan's Labour government after the 'winter of discontent' in 1979, the new Conservative government, with a widely proclaimed radical agenda, set about rolling back trade union power and state bureaucracies. During this time, 'consensus' became a term of some scorn. A series of occupational groups was confronted and faced down; these included steelworkers, coalminers, firefighters and teachers. Compulsory competitive tendering and internal market mechanisms were used in order at least partially to dismantle traditional arrangements in local government and the health service. Fully versioned privatization was implemented in whole swathes of erstwhile public sector areas including, as a surprise to many, the oft-assumed natural public monopolies such as water, gas and electricity.

The state education system was, in such a context, an inevitable target for change and in the struggle which was to follow the concept of 'teacher professionalism' itself was severely tested. The strike actions and working-to-rule by teachers in the mid-1980s heightened the sense that education and those who controlled it were core political issues. Value for money and accountability became new touchstone concepts. The introduction of the National Curriculum, and in England and Wales, of school inspections by Ofsted, Key Stage testing, the publication of results and league tables as indications of a school's performance, and appraisal systems were, it is argued, some of the control systems placed upon teachers and schools to check power and to produce improved levels of consistency in educational achievement. Nor was the new agenda simply a temporary phase to be thrown into reverse by a change of government. New Labour pressed ahead with many of the same ideas and mechanisms. Familiar versions of professionalism in teaching, based on notions of autonomy, individual creativity, and resistance to state interference in matters of curriculum or methods, became the source of prolonged confrontation with a series of governments intent on driving through far-reaching changes relating to consistency and higher standards in an education system.

Performance management systems, to include appraisal, classroom observations and quality-control systems to ensure consistency in a nationally provided service came next – along with a new career structure, better pay for good performers and the notion of career-long professional development to support a newly-versioned educational agenda.

The 1998 Green Paper proposals for reforms in teaching and learning

The Fast-track references, mentioned several times in this chapter, embodied a great deal of what the 1998 Green Paper proposals were about, and these were confirmed and expanded in the 2001 Green Paper, *Schools: Building on Success*. Rapid change and its management were at the heart of the programme for the 'imperative' modernization programme described in these publications. In 1998, teachers were urged to join the government's crusade, launched in its 1997 *Excellence in Schools* White Paper, to provide top-quality education consistently offered to pupils, and by so doing to raise achievement in schools. Nothing less than a 'world class education system', internationally recognized and valued, was to be sought. Old structures, particularly those which had appeared overly weighted to rewarding experience and continuity at the expense of flair and innovative approaches and which had not remunerated talented classroom practitioners in fair measure compared with management positions in teaching, were to be re-versioned.

The rationale for radical change was that 'the present reality of teaching too often compares unfavourably with the growing range of alternative careers for successful graduates' (DfEE 1998: 16, para. 14). This 'reality' touched other spheres of educational life. Cutting-edge schools, for example, were seen as too isolated from other school institutions which could benefit from planned contact. The bureaucratic burden on teachers was described as too large and many administrative tasks well able to be undertaken by support staff or by mechanical means. Working conditions were judged to be 'below the standard which well-qualified graduates in other fields take for granted' (ibid: para. 22).

Support was to be directed to these areas of concern and to pay structures, which were described within a performance management system which comprised appraisal, professional development and better career opportunities. Four major strands of the modernization plan, incorporating better leadership, better rewards, better training, better support and new possibilities, were outlined and the better training facet of the scheme was directed to 'a career of learning' to facilitate the teaching and learning gains envisaged. Chapter 14 addresses this aspect of teaching-learning life in detail. What is notable is that within two years of these proposals, over 80 per cent of eligible teachers had applied for assessment for threshold-competence teaching posts, responding to the new career structure on offer.

Wider opportunities and rewards for teachers

From 2000, differential pay for exceptional performance was deployed as a deliberate strategy to provide leaders, and successful approaches to teaching and learning for all schools through active dissemination, practical impacts and improved pupil performance. Fast-track teachers (the term will undoubtedly change and the role certainly has connecting functions with that of Advanced Skills Teachers) are essentially viewed as catalysts in the move to modernization. Their role is to agitate, provoke, support, challenge and provide practical insights into what might have been seen as intractable problems in the teaching and learning dynamic.

Figure 1.1 summarizes the rationale and the expected outcomes of their influence. Again, the acknowledgement that alternative career paths are available to such talented practitioners is stated. Significant, too, is the recognition that teaching might employ them for less than a career-span of time. This is turned into a positive: such capable entrants can be welcomed on this basis.

The 'cross-fertilization' referred to is, by definition, a connecting process. Other talented workers from different professions, it was argued, would be more likely to enter into teaching after a period of time elsewhere, if conditions and the duties attached to it were appropriate.

Advanced Skills Teachers (ASTs), expanded as a group and pressed as a force for rapid and productive change in and between schools in the 1998 Green Paper, were placed firmly in the Fast-track framework. Outreach work, a 20 per cent allocation of their teaching time, was designed to help to support and develop teaching and learning in other schools, after, in some cases, a first year of this allocation being directed to their own school's development. The impact of 'a teacher who has passed a national assessment and been appointed to an AST post' was clearly potentially a tangible one. Such posts would enable 'excellent teachers to concentrate on using and sharing their skills in classroom teaching' (DfEE literature). This was no mean advance in thinking in a profession in which traditionally large numbers of the best practitioners had often been dispersed to better-paid (largely non-teaching) management posts.

The changing nature of leadership in schools

The ultimate outcome of the modernization drive will, one argument goes, succeed or fail in relative measure to the quality of the leadership that attends it. The 1998 Green Paper acknowledged this:

> All the evidence shows that heads are the key to a school's success. All schools need a leader who creates a sense of purpose and direction, sets high expectations of staff and pupils, focuses on improving teaching and learning, monitors performance and motivates the staff to give their best.
>
> (DfEE 1998: 23, para. 36)

> The best heads are as good at leadership as the best leaders in any other sector, including business.
>
> (ibid)

In this document, heads were charged with overseeing the performance management and appraisal processes in their own school; the *Technical Consultation Document* which closely followed it outlined further details of how this would be managed (DfEE 1999b). A broader leadership group would enable heads to meet the stringent requirements for their re-shaped role – one of leading as well as managing change to secure higher standards of achievement, particularly since 'shared leadership responsibility is a characteristic of successful heads' (DfEE 1998: 25, para. 48). Assistant heads and ASTs would join the leadership group, to drive through the training, support, rewards and performance management elements outlined. They were reminded of

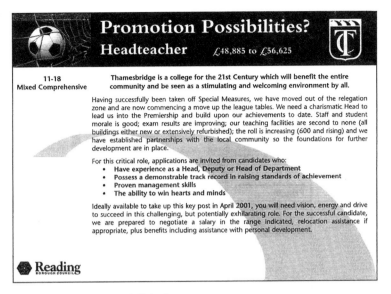

Figure 1.2 Promotion possibilities?

Source: Adapted from 'TES' 22 December 2000.

the standards agenda set in the 'Excellence in schools' initiative and the declaration there that 'our goal is that every school should be excellent, improving or both' (ibid: 22, para. 37). Heads were expected to determine the nature of the 'new professionalism' advocated (ibid: 13, para. 11), and to make links and partnerships with business so as to gain 'an outside perspective' (ibid: 22, para. 38). The National College for School Leadership, its virtual college, fast-tracking towards headships, movement of outstanding heads to other schools to help them to innovate and raise standards, were other aspects of this part of the framework. Moreover, the leadership potential of all teachers needed to be identified and used at an early stage of their careers – an issue taken up in the final chapter of this book.

The sense of urgency to produce all-round better standards of training, 'professionalism', leading innovation, securing rapid enhancements of teaching and learning in the classroom became a refrain. The pressure for good leadership in education quickly transmitted itself to descriptions of what such leaders were seen to be and could do. It was a tall order. The advertisement in Figure 1.2 which appeared in the *Times Educational Supplement* was one example which sought such a leader.

The head required here would be 'charismatic', with 'the ability to win hearts and minds' and would need 'vision, energy and drive' in this 'challenging but potentially exhilarating role'.

This is a school seeking to succeed, is 'improving', has had investment in its physical fabric and its teaching facilities 'are second to none'; moreover, 'staff and student morale is good'. The proposed salary range is sound for such a post and there is willingness to negotiate within the range indicated. Relocation and personal development assistance is available. There is much here that is attractive to potential candidates.

Yet there are elements to prompt caution, too, perhaps. The football metaphor is revived here in a different guise and for the purpose of signalling that what might seem possible in visions of success on the field of sport is as appropriately relevant in the domain of academic endeavour. The school has been 'moved out of the relegation zone'. It is 'commencing a move up the league tables.' The new head is needed 'to lead us into the Premiership' and the headline 'Promotion Possibilities' is double-weighted in value. The goal-in-the-net illustration completes the meaning.

Two elements of significance emerge here: first, that, arguably, the clear association of a new reforming head with a football manager is not entirely unladen in the UK with associated meanings. The world of football, and notably the England team, is littered with the names of hopefuls (exclusively male) who failed to 'deliver' their team's winning goals quickly enough. Second, all heads, male or female, cannot be like this. There are many routes to effective leadership. Some common threads uniting successful heads are indeed identifiable, but the emergence of a thrusting prototype, for example, may deter talented practitioner-leaders, as may the expectation of rapid success in challenging schools – one expectation of the unsuccessful SuperHead scheme, tried in the late 1990s.

But success stories there have been, and in sufficient numbers to encourage and enthuse, but insufficient, currently, to fill all leader-headteacher positions in the secondary sector. Education Action Zone schools and City Academies, both developments of the modernization programme to raise standards (the latter a reformulation of Fresh Start Schools), require talented, resilient leaders yet are statistically likely to attract fewer applicants than a Beacon School, a best performing school, judged by attainment and inspection evidence and other factors.

Yet it is well to acknowledge in this era of quality control (Storey and Hutchinson 2001) that individuals *still* enter teaching for the sense of a job well worth doing, and for other elements of personal satisfaction and ambition, as well as the requirement of a fair remuneration for their skills and personal attributes.

In these respects, the Schools Plus Policy Action Team, one of 18 teams set up by the Social Exclusion Unit in 1998, to reduce failures in school and using schools as a focus for other community services and activities, had a great deal to commend it. These schools, sited in socially disadvantaged areas, had real stories to tell and their enduring gains will not be the result of quick fixes – however needful these are in some respects. Indeed, a number of the key heads involved here were working for accumulative change in their schools within the community for a significant amount of time before the creation of the Policy Action Team (PAT). Reading 1.1 gives some indications of their achievements, exemplified by Garibaldi School, Mansfield.

It is a difficult dilemma for any government to solve; parts of some initiatives in the secondary sector *have* achieved success, over time and by different routes; the challenge of providing consistently high levels of teacher and pupil performance nationally remains, for reasons indicated earlier. The pressure for rapid success has been exciting. It has also been daunting, where best efforts have been applied previously

Reading 1.1 Schools and communities: working for change

Garibaldi School, Mansfield

What was it like?

In 1989, when the current head took over Garibaldi School the picture was one of:

- Derelict buildings
- £42,000 spent per year as a result of vandalism
- Third lowest GCSE pass rate in Nottinghamshire
- 580 pupils, a sixth form of eight pupils
- 50 pupils leaving each year to go to another school
- Very low levels of parental involvement
- Difficulty in recruiting teachers
- A school parents did not want to send their children to.

What was done to change it?

- Flattened management structure – no heads of faculties
- Collaborative arrangements with FE college for the vocational training of adults and students – extending the range of courses on offer
- Needed to get people, especially parents, into the school. Changing perception of school
- Much improved customer care programme to make first contact 'welcoming and friendly'
- Half a day a week for a teacher to go out into community and talk to parents and others about what school was doing – finding out what parents thought school was doing well and badly;
- Marketing school in community – including introduction of uniform
- Breakfast Clubs for pupils and parents to meet teachers informally
- Parenting courses, volunteer training, help with numeracy and literacy courses undertaken by Garibaldi and its feeder primary schools – most leading to initial qualifications and later NVQs
- Incentive schemes for pupils – including luncheon vouchers. These were just a wider part of a reward system which was initially funded through industry
- Opening up the sixth form to adults – with new Under Fives' block offering childcare. Further Education Funding Council (FEFC) funding
- Drop-in IT centre for adults: 9.00am–9.00pm
- Working with industry
- Community Award evenings
- Huge increase in administrative staff (eight full-time secretaries) because of the additional work to relieve teachers of burden, and

extra funding into school through additional activities pays for this. Extra funding was raised by having an 'entrepreneurial culture'

- Job Centre outpost on the premises
- 'Virtual organization' of courses in venues across the town offering courses to parents and students in literacy, parents as classroom assistants and ICT FEFC funding
- organization of courses for parents in the five feeder primary schools. These link to national initiatives (e.g. literacy and ICT) – FEFC funded.

What is it like now?

- Well equipped school – new maths block; all-weather pitch; three computer rooms; new sports hall; fitness room – all built with self-help schemes and now fully open to the community
- A*–C rates for GCSE approaching national average – now 52 per cent maths GCSE at A*–C
- 1,100 pupils on roll
- 180 in sixth form.

Source: Schools Plus Policy website at www.dfee.gov.uk/schoools-plus/

and not generated, unlike the example above, gains in achievements that are systematically measurable. The root-and-branch reforms that attempt to link school, community and development, to reduce truancy and exclusion rates, as in the example in Reading 1.1, have meshed to produce real challenges for teachers at any stage of their career, whether beginning teachers or leaders of them.

Clearly then, in such demanding times, all teachers need support and challenge in a balanced whole that enables them to feel able to tackle the duties attached to their professional lives, teaching their subject and meeting wider professional obligations that 'make a difference'. Schools are tightly organized institutions with limited freedom to risk scarce resources on ventures which might fail. This is a key problem. Leaders are expected to innovate yet, whereas in the commercial world risk-taking and failing is accepted culturally, and costed-for, on the premise that if five innovatory approaches fail, the sixth might well be very successful, the culture of schools is necessarily more cautious for the sake of continuity, known and safer routes to success, and because young people and their futures are involved. High-risk strategies have costs and the debates continue among leaders in education about the nature and impacts of these.

The organization which has promised much in terms of supporting teachers and their leaders to aspire to greater professional weight and status, through self-regulation and career-long professional development, is the General Teaching Council, an independent body for teachers and with which all teachers now register. Its initial policy statements made it clear that the time had come for teachers to seize the opportunities available to them to 're-professionalize'. It is an examination of this organization that provides the focus of the last substantive section of this chapter.

The role of the General Teaching Council in the professional lives of teachers

All teachers in English and Welsh schools are being encouraged to register with the General Teaching Council (GTC), the standards and disciplinary body for teachers. A Scottish General Teaching Council was established in 1965. Teachers' certificates have to be validated by this body and this is done automatically for a beginning teacher when she or he begins to work in a school. A small registration fee is also automatically deducted from the earnings of all certificated teachers each year.

These rather pedestrian details disguise much drama and many set-backs for well over a century before the foundation of what has been described as 'a louder voice for teachers' (*TES* 2000b). The foundation itself, in England and Wales, came in September 2000; the chief aims were described as seeking to:

- raise the professional status and public standing of teachers
- provide an independent and influential voice for teachers
- maintain and guarantee high professional standards of teaching.

That the creation of this body had been so long in coming is, at the least, a source of interest and a statement about how, for an admixture of reasons, teachers' frequently-divided professional associations had largely failed to provide these benefits for their members in the recent historical perspective outlined in an earlier section of this chapter. It is worth citing here the chief points on the 'the long road to the GTC' (*TES* 2000b).

It has been one of the intentions of this chapter to indicate the intrinsic difficulty of achieving a sustained balance of the rights and responsibilities of the major (non-political) parties in education. It is clear that parents and their children have a right to be recipients of a high-quality, consistently-offered national education service. It is appropriate that the highest levels of endeavour should be offered by teachers and that they, in turn, should be given terms of employment which make a statement about parity with other multi-skilled professionals. It is apparent, too, that on a number of occasions, the electorate has baulked at paying increased levels of public taxation to secure the high levels of resourcing which would be needed to match the rhetoric of outlined ideals of recent governments. Nevertheless, it was clear that the 1998 and 2001 proposals made a statement about and a commitment to improvements in education, training, remuneration and restructuring not matched in the recent history outlined in this chapter. Radical change applied to ossified perspectives and dead-wood practices can indeed be beneficial. The debate centres on which perspectives and practices are ossified and these need to be weighed with the interest of pupils in organizations whose work is about routines, continuity and stable communities, where staffing is constant and professional adults behave fairly predictably and reliably, within the somewhat small elastic ranges of personality differences. From this view it is, then, inappropriate to dismiss lightly or politically one set of arguments vying with another. Many in the profession continue to look, then, to the General Teaching Council to be the body that will help teachers and others to resolve these competing and legitimate claims.

1862   College of Preceptors proposes a 'scholastic council'.

1879   Dr Playfair sponsors a Bill to Parliament and in 1889, a Select Committee considers two Bills.

1899   Education Act makes provision for setting up a register of teachers.

1901   Education Act lays a duty upon the Board of Education to establish a Teachers' Registration Council, but this is scuppered by difficulties between teachers and Robert Morant, the civil servant at the Board. The Council is abolished in 1906.

1910   First solo edition of the 'TES' calls for a professional organization and the establishment of a Teachers' Register.

1912   A voluntary Teachers' Registration Council is established, which becomes the Royal Society of Teachers in 1929.

1944   Education Act fails to make registration compulsory, and the Royal Society of Teachers is wound up by an Order in Council in 1949. The McNair Committee considers the principles of professional status, but this is ignored by Government.

1950s   Teachers' associations and civil servants such as John Maud and Derek Morrell keep the idea alive.

1959   English education ministers take it in turn to reject the idea: Tory minister David Eccles says no in 1959 and Labour minister Anthony Crosland is equally dismissive in 1965.

1965   A General Teaching Council is established in Scotland.

1968   Education minister Edward Short announces his intention to create a General Teaching Council in England but the Weaver report recommends two councils (separating registration and discipline) and the proposal fails again.

1972   James Committee on teacher training recommends a National Council for Teacher Education.

1978   Different groups take turns to support the concept of a General Teaching Council but the success of the idea rests with the teachers' associations, who begin meeting regularly this year.

1980   The Campaign for a General Teaching Council (CATEC) is set up at the instigation of Robert Balchin, treasurer of the College of Preceptors. Keith Joseph becomes Secretary of State for Education and Science. Balchin reports that 'Sir Keith Joseph finds himself totally out of sympathy with the kind of professionalism for teachers we support'.

1981   CATEC is wound up.

1983   Teachers' associations start again, and ask the Universities' Council for the Education of Teachers (UCET) to lead negotiations. The campaign inches forward.

1988   John Sayer publishes 'Towards a General Teaching Council', the fruits of a UCET/teachers' association working party.

1989   John MacGregor takes over at the Department of Education and Science and reveals his personal sympathy for the idea. The Education Select Committee recommends 'that the Government create a General Teaching Council to work for the profession', but the Government continues to be resolutely against the idea.

1990s   Detailed proposals now exist in print and a company is formed by the Forum of Associations. The UCET initiative ends and GTC (England and Wales) is created with John Tomlinson as chair. Every year sees a debate in Parliament. The National Commission on Education and a second select committee endorse the GTC; a private member's Bill is promoted by the Tory chair of the Select Committee, Sir Malcolm Thornton. Lobbying gains pace.

1998   The Teaching and Higher Education Act makes provision for the establishment of General Teaching Councils in England and Wales.

2000   The GTC (England and Wales) group dissolves itself, believing that the General Teaching Council will be the organization the profession has fought so long for.

Figure 1.3 The long road to the GTC

Source: 'TES' 15 December 2000.

The GTC's stated aims were designed to provide a balance of support and challenge to teachers and in so doing to help teachers themselves, rather than any other organization, to strengthen their professional status and to regulate the standards required of a professional body – the national standards of performance for teachers deemed to be effective at different stages of their career, from induction, through fast-tracking or some other variant, to threshold, to AST, to fuller leadership roles. The challenge remains one of balancing regulation and career-long professional development and support which the GTC has seen as a major route to enhanced professional status. Chapter 14 examines in detail the professional development support role of the GTC.

Within a standards framework for professional conduct and competency, cited by the GTC as the lynchpin to a revived professional status for teachers, will rest the fully-honed versions of models of teacher effectiveness, such as that supplied by Hay McBer in 2000 in a study of what effective teachers actually do in the classroom. One development here was a recognition that the context of teaching and differences among teachers are important, as well as standards of effectiveness. Effective teachers, like leaders, come in many varieties.

There emerged in this study, commissioned and funded by the government, a recognition that real life in classrooms – and this in many contexts – had to be part of any creditable assessment of what teachers need to do and how they do it. In tune with this, a model emerges of what being 'effective' can be taken to mean. Here it was tellingly given a much wider definition than hitherto.

It may also be argued that the report's descriptions of 'effectiveness' arising out of its study constituted a more realistic recognition about the need to look at the wider picture in terms of what a teacher actually does and ought to do in order to take future practice beyond the narrow confines of what practitioners and writers have characterized as trends to de-skilling. This Phase II Report (Hay McBer 2000) recognized that teaching is 'a cultural activity' (5.1.6.), that because of this 'changes in teaching practice can only take place over a long period of time' (6.2.3.), and that the 16 professional characteristics outlined 'do[es] not provide a one-size fits-all picture' (2.3.2.) since 'teachers are not clones'. The final chapter of this book returns to other aspects of this report.

Conclusion

The formulation of national standards, aligned to teachers' career stages, is part of the regulation responsibility of the GTC in relation to its registered members.

Ten years from now, of course, teachers will be better able to judge its achievements and, if arguments are advanced to moderate radical, fast changes to root as well as branch in the educational world, then the GTC might also present the view that an appropriate time-frame is essential to assess its own impacts on some key aspirations of teachers. Its own words in relation to an ITT education and training programme are typical of its ambitions for all teachers, beginning and experienced:

> The ITT framework needs to inspire and enthuse new teachers and those in higher education who support them – with a sense of what it means to be a professional and the challenges, rewards and commitment of being a teacher, today and in the future.
>
> (Carol Adams, Chief Executive, GTC 2000)

There is little doubt that more thought about the practical aspects of recruiting and retaining capable teachers, and the targeted schemes to reward teachers differentially at different phases of their career have been evidence of this. Attention during this period was also applied to shorter stays in teaching – not just for the struggling practitioner but for the very able too. Experience in other career fields was pressed as valuable in relation to new recruits to teaching; and the multiplicity of skills owned and demonstrated in action every day by successful teachers received a public recognition notably absent previously. Teachers, demonstrably so, transfer rich management and leadership capacities as well as the ability to multi-task that is valued and remunerated appropriately in other work spheres. Their 'can do' capabilities are patently visible in the flexible, team-working, problem-solving practices of the current work world.

It is to the detail and discussion of these 'can do' aspects of teaching and the challenges and rewards relating to them for beginning teachers that the following chapters of this book are directed.

References

DfEE (1997) *Excellence in Schools*, London.
—— (1998) *Teachers: Meeting the Challenge of Change*, London: The Stationery Office.
—— (1999a) *A Fast Track for Teachers: A Prospectus*, London: DfEE.
—— (1999b) *Teachers Meeting the Challenge of Change: Technical Consultation Document on Pay and Performance Management*, London: DfEE.
DfES (2001) *Schools: Building on Success*, Norwich: The Stationery Office.
Golby, M. (1998) Editorial, *Teacher Development* 2(3).
Harris, A. (1997) 'The deprofessionalization and deskilling of teachers' in K. Watson, C. Modgil and S. Modgil (eds) *Teachers, Teacher Education and Training*, London: Cassell.
Hay McBer (2000) *Research into Teacher Effectiveness: Phase II Report: A Model of Teacher Effectiveness*, London: Hay McBer.
Hodkinson, P. (1997) 'Neo-Fordism and teacher professionalism', *Teacher Development* 1(1): 69–82.
Quicke, J. (1998) 'Towards a new professionalism for new times: some problems and possibilities', *Teacher Development* 2(3): 323–38.
—— (2000) 'A new professionalism for a collaborative culture of organizational learning in contemporary society', *Educational Management and Administration* 28(3): 299–315.
Storey, A. (2000) 'A leap of faith? Performance pay for teachers', *Journal of Educational Policy* 15(5).
Storey, A. and Hutchinson, S. (2001) 'The meaning of teacher professionalism in a quality control era' in A. Shelton-Mayes and F. Banks, (eds) *Early Professional Development for Teachers*, London: RoutledgeFalmer.
TTA (2001) 'Annual Report', TTA.
Times Educational Supplement (*TES*) (2000a) 'Hope for recruiters', 22 December 2000.
—— (2000b) 'The long road to the GTC', 15 December 2000.
Welch, G. and Mahony, P. (2000) 'The teaching profession', in J. Docking (ed.) *New Labour's Policies for Schools*, London: David Fulton.
Whitty, G. (1989) 'The New Right and the National Curriculum: state control or market forces?', *Journal of Educational Policy* 4(4).

2 Teachers' curriculum understanding and the secondary school curriculum

Introduction

Curriculum understanding lies at the core of the teacher's classroom practice. This understanding takes different forms. Some of it is clearly propositional and is relatively easy to articulate. For example, part of the process of developing as a teacher is acquiring the common technical language used to describe the curriculum. The National Curriculum uses a particular terminology which is part of the daily repertoire of teacher discourse, such as Programmes of Study, Schemes of Work, Attainment Targets, or Level Descriptions, etc. Other aspects of curriculum understanding are implicit in the way teachers interact with their pupils, organize their lessons and carry out their wider professional role. This understanding is embedded within their action, and as such is more easily demonstrated than talked about.

In making sense of their lessons, in monitoring and shaping their classroom routines and behaviours, experienced teachers have access to a wide range of curriculum knowledge which they use to inform how they approach classroom situations, and which can help in interpretation and responses to them. Part then of teachers' professional knowledge is an understanding of the often competing and conflicting factors that shape and influence what is taught in schools, and how it is taught. Teachers' professional knowledge includes the development of their own views, grounded in a clear rationale, about how further curriculum development could be planned and implemented. This critical dimension of a teacher's work grows as s/he gains practical experience and think about the issues and ideas involved.

This chapter:

- introduces the beginning teacher to a range of definitions of curriculum;
- presents an overview of a history of the secondary school curriculum from the nineteenth century to the introduction of the National Curriculum and beyond;
- considers the development of the post-16 (post-compulsory) curriculum;
- explores approaches to curriculum organization and development in secondary schools.

Definitions of curriculum

The two extracts overleaf (Figures 2.1 and 2.2), written almost a hundred years apart, the one taken from the Day School Code of 1902 and the other taken from the prospectus of a large inner-city comprehensive school in 2000, give us two definitions of the school curriculum. There are, surprisingly or not, many similarities between the two. Both have core subjects which all pupils must take, and these core subjects cover the basic skills. Significantly there is a nuanced difference in the definition of these basic skills – a shift from an emphasis on arithmetic to mathematics and numeracy. There are also significant differences indicating the wider social changes which have taken place over the last century. The 'Curriculum Statement 2000' gives an emphasis to the principles of access and equality: that all pupils have the opportunity, regardless of gender, ethnicity or attainment, to follow the same curriculum. The latter curriculum statement is also clearly addressed to the pupils' parents.

These two extracts indicate the links between what is taught in school, and the form and function of education. They demonstrate links between the school curriculum and the labour market and society's 'vision' of the skills, knowledge and understandings adults, in, the twentieth or, in the case of the present-day curriculum statement, the new twenty-first century, require. In defining the school curriculum and the teachers' curriculum knowledge, we are defining more than subject titles. 'Curriculum' definitions also include values and attitudes. So, in the above statements about what should be taught in schools, the statement from 1902 draws a clear distinction between the curriculum for girls and the curriculum for boys, linked to the expectations about future employment and gender roles. The curriculum statement from the secondary school in 2000 emphasizes that the whole school curriculum is much more than the separate National Curriculum subjects to be taught, and that the aims of the curriculum, not just the content of the curriculum, need to be clearly stated. Here the emphasis is on entitlement and transparency, providing a curriculum which aims to provide all pupils with the same educational opportunities and making that curriculum explicit to parents.

Until the 1960s, however, the term 'curriculum' was not widely used in the UK. Here, most schools used the term 'timetable' rather than 'curriculum'. The concept of curriculum came to the UK from the USA where it had begun to take root in the 1920s and 1930s. Here the term was used by a number of writers not only to describe the subjects being taught, but also the methods used, the resources available and the wider environment in which the teacher had to work. Understanding and managing the curriculum, therefore, became more than knowledge and awareness of the knowledge base of a subject or subjects. These ideas gained common acceptance in the UK in the 1960s and 1970s. What is included in the curriculum and the principles underpinning the design of the school curriculum have been hotly debated terrain. Figure 2.3 gives a list of representative samples of the different emphasis given at different times over the past thirty years to the school curriculum.

As these definitions demonstrate, curriculum statements include assumptions about society's values and attitudes. For example, Hirst argues that a curriculum can be constructed on the basis of the nature of knowledge and makes academic knowledge the heart of the curriculum. This view would appear to match the

The Day School Code

Curricular requirements were laid down in some detail:

Course of Instruction Article 15

(i) The Course of Instruction for older scholars (i.e. 7+) is as follows (to be taken as a rule in all schools):

English, by which is to be understood reading, recitation, writing, composition, and grammar insofar as it bears upon the correct use of language
Arithmetic
Drawing (for boys)
Needlework (for girls)
Lessons including object lessons on geography, history and common things
Physical training

N.B. It is not necessary that all these subjects should be taught in every class. One or more may be omitted in any school which can satisfy the Inspector and the Board that there is good reason in its case for the omission.

For the purposes of Section 1(1)(a) of the Technical Instruction Act 1889, reading, writing and arithmetic are obligatory or standard subjects.

(ii) One or more of the following to be taken when the circumstances of the school, in the opinion of the Inspector, make it desirable:

Algebra	Euclid
Mensuration	Mechanics
Chemistry	Physics
Elementary physics and chemistry	Animal physiology
Hygiene	Botany
Principles of agriculture	Horticulture
Navigation	Latin
French	Welsh (in Wales)
German	Book-keeping
Shorthand	Domestic economy or domestic
Drawing (for boys)	science

(iii) For girls: cookery, laundry work, dairy work, household management. For boys: cottage gardening, manual instruction, cookery (for boys in seaport towns).

Figure 2.1   1902 Board of Education Regulations

Source: Board of Education, 1902.

Curriculum Aims 2000

The School curriculum endorses and builds upon the principles underlying the LEA's (i.e. Birmingham LEA) Curriculum Statement. We see the curriculum as representing all the learning experiences each student receives both through the formal and informal programmes and through the values and attitudes embodied in the stated aims of the school. These aims are:

- to ensure that the process of education is a partnership between the learners, the school and the parents, together with the government, employers and the community;
- to keep the child at the centre of this process;
- to strive to equalise the opportunities for each child to develop their talents to the fullest extent;
- to make the curriculum equally accessible to all students, raising their own expectations and society's expectations of them;
- to provide each student with the experience of challenging learning styles that value not only individual thinking, but also the collaborative skills of investigating, experimenting, discussing and communicating;
- to engender in each student a thirst for knowledge that will be enjoyed throughout her or his life.

Curriculum delivery

The curriculum for all our students achieves breadth and balance through the framework of the National Curriculum core and foundation subjects with extended learning experiences through cross-curricular themes.

It is delivered by Curriculum Teams each with their own co-ordinator.

The Curriculum Areas are: English, Mathematics, Science, Design Technology including Information Technology, Home Economics and Textiles; French, the Humanities, with Geography, History and Religious Studies; the Expressive Arts of Art and Design, Pottery, Music and Drama; and Physical Education.

These areas are all serviced by the Programmes of Study in Personal and Social Education and Careers Education, and the Pastoral and Supportive curricula, which are each led by a co-ordinator.

Sex Education is offered through teaching that complements and supports the role of parents and encourages students to have due regard to moral considerations and the value of family life. It is delivered across different learning programmes and is part of the Personal and Social Education Programme. In Years 7, 8 and 9 the content is centred on the National Curriculum Science Attainment Target 6 which looks at an understanding of the physical and emotional changes that take place during adolescence, the process of conception in human beings, and the need for a responsible attitude to sexual behaviour. In Years 9, 10 and 11 the moral and legal dimensions of current social issues are sympathetically addressed.

Figure 2.2 Curriculum Aims 2000 (Statement from Bartley Green Comprehensive School, Birmingham)

Definition A

A curriculum is a series of content units arranged in such a way that the learning of each unit may be accomplished as a single act, provided the capabilities described by specified prior units (in the sequence) have already been mastered by the learner.

(Gagné 1967: 79)

Definition B

The term 'curriculum' is, of course, used very variedly, but I shall take it to mean a programme of activities designed so that pupils will attain by learning certain specifiable ends or objectives. I do not wish to imply by this that a curriculum must be a programme or sequence of activities that is not to be changed in any respect by the pupils, that it must be completely determined by teachers. Nor do I wish to imply that curriculum activities are teachers' activities as distinct from the activities of pupils. I am concerned, of course, with both.

(Hirst 1974: 2)

Definition C

It (i.e. the curriculum) is a term which is used with several meanings and a number of different definitions of it have been offered … It will be helpful if we distinguish between the use of the word to denote the content of a particular subject or area of study from the use of it to refer to the total programme of an educational institution.

(Kelly 1989: 10)

Definition D

The emerging curricular concerns about gender equity, human sexuality education, racial and ethnic bias in hiring practices and classroom interaction, sexual orientation, minority representation, multicultural literature, cultural and civic literacy, and a litany of other volatile issues, remind us of the importance of integrating race, gender and ethnicity into the fabric of our understanding of curriculum development.

(Slattery 1995: 143)

Definition E

Actually, it isn't a cube. It's a multi-dimensional hyperspace, but the 'Multi-dimensional Hyperspace Curriculum' does not exactly have a ring to it … The argument put forward for the cubic multi-dimensional view of the curriculum is founded on a number of linked propositions. The first is that **education must incorporate a vision of the future** … . The second proposition is that **there are escalating demands on citizens** … . Coping with adult life in the future will require a mixture of personal, social and professional competence … . The third proposition implicit in the cubic curriculum is that if they are to

> manage the increasing complexity **children's learning must be inspired by several influences**. Important though subject matter is, in certain circumstances how something is learned may turn out to be as important as what is learned … . The fourth and closely related proposition … it is essential to see the curriculum as much more than a mere collection of subject syllabuses. The whole of what is experienced in schools and colleges can make an impact on those who attend them. This includes, among other factors, the subject matter being taught, the knowledge, skills and attitudes and patterns of behaviour being learned, the explicit and implicit values and beliefs in education, the form of teaching and learning which are employed.
>
> (Wragg 1997: 1–2)

Figure 2.3 Definitions of the school curriculum

emphasis given in the 1988 National Curriculum to subjects as the curriculum's organizing framework. Wragg's view of the curriculum has the needs of society, or the needs of the individual, as its starting point. 'Needs', however, is a value-laden term and defining an individual's or a society's needs in a pluralist society inevitably raises different interpretations and versions of what those 'needs' are. Should the school curriculum include elements of vocational training? What should be included in sex education and should this be a compulsory curriculum topic in secondary schools? What is the place of creative arts in the curriculum, and so on? These debates and considerations are an ongoing aspect of the teacher's work.

A further important point which emerges from these various definitions of the curriculum is that it is now commonly perceived in a broad sense to include all those aspects of school life and organization that affect teaching and learning, not just the content or syllabus. The way in which pupils are grouped – mixed attainment or setted; the organization of the timetable; the way school assemblies are run; the system of pastoral care to be found in a school and attitudes to school uniform are all part of the pupils' learning environment. These systems convey messages about what the school does and does not value. For example, having displays of pupils' work around the school and in the classroom is not just to make the room look attractive. A display provides a clear signal to the pupils that in this room their work is important, in this room learning is valued.

Importantly, the school curriculum is more than the National Curriculum which government departments and agencies are keen to stress should not be equated with the whole curriculum of a school. Regulations now require all maintained and foundation schools to have a school policy for the whole curriculum, formally promulgated by the school governors and made widely available to parents (see Figure 2.2).

More recently the term 'curriculum' has been extended to include the 'extra-curricular activities' which pupils experience outside the formal school timetable. These activities include work experience, after-school clubs, sporting activities, school journeys, homework clubs, etc.

Curriculum, in this broad definition, must therefore be the central concern of the school; the way it is designed, developed and reviewed is a key task at all levels of the education system. Understanding of this contemporary picture of the school curriculum is therefore rooted, in part, in the historical genesis of prevailing ideas.

The historical origins and recent antecedents of the secondary school curriculum

The nineteenth century to 1944

A history of the school curriculum provides insights into the ways in which schools reflect the values, interests and priorities of society and identifies some of the factors which have influenced change and which influence individual teachers' thinking about curriculum development.

> An educational curriculum, as we have seen again and again in past periods, expresses a compromise between an inherent selection of interest. At varying points in history, even this compromise may be long delayed, and it often will be muddled. The fact about our present curriculum is that it is essentially created by the nineteenth century, following some eighteenth century models and retaining elements of the medieval curriculum as well.
>
> (Williams 1975)

The curriculum, as Raymond Williams suggests, can only be understood in its historical context. Why certain subjects are taught, and how certain areas of the curriculum have become more important than others, are often the consequence of debates that stretch back into intellectual and political history.

The secondary curriculum found in schools today has its origins in the 'classical education' of the fee-paying public schools that flourished in the latter half of the nineteenth century. These schools were set up to provide an education (generally for boys) and organized their curriculum around the teaching of classics, political economy, mathematics and natural science. In some cases modern languages were taught. Arnold's Rugby School, for example, typified the development of an elite institution which took responsibility for the moral training of those going on to the government bureaucracy or the running of the colonies:

> These moral purposes made humanistic studies central in the curriculum. In the nineteenth and early twentieth centuries, the classics – particularly Greek and Latin literature, philosophy and history which were the main subjects of the prestigious Literae Humaniores degree course at Oxford – were regarded as the most important subjects.
>
> (Holmes and McLean 1989: 27)

The extension of secondary school provision to a wider population was made possible by the Education Act of 1902, and this was followed by fierce debates about the nature and content of what should be taught. Morant, the first Permanent Secretary

1904	1935	1988
English language	English language	English
English literature	English literature	
One language*	One language	Modern language (11–16 only)
Geography	Geography	Geography
History	History	History
Mathematics	Mathematics	Mathematics
Science	Science	Science
Drawing	Drawing	Art
	Physical exercises and organized games	Physical education
	Singing	Music
Due provision for manual work and physical exercises (housewifery in girls' schools)	(Manual instruction for boys, dramatic subjects for girls)	Technology
		(Welsh)

*'When two languages other than English are taken, and Latin is not one of them, the Board (of Education) will be required to be satisfied that the omission of Latin is for the advantage of the school.'

Figure 2.4 Compulsory curriculum subjects in 1904, 1935 and 1988

of the Board of Education, was determined that the new secondary schools should develop in the mould of public schools, teaching traditional subjects. The compulsory curriculum subjects laid down by the 1904 Code formed the basis of the secondary school curriculum throughout the twentieth century. Figure 2.4 sets out the subjects and juxtaposes the regulations pertaining in 1935 and the National Curriculum of 1988.

Morant won his struggle against those in government and the civil service who suggested that the curriculum should include some vocational elements. The 1904 Regulations laid down the grammar school curriculum and Figure 2.4 indicates a striking continuity in curriculum organization through the last century, despite the introduction of some radical education legislation like the 1944 Education Act, and despite heated debates in the 1960s and 1970s about the nature and form of the curriculum.

The evolution of the secondary curriculum 1944–88

Any notion of a prescriptive, state-imposed curriculum was, in the aftermath of the Second World War, viewed as an undesirable concept linked to totalitarian Fascist or Communist regimes. The consensus viewpoint on the curriculum was that teachers should have the freedom to determine the curriculum and methods of teaching. For nearly fifty years, the dominant piece of legislation affecting the conduct of schools was the 1944 Education Act. This act was held as being a radical piece of legislation, far-reaching in its provision of secondary education for all. As such, it provided the cornerstone of the Welfare State, yet it made no attempts to define the content of the primary or the secondary curriculum (Chitty 1996). In the period after 1944 until the 1988 Education Reform Act, schools had a great deal of freedom to make decisions about the structure and form of the curriculum, within certain limitations, such as the detailed syllabuses laid down by the examination boards for examinations at 16 and 18 and the influences exerted by the universities on the form and structure of the school curriculum at sixth-form level. Parental expectations also ensured that the majority of schools had very similar forms of curriculum.

This devolved and decentralized tradition did, however, generate a series of curriculum initiatives. A number of educational philosophers began to present arguments for the curriculum conceived of in terms of areas of experience. One of the leading protagonists of this view was Paul Hirst, whose views on the curriculum we have already referred to. Hirst argued that there was a finite and fairly small number of distinct 'forms of knowledge', each with its own concepts and its own ways of testing the claims it makes. The original 'forms of knowledge', which were later refined, contained seven forms: mathematics, physical sciences, human sciences, history, religion, literature and fine arts and philosophy.

The attraction of the concept of 'areas of experience' was taken up by HM Inspectorate. A number of publications in the late 1970s and early 1980s began to talk about the need for a common national framework for the curriculum (Moon 1995: 16). This was partly in response to the challenge thrown down by Prime Minister James Callaghan in his speech at Ruskin College in 1976. In this speech he argued that it was time to examine the case for a so-called 'core curriculum' of basic knowledge and that, as far as the secondary curriculum was concerned, it was essential that one of the chief objectives should be to prepare pupils for the world of work. It has also been argued that the Ruskin speech acknowledged the need to define and limit boundaries of teacher autonomy (Chitty 1996: 19).

This period also saw the return of debates about the place of vocational education in secondary schools. A major new initiative, the Technical and Vocational Education Initiative (TVEI), was launched by the Manpower Services Commission in the early 1980s. This initiative fitted with the views, heralded by the Ruskin Speech, that there should be a concerted attempt to build a new educational consensus around more central control of the curriculum, greater teacher accountability and a more direct link between the secondary school curriculum and the needs of the economy (Chitty 1996: 18). TVEI was an attempt to introduce a technical/vocational component into what was seen as an overly academic curriculum for 14–18-year-olds. It was eventually extended to most LEAs and was influential in developing more active and experiential approaches to teaching and learning as well as launching a series of programmes linked, for example, to extended ideas of work experience, school–FE co-operation and career guidance (Moon 1995: 17).

The introduction of TVEI provoked further debate about a government move towards the imposition of a curriculum framework, and the nature and form of the school curriculum. From 1976–81, the DES produced a series of documents that fell into one of two opposing camps in terms of framing the secondary school curriculum. On the one hand, there were documents such as *Education in Schools: A Consultative Document* (DES 1977) which emphasized the general accountability of education to society at large and which argued for a compulsory core curriculum consisting of a limited range of subjects. The 'core curriculum' was developed further in two DES publications, *A Framework for the School Curriculum* (DES 1980), and *The School Curriculum* (DES 1981). The latter went so far as to specify what proportion of school time should be spent on the core curriculum. Then, on the other hand, there were documents presenting the 'professional view', produced by HMI, such as *Curriculum 11–16 Working Papers* (1977), which advocated a common curriculum and 'area of experience' approach. Without suggesting that there was only one model of good practice, *Curriculum 11–16* put forward a checklist of eight 'areas of experience' to be used as the basis of curriculum construction. These areas, the aesthetic and creative, the ethical, the linguistic, the mathematical, the physical, the scientific, the social and political and the spiritual, were all equally important components.

Underlying HMI's 'areas of experience' approach, was the notion of entitlement:

- pupils have common needs to develop, with maximum enjoyment, skills and attitudes necessary for their individual autonomy now and in the future and for work and political and social participation in the democratic society to which they belong;
- they face the common experience of living in a world which is increasingly international, multi-ethnic and interdependent both economically and politically;
- their curricula should be based on a common framework which provides coherence, and, while taking account of individual needs and abilities, will ensure the provision of a broadly based common experience.

(HMI 1983: 25)

From the mid-1970s there was a growing body of opinion which had been arguing the case for a core or entitlement curriculum. The introduction of the National Curriculum in 1988 was a victory for the bureaucratic camp with its emphasis on accountability and a subject-based curriculum. With its ten foundation subjects, three of them initially forming the 'core curriculum', it appeared to represent an extension of the earlier DES framework of 1980. The introduction of the National Curriculum in 1988 was a bold and audacious political decision. Presented in a subject format for both primary and secondary schools, it marked a sharp break from the evolving MHI and schools' consensus about national frameworks and entitlements. The political background to the decision and the advantages and disadvantages of the model adopted have been widely discussed; there is now an extensive literature that considers both the curriculum as a whole and the specific subjects within it. The style and form in which Statutory Orders were laid down involved a level of central control and direction that contrasted strongly with the decentralized traditions of the period after the Second World War.

In considering this historical overview, it is clear that planning and implementing a curriculum is a process of selection from the available knowledge. At different times and in different places there are different and contrasting views about what this should be. Any form of curriculum represents a synthesis of numerous, possibly overlapping, historical traditions, any selection of knowledge reflects an accommodation between prevailing social forces or movements (economic, political, social) and individuals or interest groups in pursuit of particular ends, and significant change in the curriculum is almost habitually associated with conflict at some level as interests or groups are displaced to make way for new ideas.

The era of a National Curriculum

For teachers and schools, 1988 and the introduction of the National Curriculum marks a key turning point in the development of the school curriculum. It marks the point at which an education system which was often quoted as a prime example of a decentralized, schools-based model of curriculum organization became, almost literally overnight, one of the most centralized in the world. However, it can be argued, as illustrated in the quotes at the beginning of this chapter, that the question of centralized control over the school curriculum was by no means a new development, and that various Education Acts throughout the twentieth century had defined and determined the curriculum in state schools.

The introduction of the National Curriculum produced strong reactions and an extensive list of publications offering critiques of its introduction (Aldrich 1998; Tomlinson 1993; Whitty 1990; Young 1998). One of the areas which excited strong criticism was the introduction of a subject-based curriculum. This move appeared to ignore the curriculum development work of some thirty years, for example the moves to vocational courses and cross-curricular working, and the organization of the curriculum around areas of experience.

Alongside the emphasis given to a subject-based curriculum, the subjects themselves within the National Curriculum were attributed different statuses. The curriculum was seen as having a 'core' – English, Mathematics and Science – whilst the remaining subjects were categorised as 'foundation subjects'. School effectiveness and pupils' attainment in school are now judged against assessments (Standard Assessment Tasks – SATs) in the core subjects. The predominance given to these subjects has been justified on the grounds that they are prerequisites for the knowledge and understanding required in other subject areas.

Defenders of the National Curriculum argued that it heralded an important turning point in curriculum history with its establishment of the notion of the 'entitlement curriculum'. Up until this point, 'entitlement' had been a notional concept. Now it was a legal requirement. All pupils in state schools, regardless of class, gender and ethnicity, are now offered access to that knowledge which is considered worthwhile. It thus aimed to avoid the weaknesses of offering some pupils a high-status 'academic curriculum', and others a low-status 'vocational' curriculum. It was also argued that the National Curriculum, whilst it regulated content, did not regulate pedagogy, so an important aspect of teachers' professional judgement was required in implementing and teaching it (McCulloch et al. 2000).

The challenge facing secondary schools, however, in putting the National Curriculum orders into practice, was the struggle to fit in all the subjects, particularly at Key Stage 4. Subsequent reviews, the Dearing Report (1993), and the revised National Curriculum implemented in schools in September 2000, have all significantly reduced the content of the curriculum. This, together with the increase in the number of foundation subjects made optional at Key Stage 4, has eroded the principle of the 'entitlement curriculum'. Other principles of the National Curriculum, such as the specified Programme of Study and statutory assessment together with stated compulsory subjects to be taken at each Key Stage, have not been radically altered. However, schools, in the light of evaluations of the National Curriculum, are being offered more flexibility in the number of statutory subjects. Design and Technology and Modern Languages join the other foundation subjects of History and Geography as no longer being compulsory at Key Stage 4. This flexible provision aims at enabling schools to accommodate a wider range of vocational qualifications, to allow pupils making significantly less progress than their peers to study fewer National Curriculum subjects in order to consolidate their learning across the curriculum, and to allow pupils, in response to individual strengths and talents, to emphasize a particular curriculum area by exchanging National Curriculum subjects for further courses in that curriculum area, particularly at Key Stage 4. The 'skills' of literacy and numeracy have strengthened. Citizenship has been introduced as a statutory foundation subject at Key Stages 3 and 4 (from August 2002), and non-statutory guidance for personal, social and health education (PSHE) across all four Key Stages has been added. In the rhetoric of 'diversity' which typifies more recent DfES publications, such as the White Paper *Schools Achieving Success* (2002) and *The Revised National Curriculum 2000* (1999), the pendulum appears to be swinging back. A greater focus is being placed on vocational courses and more option choice and specialism at Key Stage 4.

Within this subject-based curriculum, which, it can be argued, is Morant's legacy to secondary schools, the question he struggled over, that of vocational education, continues to raise its head. TVEI became subsumed and submerged under the plethora of educational initiatives following hard on the heels of the 1988 Act. Now, a decade or more later, the place of vocational education in the secondary curriculum is once more being appraised. The White Paper *Schools Achieving Success* (DfES 2002) comments:

> Particularly in the upper secondary years, the education system must respond to the needs, talents and aspirations of each student. Despite serious attempts over many years to solve the challenges of upper secondary education and to raise the status of vocational education, the problems remain. We now want to begin a debate about the best way to develop a coherent phase of 14–19 education, which responds effectively to students and provides real choice. We believe that key components of a new phase include:
>
> - recognition of achievement in both academic and vocational subjects, perhaps through an overarching award
> - creating space in the 14–16 curriculum to allow students to pursue their talents and aspirations, while maintaining a strong focus on the basics
> - making high quality vocational options available to all students, which are widely recognized and offer the opportunity of entry to Higher Education.
>
> (DfES 2001: Section 4)

There has then been a subtle shift in the balance of the curriculum away from the subject base, although this is still strongly in evidence, to coverage of basic skills and a renewed emphasis being given to vocational education. It is clear that the curriculum picture is never a static one. There have been suggestions that pupils will be able to drop subjects such as History, Geography and Modern Foreign Languages at the beginning of Key Stage 3 in 'good' schools (as defined by the DfES), in order to 'prevent them becoming disillusioned with education' (*TES* 14 September 2001). This suggestion, together with the proposals in the White Paper *Schools Achieving Success* (DfES 2001), that 'specialist schools' such as technology and language colleges are to expand and new specialist schools for science and engineering, business and enterprise and mathematics and computing are to be developed, heralds a phase of further curriculum change. (For details of current curriculum requirements see the following websites: Qualifications and Curriculum Authority (QCA) for England, the Northern Ireland Council for Curriculum, Examination and Assessment (CCEA) and the Qualifications, Curriculum and Assessment Authority for Wales (ACCAC).)

Curriculum change, design and debate are an ongoing aspects of the teacher's work. The questions posed in the 1960s and 1970s about the nature and form of the curriculum are still relevant today, although the answers and priorities will be different. The presentation of a clearly argued case and rationale for the construction of a particular school curriculum becomes all the more pertinent, however, at a time of an externally driven agenda. This is the case with the post-16 curriculum.

The post-16 curriculum: a brief overview

The post-16 curriculum in schools has emerged (QCA 1998a; DfEE 2000) through a long period of ideological debate, during which the status of A levels as 'the gold standard' for achievement at 18+ has been maintained. Whilst the Education Reform Act (1988) revolutionized the 11–16 curriculum, it left much undone in relation to the 16–19 curriculum. Two major aspects of the post-16 curriculum were not addressed. The first of these concerned the A level curriculum, which offered:

- no linkages to vocational alternatives
- no perceived relevance other than as preparation for higher education
- increased evidence of 'specialisation' in a small number of subjects and little breadth to the range of subjects it was possible to study
- little value to those pupils who wanted to spend only one year in the sixth-form context
- nothing to show for the 25 per cent of pupils who attempted A levels and failed to pass.

The second aspect centres on those pupils who left compulsory schooling to receive no further education and training at all, due to the limited nature of post-16 courses. These issues are hardly new. Three years after the introduction of A levels as single-subject examinations to replace the older Higher School Certificate (organized on a subject group basis), the Early Leaving Report (1951) criticized the wastage of talent, a view endorsed by the Crowther Report of 1959. Over-specialization and a lack of breadth were highlighted in an agreement to broaden the post-16 curriculum in 1961. These good intentions were sidelined by university demands for higher A level grades. Curriculum bodies such as the Schools' Council battled with the problem of the lack of breadth in the 16–19 school curriculum for almost a decade, with various recommendations over this period, such as different levels of qualification in Years 12 and 13. All were rejected, partly out of a concern that pupils should not be subjected to three successive years of public examinations, and partly out of university fears that lower standards would necessitate longer degree courses.

There were some successful attempts to broaden the post-16 curriculum and to complement academic subjects. Advanced Supplementary (AS) levels were proposed by the DES in 1984 and introduced into schools in 1987. Examined to the same standard as A level, but with half the content and study time, the AS was always optional, and take-up for a 2+2 model (that is, two A levels and two AS levels) was modest, with most schools and pupils choosing to stick with a traditional three-A level programme. The Higginson Report (DES 1988) advocated a five-subject mix of AS and (leaner) A levels, but this was rejected by the then government's publicly stated firm intention of preserving what it declared as the 'gold standard' of specialized A level.

Throughout the 1990s, governments favoured clinging to specialist A levels as a globally recognized academic award. There were some minor changes, reflecting the shift in assessment practices following the introduction of GCSE, and there was an increase in the amount of coursework options. This move to reform was, however, curtailed following the introduction of the 'Code of Practice' (SCAA 1994) which imposed a general subject core in an attempt to promote equality and consistency across the examining boards, and to help HE and employers know what had been studied and assessed. Modularisation was the main attempt to modify A levels in a more flexible direction, with discrete units or modules which could be assessed at up to three points during the academic year. The shorter-term goals and the facility to bank modules was an ongoing attempt to increase pupil motivation, but even here synoptic assessment was included to test understanding of the connections between the subject elements.

In 2000, the results of a two-year consultation on A, AS and GNVQ Advanced levels were implemented. This has resulted in key reforms to the post-16 curriculum. The original government rationale had been a desire to broaden A levels and upgrade vocational qualifications, underpinning them (as was consistently reiterated), with rigorous standards and key skills. The traditional post-16 curriculum was considered too narrow and inflexible for the modern world, while European competitors tended to offer broader but more demanding programmes of study, including vocational elements. The process of consultation highlighted specific concerns. These were:

- the need for learners both to improve their adaptability and keep career options open;
- the requirement for a more flexible system to allow the combining of different types of qualifications according to developing interests and needs;
- the need to promote real parity of esteem between different types of programme through an underpinning quality standards framework.

The current framework is designed to:

- ease the move between, and combination of, different types of qualifications;
- retain specialism where necessary for progression;
- ensure coherence of provision without unnecessary duplication;
- promote confidence in the relevance, consistency and intelligibility of all accredited awards.

The key reforms in the post-16 assessment structure are summarized below.

A level

In the first year of A level study, a student is able to take four or five subjects to AS level. Typically, three of these subjects might be studied for a further year to gain a full A level. This second year is termed A2 but does not make up a qualification in its own right. Examination boards provide specifications (formerly syllabuses) made up of six equally sized units (see GNVQ), to the same standard as the previous A level, with choice of linear or modular assessment in each. Synoptic assessment, testing understanding of the syllabus as a whole, regardless of the assessment option chosen, is included. Coursework is generally limited to a ceiling of 30 per cent in order (it is argued) to enhance the validity of overall assessment without compromising on rigour. A level module results will be certificated individually for the shelf-life of that particular module. Pass grades are awarded from A to E, in line with the old A level grading system.

AS (Advanced Supplementary)

This is a reformulated three-unit AS qualification representing the first half of the full A level and worth 50 per cent of the marks. It is designed to encourage greater take-up of subjects, especially in Year 12, to provide better progression from GCSE into advanced level study, and to reduce the numbers dropping out with nothing to show for their efforts. It counts as a qualification in its own right, and parallels the A level grading system of A to E. Opportunities to develop and assess key skills are identified within the syllabus.

Vocational A level (formerly Advanced GNVQ)

This has been revised and renamed from the previous General National Vocational Qualification with a more rigorous and manageable assessment regime for teachers, in order to reduce confusion over the relative standard of Advanced GNVQ. A five-grade A to E scale mirroring A level standards is now in place. The full twelve-unit Vocational award is equivalent to two A levels and is taken in subjects explicitly related to the world of work, such as health and social care or business. The six-unit Vocational A level is equivalent in size and demand to a single A level, and can be combined with them for those pupils wishing to pursue both vocational and academic learning. Some three-unit awards, equivalent to AS qualifications, are available. The link to relevant occupational standards on related NVQs has been made more explicit.

AEA (Advanced Extension Awards)

These are 'world class' tests in 13 major A level subjects aimed at the most able and designed to be more accessible than the S levels they have been designed to replace. They are intended to stretch the brightest advanced level students and allow them to demonstrate their understanding in greater depth. (Unlike the majority of changes to the post-16 curriculum, which were introduced in September 2000, these were unavailable until 2002.)

Key skills

It has been considered essential by employers that post-16 pupils develop and demonstrate key skills to a higher level of competence. Communication, Application of Number and Information Technology are promoted as the first three key skills. These are integral to Vocational A level courses but are separately certificated. A new key skills qualification draws out evidence from pupils' Programmes of Study and is graded at level 1 to 4. Working with Others, Improving Own Learning and Problem-Solving are termed the wider key skills and the reporting of achievement in these areas can be through the Progress File. For existing teachers, this development in particular has necessitated significant staff development.

Towards an overarching certificate

The QCA consultation revealed an opinion shift in favour of an overarching certificate for advanced level qualification (i.e. a baseline equivalent to two A levels, or a 12-unit Vocational A level award or NVQ level 3, plus the first three Key Skills at level 3). The chief rationale was expressed as a desire to reward a breadth of achievement. Trainee teachers would be well advised to ask practitioners for their opinion on this when on school placement.

Figure 2.5 Key reforms in the post-16 assessment structure

The span of curriculum change throughout the 11–18 curriculum and the introduction of new initiatives would result in a fragmented, incoherent curriculum unless it was developed around a set of guiding principles to underpin curriculum planning. The next section of this chapter explores some of the different approaches to curriculum planning which can be found in schools.

Contexts for decision-making in the curriculum

The curriculum design process represents one of the creative dimensions of the teacher's role. Many teachers acknowledge the excitement of working out how to teach a series of lessons or unit of work, particularly if this is well prepared in advance and the time is available. Even parts of the curriculum that have been taught many times before offer new possibilities as new groups of pupils arrive and new resources become available. The stimulus of curriculum planning is almost always enhanced if done by a team, a department or year group, for example. Courses of teacher education aim to provide the skills and expertise required to play a full part in such processes.

Decision-making about the curriculum can be approached in a number of different ways. One perspective is to think in terms of contributions from the different stakeholders – the external requirements in terms of the National Curriculum, the school governors, parents, etc., as well as teachers. What is decided nationally, locally or within the school? In all parts of the United Kingdom the balance of decision-making has shifted in recent years with government claiming a far greater say than was traditionally the case.

However, despite this increasingly centralized control of the school curriculum, there is still great latitude in the way schools can implement, organize and interpret the statutory requirements. In secondary schools, pedagogy still remains within the professional repertoire of teachers, as do pupil grouping, classroom methods and the physical organization of the learning environment. In terms of their accountability to their communities, parents, pupils, LEA or central government, schools not only issue curriculum statements (see Figure 2.2), but also identify how this curriculum statement supports the values they collectively see as underpinning the curriculum.

It is important to remember that the design process (and here architects, lawyers and doctors would again have similar observations to make) is the point where values impinge heavily on the way expertise is deployed and plans are made. Just as there is more to effective teaching than effective techniques, there is more to an effective curriculum than the various activities of designing, implementing and reviewing that make up the curriculum process. Widespread media debate about the organization and structure of the school curriculum has illustrated how value laden any discussion of the curriculum is.

There are several dimensions to curriculum planning which schools need to take into account:

The content of what is being taught   The selection of the subject matter of the curriculum.

The objectives of the curriculum   The identification of the learning aims and objectives. These are linked to and draw from the knowledge, skills and understanding covered through the different subjects, but embrace wider objectives linked to the values and ethos of the school.

The cognitive processes   This requires a consideration of what is understood about pupils' developmental needs at different stages of maturity and a consideration of how pupils learn in the different curriculum areas.

The social and geographical context of the school   Teachers are challenged in different ways by the social and geographical contexts of the school. This may have implications for the way in which the curriculum is organized and implemented. For example, over the last twenty years or so a number of urban schools have attempted to develop forms of curriculum that respond to the problems of disaffection or alienation. New forms of curriculum development programmes have been mounted, often involving a greater stress on links with the community and home–school liaison. This could be contrasted with remote rural schools, often small in size, where finding the staff expertise to cover the full range of subjects might be difficult.

Issues raised by the geographical and social context of the school are central to some of the major educational concerns of the day. There is, for example, plenty of evidence to show that attainment as measured by examination results varies from area to area but correlates strongly with the socio-economic characteristics of home background. This is an enormously important issue and one that has been the source of a great deal of debate, policy formulation and experiment for most of the second half of the twentieth century. For the curriculum this raises a series of important questions. Should different provision be made to compensate for the disadvantages that some children bring to their schools? If so, when and in what form? Is there a case for changing the form of the curriculum to allow pupils from a variety of social contexts to show their capability?

There is a range of other questions and issues that impinge on decisions about the curriculum:

Staffing and resource organization   How teachers are deployed and the resources available to them are further crucial dimensions to curriculum implementation. What percentage of a week should be devoted to teaching? How much planning time should teachers have? Do they have their own room? Do they work on their own or as part of a team? Are non-teaching support staff available? What range of technical aids do teachers have at their disposal? Can the pupils take textbooks home? Are there textbooks? Is access to a library or resource centre provided in all lessons? Who in the school makes these decisions and how are they made?

The list of issues and questions is again almost endless. A well-planned curriculum anticipates these questions in the general sense just as a well-planned lesson does so in a specific way. But the technicality of these concerns also raises a number of more policy-oriented, strategic questions. How are resources allocated in the school? Prior to that, how are resources made available to the school and in what terms can they be judged adequate or otherwise? As with timetables, what appears a relatively low-level issue in the scale of the educational system may originate in debates that reflect major issues of value in terms of prioritizing and valuing certain forms of staffing or resource.

The use of time and the organization of the timetable   There are no statutory requirements or guidelines. There is custom and practice which, for example, indicates that a GCSE subject requires 10 per cent of the total subject time during Years 9 and 10. But the length of the school day and week varies from school to school and 10 per cent therefore is rather an elastic concept, not least because of the introduction of short-course subjects within and outside the GCSE framework. Debates about the allocation can be quite fraught, with different subjects and subject teachers seeing time in terms of territory to be defended or claimed from one year to the next. This debate often swirls around the completion of the school timetable.

Timetabling can become a very technical process. It is important, however, to remember that the first decisions about a timetable say important things about a school's curriculum aims and priorities. In most schools the process of preparing the timetable begins in the spring term but in a few the process may begin even earlier.

There are very different ideas about the way time, and therefore teachers, should be organized. The timetable as such does not necessarily say anything about the form of the curriculum or the way it is taught. It is, however, an important influence on how flexible teachers can be or how constrained they are in planning and organization (in developing cross-curricular forms of planning, for example). There are significant links between the technical issues of timetabling and the big questions and issues we might ask about goals and purposes. It is of no value, for example, for a school to say that older pupils should have more opportunity to plan and develop their own learning and achieve a degree of autonomy in learning but at the same time organise teaching time in ways that considerably constrain the use of time for teaching and learning. The organisation of time links directly back to the fundamental aims and purpose that can be ascribed to the school curriculum.

The task of disentangling all these facets is a fascinating process.

Anyone entering a British secondary school will immediately perceive evidence of each of these dimensions. Most schools now must have schemes of work, which show how whole-school policies and the National Curriculum are brought together in practice. This substructure is, arguably, much more visible now than in the period before the 1988 Education Reform Act although that form of visibility says nothing about what actually happens in practice. In preparing a school's curriculum policy numerous interest groups come into play, within the staffroom and through the wider community of governors or parents.

More often, however, the social and political processes operate at the more local-ized level of micro-politics within a school. Does science have a sufficient resource budget to meet the needs of the National Curriculum? How will time be found to introduce a new course in personal and social education (PSE)? Should pupils learn one language in depth or gain an introductory level of competence in two or three?

Once these sorts of questions have been resolved other issues come to the fore. Some are of a fairly mundane nature. How is the timetable organized to ensure that every class in Year 7 has access to a twenty-minute daily burst of the MFL (modern foreign language) department's audio-visual equipment? Others are more signifi-cant. Is PSE best taught in tutor groups by tutors, or would a specialist team be more effective? Is the science faculty's reliance on worksheets rather than textbooks the most appropriate approach? These considerations apply at the level of the whole-school curriculum as well as within specialist areas.

Take, for example, the subject of history. This is hardly a new subject on the school curriculum, but it is one which has excited a lot of public debate, particularly around its relationship with the idea of 'Britishness' and 'identity', and the 'history as content' or 'history as process' debate.

In any secondary school considering the debates about history the issues are likely to be focused on:

Content   Discussion about the substance of the subject. What exactly do we mean by history? Whose history are we covering? Should the question of histories, rather than history, be addressed? How do we reconcile the history Programmes of Study with the developments in academic history? Is the content of historical significance?

Objectives   How does the history curriculum cover historical knowledge, skills and understanding? Which topics are best fitted to teaching about continuity and change in history? How do we approach the teaching of interpretations? How do we cover the teaching of history from a variety of perspectives? What contribution does history make to ICT and Citizenship?

Pupils' learning   What do we know about the development of conceptual under-standing in history? Do the attainment levels reflect progression here? How do we counter the stereotypes that pupils have of earlier periods in history being somehow 'primitive'?

Resources   Is the time allocation adequate? How is history in the field to be resourced and how is it to be supported by the structure of the timetable? And so on.

These processes of curriculum planning and implementation go beyond the plan-ning, managing and assessing which are at the core of the teacher's task; they reflect a range of values and beliefs, and have to take account of a number of different dimen-sions influencing curriculum decisions. Curriculum planning in secondary schools has become particularly complex at Key Stage 4. Here, there are so many variable ingredients to the curriculum that the way schools combine the compulsory subjects, options, short-course GCSEs and GNVQs, etc. is variable and very specific to a school. Schools approach this curriculum organization in different ways depending on their aims and ethos.

In addition to these considerations, there are new ones for schools to accommo-date in their curriculum planning. ICT is propelling the school curriculum towards a radical transformation. This operates at many levels. How do schools ensure that their teachers have the necessary skills and knowledge to use ICT in their teaching? How do schools organize the timetable so that pupils and teachers have access to computers? The use of ICT requires teachers to have not only the technical skills of using the various applications – word-processing skills, Internet skills, presentational skills (using Powerpoint, for example) – but also a knowledge and understanding of the relationship between their subject area and the way in which their subject area can be transformed through the use of ICT which is having an impact on the school curriculum in three main ways:

- it provides a more *effective* way of doing what is already being done;
- it has the potential to *extend* what can be achieved; and
- it has the potential to *transform* the nature of the subject at a most funda-mental level.

(These matters are taken up in more detail in Chapter 7.)

Whichever model of the curriculum schools choose to implement, and what-ever way they choose to manage the ICT curriculum, curriculum evaluation is an essential dimension to a teacher's work. Evaluation acts as both an end point, a review of how things have gone, and a beginning point, influencing how it should be done in the future.

Curriculum evaluation

Curriculum evaluation is a specialist field which raises a number of issues that form an important part of an initial teacher-training course. For example:

- assessment of pupils
- pupils' self-evaluation
- teacher evaluation and review

- teacher appraisal
- procedures for schoolwide monitoring and review (including perhaps the use of performance indicators)
- school inspection
- governors' reports to parents.

Figure 2.6 illustrates guidance from the QCA (1998) on an approach to curriculum evaluation. This applies to the general school curriculum framework. In addition, departments or faculties have additional discussion points for their own particular curriculum area.

Discussion points for staff, governors and parents

A selection of points for discussion is set out below. Schools will be able to add others and focus on the matters most pertinent to them.

Curriculum models

Purposes and principles

- What educational aims and principles should guide our curriculum planning?
- Are we meeting statutory curriculum requirements in a way that reflects our aims and principles?
- What entitlements and opportunities do we wish to establish for our pupils at Key Stage 4?
- What do we regard as essential elements of the curriculum for all pupils and why?
- Are we providing a broad and balanced curriculum at Key Stage 4? Have we achieved an appropriate balance between choice and flexibility?
- Does our Key Stage 4 curriculum build effectively on pupils' learning at Key Stage 3 and prepare pupils appropriately for progression post-16?
- Are we developing the skills pupils will need in adult life?

Areas for development

- What are our current strengths and weaknesses (staffing, timetabling, resourcing)? How can we build on our strengths? How are we addressing our weaknesses?
- What are our pupils' strengths?
- Are we fully informed about the range of new curriculum possibilities and qualifications which we can use to meet the aims and objectives we have identified?
- What changes do we need to make to our current arrangements for careers education and guidance? Has career management been considered?

- What changes do we need to make to our pastoral curriculum?
- How effectively do we communicate our curriculum to parents, pupils and employers?
- How do we monitor, evaluate and review our curriculum?

Next steps

- What are the next steps for us?
- What do we wish to protect and what do we need to change?
- Are there any subjects or areas threatened by the changes? What action do we need to take now?
- Can we achieve our plans immediately, or do we need to make transitional plans?
- Have we maximised our resources to achieve our aims?
- Have we considered the implications of our decisions in terms of training needs, workload for pupils and staff, impact on other key stages, costs, time and presentation?

Figure 2.6 'Key Stage 4 curriculum in action: a discussion document for secondary schools' (QCA 1998)

All of these questions interrelate, although they may impact on different parts of the school and education system. The beginning or new teacher is likely to be more concerned with classroom evaluation than the preparation of, for example, reports to governors. Very quickly, however, all teachers are drawn into broader issues. Important issues for curriculum evaluation are how individual teachers critically appraise their own teaching and the progress that their pupils have made.

Conclusion

This chapter has emphasized just how wide the influences on the school curriculum are. Within the study of curriculum there are a number of competing ideas and theories, some of which derive from parallel disputes in the disciplines of history, philosophy, psychology or sociology and others which have particular significance for issues of curriculum. We have considered:

- why knowledge of the curriculum is an important aspect of a beginning teacher's professional knowledge;
- a brief history of the school curriculum;
- a consideration of the concept and definitions of the curriculum;
- issues in curriculum development since the 1988 Act;
- the post-16 curriculum;
- school approaches to curriculum organization and development.

Curriculum enquiry is now established as an area of enquiry in its own right. There are specialist journals available in Britain (*The Curriculum Journal* published by Routledge, for example) as well as internationally, and at least two curriculum encyclopaedias exist (published by Pergamon Press and Macmillan). The debate about curriculum ranges across academic, policy and practical concerns and provides an important reference point for the implementation of any particular curriculum programme and plan. This is an important debate for teachers, and one in which they are increasingly engaged.

References

Accac website: www.accac.org.uk

Aldrich, R. (1988) 'The national curriculum: a historical perspective' in D. Lawton and C. Chitty (1988) *The National Curriculum*, London: Kogan Page.

—— (1998) *The National Curriculum beyond 2000: The QCA and the Aims of Education*, London: Institute of Education.

Board of Education (1902) *Code of Regulations for Day Schools 1902*, London: HMSO.

CCEA website: www.ccea.org.uk

Chitty, C. (1996) 'Organisation and control of schooling. Unit 2. Generating a national curriculum', *EU208 Exploring Educational Issues*, Milton Keynes: Open University.

Dearing, R. (1993) *The National Curriculum and its Assessment – Final Report*, London: SCAA.

DES (1977) *Education in Schools: A Consultative Document*, London: HMSO.

—— (1980) *A Framework for the School Curriculum*, London: HMSO.

—— (1981) *The School Curriculum*, London: HMSO.

—— (1988) *Advancing A Levels* (The Higginson Report), London: HMSO.

DfEE (2000) *Qualifying for Success: Changes to Post-16 Qualifications*, London: HMSO.

DfES (2002) *Schools Achieving Success* – (White Paper), London: HMSO.

Gagné, R.M. (1967) 'Curriculum research and the promotion of learning' in R. Tyler, R.M. Gagné and M. Scriven (eds) (1967/8) *Perspectives of Curriculum Evaluation*, Chicago: Rand McNally.

Hirst, P.H. (1974) *Knowledge and the Curriculum*, London: Routledge and Kegan Paul.

Hirst, P.H. and Peters, R. (1970) *The Logic of Education*, London: Routledge and Kegan Paul.

HMI (1977) *Curriculum 11–16 Working Papers*, London: HMSO.

—— (1983) *Curriculum 11–16: Towards a Statement of Entitlement*, London: HMSO.

Holmes, B. and McLean, M. (1989) *The Curriculum: A Comparative Perspective*, London: Unwin Hyman.

Kelly, A.V. (1989) *The Curriculum. Theory and Practice*, London: Paul Chapman.

McCulloch, G., Helsby, G. and Knight, P. (2000) *The Politics of Professionalism: Teachers and the Curriculum*, New York: Continuum.

Moon, R.E. (1995) *The Secondary School Curriculum: Teaching in Secondary Schools Secondary Document 1*, Milton Keynes: Open University.

QCA (1998a) 'QCA proceeds with developing post-16 qualifications', QCA Press Release, 3 April 1998.

—— (1998b) 'Key Stage 4 curriculum in action: a discussion document for secondary schools', London: QCA.

QCA website: www.qca.org.uk

SCAA (1994) *Code of Practice for GCE A and AS Examinations*, London: SCAA.

—— (1995) *Managing the Curriculum at Key Stage 4, a Discussion Document*, London: SCAA.

Slattery, P. (1995) *Curriculum Development in the Post-modern Era*, New York and London: Garland.

Taylor, A. (1985) 'An early arrival of the fascist mentality: Robert Morant's rise to power', *Journal of Education Administration and History*, 17(2): 48–62.

Times Educational Supplement (*TES*) September 14 2001, p. 1, London.

Tomlinson, J. (1993) *The Control of Education*, London: Cassell.

Whitty, G. (1990) 'The new right and the National Curriculum: state control or market forces', in M. Flude and M. Hammer (eds) *The Education Reform Act 1988: Its Origins and Implications*, Basingstoke: Falmer Press.

Williams, R. (1975) *The Long Revolution*, Harmondsworth: Penguin.

Wragg, E.C. (1997) *The Cubic Curriculum*, London: Routledge.

Young, M.F.D. (1988) *The Curriculum of the Future: From the New Sociology of Education to a Critical Theory of Learning*, London: Falmer Press.

3 Subject knowledge and preparation for teaching

> The image of good 'history' teaching … is one that is grounded in subject matter. It is a disciplinary conception of history teaching that pre-supposes that one major goal for teaching history is the communication of historical knowledge – the central facts, concepts and ideas of the discipline – and the nature of the methods employed by interpretation and narrative.
>
> (Wilson 1991)

Introduction

The skills, knowledge and understandings which beginning teachers bring with them to their postgraduate teacher education to qualify as secondary school teachers are located initially within their subject knowledge. Subject knowledge in turn is generally determined by the undergraduate degree they studied. Other qualities, such as the personal qualities required by the professional demands of teaching, previous experience and skills, together with the ability to communicate effectively in spoken and written English (or Welsh), are also requirements for initial teacher education courses. However, for beginning teachers in secondary schools, it is their subject knowledge that mainly determines what they will teach. This in turn defines them as teachers and the subject culture in which they work, as well as their longer-term career opportunities and prospects. They are trained and educated to be science teachers, history teachers, English teachers, or music teachers. The old adage of primary teachers teaching children rather than a subject springs to mind, and underlines not only some of the differences in expectations about the place of subject knowledge in pupils' learning, but also raises questions about the place of subject knowledge in learning to teach.

Across all phases of education, there is a renewed focus on the influence of a teacher's subject knowledge on pupils' learning. What sort of degree background provides the best basis for future science, maths, music and other subject teachers? Are there any links to be made between teachers' knowledge of their subject, say, for example, their knowledge of post-colonial studies, and pupils' learning? Does teachers' subject knowledge influence the pedagogic strategies they adopt in teaching, and does this result in more successful pupil learning? How do teachers up-date their subject knowledge? This chapter explores:

- the place of subject knowledge in teaching;
- subject knowledge and effective teaching;
- subject knowledge and teacher development: beginning teachers and continuing professional development.

The place of subject knowledge in teaching

In 1942, 9 per cent of teachers were graduates who had additionally studied education or followed an initial teacher training course. Until the 1970s, and for teachers of some shortage subjects (principally mathematics and science) well into the 1980s, a degree was all that was required to gain qualified teacher status to teach in maintained secondary schools. The reason for this is mainly historical. With the post-1944 expansion of education, both secondary and higher, and the raising of the school leaving age to 16, the nature and purpose of secondary education underwent a transformation. Throughout the 1960s there were fierce debates about the need for different types and organization of secondary education – grammar schools for those who passed the 11+, secondary modern schools for those who didn't, technical schools for the education of future industrial apprentices. The push to establish comprehensive education, which put an end to secondary modern schools, had an impact on what was considered to be 'effective' teacher education. The learning needs of pupils, and the development of the school curriculum (see Chapter 2), determined definitions of a teacher's knowledge, skills and professional identity. For the 11–16 age-range, an 'academic' education, one based firmly in the different disciplines and originally aimed at establishing a grammar school elite, was only one aspect of the whole curriculum. Teachers entering the comprehensive schools of the 1960s and 1970s needed to teach an increasingly diverse pupil population. This diversity embraced attainment, gender, ethnicity and social class, as well as the acceptance of a wider definition of the school curriculum to include pastoral and extra-curricular activities. A grounding in the academic discipline of the chosen subject on its own was no longer considered to be an appropriate qualification for teaching.

At the same time, the whole of initial teacher training and education was being reviewed. At the heart of this review was a concern about the academic standing of education courses within higher education, and the status of teaching as a 'profession'. Figure 3.1 indicates some of these main reforms.

Graduates wishing to teach in maintained secondary schools were only *required* to have some postgraduate training after 1973. This date also coincided with the predicted fall in the school-age population, and longer-term planning to reduce the number of teachers. Ratcheting-up the educational requirements for qualified teacher status at a time of teacher surplus was no coincidence. Maintaining the balance, however, between teacher supply and demand, and between professional standards and supply, is a delicate operation, particularly as demand for different subject specialisms across secondary schools is uneven, influenced not only by the school curriculum but by wider social and economic shifts. Even as the requirement for all graduate entrants into teaching to complete an initial teacher education course following a first degree was announced (*TES* 19 January 1969), teacher shortages in some subjects were becoming apparent. Under the headline of 'Maths and Science places go abegging', the *TES* announced that applications to fill college places for

A chronological list of the major reports and policy documents in initial teacher education, issued by the Board of Education and its successors

1944   McNair Report 'Teachers and youth leaders'
Recommended one grade of teacher with qualified teacher status from an approved training course.

1944–50   One-year Emergency Training Scheme for Elementary Teachers
Mature students from the forces. [Produced 35,000 teachers.]
Others continued to do two-year courses or university courses.
Training programme to qualify uncertificated teachers.

1949   Circular 211. 'Probation of qualified teachers'
Requirement for one year's probation removed.

1950   Circular 213. 'Minimum examination qualifications for candidates seeking admission to training colleges'
At least 5 GCE O levels or combinations of O and A levels.

1950s   National Advisory Council on Training and Supply of Teachers produces a number of reports on the implementation of the McNair recommendation for three-year courses.

1950   Circular 230. 'Training of technical teachers'
Special one-year courses for teachers of technical subjects to continue to be run by LEAs.

1957   The Training of Teachers: suggestions for a three-year training college course. Ministry of Education Pamphlet no. 34.

1960   Three-year Certificate of Education Courses at training colleges begin.
Last two-year course finished in 1961.
Number of college places doubled 1960–64. By 1962, 60 per cent of entrants had GCE A levels.

1963   Robbins Report 'Higher education: report of the Committee appointed by the Prime Minister' Cmnd 2154.
Recommends enlarging training colleges to over 750 students and renaming as colleges of education. Suggests four-year courses with final Bachelor of Education degree awarded by a university.

1963   Post Graduate Certificates in Education begins.
Further massive increase in college places to reach 119,000 in 1971.

1967   The Training of Teachers Regulations 1967. SI 1967/792 and Circular 4/67.

1968   First Bachelor of Education degrees awarded.

> **1969** The Schools (Qualified Teachers) Regulations 1969. SI 1969/1777.
> As explained in Circular 18/69 'Professional Training for Teachers in Maintained Schools', requires all graduate entrants to teaching to have a professional one-year qualification by 31 December 1973.
>
> **1970–71** James Report 'Teacher education and training'
> Recommends two-year courses for diplomas in higher education followed by two-year courses leading to Bachelor of Arts degree.
>
> **1972** School leaving age raised to 16.
>
> **1973** Birth rate falls. Plans for reducing teacher training to 85,000 by 1981.
>
> **1973** The Schools (Qualified Teachers) Regulations 1973. SI 1973/2021.
> Circular 11/73 'The Qualification of Teachers' explains that all teachers must have qualified teacher status.

Figure 3.1 Teacher education reforms: 1944–73

Source: DfEE Library.

October 1970 had dropped by 13 per cent and that recruitment to maths and science courses was proving particularly difficult. When the requirement to complete a post-graduate education course to qualify as a teacher was about to come into force, the then Minister for Education, Margaret Thatcher, rushed through legislation exempting maths and science teachers from this requirement. So even relatively recently, teachers of some subjects in maintained secondary schools have not had to follow a course in education. The need to recruit and maintain suitably qualified teachers is an on-going theme of educational policy-making.

New concepts of teaching were also developed in response to the growth of research findings into pupils' learning. The shift from seeing learning as 'knowledge as transmission' to ones which saw it as 'knowledge as construction' was significant here. This work challenged the view that 'good' teaching was the product of a thorough knowledge of subject combined with work-based experience in schools. Subject knowledge was seen as only one component of a teacher's professional knowledge.

At the same time, work on a theory of mental structures in the organization of knowledge domains shifted the focus from the place of teachers' subject knowledge to the development of pupils' learning and understanding. A consideration of skills and conceptual understandings as the principles upon which pupil learning could be organized, rather than on subject disciplines, was taken up in England by HMI. In the 1980s HMI developed a model of a curriculum organized around nine 'areas of experience':

- linguistic
- mathematical
- scientific
- technological
- human and social

- aesthetic and creative
- physical
- moral
- spiritual.

(HMI 1985)

This curriculum was influenced by earlier thinking from HMI which moved beyond the notion of 'disciplines' to the concepts, skills and understandings which underpin them.

> ... it is necessary to look through the subject or discipline to the areas of experience and knowledge to which it may provide access, and to the skills and attitudes which may assist their development.

(DES 1977)

The concept of the teacher which emerges from this view of pupil learning is not of an academic subject knowledge specialist, but of a facilitator of learning who covers all areas of the curriculum. In secondary schools, there were moves to present a more 'holistic' view of the world, and therefore of knowledge, to pupils, through initiatives such as the development of humanities. This aimed to seek ways in which pupils' understanding of the world around them would be more effectively developed through offering a 'coherent' curriculum which allowed the social, political, environmental, economic and religious aspects of human interaction to be addressed. Similar frameworks which identified skills and concepts were used in the development of schemes for cross-curricular work (the skills of numeracy, literacy and ICT or the theme of citizenship, for example). Yet in secondary schools, subject knowledge and understanding remained the central organizing principle underpinning the school curriculum and pupil learning.

All teachers, however, whether in primary or secondary schools, have been affected by a resurgent interest in the place of subject knowledge in teaching and learning and a move away from 'topic' or 'integrated' work. This resurgence was largely precipitated by criticisms of the 'topic' work carried out in primary schools, in which learning was organized around areas of experience and taught through one topic, such as 'electricity'. The 'child-centred' view of the curriculum was challenged as being as 'artificial' as the 'subject-knowledge'-centred curriculum. There certainly were some 'distortions' of the disciplines here as teachers struggled to 'fit' all areas into a chosen topic. For example, one primary school has gone on record for covering the Black Death in its work on 'Colour'!

The clearest attack on the 'topic' approach to teaching came from a specially commissioned report into primary teaching, *Curriculum Organisation and Classroom Practice in Primary schools* (Alexander *et al.* 1992). The authors of this report, Alexander, Rose and Woodhead, argued that to deny pupil access to discrete subject knowledge was to deny them access to powerful ways of looking at the world. This work was echoed in a series of HMI reports into the primary school curriculum which stated that, at the upper end of the primary school, subject and subject-specialist teaching might bring depth to pupils' understanding. The question of teachers' subject knowledge then became part of the 1990s' debates about standards in education. A teacher with a subject specialism could raise standards because they could better diagnose a pupil's learning need and plan more carefully for differentiation and progression (Morrison 1986).

The focus given to subject knowledge and its place in raising educational standards has been reflected in the renewed emphasis given to teachers' subject knowledge in teacher education. The concern expressed in government reports is echoed by research being carried out into teachers' professional knowledge. Here findings indicate that 'it must be of some concern that students' understanding of subject matter and of children's learning appear to remain at a superficial level throughout training. Student teachers, it appears, are learning to manage activities, rather than becoming experts in particular subject matter and the pedagogy associated with it. Their ideas about children's learning appear to focus on motivation, engagement and relationships, rather than subject matter, (Calderhead and Shorrock 1997).

This renewed emphasis on subject knowledge has had an important impact on regulations for initial teacher education. In the 1990s, a National Curriculum for Initial Teacher Training (ITT) for both primary and secondary English, mathematics and science, and ICT was introduced (DfEE 1998). An increasing emphasis on the connection between the 'what' and 'how' of the secondary school curriculum, and the place of subject knowledge as a significant factor within it, was brought into sharper focus through the inclusion of subject knowledge in the National Curriculum for Initial Teacher Training. Beginning teachers are required to demonstrate that they have a secure knowledge in the skills and concepts of their specialist subject together with the 'basic skills' of ICT, literacy and numeracy.

The introduction of the National Curriculum for ITT was highly controversial. The principle of government intervention into the detail of initial teacher education was seen as being an attack on higher education through controlling the curriculum and as undermining the autonomy and professionalism of teachers and teacher educators (Richards *et al.* 1997; Maguire *et al.* 1998). Other concerns are linked to the 'unauthored' nature of the ITT National Curriculum, which was drawn up by the Teacher Training Agency in collaboration with teams of invited, but unnamed, teams of 'subject experts'. Whilst many on the curriculum teams were themselves involved in teacher education, the fact that they remained anonymous contributors has raised questions about the nature of subject knowledge. The subject knowledge content of the ITT National Curriculum has not been defined by the wider academic subject knowledge communities who debate, change, challenge and transform subject knowledge. Instead, it has been defined by a government quango. In relation to English, the ITT National Curriculum is seen as a thinly veiled political attempt to reassert a traditional conception of English and English teaching by championing traditional views and implying that there is a 'simple, right answer in English that is always and everywhere correct and that it has to be learnt by heart' (Richards *et al.* 1997). The National Curriculum for ITT was followed by the Green Paper *Teachers Meeting the Challenge of Change* (DfEE 1998b) which asked the TTA to strengthen the pre- and in-course study to give trainee teachers opportunities to improve their subject knowledge. The initiative supported the production of study support materials in some subjects only – primary English, Mathematics and

Science; secondary Science, Design and Technology and Physical Education (see http://www.canteach.gov.uk/ and the TTA publication '*Supporting Trainee Teachers – Subject Knowledge Materials*' TTA 2000).

Evidence from Ofsted inspections of initial teacher education courses (Baker *et al.* 2000) has pointed to ways in which the level of subject knowledge has an impact on beginning teachers' development:

- It helps beginning teachers to feel confident in the classroom. This confidence underpins their planning and teaching. They are able to focus on developing their subject knowledge pedagogy, to structure individual lessons and sequences of lessons and to select appropriate teaching methods.
- Feeling confident about subject knowledge facilitates the production of classroom resources and learning materials.
- Their teaching reflects their depth of subject knowledge. They rarely make errors and are able to include in their teaching relevant analogies and anecdote.
- They are able to cope with unexpected questions and are able to respond to complex enquiries. Lack of subject knowledge produces incorrect or generalized answers.
- They are adept at helping pupils understand the language and organizing concepts of their subject. Where beginning teachers themselves have a clear conceptual framework, they are able to recognize potential difficulties of understanding, and develop their teaching accordingly.
- Understanding how the subject teaching links to basic skills. Particular literacy and numeracy requirements, for example, moving from narrative to analytical writing, and cross-curricular themes such as citizenship, are more effectively taught from a strong subject knowledge base.

In terms of policy initiatives, subject knowledge is seen as one of the main planks for raising the standards in the profession. It is tautological to say that, without feeling confident in their subject knowledge, teachers will be unable to develop varieties of strategies in the classroom for teaching. If teachers are always having to refer to their notes for details, or are just one step ahead of the pupils through reading a textbook, they can hardly focus on pupils' work and learning, or understand the conceptual processes the subject demands. For example, a history teacher, teaching the Medieval period, would find it difficult to explain the concept of feudalism if concentrating on imparting the factual knowledge of the Battle of Hastings only and then following the diagram on the feudal structure in the textbook. The significance of land tenure resulting from the establishment of a feudal monarchy and the complex interplay between the knowledge, skills and concepts of history would be limited, as would the ability to explore the power relationships implicit in this social organization. Inevitably, the learning opportunities for pupils to develop their understandings would likewise be limited. Is there then a link between teachers' subject knowledge and effective teaching? Does a deeper understanding of the subject encourage the flexibility of teacher conceptions and yield knowledge in the form of multiple and fluid conceptions?

Research into the place of a teacher's subject knowledge and its links to effective teaching is part of the wider body of research into the professional knowledge held by teachers. 'Initially much of the literature was based on the ideas of the great theorists from Rousseau to Dewey, while later it found its natural home within the psychology, sociology, philosophy and history of education disciplines. In focusing on these four domains of knowledge, teaching could claim to be gathering intellectual respectability and professional status along the lines of traditional professions. Applying the methodologies of the social science disciplines therefore gave credence to much of the highly operationalized and fragmented theorizing that had proceeded it.' (Hoyle and John 1995). Numerous taxonomies that claim to describe and delineate teachers' professional knowledge have been produced over the past thirty years as a result of intensive research. These different taxonomies are underpinned by rival epistemologies (positivist, interpretative, critical, etc.). Whilst these different epistemologies are often oppositional, most of the research into teachers' professional knowledge rarely draws on one approach exclusively, and more recent typifications of professional knowledge adopt an eclectic approach. This research offers several definitions of teachers' professional knowledge as well as explanations of the different forms of knowledge teachers hold (for example, see Dewey 1904; Schulman 1987; Brown and McIntyre 1993; Cooper and McIntyre 1996; Calderhead and Shorrock 1997).

> Research in teacher education cannot at present offer one comprehensive theory of professional development … Nevertheless, inquiries into the professional growth of teachers have tended to cluster around five particular models that emphasize specific aspects of learning to teach, and that construe the learning process in particular ways.
>
> (Calderhead and Shorrock 1997)

Calderhead and Shorrock identify these five models as being:

1   enculturation or socialization into the professional culture. This emphasizes the socializing process of professional development;
2   technical or knowledge and skills model, which emphasizes the knowledge and skills teachers acquire that contribute to classroom practice;
3   subject knowledge and pedagogical content knowledge – knowledge of examples, anecdotes, experiments, knowledge which helps teachers to communicate the subject matter;
4   teaching as a moral endeavour;
5   the close relationship between personal development and the professional in teachers' work.

The most influential work on the place of subject knowledge in teachers' professional knowledge was carried out in the late 1980s by Shulman. He identified that the 'missing paradigm' on research into teachers' professional knowledge was their subject knowledge. He suggested the following categories of teacher knowledge:

- content knowledge
- general pedagogical knowledge i.e. the broad principles and strategies of classroom management and organization that appear to transcend subject matter
- curriculum knowledge i.e. this includes knowledge of the way in which subjects are organized in schools, a knowledge of the National Curriculum, knowledge of literacy, numeracy and ICT, etc.
- pedagogical content knowledge – the way in which teachers transform their knowledge of the subject for the classroom through their knowledge of explanation, styles of teaching and learning, activities and tasks, etc.
- knowledge of learners and their characteristics
- knowledge of educational contexts, ranging from the working of the group or classroom, the way in which schools are financed and governed, etc.
- knowledge of historical ends, i.e. purposes and values of education together with its history and philosophy.

It was Schulman's identification of pedagogic content knowledge which provided the analytical tool and framework for further research into teachers' use of subject knowledge (see Banks *et al.* 1999). Other models of teachers' subject knowledge have focused on ways it is held in an intellectual way and transformed into classroom activity and pupil learning. Prestage and Perks, through their study of students on an initial teacher education maths course, identified 'that teachers' subject knowledge in mathematics might be held in two forms, either as learner-knowledge in mathematics or as teacher-knowledge in mathematics. The former is the knowledge needed to pass examinations, to find solutions to mathematical problems; the latter the knowledge needed to plan for others to come to learn mathematics' (Prestage and Perks 2000). They also argue that teachers in evaluating their lessons need to consider not only the 'teacher-knowledge', such as how well the lesson achieved its objectives, how well the class was managed, what pupil learning took place, etc., but also the 'learner-knowledge', the concepts, skills and understandings which underpin the content of the lesson.

These models of teachers' professional knowledge provide useful insights into our understanding of developing teaching, how subject knowledge is used, transformed and integrated with other forms of professional understanding in order to provide effective teaching and learning. However, all models and theoretical frameworks, whilst offering concrete representations of something as abstract as teacher knowledge, provide only partial answers to the complex process of teaching, and are often derived from external unsituated testing. They do not necessarily answer the question as to why subject knowledge is at the heart of teachers' professional knowledge. What are the links then between subject knowledge and effective teaching?

Subject knowledge and effective teaching

By the time of their final assessed school placement, graduates entering teaching need to demonstrate that they have a

> secure knowledge and understanding of the concepts and skills in their specialist subject(s) at a standard equivalent to degree level to enable them to teach it (them) confidently and accurately at … Key Stage 3 and Key Stage 4 and, where relevant, post-16 for trainees on 11–16 or 18 courses.
>
> (DfEE 1998a)

The extent to which beginning teachers are able to do this depends to some extent on their degree profile. There are also different challenges in matching some subjects to the school curriculum. Reading 3.1 identifies some of these.

Reading 3.1 Subject knowledge and the secondary school curriculum

Science

Some schools organize their science timetable in separate subjects or modules so that teachers do not have to move outside their specialism. However, it is very likely that at some point in a teaching career, science teachers will have to teach outside the subject range they feel comfortable with. For science graduates, it is likely that there are areas such as earth science and space science which they may not have studied before. If they are physics graduates, for example, who did not study any life sciences, then they may find that the area of life processes and living things might present something of a challenge.

Music

The National Curriculum in music does not prescribe specific examples of music to be studied, but rather articulates its intentions more broadly, in terms of the 'opportunities', 'experiences', 'knowledge' and 'skills' which children should enjoy. Consequently, each school's music curriculum can, within certain parameters, reflect the particular needs and interests of children and teachers alike. This should include a range of live and recorded music from different times and cultures. Teachers need to be aware of the implication that this has for the development of their own subject knowledge and musical skills.

Many music degrees have, until recently, concentrated upon western music and the acquisition of advanced performance skills. Composition and the study of electro-acoustic music, jazz and world musics, if they were available at all, tended to be specialist options. Effective music teachers therefore need to have a developing familiarity with a wide range of musical styles and an awareness of the potential of different musical mediums – including electro-acoustic, computer technology and non-western instruments. This does not mean, of course, that a music teacher cannot have musical likes and dislikes. A music teacher's enthusiasms are the life-blood of their teaching. Indeed, to have no strong opinions about music would almost inevitably lead to an insufferably bland teaching style. What is to be avoided, however, is a musical perspective based on preconceived notions of what music is and a knowledge of music which is restricted to the narrowness of one's own tastes. Teaching music is a marvellous opportunity to develop musical skills and interests. In this respect, as in many others, the children should be treated as partners. They will introduce different types of music, which although often transient, will offer invaluable opportunities for teaching and learning.

English

From 'Beowulf' to 'The Color Purple', prose, poetry and drama, the range of children's literature, knowledge about language – with such a vast field, it would be most unusual to find an English teacher who did not have gaps in their personal subject knowledge. Neither, of course, does the range of literature have an end point. New books are constantly appearing. Teaching new texts means knowing about the relevant period, the traditions and other authors writing at that time.

Modern Foreign Languages

A language teacher's priority must be their own linguistic competence. It may be some time since they spoke their second language for a prolonged period, but they should be spending much of the day speaking this in school. Teachers offer a linguistic model for pupils. In view of the range of themes to be covered, language teachers may need to up-date their knowledge of the areas of the world in which the target language is spoken. Language is not static, nor does it exist separately from its culture. If a language teacher's knowledge of, say, French culture, was acquired some years ago, then it will need up-dating.

Source: Open University Initial Teacher Education Programme Team.

As these examples show, up-dating subject knowledge is a central feature of developing as a teacher. A review of research into teacher knowledge suggests a few features of subject knowledge that influence teaching:

- Whilst defining 'depth' of subject knowledge is highly problematic, there is some evidence that deeper subject knowledge results in more emphasis on conceptual explanations (Ball 1991).
- Work by Leinhardt and Smith (1985) indicates that where teachers had a large mental map of their subject matter, they were more able to understand

the relationship of individual topics or skills to the more general topics. This had an impact on their organization of knowledge for pupils.

• Work by Grossman *et al.* (1989) indicates that there are four dimensions of subject knowledge that influence the teaching and learning of beginning teachers. These four dimensions, content knowledge, substantive knowledge, syntactic knowledge and personal beliefs, merit further exploration.

Content knowledge

As Grossman *et al.* indicate, content knowledge is by no means a straightforward concept. It includes factual information, but also the central concepts and organizing principles of the subject. So, for example, in history, content knowledge is not synonymous with factual knowledge. It embraces both a knowledge of, say, the French revolution, together with an understanding of the organizing principles – revolution, monarchy, republicanism – together with historical concepts such as causation and chronology.

A lack of content knowledge can cause teachers to avoid teaching topics with which they are unfamiliar. In their research sample, Grossman *et al.* found that English teachers who were uncertain of their own knowledge of grammar avoided teaching it. A lack of content knowledge may also mean that teachers rely heavily on textbook interpretations. Often they have access to only one textbook covering the topic.

> Given teachers' lack of time, the textbook provides a convenient source of relevant facts and information. Textbooks become for many teachers, major sources of new content knowledge … . Unfortunately, without adequate understanding of the concepts and content of a subject matter, teachers are unable to appraise critically the adequacy, accuracy and salience of the text.
>
> (Grossman *et al.* 1989)

Additionally, teachers' lack of content knowledge can also affect how they teach. For example, teachers who are uncertain of their content knowledge often choose to lecture rather than engage in open discussion and exploration, which might lead pupils to raise questions the teacher was unable to answer.

Substantive knowledge and syntactic knowledge as dimensions of teacher subject knowledge are drawn from work done by Schwab (1978) on the structure of disciplines. These structures are not always made explicit in the study of particular specialisms, but are implicit in its methodology.

Substantive knowledge

This is the framework, or model of explanation, which guides the inquiry in a discipline, and which varies from subject to subject. Grossman *et al.* found that 'a teacher's knowledge of substantive structures has important implications for how and what teachers choose to teach. For example, history teachers are more likely to present historical information that is relevant to the questions they find most interesting, be they social, cultural, political or intellectual' (Grossman *et al.* 1989).

Syntactic knowledge

This provides the procedures and processes of enquiry in a subject area, for example what constitutes scientific or geographical enquiry. A lack of syntactic knowledge may mean that the process of subject enquiry is not taught to pupils. For example, teachers who do not understand the process of historical enquiry may well see teaching history as consisting of learning a string of facts only, rather than interpretation and the critical evaluation of historical evidence. In addition, without a knowledge of the process of enquiry, teachers will be unable themselves to learn new information in their fields, or to question new theories and explanations.

Beliefs about subject knowledge

This dimension includes teachers' personal subject constructs, their own experiences of learning, their gender and ethnicity and beliefs. It is this personal construct, this view of the world, which can determine the extent to which beginning teachers are open to examining the assumptions they hold about their subject knowledge and about approaches to teaching and learning.

What emerges from the discussion of the role of a teacher's subject knowledge in teaching is that up-dating subject knowledge is central both to initial teacher education and to a teacher's continuing professional development.

Subject knowledge and teacher development – beginning teachers and continuing professional development

How then do experienced teachers in practice integrate and up-date their subject knowledge whilst developing their subject related pedagogy? Reading 3.2 identifies how an experienced history teacher tackled this issue.

Reading 3.2 A teacher's subject knowledge

This information was provided in response to an email asking about the place of subject knowledge in the organization of the curriculum.

(Helena teaches history in an 11–18 inner-city comprehensive school. It has 7 forms of entry and draws its intake from the local area which includes council estates with some privately owned housing. Pupils come from ethnically diverse communities and housing estates.)

I have just up-dated our Scheme of Work for Year 9, mainly to accommodate the new National Curriculum and the use of ICT which we have been developing in the department. With the topic on public health in the nineteenth century I've incorporated new material. This includes resources – letters and petitions – taken from the Public Record Office website (www.pro.gov.uk). This includes a collection of teachers' notes and pupil materials organized around themes on Victorian Britain around 1851 (the date of the Great Exhibition). I find some of the background information useful; for example, it gives a succinct biography of Chadwick and Snow, contrasting their characters. I find the original documents (well, the electronic versions) and the transcripts of these valuable resources. In addition, I've found the Institute of Historical Research website really useful. It has links with all the history journals. www.historytoday.com has had a discussion recently on the standard of living debate which includes a lot of new findings on life expectancy and so on. In this way I find ICT an excellent way of keeping in touch with recent developments in history research.

I do find that the standard textbook versions are limited, particularly when it comes to gender and history – despite all the work that's been done on this over the years. I can't quite believe the way in which textbook authors still stick to the old frameworks for the definition of the content of history – possibly they are too obsessed with source evaluation, or historical skills, rather than exploring some of the organizing concepts of history, such as gender. I can't see the point of using materials that are out of touch with the academic debates. I've included some work on the Ladies' Sanitary Association:

> By some means or other, the grand political agencies of Parliament with their Acts and their Boards, must be narrowed down to minute domestic application. The cesspool … must not only be closed and got rid of … the chimney must be cured of smoking, the butcher must not sell bad meat. The infected clothes must be burned after an epidemic.
> (Ladies' Sanitary Association Annual Report 1859)

This raises discussion about the different approaches to public health – the domestic and the policy areas, and there is possible further work here on the role of charity and attitudes to the working class – how inappropriate the suggestions for food were when many people didn't have anywhere to cook other than an open fire. I've also found some new work which considers the impact of levels of spending on public health in England and Wales. It examines the links between sanitary reforms and declining mortality rates – it allows for some database work and presents an argument for the impact of reform and expenditure, particularly on the declining infant mortality found at the end of the nineteenth century.

I've revised the pupils' activities and integrated the evaluation of sources in a structured enquiry into the impact of sanitary reforms on public health. I always found the evaluation of historical sources taken out of their historical context, an exercise in 'source evaluation', a particularly sterile activity. It led to teaching to a formula based on notions of progression – moving from communicating information from an historical source, to putting together information from different historical sources, to understanding that the value of the source depends on the questions asked. Defining progression in source evaluation is to define a hierarchy of activities which have no meaning in terms of the historical process itself.

In doing this work I rely on other members of my department to discuss issues and plan activities. We discuss teaching history with a wider group of history teachers through annual conferences, journals and on-line discussion links. I also depend on the academic history journals and websites for the latest research.

The academic network

The experiences of this teacher highlight the importance of keeping in touch with academic debates in the subject – the areas of controversy, competing theories, different schools of thought and hard-fought terrain. Without these links, Helena would be limited in the ways in which she could interpret the National Curriculum. A heavy reliance on textbooks to teach a prescribed National Curriculum would leave subject knowledge closed to question. The further the school curriculum is removed from its academic roots, the nearer it can be said to resemble propaganda. For what then is the basis for this knowledge other than a state directive, and assumptions about what is relevant to teach to pupils? Whilst the school curriculum, and therefore teachers' subject knowledge, do need to contain those aspects of knowledge considered important by the wider society, subject knowledge also needs to be informed by the shared understandings and differences, the nuances of debate and uncertainty which characterize interactions within each subject's shifting and changing academic community. Maintaining the network with the academic community is therefore an important part of teachers' subject knowledge development. This can be done through:

Subject associations   In addition to supporting teachers' pedagogic subject knowledge, and representing the views of subject teachers to a wide audience, subject associations such as NATE and ASE provide advice on up-dating subject knowledge, have links to relevant academic journals, and hold annual conferences. Some subject associations provide a review of the year's academic publications, which provides a useful and quick route to finding the latest work on a particular subject.

Websites   The Internet provides one of the fastest growing sources of subject knowledge support for teachers. Education websites, such as the National Grid for Learning, include forums where teachers can discuss at a national level issues of teaching and learning. Subject-specific websites are now legion: the English and Media Centre site at www.rmplc.co.uk/orgs/emedia.index.html is one such.

Continuing academic study in the area of subject knowledge   Teachers' own individual interest and enthusiasm for their subject often leads them either to undertake further academic study in their subject area, or to practise, in cases of art, music, drama, English and Modern Foreign Language teachers, some of the knowledge, skills and understandings they teach. This study is invaluable in terms of helping teachers to understand the conventions of subject knowledge which can be ever-changing and questioned, and approaches to subject knowledge enquiry. Considering their own academic learning often enables teachers to understand more clearly the processes and conceptual explanations which facilitate pupil learning.

It is perhaps unfortunate that over the past twenty years or so, the emphasis given to teachers' professional development, through school or LEA in-service courses, has neglected to include programmes which specifically address the development of subject knowledge, concentrating instead on pedagogy. Traditional forms of teacher development have mainly focused on generic learning and teaching skills, such as group work, which do not necessarily help teachers to develop teaching strategies aimed at developing pupils' understanding of important subject concepts. Teachers need the opportunity to explore subject knowledge themselves before grappling with how to teach it (Ball 1991).

The teacher education network

At the same time as maintaining links with the academic subject network, links with other teachers lead to the development of new insights into pupils' learning. Involvement in action research programmes enables teachers to integrate the demands of the subject with the knowledge of pupil learning. Figure 3.2 shows the different spheres of influence on effective subject teaching and learning.

Within government initiatives to support teachers' continuing professional development, there is an increased emphasis placed on teaching as research and evidence-based practice. This initiative accords with the view of teacher development implicit in action research into classroom practice.

'Teachers who use research and evidence effectively in order to improve their practice and raise attainment' know how to find and interpret existing high-quality evidence from a range of sources; see professional development as a means of improving classroom practice rather than as an end in itself; and regard pedagogy as integral to learning' (TTA 1999).

Many educational researchers would question the purpose of educational research being focused mainly on 'raising standards' but would place the emphasis rather on understanding teaching and learning, which in turn raises standards. There is also considerable controversy surrounding the simple causal links implicit in the above statement, about teacher input and pupils' standards. However, this initiative indicates the importance being placed on teacher and action research in the development of teachers' professional practice. Action research, undertaken by teachers and teacher educators and aiming at improving understanding of practice and the situations in which practices are carried out, is well established as an approach to educational research. Action research is best carried out collaboratively by, for example, people in a department or a group of teachers across subjects interested in, say, thinking skills. Teachers often work collaboratively with their local education authority advisers, or staff from Higher Education Institution's education departments. In terms of method, a self-reflective spiral of cycles of planning, acting, observing and collectively analysing is central to an action research approach. In education, this has been employed in school-based curriculum development, professional development and school improvement programmes. Action research forms the basis of much effective professional development. Co-teaching, collaborative planning and observing lessons give teachers new insights into their day-to-day practice. The emphasis here then is on the importance of teachers' own theorizing, on their own development of insights into learning informed by wider research and evidence-based practice. Teacher research grants have been made

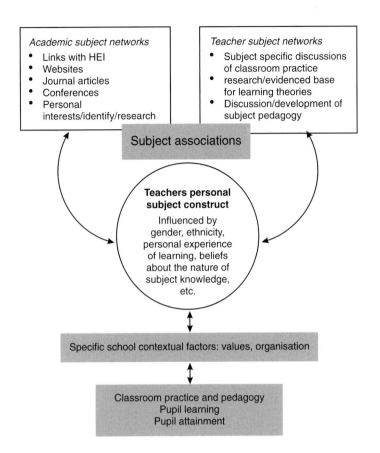

Figure 3.2 Networks of support, teachers' subject knowledge and pedagogy

available by the TTA to fund small-scale, classroom-based research. Funding is now available from the DfES under the Best Practice Research Scheme. Reading 3.3 (overleaf) is an example of one such research project.

Beginning teachers and subject knowledge

The final section of this chapter returns to the question of beginning teachers' subject knowledge. Teacher educators have developed various approaches to supporting beginning teachers' development of subject knowledge. These include:

- An audit of subject knowledge at the outset of the course. This audit is usually carried out against the National Curriculum at Key Stages 3 and 4 and the most common topics found at post-16. The audit identifies beginning teachers' depth of subject knowledge and their levels of confidence to teach their subject to particular age groups. This initial audit identifies the focus for beginning teachers to up-date their subject knowledge.

Reading 3.3 Language issues in the teaching and learning of school algebra

Aim

To investigate the link between language and competence in algebra, highlight the problems experienced by pupils when learning algebra, and suggest some strategies for teachers.

Dimensions of this case study

The research was carried out from September 1997 to May 1998 with 55 pupils aged 14–16 and two teachers.

Summary of findings for this case study

For pupils

- A significant number of pupils with low reading ages and poor problem-solving skills demonstrated competence with algebra.
- Common misconceptions occurred because pupils could not relate to teacher language which reflected a sophisticated understanding of algebra.
- Pupils found it difficult to describe and discuss the algebra they used and generally did not use the language used by their teachers.

For teachers

- It appeared that the main stress was on the learning of methods and building the confidence of the pupils.
- The skills and level of understanding associated with school algebra were accessible to many pupils where the teaching approach was appropriate.
- The vocabulary of algebra needed to be explicitly taught, practised and revised.
- Confidence was central to achievement in algebra. When planning the curriculum, emphasis needed to be on those areas where skills and understanding could develop together.

Source: Gerry Wearden (TTA 1999).

- Initial teacher education courses include materials or seminars which enable beginning teachers to explore their subject knowledge and understand the nature of the discipline. For example, materials or discussion on GCSE could give beginning teachers not only an understanding of GCSE, but also effective opportunities to enhance their own subject knowledge. During the course of their training, beginning teachers are also introduced to a wide range of textbooks, articles and other materials. With many courses now having a web-based component, this also allows beginning teachers to be directed to relevant sites for the purpose of subject knowledge update materials. E-conferencing allows the subject knowledge expertise of some teachers to be shared with the wider group, as well as allowing for links with a 'Guest Speaker' on aspects of subject knowledge.

- Subject mentors also make a contribution to beginning teachers' subject knowledge through, for example, identifying relevant reading and pointing out the specialization of other members of staff.
- School-focused and written assignments are designed to encourage beginning teachers to develop an area of subject knowledge weakness, analyse the learning processes involved, and then consider the implications for teaching.

This chapter has considered the place of subject knowledge in the development of a teacher's professional knowledge, and approaches to up-dating and keeping in touch with subject knowledge. Through teaching, experienced teachers improve their knowledge of certain topics and gain fresh insights into whole new areas of their specialist subject. Many people are attracted into the profession by a desire to share with young people their own interest in and enthusiasm for learning their subject specialism. Maintaining links with specialist subject academic networks, through such means as reading, lectures, websites, fieldwork, etc., is central to teachers' professional knowledge. Just as teachers have to 'theorize' about pupils' learning and the effectiveness or otherwise of the teaching and learning strategies they use in the classroom, they likewise need to maintain authority in relation to their subject matter knowledge. How else are they to measure the accuracy of the resources they use and avoid the ossification of subject knowledge? How else are they to maintain a creative and lively enthusiasm in their teaching and avoid the stale, rigid and mechanistic approach to teaching? Without teacher enthusiasm, how can pupils' interest and engagement flourish?

References

Alexander, R., Rose, J. and Woodhead, C. (1992) *Curriculum Organisation and Classroom: Practice in Primary Schools*, London: HMSO.

Baker, C., Cohn, T. and McLaughlin, M. (2000) 'Inspecting subject knowledge' in J. Arthur and R. Phillips (eds) *Issues in History Teaching*, London: Routledge.

Ball, D.L. (1991) 'Research in teaching mathematics: making subject knowledge part of the equation' in J. Brophy (ed.) *Advances in Research on Teaching. Vol. 2. Teachers' Knowledge of Subject as it Relates to their Teaching Practices*, pp. 1–48, Greenwich, CT: JAI Press.

Banks, F., Leach, J. and Moon, B. (1999) 'New understandings of teachers' pedagogic knowledge' in J. Leach and B. Moon (eds) *Learners and Pedagogy*, London: Paul Chapman.

Brown, S. and McIntyre, D. (1993) *Making Sense of Teaching*, Buckingham: Open University Press.

Calderhead, J. and Shorrock, S.B. (1997) *Understanding Teacher Education*, London: Falmer Press.

Cooper, P. and McIntyre, D. (1996) *Effective Teaching and Learning: Teacher and Student Perspectives*, Buckingham: Open University Press.

DES (1977) *The Curriculum 11–16*, London: HMSO.

DfEE (1998a) *Teaching: High Status, High Standards* (Circular 4/98), London: DfEE.

—— (1998b) *Teachers: Meeting the Challenge of Change* (Green Paper), London: DfEE.

Dewey, J. (1904) 'The relation of theory to practice in education', in C.A. Murry (ed.) *The Relation of Theory to Practice in the Education of Teachers (Third Yearbook of the National Society for the Scientific Study of Education, Part 1)*, Bloomington, IL: Public School Publishing.

Grossman, P., Wilson, S. and Shulman, L. (1989) 'Teachers of substance: subject matter knowledge for teaching', in M.C. Reynolds (ed.) *Knowledge Base for the Beginning Teacher*, Oxford: Pergamon Press.

HMI (1985) *The Curriculum from 5 to 16*, London: HMSO.

Hoyle, E. and John, P. (1995) *Professional Knowledge and Professional Practice*, London: Cassell.

Leinhart, G. and Smith, D. (1985) 'Expertise in mathematics instruction: subject matter knowledge', *Journal of Educational Psychology* 77: 247–71.

Maguire, M., Dillon, J. and Quintrell, M. (1998) *Finding Virtue, Not Finding Fault: Stealing the Wind of Destructive Reforms*, London: Association of Teachers and Lecturers (ATL).

Morrison, K. (1986) 'Primary school subject specialists as agents of school-based curriculum change', *School Organisation* 6(2): 175–83.

Prestage, S. and Perks, P. (2000) 'Subject Knowledge: Developing a Fourth Sense', paper presented at the British Educational Research Association Conference, Cardiff University, 7–10 September 2000.

Richards, C., Harding, P. and Webb, D. (1997) *A Key Stage 6 Core Curriculum: A Critique of the National Curriculum for Initial Teacher Training*, London: Association for Teachers and Lecturers (ATL).

Schwab, J.J. (1978). 'Education and structure of the disciplines', in I. Westbury and N.J. Wilkof (eds) *Science Curriculum, and a Liberal Education*, Chicago: University of Chicago Press.

Shulman, L.S. (1987) 'Knowledge and teaching: foundations of the new reforms', *Harvard Educational Review* 7(1): 1–22.

TTA (1999a) *Improving Standards Research and Evidence Based Practice*, London: TTA.

—— (1999b) *Teacher Research Grant Schemes. Summary of Findings – 1998*, Publication No. 66/8–99, London: TTA.

—— (2000) *Supporting Trainee Teachers: Subject Knowledge Materials*, London: TTA.

Times Educational Supplement (*TES*) 19 January 1969.

Wilson, S.M. (1991) 'Parades of facts, stories of the past: what do novice history teachers need to know?' in M. Kennedy (ed.) *Teaching Academic Subjects to Diverse Learners*, pp. 99–116, New York: Teachers College Press.

4 Language and learning

Introduction

This chapter seeks to raise some key issues about language and learning and their practical impacts upon teaching and learning in the classroom. The beginning teacher will be aware of the many theories about language and learning that are available for consideration and the need for a thoughtful and practical synthesis of these. It is the task of other texts to present the key facets of these learning theories and to debate their detail and weight (Moon *et al.* 2001). This chapter does not argue for any easy relationship between the two elements of theory and practice; and still less does it present a case that the school placements of trainee teachers are simply about 'applying' theories about learning to practical contexts. It does press the view that what is regarded by educational communities as authoritative, supportive theory about learning (and teaching) needs to be taken and given shape by practical reworkings so that new understandings emerge. In addition, what is essentially a symbiotic relationship between the theory and practice of teaching and learning means that each element – theory, teaching, and learning – is changed by the relationship. Each is enhanced by the others and new supports for teaching and learning are created.

It is the purpose of this chapter to raise some central aspects related to learning processes and attempt to frame these so that the beginning teacher might make an understanding of these work productively in the classroom. Five core sections examine:

- issues relating to practical perspectives and learning theories
- issues and practicalities of language and learning processes
- implications for departments and schools
- the Key Stage 3 Strategy and literacy across the secondary curriculum
- thinking and accelerated learning issues.

Later chapters of this book, in Part 2, focus in much greater depth on constituent, supporting and interrelated parts of an effective subject teacher's role: those on planning, classroom methods, classroom management and assessment processes, for example. What is offered there is predicated upon commonly shared understandings of the rationales of learning processes and practical implications for the teaching–learning dynamic.

Issues relating to the practical perspectives of learning theories

A beginning teacher will find the array of learning theory texts available for perusal not far short of bewildering (examples are: Piaget 1926; Brainerd 1978; Beard 1969; Britton 1987; Bruner 1966a, 1966b, 1983; Eysenck and Kamin 1981; Skinner 1974; Gardiner 1993, 1999; Jensen 1969; Vygotsky 1962, 1978; Perkins 1995). Decades of research studies, critiques of established theory, models for organizing propositions about how learning occurs and in what contexts, variables identified as impinging positively and negatively, variables which have been perceived as inert and later are challenged as impactful upon learning processes, all offer their own contributions to the central discourse of educational communities. All of these concerns properly belong both to academics and to teachers in schools.

Some of the possible and actual applications of the work of educational theorists referred to above can only be indicated here. Gardiner's contributions to concept-ualizations of learning, for example, not least that of 'multiple intelligences', reminds us that a 'one size fits all' method of teaching and learning is unlikely to produce uniformly high learning gains in classrooms, since individuals have predispositions to learn effectively using different abilities, senses, skills and learning routes. The move to differentiation in teaching strategies to foster learning – of task, resource and support, for example – can be seen to have links with this concept. Subtleties and details of the concepts and arguments pursued in the text references indicated above will rapidly reveal themselves to the interested student of such areas of educational debate and practice. Any beginning or experienced teacher will find that both the theories and the practical manifestations of them in school will produce a tranche of further understandings and re-shapings of existing ones. It is arguably the reification of their theories and research studies that these writers would have least liked. New meanings and recognitions, created in practical contexts by thinking professionals, might be the greatest outcome of and tribute to these conceptual starting points by subject teachers in the classroom. And how might these new recognitions and reworkings occur? They can only emerge from 'deep' or 'profound learning' (Bowring-Carr and West-Burnham 1997). The salient features of learning, and the teaching that accompanies it, may show themselves in the classroom in the ways suggested below:

- Pupil and teacher are continuously aware of and discuss the processes of learning;
- Pupil and teacher will ensure that assessment procedures embrace process as well as product;
- Pupil and teacher will look together for a range of ways in which learning can best be demonstrated;
- Before a new topic is started, time will be given to an exploration of the 'mind map' of the pupils to establish their (varying) understandings, strengths, and starting points;
- Pupil and teacher together ensure that over a period of time all intelligences are stretched and engaged;
- The purpose of the learning will be focused on enabling an individual to change, grow and become autonomous;

- Quality investigation of less material will benefit pupils' learning more than coverage of larger areas more superficially.

(adapted from Bowring-Carr and West-Burnham 1997)

These are the kinds of practical ramifications alongside which we need to place educational theories. Testing them, reworking them, with pupils engaged with teachers in the learning processes, forms the business of good teaching.

Issues and practicalities of language and learning processes

The commonly expressed phrase 'language and learning' describes symbiotic and complex relationships. Learning takes place through language use; language use and its development shape thinking and learning. Language use relates to the interplay of all the language modes: speaking, reading, listening, writing, and its fifth representation, thinking. The concept of 'literacy' and literate outcomes from pupils at different Key Stages of education has come to dominate a national standards agenda and a professional discourse which formerly addressed what were referred to as 'language and learning' issues. In professional debates relating to this, among teachers of English, for example, speaking and listening and the range of activities and processes related to drama have consistently been included as part of any definition of literacy. Such definitions went beyond an early, narrower official view of the term which focused heavily on reading and writing competence. A gradual, formal recognition in the later years of the twentieth century that quality, structured writing, for example, is the complex outcome of things seen, experienced, heard, overheard, read, discussed and thought about, resulted in a wider definition of the terms 'literate' and 'literacy'. Interestingly, this development occurred in the same time period as a more directed, prescriptive version of the term, embodied in the 'Literacy Hour' which has been more about a publicly declared, politically propelled push for improved across-the-board consistency of teaching practice and pupil achievement at a national level, initially in primary schools.

The wider, well-established practitioner-professional definition of literacy, then, clearly forms an integral part of discussion about language and learning processes. It supplies, too, a support for thinking, to allow children to consider the 'possible worlds' (Bruner 1983) beyond the immediate, physical present.

Language and achievement or underachievement

Language is not only the medium through which ideas are communicated and relationships formed. It is also the medium through which teachers assess learners (and through which learners come to know and sum up their teachers). Accents, dialects and ways of talking and writing are markers through which we consciously and unconsciously establish our identities and social allegiances. They are also used by others in the judgements they form about people's backgrounds. Through the medium of language, notions of an individual's class identity, ethnicity, and potential ability are all formed. When they enter the classroom, teachers and pupils bring with them the range of social stereotypes and pre-judgements that are found in the wider society of which the school is a part.

These issues are clarified in Wood's *How Children Think and Learn*, which in part focuses on language and underachievement in relation to social class. Wood argues that linguistic and intellectual development occur together. Through language, children learn to evaluate, monitor and plan their own intellectual activities. In the first edition of his book, Wood explained how effective teaching exposes children to:

> ways of thinking that characterise different disciplines ... Ways of thinking, in mathematics, history, geography or whatever, have developed to achieve certain ways of making sense of and understanding the world. Unless the child practises the role of being a mathematician, historian or geographer, learns the issues that excite such people, the problems that interest them and the tools that help them to resolve and solve these, then the child may only learn empty tricks or procedures and will not inherit the discipline itself.
>
> (Wood 1988: 84)

Wood makes the point that a major part of the practice of different intellectual disciplines concerns the language they use, through which they construct their concepts and make sense of the world. Language learning cannot be separated from curriculum learning and every subject teacher needs consciously to take on the role of a teacher of language development. Chapter 12 of this text refers to the teacher-tutor's contribution to whole-school endeavours, of which this is one part. All teachers, then, whatever their specialist subject area, need to be aware of the role of language in teaching and learning, to develop their knowledge about the way language is used within their particular subject areas and to plan for literacy gains for their pupils. This awareness needs to have practical results. Wood poses a question which he himself answers in relation to this: 'how active should teachers be .... In aiding a child in ... problem-solving and ... conceptual constructions? Very active.' (ibid: 183).

In a different, impactful text, *How is Language Used as a Medium for Classroom Education?*, Mercer (2000) places an accent on spoken language in his discussion of his own research findings and those of others. The outcomes here also suggest a key brief for teachers in their planning to enable pupils to negotiate the different genres of discourse that have been revealed in a range of subject areas. So:

> Teachers have a responsibility for guiding students' use of language as a social mode of thinking and to express their understanding in the appropriate language genres or discourses ... (p. 109) ... [Such a genre approach] offers teachers and students an analysis of how English or any other language is used in specific social contexts and attempts to make explicit the 'ground rules' for producing ... appropriate ways of writing (p. 125).
>
> (Mercer 2000)

Wood (1998), though, warns against an over-reliance on teacher-directed talk and questioning. If pupil talk, in pairs or groups, for problem-solving and exploration, is essential to discovery and the writing process, as proposed in Reading 4.1, as well as for other learning gains, then the truncation of this activity creates special problems for language development and learning. Wood writes that if talk is teacher-dominated:

involving frequent teacher-directed questions, [this] may be effective in achieving certain managerial and instructional ends, but it seems unlikely to provide good conditions for developing children's powers as narrators, informants and, perhaps, self-regulating learners. The challenges confronting the teachers are far from trivial and demand considerable expertise in what are very special forms of communication.

(Wood 1998: 179)

The subject-specific gains potentially to be made, as well as the generic ones relating to literacy and other achievements, are taken up and reaffirmed in the Curriculum 2000 documentation from the DfEE. Reading 4.1 raises some practical implications and developments arising from them in whole-school considerations relating to language use in subject areas and wider literacy programmes. The role of the English department in these processes is also addressed.

In relation to Reading 4.1, it may well be fruitful for the beginning teacher of any subject specialist area to respond to key considerations which appear to arise from what is a renewed emphasis on all teachers' contributions to the language, learning and literacy enhancement being sought in all schools as part of the national standards and school development agendas. These are:

- the idea that language development and cognitive development are inextricably linked, that curriculum learning cannot be separated from language and literacy learning and that all teachers are, necessarily, teachers of this;
- the importance of valuing, building upon and extending the different language understandings and practices children bring to school;
- the roles of teacher talk and peer-group talk in the classroom, and how these can be developed to create an effective medium for learning for all children, whatever their backgrounds, gender or ethnicity;
- the importance of a growing familiarity with the range of written language necessary for academic achievement across the curriculum, and the practical ways in which pupils' reading, writing, speaking, listening and thinking skills can be extended;
- the concrete effects of a whole-school literacy-across-the-curriculum strategy in supporting teaching and learning processes.

Some practical implications in departments and schools

Literacy across the curriculum and learning gains

Potential contributions to pupils' language development, thinking, and other learning gains, in particular subjects and generically, have been indicated above. There is a distinction to be made here between cross-curricular literacy inputs and the extension of some Literacy Hour practices from primary into secondary schools. This latter development, an attempt to deepen further the perceived gains of the primary school variant, has had its critics, NATE – the National Association for the Teaching of English – among them. Historically,

Reading 4.1 Use of language for learning across the curriculum

One of the models of English [discussed by Cox], focused on a view that saw the potential of English as a cross-curricular vehicle for learning, servicing other subject domains. This view or expectation of English has been re-fashioned somewhat with a growing recognition that all subject areas have a vital role to play here, not simply in terms of posting-up and testing for subject-specific vocabulary, but to contribute more forcefully to the language-learning dynamic rehearsed so eloquently in the Bullock Report of 1975 (DES 1975). In its 'Language for Learning in Key Stage 3' (QCA 2000), the Qualifications and Assessment Authority makes the point that:

> It is important to distinguish between teaching language and literacy across the curriculum and the teaching of language, literacy and litera-ture which continues to be the province of English … . Teachers of subjects other than English need to teach pupils those aspects of language which are vital to success in the subject and reinforce pupils' general skills in writing, talk and reading. In the past, in many subjects in the secondary curriculum, there have been moves to reduce the language demands, particularly in writing, as these were seen as barriers for pupils. In the longer term this is likely to be counter produc-tive, since continuing progress in many subjects is dependent on examination success which relies on pupils' ability to read and to express themselves in language.
>
> (p. 4)

The revised National Curriculum, then, is much more explicit about how all subject teachers might contribute to pupils' ability to use language in different contexts. The requirement is placed upon every subject area to contribute to the development of pupils' skills to:

- express themselves correctly and appropriately and to read accu-rately and with understanding. Since standard English, spoken and written, is the predominant language in which knowledge and skills are taught and learned, pupils should be taught to recog-nize and use standard English;
- use correct spelling and punctuation and follow grammatical conventions; to organize writing in logical and coherent forms.
- use language precisely and cogently in speaking;
- Listen effectively, responding constructively;
- read with understanding, to locate and use information; to follow a process or argument, to synthesize and adapt what they learn from their reading;
- know the specialist vocabulary of subjects and how to spell these words; to use the patterns of language necessary and commonly used for individual subjects.

The Literacy Hour and literacy in the secondary school

The influence of the Bullock Report can be seen in the requirements described above. These mesh, too, in a more functional way with the government's resolve to support enhanced performance from pupils in key literacy skills. The National Literacy Strategy (NLS) was implemented in Key Stages 1 and 2, following the report of the Literacy Task Force of summer 1997. A national target for literacy was set, linked to the Attainment Levels of the National Curriculum for English: by 2002, 80 per cent of 11-year-olds will be expected to reach Level 4 (a satisfactory attainment for Key Stage 1 is set at Level 2) or above in the Key Stage 2 English tests.

Pupils who have experienced the daily Literacy Hour, effectively universally present in primary schools, and the regular word, sentence and text-level activities which have largely composed it, are now in secondary schools. The gains made at primary level are to be used and strengthened in the secondary sector ... . [Other] findings, related to pilot schemes of secondary whole-school literacy initiatives, will be used in order to offer effective classroom strategies to individual subject areas. What follows will be a move to embed in practical terms the statement of principle in the document, Implementation of the National Literacy Strategy:

> Every secondary school should specialise in literacy and set targets for improvements in English. Similarly, every teacher should contribute to promoting it ... . In shaping their plans it is essential that secondary schools do not see work on reading and writing as exclusively the province of a few teachers in the English and learning support departments.
>
> (DfEE 1997: 38)

Source: Storey (2001).

literacy-across-the-curriculum initiatives in schools have had a strongly developed professional practice impetus to them, focused on raising achievement and pooling resources and methods across departments. These certainly stretch back to the 1975 Bullock Report and, in alert, enquiring schools with a collegiate ethos, way before this, of course.

The main findings of the Ofsted *Report on Cross-curricular Literacy 1997–2000* (Ofsted 2000) based on visits to 170 secondary schools were that effective literacy projects were characterized by good school management and a clear priority for literacy in school development plans. Successful practice was well-focused on literacy and was often supported by cross-curricular initiatives as well as what was initially termed 'catch-up' work for low achievers, afterwards referred to as Progress Units. Many schools, it was found, were still at the early stages of literacy development and the most successful had drawn upon external support. Secondary schools had recognized the gains of the primary Literacy Hour but most usually had not acted upon this with any kind of Year 7 intervention programme. The most common failure in evidence was the lack of a coherent strategy to link different approaches across subject departments.

Areas of weakness identified in the survey are informative and present all teachers with pointers about the ineffective uses of data, or about unproductive classroom practice and response. These relate to:

- a lack of focus on literacy development in lesson plans;
- pupils not always offered good models of literacy by those who worked with them;
- underdeveloped systems to support the transfer of literacy learning;
- little tracking of the progress of pupils involved in literacy intervention programmes;
- learning support assistants not always used effectively to enhance pupils' literacy development;
- literacy policies which insufficiently supported or represented whole-school classroom practice.

Nevertheless, those features which composed *effective* literacy development in schools were clear, too, and equally important to consider as strategies for classroom teaching and learning:

- a staged approach aligned to staff development, costed and with accompanying success criteria;
- a multi-layered approach, as opposed to reliance on a single intervention;
- the active involvement of a majority of staff;
- a literacy management group with representatives of different departments with a remit to audit practice, and a responsibility for development, monitoring and evaluation;
- teachers aware of literacy issues who managed opportunities for literacy development in their lessons;
- classrooms visibly supportive of literacy;
- good use of expertise outside the school, such as LEA advisers.

Findings positive and negative are clearly markers for consideration and for practical application for all secondary teachers, beginning and experienced.

Developments such as co-ordinated and pedagogically oriented approaches to extend pupils' learning skills through language and literacy enhancement, effective planning, inclusion of all staff and pupils, with appropriate monitoring and evaluation systems, are simple to recommend and complex to implement. Senior management of a school may not take a lead on this until really pressed to do so, given multiple other requirements of them, and staff turn-over may provide a barrier to sustained development. Moreover, not all pupils, as one of the desirable components of the 'co-ordinated school approach' advised, may be willing to 'take some responsibility for developing their own literacy' (QCA 2000).

Nevertheless, the rewards for such an approach are visible in best practice situations. Despite the difficulties, different department colleagues might well refer to the learning theories and practical findings referred to earlier in this chapter. They remind us that learning is supported by language and literacy development, writing helps to sustain and to structure thought, and reading enables pupils to learn from sources beyond their immediate experience. Language use itself allows pupils opportunities to reflect, revise and evaluate, respond to higher-order questions and encourage the development of thinking skills and enquiry. And improved literacy and learning can have impacts on pupils' motivation, self-esteem and behaviour in class. It can be for pupils literally empowering and at the heart of any classroom teacher's responsibility to them.

Talking, listening, learning and feedback

In relation to the narrow definition of being literate, 'the ability to read and write', subject teachers are often well-versed in what kinds of reading and writing activities are required to meet a tranche of syllabus requirements at different Key Stages. They are sometimes less familiar or confident with the benefits that arise from their pupils' speaking, listening, thinking, problem-solving and sharing feedback processes. For this reason, and in terms of pressing the point about extending approaches for learning gains in all departments, and the wider definition of literacy, this aspect is accented at this point. The learning gains here are legion. Planning for appropriate learning outcomes, though, is essential. There are benefits and limitations attached to variants of talk-thinking-listening-talk processes designed for pairs, small groups (3–4), large groups (5–7), the whole class or for individuals. There are pros and cons too, in relation to group compositions: of friendship, ability, random, structured mixes or of single sex. Simply to ask for talk, listening and feedback without giving attention to these vital elements will limit or even actively undercut learning outcomes relating to knowledge, understanding and skills. Chapters 5 to 8 in Part 2 address these issues in more detail. At this point, though, it is sufficient to post this general caution; and more especially so for departments where active talking and listening, planned for a range of language, literacy and learning outcomes, have not been commonplace. Such scenarios might be: mathematics lessons where pupils work individually in (predominant) silence, history lessons where it is not the norm to share ideas about essay structure or to quiz pupils in role as historical characters; lessons in the science department where 'research' is confined to the lab and 'finding out' things rarely extends to a visit to the school library, or where discussion of thesaurus options of a word or term does not occur. Overleaf, a selection of practical and wide-ranging classroom activities available is indicated. These relate to: thinking, talking, listening, finding out, re-working first thoughts, engaging with others, recounting findings and commenting upon them. Following these processes, a return to whole-class considerations of progress made and understandings and learning gained may well expand and establish learning.

Such strategies as the ones outlined above, embedded in the practice of many successful English departments for years, present pointed implications for planning and organization of lessons across the curriculum. But more than this, possibly, they tackle the issue of the teaching–learning dynamic and especially the notion of placing responsibilities and roles upon pupils and enabling them to play to their strengths and to develop emerging skills, as a commonplace happening of lessons, individual and in sequence. One can see clearly the opportunities available in these descriptions of multiple ways of teasing out the interests and strengths of individuals and the socially dynamic approaches represented by them. What becomes apparent in practice, too, is that 'progress' and 'learning' are messier, more interactive, less static processes than the shaped, theoretical perspectives briefly alluded to at the beginning of this chapter might, at times, suggest.

Pair talk

Easy to organize in cramped classrooms and for high levels of participation. Can be used productively in the early stages of learning. Good for organizing a system of 'response' partners in drafting work; provides essential thinking time and the rehearsal of ideas before whole-class discussion.

Pairs into fours

Pupils work together in pairs, perhaps in friendship or boy-girl pairs, as appropriate. Each pair then joins with another pair to explain and compare ideas.

Listening triads

Pupils work in groups of three. Each pupil takes on the role of speaker, questioner or recorder. The talker explains an event or states a point of view about an issue. The questioner seeks clarification. The recorder makes notes and gives a report at the end of the conversation. Roles are then changed.

Envoys

When groups have completed a task such as the one above, one person from each group acts as an envoy and moves to a new group to explain or summarize and also to find out what a different group thought or decided. The envoy returns to the home group and feeds back. This avoids time-consuming and tedious repetition of the same points in a whole-class reporting-back session. It also places responsibility upon the envoy to be an effective listener and accurate explainer.

Snowball

In pairs, pupils discuss a topic or map out some initial ideas, then double to fours and then into a group of eight in order to decide a course of action or responses to a proposal. The whole class then hears the spokesperson for each group of eight in circumstances that are nearer to and often more effective than formally planned-for public discussion or debate.

Rainbow groups

This is a way of ensuring that pupils work with a range of other individuals. After small groups have had a discussion, pupils are allocated a number or *a colour. Pupils given the same colour or number join up in their new group. Pupils take turns to report back on their new group's work.*

Jigsaw

A topic is divided into sections. In 'home' groups of four or five, pupils allocate a section each, and then regroup into 'expert' groups. In these groups, experts work together on their chosen topic, then return to the original 'home' groups to report back on their area of expertise. The 'home' group is then given a task which requires the pupils to use the different aspects of expertise they have to contribute to a joint outcome. This formulation requires careful planning but ensures the participation of all pupils and the need for them to practise effective listening, thinking and speaking.

Spokesperson

- *Each group appoints a spokesperson to report back findings or views of a group. The first group gives a full feedback to the class. To avoid repetition, additional points are contributed by other groups only if they have not been offered.*
- *Each group is asked in turn to offer one new point until every group 'passes'.*
- *Groups are asked to summarize their findings on A3 sheets which are then displayed. Responses from other class members are invited and views are exchanged with the main group.*

(Adapted from 'Transforming Key Stage 3: National Pilot Literacy across the Curriculum', DfEE 2000)

Key Stage 3 strategy and literacy across the secondary curriculum

This initiative was introduced into secondary schools in September 2001, following a national pilot scheme and as one part of a Key Stage 3 Strategy in order to build on the success of gains made in the primary sector, as indicated in Reading 4.1. It sought also to sustain the strengths and minimize the weaknesses identified in Ofsted's *Report on Cross-curricular Literacy 1997–2000*.

Key Stage 3 national strategy

Some of the explanation of the rationale for this has already been indicated. Specifically, between 1998 and 2000, the number of pupils at Key Stage 2 reaching Level 4 in English reached 75 per cent, a rise of 13 per cent points, and in Mathematics 72 per cent, a rise of 13 per cent points. The logic of this success, seen in these terms, was to build upon it and 'transform' standards in Key Stage 3.

Specifically, too, problems requiring solutions at Key Stage 3 were seen as:

- the dip in pupil performance at the beginning of secondary education;
- the quality of teaching in Key Stage 3; and
- the slow rate of progress of pupils between the ages of 11 and 14.

The breadth of the National Curriculum at Key Stage 3, of 11 subjects, as well as religious education, careers education, sex education, citizenship and personal, social and health education (PSHE), has provided a challenge in that pupils need to be taught enough to experience the distinctiveness of different disciplines in order to make informed choices for study beyond this Key Stage. HMCI's report for 1998/9 indicated that boy–girl achievement differences, the range of attainment between similar schools and the variable achievement of particular minority ethnic groups, remained problems to be addressed. This set of needs was cited as a driver to the Key Stage 3 strategy and was repeated in documents such as *National Literacy Strategy: Review of Research and other Related Evidence* (1998). Raising aspirations of pupils by transformed teaching and learning processes was seen as a catalyst to the transformation. A four-pronged approach was outlined as being at the heart of the Key Stage 3 strategy, and in its cross-curricular and key-subject strands. The four elements of the approach were directed to:

- ensuring continuous progression from Key Stage 2 to Key Stage 3 and beyond in teaching and learning;
- providing opportunities for all pupils to benefit from a range of teaching approaches and contexts designed to promote their motivation and engagement;
- setting high expectations of every pupil in every subject;
- providing a programme of professional development to enable teachers to use a wide range of pilot-tested teaching approaches to underpin the planned transformation of teaching and learning at Key Stage 3.

So, it was to this agenda of needs that pilot-study work and the Key Stage 3 strategy was developed; it included generic whole-school requirements about achievement levels, a Key Stage 3 English strand which sought to build on primary school achievements in literacy and English, as well as a cross-curricular initiative relating to literacy achievement (as well as numeracy and ICT). In this chapter on language and learning, this section focuses on the initiative related to literacy across the secondary curriculum.

Literacy across the curriculum

The 1999–2000 Key Stage 3 National Literacy pilot scheme involved 17 LEAs and 205 schools. One of its participants, a secondary school in Gloucestershire, provides a revealing case study for beginning teachers to consider. The school focused on issues not dissimilar to those identified as areas of need in many other secondary schools: 'the improvement of spoken and written expression'; the 'attainment of boys'; 'monitoring the effective learning policy' of the school; and 'improving the teaching and learning in Key Stage 3'. These central issues identified by the school arise from a mix of post-Ofsted priorities and the school's own Development Plan. The details of the school's strategy are set out in Reading 4.2.

Reading 4.2 Whitecross School Literacy Learning Strategy

Key Stage 3 pilot – case study

School Name: Whitecross School   LEA: Gloucestershire

School's priorities

From Ofsted action plan

- Improving standards of spoken and written expression
- Attainment of boys

From School Development Plan

- Monitoring the effective learning policy
- Improving the teaching and learning in Key Stage 3 (with particular reference to the Key Stage pilot)

The emphasis on the pilot has been to improve the quality of teaching and learning throughout the school. When the training was initiated I was struck by the emphasis on pedagogy and how adopting the four-part lesson structure for all subjects could reinforce the interactive teaching and learning philosophy. The school was also aware of the lack of pace in a lot of lessons in Years 7 and 8, and felt the need to look for ways in which this could be improved. There was also an issue to improve written and spoken expression throughout the school. The cross-curricular approach to literacy, which we had initiated, to some success, in September 1998 was given a higher profile with the new framework and the cross-curricular 'Language for Learning' objectives. It also allowed us as a school to feel confident about going forward with this initiative as we had started to take some of the steps already. It did, however, give us a focus to address the issues of our Ofsted action plan. Finally the underachievement of boys, at Key Stages 3 and 4, has been an issue that we have wrestled with. The school felt that the pilot would give us a structure in which to address these issues of underachievement.

Strategy and its benefits

The strategy has helped in the following ways:

- It has allowed English and Mathematics departments the opportunity to focus on improving teaching and learning. The extra resources have been invaluable in allowing this to happen
- It has given the school an opportunity to focus its work to address weaknesses the school has in its provision for pupils as identified in the Ofsted action plan
- It has given an impetus to teachers to develop their planning, teaching, focusing on learning outcomes for pupils and the use of assessment, which they would otherwise not have had

- It has given an opportunity for whole-school planning, on key issues at middle management level
- It has improved the quality of experience for pupils in Years 7, 8 and 9 and given them ways to address their own learning agenda
- There is a sense of optimism for teachers about some aspects of their teaching, which has been missing for some time
- Use of booster groups has allowed the school to target pupils who would not normally be part of any special needs provision and yet the school has recognized that these pupils have needed input.

Support provided by the LEA

- At consultant level the support provided has been outstanding with the core subjects
- Support from the advisory level in the LEA is also outstanding.

What next

- Improving schemes of work at Key Stage 3 explicitly to teach literacy and numeracy objectives in all subjects
- Revising the school's assessment policy to support this initiative
- Introducing the four-part lesson into the pedagogy of teachers at Whitecross
- Evaluating the impact of the pilot particularly on boys and all students who were at Level 3 or below on entering Year 7 at Whitecross.

School management (reworking practice)

The school leadership team has implemented the following activities to improve the delivery of the Key Stage 3 pilot. With hindsight some of these would be augmented:

- The allocation of a senior manager to take responsibility for the pilot with additional time for planning, teacher observation and evaluation
- The allocation of additional time for our Head of English successfully to develop her role as the school's literacy co-ordinator and to support her department
- The use of protected time in Mathematics to allow teachers to meet and plan the next stages of their teaching; with hindsight this should have been implemented for the English Department also
- Having a strong management focus on literacy and raising its status with all staff, including:
  1 Having clear aims for the pilot including an INSET day at the beginning of the year to get the process started on the right foot
  2 A Key Stage 3 Management Team largely consisting of middle managers to focus on allocation of resources (subject

development literacy bids), evaluating what is working well and focusing departments on the next stage of the process

3 Being proactive in sharing content and materials with staff from progress units and from other individual sources

4 Using an INSET day half way through the year to celebrate with all staff our successes, looking at issues and giving departments time to prepare for the next stage of the pilot

5 The use of subject reviews to evaluate whether policy has become practice.

This has resulted in a general willingness to embrace change and therefore created an understanding and support for the activities (including withdrawal groups) that have taken place across the curriculum.

- Employing an LSW specifically to teach and deliver the Year 7 intervention classes, including preparation and feedback time
- Employing an ex-teacher from the school for the Year 9 booster classes and to use him as a supply teacher for our Head of English to ensure consistency of teaching when she is required to attend training and evaluation meetings.

Comment

What emerges from Reading 4.2 is that the benefits of the strategy have been seen as multi-faceted and not always predictable. The infusion of impact into other areas of the teaching–learning dynamic, such as opportunities for teachers to reflect, to focus more pointedly and to target particular provision for pupils outside those formally identified as having 'special needs', are planned for and pleasing; the 'sense of optimism' of teachers about some aspects of their teaching which 'has been missing for some time' is telling and possibly a profound outcome for the school.

Two of the strengths of the large-scale pilot which occurred were that, firstly, it tapped strongly into best practice and regional strengths; and secondly, many of these strengths were incorporated into training materials available for the national professional development programme. The appearance of the strategy, as another top-down initiative, may well have vitiated some of the power of the materials initially, but as tools for organized and consistent department and cross-school development, they have force. Moreover, the accent of the resources on a particular department's starting point and the process of self-audited (practically attainable) targets for development, as well as pointers to possible next steps, are attempts to moderate reasonably the national requirement for compliance.

In the cross-curricular training pack, in relation to the question: 'What's in it for departments?', an attempt was made to specify the needs of pupils and the outcomes of enhanced literacy awareness. These were identified, in essence, as:

- Supporting language and literacy supports learning. Pupils need vocabulary, expression and organizational control to cope with the cognitive demands of subjects.
- Reading enables pupils to learn from sources beyond immediate experience.
- Writing helps to sustain and order thought.
- Language enables pupils to reflect, revise and evaluate things done, as well as the things that others have said, written or done.
- Responding to higher-order questions encourages the development of thinking skills and enquiry.
- Improving literacy and learning can have an impact on pupils' self-esteem, on motivation and behaviour. It allows them to learn independently. It is empowering.

Planning for progress in Years 7, 8 and 9

Cross-curricular priorities for Years 7, 8 and 9 in relation to organizing ideas, to improving accuracy, enhancing writing styles and using talk for learning are four key facets of planning for progress during Key Stage 3. All subjects are required to identify the ways in which they actively teach and consolidate the learning involved for these priorities. Whole-school implementation involves the monitoring of progress in the main forms of reading and writing undertaken in each department and the completion of an annual review of pupils' performance at text, sentence and word level, covering reading, writing, and speaking and listening, followed by the adjustment of teaching plans to take account of the review.

What, then, might key features of part of a department's training and development programme for literacy enhancement typically look like? Space here precludes the detail offered by the training materials available in all schools, and so available to beginning teachers, but an indication of the processes involved for teacher training and education and pupil learning, targeted at writing non-fiction, in a typical workshop format, is offered in Figure 4.1.

Comment

The point was made earlier that although these materials relate to a large-scale pilot study, nevertheless, with appropriate modifications resulting from the pilot responses (for example, amendments to the video footage of some of the training materials; an emphasis on a text-to-sentence-to-word sequence of approach rather than vice versa), it is clear that, although detail will change over the next few years, nevertheless, the principles were clearly in place by 2001. These principles have been designed to enable pupils to achieve more in terms of levels achieved for SATs: half of all pupils add only one level during the three years of Key Stage 3; only one in three pupils progresses by two levels; 4 per cent of pupils are, on average, absent for Key Stage 3 tests. Responses which have been offered to these points are that: the Programmes of Study for Key Stages 2 and 3 are different, so that like is not being compared with like; SATs' results are one measure only of a range of achievements and learning gains within a Key Stage; and an absence rate of 4 per cent is smaller than that normally experienced on a school day in the secondary sector. Nevertheless, no

Department X: writing non-fiction

Training module for staff: 1 hour 15 minutes

Aims

- To show how a bridge can be built between reading good examples and writing independently
- To propose a teaching sequence for introducing new types of writing
- To demonstrate how the structure of non-fiction texts can be made plain to pupils.

Useful for

- Whole staff or departments where writing is a concern
- Schools which already use writing frames and want to probe deeper.

1   Types of non-fiction (20 mins)

OHT 1 explains the range of non-fiction types

- Instructions
- Recount
- Explanation
- Information
- Persuasion
- Discursive writing
- Analysis
- Evaluation
- Formal essay

(Category examples provided.)

2   Discussion/reflection by colleagues about particular demands upon their own pupils

3   Conventions of the categories at whole-text, sentence- and word-level explored

(An explanation of these is provided and explored. A text-level example might be a recipe with its accompanying conventions of sequence of elements, its component parts, numbered instructions and serving suggestion; a sentence-level example might be related to giving directions with its particular 'voice', prevailing tense, mood and typical sentence structure and length; a word-level example might refer to a front-page story of a tabloid newspaper with its stock phrases, specialized or typical vocabulary.)

The purpose of this exploration would be to propose a teaching sequence which could apply to any department when a specific type of writing is to be introduced or reviewed.

4   Writing non-fiction (35 mins)

(A video extract is viewed as an example of a way to introduce new kinds of written text.)

The proposed sequence is:

1   Establish clear aims
2   Provide examples
3   Explore the features of the text
4   Define the conventions
5   Demonstrate how it is written
6   Compose together
7   Scaffold the first attempts
8   Independent writing
9   Draw out the key learning
10 Review

(Participants are then invited to comment upon and seek to apply the suggested sequence to science, history, music and so on.)

5   Organising writing (20 mins)

Participants are organised into groups of about 6; each group is given an envelope containing a series of points, in note form, for inclusion in a leaflet introducing the school to prospective pupils and parents. (The example is provided.) Teachers are asked to identify the five key points and supporting points for each and then to sequence them. The exercise points to an outline structure and paragraph and detail implications. The additional activity of generating ideas through favoured choices (spider diagrams, star charts, pro and con lists, flow charts or Venn diagrams) are possibilities covered and suggest classroom formats and activities.

6   Ready for more?

This is a final activity, common to all of the training workshops, and targeted at staff in all departments. It requires teachers to move to reviewing the ways in which the workshop activities might be incorporated appropriately in their own teaching and learning. Following the activities indicated above, for example, colleagues are asked to:

■   identify the main types of writing expected from pupils in your subject, and define the conventions for each one
■   compile a portfolio of successful annotated work so that pupils can see and understand what is required
■   use the strategies mentioned in the teaching sequence when you introduce pupils to new kinds of writing
■   identify a writing assignment in the near future for which you will teach the process of generating and organising ideas, e.g. using a 'mind map' or a card-sorting activity.

Figure 4.1 Writing non-fiction across the curriculum

Source: Adapted from Unit 2, 'Writing non-fiction' (DfEE 2000).

responsible and motivated teacher will challenge aspirations to greater achievement for their pupils but probably, rather, want to debate further the processes and routes to achieving them. The *Ready for More?* component of the training programme is designed to meet these professional differences and varying school contexts.

Thinking and accelerated learning issues

Moving all pupils successfully on in their learning and beyond classrooms towards adult life and productive participation in society forms part of the brief of any teacher and Chapter 12 focuses on this aspect in detail. Relevant to the learning and thinking processes operating in all subject departments, Maclure and Davies (1991) identified five significant trends in societies across the world that demand a whole new range of cognitive skills and situations for learning. These encompass flexible workforces, capable of being retrained; production-technological tasks requiring intelligent judgement responses rather than manual dexterity; the ability to comprehend and communicate complicated processes within intricate machine and human systems; the possession of enterprise skills and the increasingly complex demands of good citizenship in pluralist societies. These are not negligible demands and it is clear that attention to the development of thinking and learning skills and processes themselves must have a distinct and important place in schools.

The research evidence on the effectiveness of thinking skills programmes, however, has been somewhat equivocal (Burden 1998). Content and syllabus-driven constraints make the implementation of such schemes run against the norm in schools. Moreover, courses which do not appear to carry marks which 'count' or have the status of established curriculum areas known already to pupils, have encountered resistance (Burden and Nichols 1997). This contextual variable is an important one: it argues for integration of this focus within subjects and as a process. A stand-alone, one-hour allocation of 'thinking skills' on a school timetable may make it appear as a non-premier division subject or as a timetabling afterthought.

Clearly, though, teaching and learning processes in subject areas which accent creative and critical thinking, problem-solving, generalizing, hypothesizing, organizing and evaluating key thinking skills and in a processual, planned-for way, will contribute forcibly to pupils' learning and their approach to learning itself. The language modes outlined at the very beginning of this chapter and related to a wide definition of literacy will both mediate and be shaped by these gains.

Cognitive acceleration

Whatever the particular accent of different post-Eysenck learning theories, what unites them is the movement away from a notion of a fixed intelligence that cannot be developed in pupils through planned-for learning processes and opportunities. Some of the strongest evidence available for the view that 'intelligence', capacities and understandings can be extended and enlarged comes from the Cognitive Acceleration in Science Education project (CASE). It is claimed that CASE materials, when used appropriately in Key Stage 3, can improve GCSE results in science, mathematics and English two or three years later (Leat 1997). The case study described and devised by Leat and his colleagues, anchored into school geography Key Stage 3 subject lessons in this instance, used a constructivist approach (basically learning through the framework of what is already known and the structures by which we know it). This chapter is not the appropriate forum to describe and debate the details, but what is notable is the scheme's purposes of making geography challenging and developing substantially the conceptual understanding (i.e., accelerating this function) of pupils. The phased nature of the project, the planned teaching processes about causes and effects, the data collection and interpretation, the requirement of pupils to make choices about (limited) resource allocations to communities in southern England and Bangladesh all contributed, it is claimed, to cognitive acceleration in this subject area. Classroom elements visible during the time period of this comparative study: talk, group work, concept elaboration, debriefings, metacognitive activity, transfer of skills, an appeal to all of the senses in a range of activities, evident in the details provided, uncontroversially perhaps can be viewed as confident re-workings and extensions of the very best teaching and learning practices. More was indicated, too, and could be explored by the alert practitioner. Bereiter and Scardamalia (1989) point to the need to press pupils to discuss what they have learned and understood that they did not before the activity or process had been undertaken. This additional level of involvement and the development of a metalanguage about it (Cordon 2000) are additional goals. In this sense, then, cognitive acceleration and learning about learning can be associated with what teachers can be challenged to seek and what pupils might have. The desire to undercut the sterility of tired approaches, voiced by the geography practitioner in this case, may profitably, as here, be replaced with an alternative model which accesses some of the appropriate learning theories, referenced at the beginning of this chapter. Doing so 'is more likely to equip pupils to handle complex information and relationships, tackle challenging tasks and transfer learning to new contexts. It is also more likely to keep them interested' (Leat 1997: 2).

Conclusion

And keeping pupils interested is not to be underestimated. It is the key to further exploration and learning and often generates the willingness to move on after trying and failing. The maintenance of a shared understanding between the subject teacher and a class of pupils about common purposes and needs, about risk-taking and daring to be vulnerable, about taking responsibility and taking a part, enables meaningful learning to take place. These matters form the substance of the chapters which follow in Part 2 of this book.

References

Bereiter, C. and Scardamalia, M. (1989) 'An attainable version of high literacy: approaches to teaching higher-order skills in reading and writing', *Curriculum Inquiry* 17: 9–30.

Beard, R. (1969) *An Outline of Piaget's Developmental Psychology*, London: Routledge and Kegan Paul.

Beard, R. (1998) *National Literacy Strategy: Review of Research and other Related Evidence* Suffolk: DfEE Publications.

Brainerd, C. (1978) *Piaget's Theory of Intelligence*, Englewood Cliffs, NJ: Prentice-Hall.

Britton, J. (1987) 'Vygotsky's contribution to pedagogical theory', *English in Education* 2(3) National Association for the Teaching of English (NATE).

Bowring-Carr, C. and West-Burnham, J. (1997) *Effective Learning in Schools*, London: Pitman.

Bruner, J.S. (1966a) *The Process of Education*, Cambridge, MA: Harvard University Press.

—— (1966b) *Toward a Theory of Instruction*, New York: W.W. Norton.

—— (1983) *Child's Talk: Learning to Use Language*, Oxford: Oxford University Press.

Burden, R.L. (1998) 'How can we best help children to become effective thinkers and learners?' in R.L. Burden and M. Williams (eds) *Thinking Through the Curriculum*, London: Routledge, pp. 1–27.

Burden, R.L. and Nicholls, S.L. (1997) Evaluating the effects of introducing a thinking skills programme into the secondary school curriculum, internal report, University of Exeter.

Cordon, R. (2000) 'Reading-writing connections: the importance of interactive discourse', *English in Education* 34(2).

Cox, B. (1991) *Cox on Cox*, London: Hodder and Stoughton.

Department of Education and Science (DES) (1975) *A Language for Life* (The Bullock Report), London: HMSO.

DfEE (1997) *The Implementation of the National Literacy Strategy*, London: DfEE Publications.

—— (2000) *Transforming Key Stage 3: National Pilot Literacy Across the Curriculum*, London, DfEE Publications.

DfEE/QCA (1999) *The National Curriculum: Handbook for Primary Teachers in England, Key Stages 1 and 2*, Norwich: HMSO.

—— (1999) *The National Curriculum: Handbook for Secondary Teachers in England, Key Stages 3 and 4*, Norwich: HMSO.

Eysenck, H. and Kamin, L. (1981) *The Intelligence Controversy: H.J. Eynsenck versus Leon Kamin*, New York: Wiley.

Gardner, H. (1993) *Frames of Mind*, New York: Basic Books (original work published 1983).

—— (1999) 'Are there additional intelligences? The case for naturalist, spiritual and existential intelligences' in J. Kane (ed.) *Education, Information and Transformation*, Englewood Cliffs, NJ: Prentice-Hall.

Jensen, A. (1969) 'How much can we boost IQ and scholastic achievement?' *Harvard Educational Review* 39(1): 1–123.

Leat, D. (1997) 'Cognitive acceleration in geographical education', in D. Tilbury and M. Williams (eds) *Teaching and Learning Geography*, London: Routledge, pp. 143–53.

Maybin, J., Mercer, N. and Stierer, B. (1992) 'Scaffolding learning in the classroom' in K. Norman (ed.) *Thinking Voices: The Work of the National Oracy Project*, London: Hodder and Stoughton, pp. 186–95.

Maclure, S. and Davies, P. (eds) (1991) *Learning to Think: Thinking to Learn*, London: Pergamon.

Mercer, N. (2000) 'How is language used as a medium for classroom education?' in B. Moon, S. Brown and M. Peretz (eds) *Routledge International Companion to Education 2000*, London: Routledge.

Moon, B. (2001) *Guide to the National Curriculum*, 4th edition, Oxford: Oxford University Press.

Ofsted (2000) *Report on Cross-curricular Literacy 1997–2000*.

Piaget, J. (1926) *The Language and Thought of the Child*, London: Routledge and Kegan Paul.

Perkins, D. (1995) *Outsmarting IQ: The Emerging Science of Learnable Intelligence*, New York: Free Press.

QCA (2000) *Language for Learning in Key Stage 3*, London: QCA.

Skinner, B.F. (1974) *About Behaviourism*, New York: Vintage Books.

Storey, A. (2001) 'English in the National Curriculum' in B. Moon (ed.) *A Guide to the National Curriculum*, Oxford: Oxford University Press.

Vygotsky, L. (1962) *Thought and Language*, MIT Press.

—— (1978) *Mind in Society*, Cambridge, MA: Harvard University Press.

Wood, D. (1988) *How Children Think and Learn*, 1st edition, Oxford: Blackwell.

—— (1998) *How Children Think and Learn*, 2nd edition, Oxford: Blackwell.

2 The practice of teaching and learning

5 Planning for teaching and learning

Introduction

Planning is for teaching and learning. It is an activity in which all teachers engage, in some way or another. In their planning, teachers interpret the National Curriculum Programmes of Study or examination syllabus requirements, the coverage of basic skills and whole-school policies, their subject knowledge and views and values about learning, into classroom activities for pupils. Planning is therefore an extremely creative activity, one which calls for solutions to highly complex questions, such as how to make abstract concepts accessible to pupils. 'To understand planning is therefore to understand how teachers transform and interpret knowledge, formulate intentions and act from that knowledge and those intentions' (John 1993: 3).

This chapter considers the following ten key areas of planning for learning:

- Approaches to planning: expert and beginning teachers
- The processes of planning
- Approaches to planning: constituent features
- Planning learning activities
- Planning: the importance of flexibility
- Planning and differentiation
- Lesson evaluation and planning
- Whole-school, long- and medium-term planning
- Schemes of work and progression
- Approaches to planning – beyond the published matrix.

Approaches to planning: expert and beginning teachers

> Entering the classroom with a well-thought out plan probably provides most teachers with greater confidence and leads to a more relaxed lesson.
>
> (Calderhead 1984: 69–89)

> Most successful lessons involve a good deal of thought and prior planning.
>
> (Powell 1997: 15)

In secondary schools, lesson plans and schemes of work often form part of the departmental handbook. These plans can be seen as teachers 'thinking out loud' about the assumptions they have about teaching and assessment in their subject areas. They can identify their beliefs about the different roles and responsibilities of the pupils and the teacher, their theories of learning, their conception of their subject curriculum, and their pedagogy. Policies about teacher planning vary from school to school, and even between departments in the same school. In some schools each teacher keeps written plans to a required format. In others this may be left to the discretion of individuals. Whatever the approach adopted, and experienced teachers produce their plans in a variety of ways, explicit and formal planning is an essential part of successful teaching.

The challenge, however, for the beginning teacher, is that lesson planning is frequently part of the implicit professional knowledge which experienced teachers take with them into the classroom. Experienced teachers are less likely to need to think through and write down in detail the way that they are preparing to teach a certain topic or lesson. They have done it many times before, they know the sorts of questions and prompts that elicit responses, and they have a well-tuned awareness of the capabilities of the pupils they will be working with. Experienced teachers have well-developed routines and procedures, together with a mental map of how long activities will take, and what they can expect to do in any one lesson. They also have a wealth of knowledge about the pupils they are teaching, which allows them to concentrate on the learning in the classroom:

> Experienced teachers have various 'plans-in-memory' as a result of their previous experiences and may rarely need to design an activity from scratch. The instructionally effective teachers appeared to be much more orientated towards learning and considerate of the difficulties of individual pupils in their planning …. Teachers' knowledge of pupils would seem to be more important in terms of designing activities which are appropriate for particular groups, classes or individuals, and also in terms of monitoring or adjusting the activity in the classroom to ensure that pupils learn.
>
> (Calderhead 1984: 69–89)

What happens in the classroom then is often largely determined beforehand in the less frequently observed processes of preparation and design. The plans teachers normally use will probably be less detailed than those required as part of an initial training course. Teachers are usually thinking about their plans for the next day or week, at all sorts of times and in all sorts of places. They have gone through the systematic process of planning already and, most significantly, they have had the opportunity of putting their plans into action perhaps hundreds of times. For beginning teachers, however, the process of planning has to be thought through and externalized. Detailed or written planning, especially of lesson plans, becomes very important as they develop their classroom knowledge and classroom routines.

As they become engaged in the multitude of activities that take place in the classroom, beginning teachers can easily overlook or forget some crucial aspects of either subject development or classroom management. Here are two examples (opposite and overleaf), one showing how planning and forethought can lead to considerable success, another illustrating how a lack of planning can lead to difficulties or, on occasions, disaster. These are true stories, and in both instances the students were mature entrants to the profession.

Example 1

Sarah was teaching a Year 10 English class. The school set its classes into broad bands, and this was the third and lowest band of one half of the year group. This particular lesson took place six weeks into Sarah's teaching practice. In the previous weeks two boys had proved rather troublesome and Sarah was nervous about their behaviour.

The class was studying John Steinbeck's 'Of Mice and Men'. They had already read the book and Sarah had planned a series of lessons around the book. She decided that the high point of the unit of work would be a 'public enquiry' into who was responsible for Lenny's death. Her lesson plan for the public enquiry session was extremely detailed. Prior to the session she had to ensure that each pupil took on the role of a character in the book and could therefore be called to answer questions 'in character' at the enquiry. She had also ensured that everyone in the class had prepared questions for the different characters.

On the day, the room had been laid out for the enquiry before the class arrived and, as they arrived, they were directed to specific seats. The two troublesome boys were apart, but both near the front! The lesson was a great success. Sarah herself asked a few questions, but as the class became familiar with the procedure most became very involved.

In the discussion that followed, the class as a whole began to appreciate how complex the issues really were and, in particular, how Curley's wife was a deeper character than many had thought at the outset. The success of the lesson depended on the planning beforehand and the organization on the day.

In the last twenty minutes (of a one-hour twenty-minute session) each of the pupils chose a character to take the role of in writing an account of what happened. The high spot of the lesson, for Sarah, was when Darren, one of the difficult pair, hit on the idea of looking at events from the viewpoint of the unfortunate dog who, before succumbing to Lennie's fatal embrace, had observed most of the events in the barn!

Example 2

Midway into a generally successful teaching practice, Pete had just taken over a Year 10 science group. The department organized its teaching of Year 10 in a modular structure, and three weeks from the end of the teaching practice Pete took over a new group, looking at 'earth and atmosphere'. Like Sarah, he had a one-hour twenty-minute 'double period', and he was implementing a modular scheme of work set out by the department. His planning, therefore, followed the scheme of work, although he had some crucial decisions to make about the form of investigations, how much group work could be organized, and what he could expect to achieve in a single lesson.

In one respect Pete's planning was excellent. He decided to organize an investigation using plastic lemonade bottles. These were to be opened (empty!) and held down in hot water. After a few minutes the tops would be screwed on and the pupils would observe the changes taking place inside the bottles. This would lead to a discussion of the atmosphere, the movement of hot and cold air, and so forth. Pete had anticipated that with a new class (which like Sarah's contained one or two awkward pupils), the use of Bunsen burners to heat the water would present management problems. He had, therefore, organized hot water tanks at the side of the room, to be replenished with hot water by a lab technician.

The opening of the lesson was good. Pete had a clear, almost 'story telling' style of exposition and the class listened in rapt attention to the plan of the lesson and the reasons for doing it. The investigation itself went well. Thereafter, however, Pete's planning, or lack of it, precipitated a number of problems. The second half of the lesson became a low-level running battle to keep the interest of the class, with one boy being sent out of the room. The difficulties arose for the following reasons.

1 The groups finished the investigation much more quickly than Pete had anticipated; he fell back, therefore, on 'chalk and talk', following the department's scheme of work rather than a developed lesson plan.

2 Crucially, as well, he failed to realize the 'disruption potential' of twenty-five wet, lightweight, superfluous lemonade bottles on the lab tables! These could easily have been put away, but as he had to grapple with an increasingly restless class, this aspect of class management was overlooked and became the focus for some very silly behaviour.

These two stories illustrate a number of issues. Planning for teaching and learning is more than the organization of knowledge and lesson content, important as that is. It needs to take account of the characteristics and background knowledge of the class and the management and organizational requirements of the way the plans will be implemented. There is a need, therefore, for the teacher to think ahead, visualize the way the lesson will go, and anticipate the opportunities and the possible pitfalls of the strategies to be adopted. The best of lessons can be compromised by the tiniest of details. As the teacher's experience grows, he or she will be able to assume certain sorts of class management techniques and approaches. At the outset, however, it is wise to write out the plan in as much detail as possible. Sarah's lesson plan recorded, for example, the way she would make the transition from the class setting, as at a public enquiry, to individuals at their desks (row by row from the back!). Pete would have done well to think about resource management in more detail, particularly about how the lemonade bottles would be collected.

In considering detailed planning at the classroom level, the whole-school curriculum plan and the department scheme of work need to be taken into account. Lesson planning is supported by these collective planning activities, but teachers are also limited in what they can plan for a particular lesson by the resources available. In many parts of the curriculum, planners have been at work outside the school. The National Curriculum requirements have to be reflected at all levels of the school's curriculum organization. Examination syllabuses, within and outside National Curriculum requirements, also have to be taken into account at the school and class level. Planning, therefore, is more than the minutiae of classroom life (lemonade bottles or the organization of chairs), important as these are.

The processes of planning

In their analysis of the different dimensions of teaching, Dunne and Wragg suggest that the planning and preparation of lessons should be based on the following:

Planning and preparation

1   Plan basic resources for children working on a given activity.
2   Plan with a clear purpose; indicate materials for teacher and children; recognize practicalities including resources, time and safety; select content to meet purposes.
3   Plan specific activities to engage a variety of identified skills and intellectual processes including enquiring, imaging, connecting, hypothesising, theorising, planning.
4   Plan a short programme of work to engage a variety of identified skills and intellectual processes and demonstrate attention to transition between activities.
5   Plan whole schemes to engage a balance of a variety of identified skills and intellectual processes with clear reference to policy guides, continuity and progression and demonstrating a sound grasp of appropriate subject and curriculum.
6   Plan to allow for imaginative adaptation of ideas to circumstances.
7   Plan for efficiency in use of time and resources with clear references to the careful management of the teacher's time.

(Dunne and Wragg 1994: 43)

This approach to planning identifies for us the different levels at which teachers plan the curriculum. At the forefront of the planning process are the skills and intellectual processes which are specific to the subject being taught. For example, in history a lesson might be planned around a study of the causes and course of the Civil War. The detailed planning of this will be influenced by the department's longer-term planning, whole-school policies (pupil grouping, for example) and the resources available. The planning considers the approach to the pupils' activities which allow them to engage in a range of intellectual skills, such as hypothesizing, enquiring, theorizing, etc. Dunne and Wragg emphasize that the planning must fit the particular contexts of learning found in the school. This would include the interests and enthusiasm of the teachers, the locality of the school and, at a classroom level, the responses and learning needs of the pupils.

The processes of planning described by Dunne and Wragg are closely echoed by the approach that experienced teachers take to planning. Listening to experienced teachers talking about their own lesson planning gives a strong indication of the elements which they consider to be important when planning lessons. One says:

> For me preparing to teach a particular group begins with a series of questions. What are my content objectives? What are the previous experiences of the group? What have they done on this topic? What sort of learning experiences have they been involved in recently? What is the nature of the group? How do they behave? How do they interact with each other and how well do they cooperate with me? Where and when is the lesson (or lessons)?
>
> At this stage my aim would be to identify some sort of framework for the lesson (or series of lessons) which would include suggestions for possible activities, resources and learning approaches. How then do I make a final decision and commit myself to a lesson plan? Decision-making at this stage perhaps reflects more of my philosophy about teaching mathematics. In choosing the activity approach resource, I am conscious of trying to fulfil certain criteria. First, I aim for variety, both to reflect the difference in pupils within any one class and also to reflect the variety of the subject itself.
>
> Secondly, I want to promote enjoyment but not in the sense of making lessons a series of games. Enjoyment of the subject can be achieved by individuals when they are successful in solving a challenge. My role in the classroom is to provide pupils with a challenge and then be available as a resource to help them solve it. The challenge for me is to give pupils ownership of the challenge so that they are solving problems for themselves and not for the teacher. With ownership and success, there can be enjoyment.
>
> (Mathematics teacher, 11–18 comprehensive school)

And a second teacher adds:

> There are definitely two things here: preparing the lesson and preparing myself. I rarely feel effective if I have done one but not the other.
>
> (Geography teacher, 11–18 comprehensive school)

In being aware of how they might facilitate pupils' learning, teachers can plan how lessons are structured and what strategies are used. If they are considering how to encourage pupils to be autonomous in their actions, their strategy might be to set an open-ended problem or to present a range of tasks from which the pupils are allowed to select. If they want to develop conceptual understanding, their strategy might be to set up a cognitive conflict situation – that is, one in which conceptual understanding is challenged by presenting pupils with an alternative solution or even an incorrect solution to a problem and asking them to resolve it.

Planning then, is about establishing the purpose or objectives of the lesson and activities, the content to match identified purposes and a variety of activities or strategies that best fit the objectives and that include skills and intellectual processes. Planning also includes choosing language and resources. It refers to official documents, the National Curriculum, the school policies and schemes of work. It takes account of progression and continuity. It allows for flexibility and efficient management.

How do teachers begin their curriculum planning? Dunne and Wragg emphasize that planning has to be flexible, be based on skills and intellectual processes and be responsive to the particular contexts of learning such as teacher interest, pupil need and particular locality. However, whilst it has been much criticized, the nature and form of lesson planning today, particularly since the advent of the National Curriculum, is strongly influenced by the work on curriculum planning done in the 1950s and 1960s.

> The dominant model of lesson planning is that associated with the rational linear framework begun by Tyler [in 1950]. This perspective has dominated curriculum texts, teacher preparation programmes and central planning criteria, in spite of contrary research evidence which shows teachers plan in a way which contrasts markedly with the linear process. The model has four basic tenets:
>
> - specifying objectives
> - specifying knowledge and skills
> - selecting and sequencing learning activities
> - evaluating the outcomes.
>
> The model assumes a close link between the ends and the means; it also assumes that the learning environments in which teaching takes place are static and controllable rather than dynamic. This technical view of planning and teaching, usually stated through the careful specification of detailed behavioural objectives, is designed to promote efficient learning and measurable outcomes.
>
> (John 1993: 11)

Within the academic education community there has been considerable debate about the merits or otherwise of what John terms the rational linear framework which identifies objectives. In the 1950s and 1960s, there were some attempts to develop curriculum and resources for the curriculum around very tightly prescribed objectives. The teachers' tasks and the pupils' required responses were all mapped out in advance. Through the 1970s and 1980s many curriculum experts and curriculum designers moved away from this model. There are a number of reasons for this. The task of tightly defining objectives, in itself, is a difficult and sometimes controversial one. Our subject knowledge and understanding are constantly evolving, and attempts to map these out are inevitably tentative. Teachers also require some flexibility to adapt to particular contexts, acknowledging, for example, the pupils' previous experience, or lack of it.

> Critics of the rational model claim that there is a mismatch between the complexity of classrooms and the specific goals laid out in a plan, they claim that classrooms and lessons have a multiplicity of goals and much of the learning that goes on in them is neither controllable nor predictable in any scientific way.
>
> (John 1993: 13)

There is a considerable literature on the subject, and controversy has continued into the 2000s, including, for example, over the way some subjects in the National Curriculum are specified. Inevitably, as in any hotly debated issue, proponents of one position tend to present that of their opponents in an extreme, stereotypical way. A way forward, given these competing views on planning, is for beginning teachers to look pragmatically at the types of planning situation they find themselves in. All new teachers need to think through what they are trying to achieve across their teaching programme as a whole and for individual lessons. This means identifying broad aims and more specific objectives, working towards fulfilling the requirements of the National Curriculum or examination syllabus.

Importantly, however, when teaching the plan, modifications may have to be made in response to the pupils' interactions and understandings. In turn, these modifications can be built into future planning. Part of the skill of teaching is to judge the extent to which new ideas and issues that arise in class should be seized on even if this diverts from the planned lesson. As is often the case, it is a question of judgement. We have all known teachers who adhere slavishly to the textbooks (their plan!). Equally, many of us can remember the teacher who could be coaxed away from the particular task in hand towards some issue or topic on which they could muse for lengthy periods of time. At this extreme it is pupil manipulation rather than pupil interest that is at work.

Decisions about the use of objectives, about how prescriptive they are, depend on the purpose of the lesson. They may refer to specific behaviours (behavioural objectives):

- at the end of the lesson pupils will be able to draw an enlargement of a simple shape using squared paper

or non-behavioural objectives:

- at the end of the lesson pupils will have an appreciation of Matisse's use of colour.

Approaches to lesson planning: constituent features

A consideration of any department's lesson plans today will generally indicate that lesson plans are organized around similar constituent features. In thinking about lesson planning, teachers consider:

- the aims of the lesson
- the objectives
- resources/ICT
- selection of content
- use of language and subject-specific language
- planning the timing of the lesson
- planning the homework
- planning the design of activities.

Each of these constituent parts of lesson planning is discussed below:

Aims

These are general statements of intent expressed in terms such as improving understanding, knowledge and skills of a particular aspect of the subject curriculum. The aims might also refer to the development of particular cross-curricular links or coverage of the basic skills.

Objectives

These are much more explicit action statements, linked to the National Curriculum Attainment Target/s, about what the pupils will be able to do or understand at the end of the lesson. In an attempt to move away from organizing lesson planning around behavioural objectives, the aims and objectives of a lesson are sometimes expressed as 'learning purposes'. Lesson planning then, is primarily about identifying the assessment and assessment opportunities being offered to pupils. The objectives, or learning purposes, for one lesson relate very closely to the medium-term aims which have been set, usually in schemes of work, for a sequence of work. Very often, the medium-term aims will be expressed in terms of a final product which enables students to demonstrate their understanding of a range of concepts, skills and techniques. For example, in Design and Technology (D&T), a seventeen-week project called 'Circus Automata' involves pupils in designing and making a small moveable manikin to entertain the queue waiting at a circus box-office. The mechanized moving figure is made out of wood and metal and costumed appropriately. In Modern Foreign Languages (MFL), Year 10 students have to design an advertising campaign for a new café opening shortly.

The short-term objectives break down the medium-term objectives into manageable chunks. So in the D&T example, the textile teacher introduces the idea of costume design by talking about and showing clothes from other times and cultures. And the resistant materials teacher explains, with the help of models and a video, different types of mechanisms such as levers, linkages, cranks and cams. In the case of MFL, the students set and agree their own objectives with the teacher, for instance to watch and listen to video adverts and make notes on the use of language and imagery.

Resources/ICT

This includes the materials needed to teach the lesson and includes specialist equipment, textbooks, artefacts, pictures, OHTs, flipcharts, ICT and videos, for example. When planning to use resources, there are many areas to review:

- Are the resources appropriate? Do they support the learning objectives? For example, if the learning outcome is to understand the difference between primary and secondary sources, then finding a balance of both sorts of source is crucial.
- Do the resources used give positive images of women and men rather than reinforce stereotypes? Do the materials reflect the diversity of society in the representation of multi-ethnic communities?
- Are the resources sufficiently varied to cater for the pupils' needs and learning styles? For example, will texts need to be modified to cater for poor readers, or to make them suitable for group work?
- If other adults (support teachers, technicians, MFL assistants) are involved in the lesson and they contributed to the planning, is there a shared expectation of the role of the teacher and the role of the support staff?
- Do the resources match the teacher's needs? For example, if the teacher is working on the management of noise levels in the class, the use of an OHP or electronic white board, rather than the chalk board, will enable the teacher to maintain eye contact with the class.
- Could ICT enhance pupil learning? ICT has the revolutionary potential to transform the ways in which classrooms are organized and learning activities are set up. In planning whether or not to use ICT in a particular lesson for a particular activity, the starting point is to be clear about its value and potential. The use of ICT should allow the teacher to teach or pupils to learn something more effectively or efficiently than would be possible otherwise. Chapter 7 focuses on this key aspect of classroom methodology and the questions and possibilities raised by its use.

Finally, in planning the resources to be used, the teacher needs to consider the practicalities of distributing and retrieving them. For example, are there enough worksheets? Are there pens and pencils to hand for those pupils who have 'lost' their pens? Will pupils be left to collect the Bunsen burners for their science work themselves, or will the teacher, informed by the work done on gender in science, hand these out in order to ensure the girls are not left with the worst equipment? Considering these practical aspects at the planning stage will help in the smooth running of the lesson and gradually become the routines and regular practices of the lesson.

Selection of the content

Both the National Curriculum and examination syllabuses play a key role in the selection of content, but subject matter knowledge is open to wide interpretation. So, for example, although the history National Curriculum for England states that Key Stage 3 should include a study of: 'Britain 1066–1500: a study of major features of Britain's medieval past; the development of the monarchy; and significant events and characteristic features of the lives of the people throughout the British Isles, including the local area if appropriate', the exact events teachers choose to focus on can vary widely. In considering the development of the monarchy they may well have chosen to explore gender and legitimacy through a consideration of Queen Matilda, or the role of queens in mediaeval England's international diplomacy. The focus of the study will depend very largely on the teacher's own subject knowledge, interest and the availability of resources. The content will form part of the learning objectives, but also it provides the vehicle through which the other learning objectives, the conceptual knowledge and understandings, are achieved.

Beginning teachers often adopt a 'transmission' model of learning in their planning, assuming that the main purpose is to deliver content to pupils. They overload their lesson plans with content, assuming that the main purpose of the lesson is to 'get through' a particular topic, without considering the pedagogy. They have to 'up-date' their subject knowledge too to cover all the areas in the National Curriculum, some of which may be new and unfamiliar to them (see Chapters 2 and 3).

Use of language and subject-specific language

Closely linked to content and activities, the language and the subject-specific language used in a lesson require careful consideration. As Chapter 4 noted, all teachers, not just English and MFL teachers, are teachers of language, and the National Curriculum clearly states in the rubric of 'Use of language across the curriculum' that 'pupils should be taught in all subjects to express themselves correctly and appropriately and to read accurately and with understanding' (QCA/DfEE 2000: 40). It details what is required in writing, speaking, listening and reading. This issue and that of subject-specific language use are matters also raised in Chapter 4.

Planning the timing of the lesson

Fitting the different activities in the lesson to the allotted time is the key to effective planning. How does a teacher fill an hour? What is an appropriate lesson structure if a 45-minute or 70-minute lesson slot is allocated? Beginning teachers often find they fail to complete all their planned activities. How long different kinds of activity take is something teachers learn from experience and timing is the device to support the teacher in keeping on track throughout the lesson.

Lesson timing, however, is not just about fitting the lesson in to the allocated time-slot. It is also about the pace and momentum of the lesson. The pace of the lesson is the rapidity and frequency with which new points of knowledge are introduced. The momentum of the lesson is the rhythm of activities. This can be affected by many factors: the voice of the teacher, the number of activities, the nature and interactions of the class, to name a few. The choice of activities and tasks, the way they are organized, the involvement of pupils, all have a great part to play in the rhythm of a lesson and these need to be carefully planned.

Planning the homework

All too often, setting homework is left to the last minute and the importance of exemplifying organization and management of time is missed. Planning needs to allot time for setting homework and ensuring that the school routines are respected in terms of where it is recorded.

Homework tasks require the same careful planning as the tasks in the lesson; they have to contribute positively to and be totally integrated in the programme of learning. They should not be a bolt-on activity given as an afterthought because 'it's homework night tonight'. As with any other tasks, homework tasks must be relevant, varied, enjoyable, differentiated and imaginative.

Design of activities

This section of the plan identifies what the pupils will do in the lessons in order to meet the learning purposes and also outlines what the teacher will do in preparing for and supporting pupils' activities. The lesson activities have to enable pupils to develop the learning purposes identified for the lesson. They also have to enable the teacher to assess and evaluate pupil learning in order to plan the subsequent lessons. As such there are many factors which have to be taken into account when designing lesson activities.

Planning lesson activities

> Essentially, teaching is a series of intentional activities, the aim of which is to bring about learning, and the quality, style and content of those activities determine their worth in an educational context.
>
> (Plummeridge 1992: 67)

There are many strategies or activities a teacher can choose from to help pupils learn. They need to be sifted and selected carefully so that:

- they are part of an overall plan which takes into account the nature of the class, the way the pupils respond to certain situations and the appropriateness of the strategy for achieving a particular aim; in other words that they are really fit for purpose;
- they are organized in a clear structure, where each task progresses incrementally from the previous one;
- they are challenging so that the pupils do not feel patronized, and are extended but still within their capability;
- there is differentiation and they cater for a range of learning styles and attainment levels;
- they provide scope for enjoyment.

Designing activities for pupils' learning merits an in-depth consideration. A more detailed discussion of approaches to this is discussed in the next section of this chapter.

Planning activities for learning

Lesson activities need to be fit for the purpose

The teaching approach chosen should accord or fit with the desired learning outcome. If pupils are to learn about the effect of resistance on electric current, for example, then the activity must be appropriate to this learning. In this case, it would be appropriate for pupils to do experiments using a variable resistor to see for themselves what happens to the current as they change the resistance. Watching a video, for example, to improve measurement skills would be an approach plainly inappropriate for the purpose.

Lesson activities need to be informed by how pupils think and learn

Lesson activities need to relate to how pupils think and learn. This does not mean there is always a direct link between an activity and a learning theory; rather, such a theory may provide a framework for the planning of activities. So, for example, an understanding of the role of language and learning needs to inform an activity designed to help pupils understand complex abstract concepts, and so will include some group discussion and exploratory talk. Bruner's work using the concept of novice and expert explores how pupils inherit culturally developed ways of thinking and learning:

> [Bruner] argues that effective teaching in school … exposes children to ways of thinking that characterise different disciplines. The 'syntax' of a subject – its formal structure, facts and 'solution' – is only one aspect of what a child needs to learn. Teaching of procedures, facts, dates, formulae and so forth will not engender understanding or facilitate generalisation unless the child understands the intentions and purposes that motivate both the discipline and the people who practise and teach it. Ways of thinking, in mathematics, history, geography or whatever, have developed to achieve certain ways of making sense of and understanding the world.

And it is worth repeating Bruner's words, referred to in Chapter 4:

> Unless the child practises the role of being a mathematician, historian or geographer, learns the issues that excite such people, the problems that interest them and the tools that help them to resolve and solve these, then the child may only learn empty tricks or procedures and will not inherit the discipline itself.
>
> (Wood 1988: 84)

Activities, then, need to allow pupils to explore the substantive knowledge of the subject, its facts and patterns and the syntactic knowledge, approaches to the 'doing' of the subject.

Lesson activities need to take into account the pupils' prior learning and attainment

In designing activities, teachers need to take into account such issues as pupils' prior learning and the attainment range of the class. Pupils bring with them some knowledge of the subject, the content, understandings and skills they have acquired from previous lessons, together with understandings and often misconceptions about the subject acquired from a range of experience inside and outside school. This understanding, the facts, knowledge, concepts and skills which learners have acquired prior to the lesson, are essential for the new knowledge to be built on. For instance, a MFL teacher planning to use a train timetable relying on a 24-hour clock to teach some parts of the past tense relies on the children being able to count up to 59 in French and to understand the concept of the 24-hour clock. If the learners cannot do either, the teaching and practice of the past tense are compromised. When planning, therefore, the teacher needs to devise an activity to check pupils' prior knowledge and present an alternative activity if the lack of acquired prior knowledge is obviously hindering pupil progress with the planned activity.

Splitting the teaching of new knowledge into small steps, increasing in complexity, is important if all pupils are to have a feeling of progress. A succession of small steps means a succession of activities that build-up knowledge and pupils feel that they are moving forward and acquiring new knowledge. The quick succession of activities makes the pupils feel motivated and they learn lots quickly. This creates a feeling of success as small amounts of knowledge are usually easier to acquire than huge chunks.

Part of planning the activities involves trying to pre-empt the misconceptions learners might have about the new content. At the beginning of a teaching career, this can be difficult, but being able to forecast where common misconceptions lie and how they might be redressed prevents things from going wrong in the lesson.

Lesson activities need to be varied and to take into account pupils' interest as well as their emotional and intellectual needs

> It is essential that individual teachers should be able to draw on a varied repertoire of teaching approaches. Clearly it is important that the approaches chosen and used are such that maximum opportunities are provided for effective and enjoyable learning by all pupils.
>
> (Curriculum Council for Wales 1989: 3)

This variety of approaches enables the teacher to choose the most appropriate task for the pupils and the circumstances. Some tasks are appropriate for pupils who arrive at the lesson exhausted after PE and who need to be 'stirred' into action, while other tasks cater for excited pupils who need to be 'settled' (Halliwell 1991). Chapter 6 considers this in further detail and the point is reinforced there that plans need to take external settings and circumstances into account.

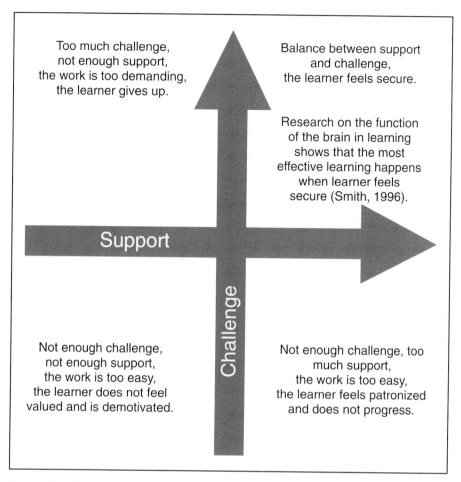

Figure 5.1 *The balance between support for learning and the challenge of activities*

Approaches also need to cater for pupils' emotional needs. The strategies adopted by teachers should offer a balance between supporting and challenging pupils so that the latter feel secure and open to learning. Figure 5.1 explores the balance between support for learning and the challenge of the activities.

Neurologists have demonstrated the effect of different cognitive activity on the brain under stress and have come to the conclusion that 'a learner who is under stress or anxiety will not learn anything! It is biologically impossible!' (Smith 1996). As well as relaxation, enjoyment provides interest and contributes to learning. Games and creative activities contribute greatly. Creativity is not the prerogative of English or MFL, music or art. All subjects offer great scope. A strategy for increasing the relevance, and hence the ownership, of the learning is to set tasks relating to the pupils' own interests and to appeal to their imagination and/or sense of humour.

So, as an experienced teacher explains, planning for enjoyment is crucial:

My general philosophy of teaching is based on the idea that if children enjoy their maths, they will want to do more and learn more. It is not always possible to prepare lessons in which everyone enjoys the work for the whole time. Some enjoy class discussions, some investigations or puzzles, and some enjoy pages of sums. When I prepare a lesson, I try to remember that a task I think the pupils will enjoy can sometimes be the complete opposite. It is important not to be afraid of letting the pupils determine the pace and the context of a lesson. Some of my most successful lessons stem from pupils' ideas brought up in class discussions.

(Mathematics teacher, 11–18 comprehensive school)

Lesson activities need to take into account the characteristics of the class and equal opportunities issues

Pupils' perceptions of their own potential attainment are influenced by gender and ethnicity (see Chapter 10), so an understanding of the different interests, behaviours, etc. of girls and boys needs to inform the planning of the activities. At the same time, the content of the activities needs to reflect the multi-ethnic society in which we live. Do activities which require social skills work better with girls than with boys? Are some areas of the subject received more enthusiastically by boys than by girls?

Lesson activities need to follow a clear structure

The lesson plan provides a timed structure of carefully planned and paced activities chosen to meet the aims of the lesson acting as 'stepping stones' for pupils to progress in their learning. Activities will normally be graded against a set of criteria which lead from:

- the familiar to the unfamiliar
- the simple to the complex
- the easy to the difficult
- the known to the unknown.

The structure of the lesson should offer pupils the opportunity to progress at an appropriate pace and needs to take account of a corpus of activities that are essential to the successful unfolding of the lesson. They include:

- routine activities: settling in time, register at the beginning of lessons, quality time to give homework, calming down close to the end of the lesson. Lesson beginnings are generally full of these routine tasks, but the lesson introduction should also arouse the maximum interest, inform the pupils about the purpose of the lesson and show them the relationship between the previous and next lesson (John 1993);
- sharing with pupils the long- and short-term objectives;
- the review of learning at the end of the lesson to provide feedback to enable the teacher to monitor pupils' understanding. Peter John suggested such

feedback strategies as pointed questions, comparisons, the summarizing by pupils of key ideas/learning points, a short quiz (John 1993).

Lesson planning, then, is not a series of single individual events, but is part of a learning review process of planning-doing-evaluating-planning-doing and so on.

Planning: the importance of flexibility

The discussion above about the component parts of the lesson plan and the areas teachers need to consider in planning their lessons, has emphasized the importance of clarity of objectives and precision timing. However, the lesson plan is not something to be followed zealously if unexpected learning opportunities arise as pupils raise questions or respond to the lesson. These questions may not have been part of the original plan, but clearly pupils are motivated and interested and the questions are relevant to the subject. The aim of planning is to enable quality learning to occur and, if the plan is not succeeding in achieving this, then bits of it are best changed or abandoned. Calderhead (1984) warns that using planning flexibly is vital to enabling quality learning.

There will also be times when doing everything that has been planned will not be possible. And there will be a whole range of reasons for this, such as:

- Overplanning – this happens frequently at the beginning of one's career, because the level of the pupils' abilities have been misjudged, because the prerequisites have not been accurately forecasted, because some tasks took longer than planned.
- Disruptions – the school dentist wants to see everybody now! The fire drill takes 25 minutes out of the lesson. A pupil fainted.
- A bright idea – the way the pupils react gives you a better idea for tackling an objective.
- The pupils worked faster than planned and are ready to move on to something more challenging.

When facing these situations, the teacher needs to decide quickly:

- Could I meet all my objectives if I cut this out, changed this, added this?
- Do I need to meet all of this objective now?

In fact, integral to the process of teaching the lesson is the development of ways of checking that the lesson is in fact working and meeting the planned objectives.

Planning and differentiation

Within any class of pupils there could be 'boys and girls, pupils with special educational needs, pupils with disabilities, pupils from all social and cultural backgrounds, pupils of different ethnic groups, including travellers, refugees and asylum seekers, and those from diverse linguistic backgrounds' (DfEE 1999: 33).

There could also be large numbers of pupils in a class who do not appear to possess a need of the particular kind indicated by these groupings. The lesson plan needs to indicate how the lesson purposes and activities meet the wide range of learning needs found in any class, whether setted or mixed attainment. Differentiation is an important approach to teaching classes with a wide range of learning needs, including special educational needs. But differentiation is equally important in classes with a narrower range of attainment, as in setted classes. It involves teachers providing differentiated tasks for pupils working at different attainment levels, or with different background knowledge of the subject. Differentiation is based on the recognition that all classes are not heterogeneous. Consider these definitions of differentiation:

> Differentiation implies that the teacher is doing something intentionally thus differentiation is about the planning that teachers do for the characteristics of individuals.
>
> (Nottinghamshire LEA)

> Differentiation is the process by which curriculum objectives, teaching methods, assessment methods, resources and learning activities are planned to cater for the needs of individual pupils.
>
> (*Science and Pupils with Special Educational Needs,*
> National Curriculum Council 1991)

> Differentiation is a process which accommodates differences in the abilities and characteristics of the learners, and also bears in mind the particular needs of students which may arise from ethnic, cultural or linguistic background and gender group.
>
> (Gloucestershire LEA)

These three definitions characterize differentiation: it is a process planned by the teacher which involves matching the learning activity and learning management to the needs of individual pupils by developing their skills, knowledge and understanding as far as possible. In focusing on differentiation in their planning, teachers generally also focus on the underlying goal of raising the attainment of all pupils.

In order to differentiate, all teachers will need:

- a clear understanding of the ways in which pupils learn
- an analysis of the knowledge and skills which comprise a particular learning task
- a heightened awareness of possible obstacles to successful learning, some of which might unwittingly be caused by teachers themselves
- procedures for observing pupils on task in the learning situation
- an understanding of the ways in which this data can be utilised in order to structure learning situations which will ensure success for pupils with special needs
- to work closely with colleagues who have specialised knowledge and expertise in the area of special needs

- knowledge of designing and implementing carefully structured programmes which enable learning to take place in successful steps.

(Barthorpe and Visser 1991)

This explanation identifies teachers' planning as critical in this process. Barthorpe and Visser also suggest we need to look hard at classroom practices that may present obstacles to effective learning.

The main approaches to differentiation used by teachers are:

- *Differentiation by resource*   Pupils could be directed to use different websites, or different written materials when exploring a particular topic. Learning support staff also contribute to differentiation by working collaboratively with the teacher to develop differentiated material.
- *Differentiation by activity*   Materials may be provided which cover the same content, but have different levels of difficulty, or offer extension activities for those pupils who complete the main task. In approaching differentiation by task, teachers consider whether there is a need to provide small steps, short, guided and more focused tasks and supporting structures. For pupils with difficulties in communication, language or literacy, the activity could enable them to use alternative and augmentative communications, to clarify their ideas through discussion, modelling, role play and the use of tape recorders, videos and photographs. The task might have a reduced amount of written work and reading.
- *Differentiation by support*   For example, once work is underway, teachers can differentiate by picking up on answers and comments, observing and assisting individuals and interacting with groups. The strength of this approach lies in the capacity of the teacher to adjust constantly to individual pupils' difficulties and insights. In order to do this, the teacher needs a detailed and internalized knowledge of each pupil's strengths and weaknesses and the ability to monitor individual progress as the lesson proceeds. 'Much differentiation takes place informally as the teacher circulates and intervenes during the activity. The skilful teacher does this in a pro-active way. The success with which pupils attempt activities will often depend on the quality of the whole class teaching that has preceded the activity. The most effective whole class teaching supports differentiation because it enthuses pupils of all abilities and provides an inclusive experience' (McAleavy 1994: 156). Differentiation also requires the organization of in-class support from the learning support staff.
- *Differentiation by outcome*   Here the activities set are the same for all pupils, but they are designed to allow for a range of responses from both high and low attaining pupils: 'every instance of differentiation by outcome depends on the setting of an appropriate task, and every attempt to differentiate by task will inevitably lead to different outcomes. Effective teachers are far more likely to use both open-ended and focused activities at different times. Sometimes it is possible to combine the two' (McAleavy 1994: 154–5).

It is true to say that using open-ended activities allows pupils to display their full potential. The advantage of this approach is that it is inclusive and concentrates on one particular activity, but it can sometimes confuse pupils with learning needs and not be demanding enough for the high-attaining pupils. The teacher must therefore monitor carefully and differentiate by response. This involves giving targeted feedback to students on the outcome of the task and giving them targets and strategies for future improvement.

The challenge facing teachers in planning for differentiation is to ensure that the plan supports the inevitable tension which arises between the teacher's commitment to respond to individual learning needs and the pressure to keep the class together in covering the particular lesson.

Differentiation is a *crucial* process. It strives to enable pupils to succeed. Individual pupils gain an enormous sense of personal satisfaction when they feel that their project is worthwhile, but they may experience an equal degree of devastation and frustration when things go wrong. Making sure that all the steps and support and challenging strategies are in place is part of planning.

Lesson evaluation

Evaluation completes the planning cycle. It is essential that the subsequnet lesson plan builds on the successes and takes into account any strengths and weaknesses which may have emerged. After the lesson, the teacher reviews what has happened in the lesson:

> I do not believe in an ideal lesson plan. Teaching involves making choices and more importantly reflecting on the outcomes of those choices. Reflection for me is a powerful tool which informs future preparation but I do not believe it will finally lead to a perfectly refined lesson plan – rather it builds up an awareness of individual needs of pupils and how to respond to them when they occur.
>
> (Mathematics teacher, 11–18 comprehensive)

In order to evaluate a lesson, criteria are required to consider the quality of planning and teaching.

> Broadly speaking there are three elements in the process:
>
> *Human* This covers the individual's learning in relation to the activities set; the role of the grouping in relation to the teaching strategy adopted; and the overall cohesion of the class and the general evaluation of the learning.
>
> *Target* This centres on the achievement of the set objectives/targets bearing in mind the differentiated outcomes. The focus will obviously be as much on the nature of the tasks as on the teaching strategy used.
>
> *Context* The outcomes need to be put into perspective given the time of the lesson, the pupils' motivation, the resources available and the tempo of the day.
>
> (John 1993: 73–4)

At the end of the evaluation, the lesson outcomes to be considered are:

- pupils' learning
- the effectiveness of the components of the lesson, including the teacher's performance. Everything will be reviewed: the teaching and learning strategies (activities and tasks) used, the resources, the classroom management, the formal and informal assessment opportunities and the approach to cross-curricular issues.

A useful checklist could contain the following questions:

- What went well? How do I know?
- What did the pupils learn which I had not planned to teach? How do I know?
- What did not go well? Why?
- What should be changed? How?

The answers to these questions can then be related to the components of the lesson listed above.

This systemic appraisal of what happened in the lesson enables the teacher to review the progress the class and individual pupils or groups have made. As a result he or she will be able to set new objectives for pupils' learning. The appraisal also makes it possible for teachers to reflect on the effectiveness of their lesson plans (including resources and management of learning) and on their performance during lessons. This appraisal and reflection serve to set new objectives not only for the pupils' learning but also for the teacher's teaching and thus to make effective use of assessment information on pupils' attainment and progress to inform planning of the next lessons and sequences of lessons.

Whole-school, long- and medium-term planning

The lesson plan forms part of the department's wider curriculum planning which includes unit plans (medium-term planning) and schemes of work (long-term planning). These in turn relate to the whole-school plan, the aims and ethos of the school. The emphasis on whole-curriculum planning is on teachers working together, not just within their particular departments, but across the whole school. This ensures that each teacher knows how the planned subject-specific curriculum contributes to pupils' learning as a whole, and how each of the different subject areas contributes to the basic skills of literacy, numeracy and ICT.

At a departmental level, the subject-specific curriculum planning usually begins with the general aims of teaching the subject, its rationale and purpose as a subject for study in school. The subject curriculum is then planned around the requirements of the National Curriculum, or examination syllabus, using a scheme of work and units. Here the QCA define these terms:

A scheme of work is the overall planned provision for (the subject) in a key stage. It is made up of units of work and shows the order in which they may be taught across the key stage.

Units are medium term plans, usually designed for a term or less. They set out specific learning objectives that reflect the programme of study, as well as possible teaching activities and learning outcomes. (…)

The complete scheme is the long-term plan. It draws parts of the programmes of study together into coherent, manageable teaching units. It shows how these teaching units are distributed across the three years of the key stage in a sequence that covers the statutory requirements and promotes curriculum continuity and progression in pupils' learning.

As part of the long-term planning, the scheme also takes account of other, broader dimensions of the curriculum. These include literacy, mathematics, ICT, financial capability, personal, social and health education (PSHE) and citizenship, together with developing pupils' creativity and thinking skills.

(QCA/DfEE 2000: 5)

Guidance from the QCA/DfEE (2000) suggests that a scheme of work should have clear aims as to how the subject should be studied and be based on the following principles. It should:

- provide a secure basis from which teachers can plan lessons on a daily or weekly basis to meet the needs of all the pupils in the class and the statutory requirements
- show how the subject specific knowledge, skills and understanding are built up in an organized, systematic and rigorous way based on the learning that has already taken place
- provide a programme for systematically building pupils' subject-specific skills
- make effective use of an activity to draw together pupils' learning
- identify what pupils are expected to learn about the subject, both within a specific topic or enquiry, and by the end of a specified period, and how pupils' learning might be assessed
- provide opportunities to develop literacy, mathematics, ICT key skills and citizenship, and, where appropriate, links with other subjects and curriculum areas
- include a range of approaches to teaching and learning
- inspire and motivate pupils.

These materials for curriculum planning provide teachers with a definition of a scheme of work, which identifies the rationale underpinning them. The current schemes of work for all National Curriculum subjects then, identify units (medium-term planning) which sequence and structure the National Curriculum requirements.

Units within all the National Curriculum subjects in the QCA's schemes of work are organized around the following:

Title of the unit   Each unit has a number and title. The unit numbers do not imply an order in which the units should be taught.

About the unit   This sets out the main focus of teaching and learning.

Where the unit fits in   This contains suggestions on where to locate the scheme of work, and how it builds on prior learning, and how it links with other units.

Expectations   These are broad descriptions of what most pupils will know and are able to do at the end of the unit. They also describe the range of responses that might be achieved by those attaining above or below the standard expected for the year group. They are based on level descriptions.

Language for learning   This contains the language for learning objectives that are referred to in the unit along with the appropriate specialist vocabulary.

Resources   This lists resources specific to the subject that are needed for the unit and are not routinely available in the subject classroom.

Prior learning   This is the knowledge and skills that it will be helpful for pupils to have before they start the unit. It includes a list of any units they need to have covered already.

Out-of-school learning/enrichment   This suggests opportunities for out-of-school learning by pupils, either on their own or with their families.

Future learning   This describes how the unit links with future work.

Learning objectives   These outline the small steps involved in building up the knowledge, skills and understandings that are the focus of the unit.

Possible teaching activities   These activities are designed to enable pupils to develop the knowledge, skills and understanding outlined in the objectives.

Learning outcomes   These outcomes are a way of assessing the extent to which the pupils have met the learning objectives. They provide the opportunity for checking progress while teaching the unit and can be used to decide if the pupils are ready to move on to the next activity.

Points to note   This section includes a range of context specific variables such as class management, health and safety, homework, extension activities, etc.

(QCA/DfEE 2000: 20–21)

It must be emphasized that these units are suggestions only. They provide a useful starting point in highlighting the features which need to be considered in planning the department's scheme of work, units of work and lessons. However, it is the professional knowledge of the teacher which will, in the end, in collaboration with colleagues in the department, determine the form and content of the planning. The main purpose of whole-school, medium- and long-term planning is to present a coherent curriculum which ensures continuity and progression within a subject specialism, the key skills and cross-curricular themes such as citizenship. This planning asks teachers to consider progression in their subject. How does a pupil move through the different levels of understanding which make up the National Curriculum level descriptors? How does the department ensure progression and continuity with a year group, between and within terms as well as between and within units?

Whether considering long-, medium- or short-term planning, clear structures need to be provided for the work of both teacher and pupils so as to maintain pace, motivation and challenge. It should take account of breadth, balance, progression, continuity, differentiation and relevance. Breadth will be achieved by covering all that is identified in the Attainment Targets and Programmes of Study. Balance concerns the weighting of parts of the curriculum, and involves judging the amount of emphasis being given to those parts.

Long-, medium- or short-term planning needs to ensure that pupils acquire and consolidate knowledge, skills and understanding in the subject they are learning. It is therefore crucial to be clear as to what the pupils' prior knowledge is, and start their learning from their base-line. And, in this and other aspects of planning, evaluation and assessment have a large part to play.

Schemes of work and progression

The schemes of work are based on a notion of progression in learning the subject across a Key Stage. The introduction of the National Curriculum presented teachers with a definition of progression in each of the subjects, defined in the level descriptors. The issue of progression raises fundamental questions which will influence the approach to teaching and the design of activities. Without a consideration of progression, there is a clear possibility that pupils will be faced with tasks beyond them or below their capabilities or which may not provide a challenge (Lomas 1992). One of the best questions all teachers need to ask as they plan their lessons is, 'What can a Year 9 pupil do that a Year 6 pupil cannot?' An easy way of answering this question is to turn to the level descriptors and parrot them. However, progression in learning is problematic. One pupil finds some aspects of the subject's knowledge, skills and understanding, identified in the level descriptors, relatively easy and others difficult, whilst another pupil will experience difficulties with what his/her peer finds easy and vice versa. As stressed in Chapter 4, pupils' learning is not neat and linear, as the level descriptors might indicate, but is eclectic, lateral and recursive.

> It is possible in some cases, to detect a logical sequence through the levels and programmes of study (...). However, a logical sequence, even if it were total, which in the National Curriculum it is not, does not necessarily imply a psychological sequence of learning.
>
> (Cohen *et al.* 2000: 86)

The QCA in its schemes of work (QCA/DfEE 2000) gives guidance on what teachers need to consider in planning for progression. This guidance is subject-specific, as each subject brings its own complexities to the issue of progression. However, some general principles to consider are:

- What is known about what pupils have already achieved at Key Stage 2 and how does this affect the pitch of the units?
- What ideas and concepts, or knowledge and understanding in the subject depend on a secure understanding of other ideas and concepts or knowledge and understanding?
- How can the units within the scheme of work be sequenced so that earlier work lays the foundations for later work?
- Are there opportunities to revisit and reinforce the knowledge, understanding, concepts and skills pupils need to understand and which some will find difficult?
- Is there sufficient challenge for pupils in Y7, Y8 and Y9?
- How are high attaining pupils, with knowledge and expertise beyond the level expected in particular years, challenged?
- Are appropriate expectations made of pupils in their use of language, mathematics and ICT?
- Does the programme constitute an adequate preparation for pupils moving from Key Stage 3 to Key Stage 4 and the GCSE examination?

(QCA/DfEE 2000: 22)

Definitions of progression differ across subjects. Analysing progression is fundamental to teachers' professional knowledge, and the understanding of progression has to come from practice and emerges from knowledge about pupils' learning. In much the same way, the whole exercise of planning is not something that can be done to a neat formula. It is a messy, unpredictable business which requires teachers to experiment, explore and above all evaluate what is happening in their classrooms. The final section of this chapter explores the limitations which can be placed on the planning process by the over-dependency on and over-use of commercially produced or government-initiated planning matrices. Again, it is the teacher's knowledge of curriculum planning, not the plan itself, which supports and promotes effective teaching.

Approaches to planning – beyond the published matrix

The developments that have taken place in the secondary school curriculum and assessment following the introduction of the National Curriculum have been accompanied by a mass of materials that set out schemes of work for teachers. Some of these are commercially produced materials, such as maths schemes which claim that all teachers need to do is to follow the scheme, or they are produced, unauthored, by government departments or agencies such as, in England, the DfES and the QCA.

There are schemes of work for National Curriculum subjects on the DfES website. These give details of the areas covered and the lessons' learning objectives, but also indicate the teaching method – for example, whole-class (plenary), individual work and so on, together with a time allocation for each lesson.

These lesson plans and schemes of work are helpful as a *starting point* for teachers' lesson planning. Certainly such resources are valuable, but to follow these plans as if they were a recipe, or to follow them uncritically, would be to ignore many of the

Date: Friday 12 March   Class: Y9   Topic: Geographical surroundings (homes)   P 7 & 8

Learning purposes (inc. NC PoS)

1 a, c, e, h, j; 2a, b, c, k, l; 3B

To learn and use vocabulary for rooms in houses and items in each room.

To be able to use vocabulary to describe things.

To be able to write a paragraph describing the different rooms in their houses.

Time	Activities	Teacher	Pupils	Resources
5 mins	Introduction Class into room; take register	Greets class Takes register	Come in and sit down Respond	
15 mins	Practise houses vocabulary On OHT – cut-outs of pictures of items found in houses – introduced last time Go over all names then play Kim's game in two teams	Explains task Manages game Keeps score	Look at pictures Hands up and suggest answers	OHT pictures of items and names
20 mins	Listening exercise Give out handout with blank plan of house with rooms labelled. I say what's in each room and they must write it down Support: leave pictures and names up on OHP, allow to draw rather than write. Go over answers together and move items into correct rooms on OHP. Pupils mark own work	Hands out sheets Explains task Reads out items in each room twice	Listen and write	Handouts OHT as above
20–30 mins	Writing exercise From this information, pupils write a paragraph describing what there is in each room: 'Dans la … on trouve/il y a …' Go over link words and write on board first. Then do more detailed paragraph about their bedrooms, describing where things are in relation to each other (differing degrees of detail acceptable depending on attainment level) Extension: use adjectives to describe items in room	Explains task Recaps 'il y a' etc. by asking questions Supervises work and help where necessary Sets new task with individuals as they finish	List Reply to questions Work individually on writing task – may confer and ask for help	
5 mins	Set homework Learn all vocab from listening exercise – take handout home or put words in vocab books	Explains homework	Listen and note down	
10 mins	Lotto (if time permits) Practise numbers if all other work is finished	Explains task Calls out numbers	Draw grid Listen and respond	
5 mins	End Clear up room, chairs on desks and leave	Supervises clearing up	Tidy up and leave	

Figure 5.2 Lesson preparation form

features which make effective classroom practice. It is teachers' professional understanding, their knowledge of the particular context in which they work, their knowledge of their pupils, the beliefs and understandings about their subject knowledge, etc., which make effective planning and teaching, not plans on grids, matrices or websites. Effective teaching cannot be done by rote!

There are, of course, many advantages to the commercially available and DfEE curriculum plans. There was a time, not in the too distant past, when departments did not have schemes of work and so did not think about such issues as progression across a Key Stage, or the coherence of the coverage of basic skills, necessarily in a systematic way. This planning activity, undoubtedly went on, but the thinking behind the planning was not necessarily made explicit through a written scheme of work. Using such matrices helps to improve the quality and consistency of curriculum planning. It helps the teachers to focus on such issues as the assessment opportunities, teaching and learning styles, the types of investigation pupils are engaged in and the ways in which the work can be adapted to meet the needs of particular pupils in the class. However, there are dangers in seeing such planning as something which is carried out in order to meet the school's policy, or to provide the relevant documentation for inspections, rather than being part of the teacher's personal conception of teaching their subject. There are other approaches to the graphic representation of planning which use the organizing principle of the underlying subject concepts to inform medium-term planning, as illustrated in the plan for a Key Stage 3 MFL lesson in Figure 5.2.

Lesson plans and schemes of work are clear statements about the pedagogic content knowledge of the teacher. The graphic representation of planning identifies the features of learning which teachers need to consider in interpreting the curriculum. These identified features transform the curriculum from statements about content, knowledge, skills and understanding into pupils' activities and learning outcomes. As such, they require a deep understanding of the reasons why the particular features have been selected, and how they are addressed in the planning process. This is a teaching activity which can be approached in many different ways, requiring flexibility and creativity, not the straitjacket of an 'off-the-web' scheme or lesson plan alone.

Beginning teachers need to start by using one of the planning matrices suggested by the course they are following. This gives them experience of thinking through the significant component parts of the lesson plans and prepares them to develop their own planning approach though reviewing the planning information they can collect in their school experience and to consider this approach to planning in the light of the discussion here.

Conclusion

This chapter has:

- discussed the importance of the planning process as a defining characteristic of the professional role of the teacher and, therefore, as a central task in the initial education and training process;

- considered the different types of planning that take place – yearly, in schemes of work; termly, in units of work; and lesson by lesson – and noted how these plans in themselves have to recognize the requirements of the whole-school curriculum plans, the National Curriculum or an examination syllabus;
- introduced the debate about progression and how aims and objectives are used in teachers' planning;
- considered the link between the planning debate to an ongoing consideration of pupils' learning, the importance of planning for active learning and the importance of planning for differentiation;
- explored some of the advantages and limitations of 'off-the-web' lesson plans and schemes of work.

Planning, as teaching, is an eminently complex process which needs to be deconstructed before it is reconstructed to become second nature. Planning is constantly under review during a teacher's career. It is therefore an ever-changing process because we plan for people, and the audiences with whom we work change constantly, as indeed do the teacher's own knowledge, skills expertise and interests.

References

Barthorpe,T. and Visser (1991) *Differentiation: Your Responsibility; an inservice Training Pack for Staff Development*, Nasen Enterprises.

Calderhead, J. (1984) *Teachers' Classroom Decision Making*, Eastbourne: Holt, Rinehart and Winston.

Cohen, L., Manion, L., Morrison, K. (2000) *A Guide to Teaching Practice* (fourth edition), London: Routledge.

Curriculum Council for Wales (1989) *Non-statutory Guidance*, Cardiff: CCW.

Dickinson, C. and Wright, J. (1993) *Differentiation, a Practical Handbook of Classroom Strategies*, NCET.

Dunne, R. and Wragg, T. (1994) *Effective Teaching*, London: Routledge.

DfEE/QCA (1999) *The National Curriculum: A Handbook for Teachers in England*, London: HMSO (www.nc.uk.net).

Halliwell, S. (1991) *Yes – But Will They Behave? Managing the Interactive Classroom*, London: Pathfinder, CILT.

John, P. (1993) *Lesson Planning for Teachers*, London and New York: Cassell.

Lomas, T. (1992) *Teaching and Assessing Historical Understanding*, London: Historical Association.

McAleavy, T. (1994) 'Meeting pupils' learning needs: differentiation and progression in the teaching of history' in H. Bourdillon (ed.) *Teaching History*, London: Routledge.

Plummeridge, C. (1992) *Music Education in Theory and Practice*, London: Falmer Press.

Powell, R. (1997) *Active Whole-Class Teaching*, London: Robert Powell Publications.

QCA/DfEE (2000) *History: A Scheme of Work: Teacher's Guide*, London: QCA. Schemes of Work for the entire National Curriculum (England) are available from the DfES (formerly the DfEE) website: www.standards.dfes.gov.uk

Smith, A. (1996) *Accelerated Learning in the Classroom*, Network Educational Press.

Wood, D. (1988) *How Children Think and Learn*, Oxford: Blackwell.

6 Teaching methods

Introduction

Our division of ideas and practical issues into chapters about planning, methods, classroom management and assessment is a convenient and useful one but also requires the reader to be vigilant. It is convenient and useful in that it enables a clear focus upon a central core aspect of the teaching (and learning) processes to be sustained but it can also over-simplify at times the complex interrelationships between these elements. Nevertheless, it is important for any beginning teacher to be able both to see the multiple skeins of what 'teaching' means and to develop each skein individually as well as in connection with the rest. This is necessary in relation both to in-course assessment and in a teaching post afterwards.

Methods might simply and usefully be defined here as the teaching strategies chosen and used in the classroom. It is an expectation that the lessons which occur as a result of this choice, and its implementation, result in high-quality learning by pupils. This aspect is important: teaching strategies, or methods, have impacts on pupils. These impacts are crucially important and embody a complex dynamic. Methods cannot simply be 'applied' to pupils since pupils themselves influence, sometimes in a marked way, the planned shape of a lesson and its learning outcomes. Teaching methods, then, are about teaching for learning. The beginning teacher is the connecting point, or bridge, between the teaching and learning which take place in a classroom (Perrott 1982). Chapter 4 tracked the importance of active, situated learning and the importance of this approach is maintained here. If required learning gains are ambitiously wide-ranging, then it is axiomatic that teaching strategies that plan for pupil participation and responsibility must be equally so.

This chapter addresses issues particularly relevant to a focus upon teaching methods. These are:

- the 'good' and 'effective' teacher
- the elements that compose successful lessons
- the essential learning purposes of a lesson: meeting pupils' needs
- connecting points between teaching strategies and learning activities
- teaching skills for teaching strategies
- methods in action: an example.

The 'good' and 'effective' teacher

During the past three decades, views on what constitutes a 'good' or 'effective' teacher have not widely differed or changed very much. Saunders (1979) offered a composite description. This is an individual who is purposeful and self-controlled and who:

- has planned the lesson carefully and builds in checks that pupils are learning
- is alert to the reactions of pupils in the class and responds to these by changing role and response appropriately
- takes positive action when it is apparent that pupils are not making sufficient progress
- shows respect for pupils
- tries to understand the point of view of the learner
- takes action to demonstrate a concern for all the pupils.

Almost two decades after Saunders, Kyriacou stressed that effective teaching is the outcome of such observable traits and responses and that this:

> can be defined as teaching which successfully achieves the learning by pupils intended by the teacher. In essence, there are two simple elements to effective teaching:
>
> - The teacher must have a clear idea of what learning is to be fostered.
> - The teacher sets up and provides a learning experience which achieves this.
>
> (Kyriacou 1997: 5)

Kyriacou cites Cattell's classic 1931 study which outlined the most commonly reported qualities of a 'good' teacher. In order of reported frequency they were: personality and wit; intelligence; sympathy and tact; open-mindedness and a sense of humour.

This set of desirable (and rather demanding) traits or characteristics is still central, of course, but an over-concentration upon them may neglect other essential variables in any teaching and learning interactive process. These might relate, for example, to coping with situations arising within school (context variables); events occurring within a classroom or the perceptions of pupils (process variables) and organizational requirements (product variables) relating to judgements about the 'effectiveness' of the teacher (Kyriacou 1997: 6). These kinds of matters were referred to implicitly above in relation to the multi-faceted dimensions required for planning. It is the process variables which are particularly potent to a discussion about classroom teaching methods. These would encompass such things as: the teacher's enthusiasm; clarity of explanations; use of questions; use of praise and criticism; management strategies; disciplinary techniques; classroom climate; organization of the lesson; types of learning tasks and feedback about them; pupil involvement in the lesson; pupil-initiated interaction with the teacher; and pupils' strategies for learning. Arising from observations and interviews, Gannaway (1976) argued that teachers are put to a systematic set of tests by pupils that determine whether the planned-for methods of a lesson are allowed to be fruitful. Their tests raised the questions:

- Can the teacher keep order?
- Can s/he have a laugh?
- Does he or she understand pupils?

The clear implication of this study and others since is that pupils expect a teacher to be able 'to keep order', be able to share humour with a class and be able to relate to and be interested in their concerns and agendas, as a class as well as assorted individuals (Cohen *et al.* 1999). These matters are taken up in Chapter 8 in a focused way but it is important to stress the point made in the introduction to this chapter: classroom methods are intricately bound with classroom planning, management, assessment and with interpersonal relations in specific contexts.

And, in terms of what teachers want from their pupils, the list is unsurprising. They want their pupils to have: increased knowledge and skills; expanded interest in the subject or topic; greater intellectual motivation; increased academic self-confidence and self-esteem; a greater degree of autonomy and expanded social development.

These are ambitious sets of requirements from the key participants and what emerges strongly in these views, the result of research findings spanning decades, is that the processes of teaching and learning together form a complex and challenging dynamic. The characteristics and outcomes outlined above are guidelines for action and achievement. What happens in the space between is challengingly complex.

'Effective' teachers

Effective teachers can demonstrate effective teaching. The professional standards for Qualified Teacher Status (QTS), induction, threshold and Advanced Skills Teacher (ATS) status are designed to enable teachers to look at and to develop their own teaching methodologies and their capacities to hone these with pupils. These professional standards 'form a coherent ladder of professional competences requiring a progressively more extensive range of knowledge and skills and the capacity to operate in an increasingly demanding range of contexts' (DfEE 1999). What effectiveness means in relation to different agencies is currently being shaped further and the multiple agencies which are concerned with this matter – Ofsted, the TTA, the DfES, the GTCS, teachers' professional associations and the Hay McBer Consultancy Group, working with the DfES – have all contributed to the debate and the schedules which have so far emerged. Hay McBer's report, *Research into Teacher Effectiveness* (Hay McBer 2000), is unlikely to be the last word on the topic but it will certainly be influential. It unambiguously associates effective teachers with being capable of providing appropriate levels of challenge and support, 'of tough caring', to their pupils, as part of 'A commitment to do everything possible for each pupil and to enable all pupils to be successful' (ibid: 12).

From its research strategy of looking at a sample of teachers perceived by their peers as 'effective', and what they actually did, the Hay Report focused its findings on three areas. These were termed teaching skills, professional characteristics and classroom climate. They were described thus:

Teaching skills   These are the 'micro behaviours' that the effective teacher constantly exhibits when teaching a class. These were clustered under seven Ofsted classroom observation areas so that teachers might have a consistent framework for self-development.

Professional Characteristics A distinction was made between outstanding and effective teachers in relation to what are termed 'these deeper-seated patterns of behaviour'. Outstanding teachers display these 'more often, in more circumstances and to a greater degree of intensity than effective colleagues'. These are further described as 'behavioural competencies or emotional intelligence competencies'. These are displayed as 'ongoing patterns of behaviour which make them effective'.

Classroom climate This related to the collective perceptions of pupils regarding those dimensions of the classroom environment that have a direct impact on their capacity and motivation to learn.

Conclusion

Much of the detail of the report confirmed a great deal of existing research in these matters and, despite criticisms about the methodology of the research which formed the report's basis, nevertheless its acceptance of the idea that school contexts rightly shape choices of teaching methods and its accent on teachers' interpersonal skills and values as well as skills and competences appear appropriate to any teacher who here is invited to 'state confidence in him or herself as a professional' (ibid: 15).

The debate about the detail and what constitutes 'effectiveness' will continue but the essentials, as described in the early part of this chapter, will remain.

Successful lessons

Successful lessons are easily recognized by teachers and pupils. They can be characterized as ones in which a learning endeavour was shared, learning was seen as successful, a sense of well-being infused the lesson and enjoyment of the time spent made time itself appear to speed up. All successful teachers have experienced the lift that such experiences provide. Clearly, being a 'good' teacher as defined by pupils in the section above will have made a contribution to this. But being pleasantly firm and understanding the class will not by themselves produce the successful lesson; many of the learning and social gains will have come from clear-sighted planning of many matters, not least the teaching strategies organized for the lesson.

Quality lessons and successful teaching link firmly with methods used within them. Ofsted inspections and professional discourse about the issue have consistently highlighted that lessons should:

- sustain pupils' interest and help to develop their confidence
- press for high expectations of pupils
- be relevant and challenging to pupils
- be well-matched to pupils' abilities and learning needs
- provide opportunities for pupil engagement in a variety of activities
- encourage a sense of responsibility in pupils for their own learning
- extend pupils' language abilities
- be well-ordered with a clear sense of mutual respect between teacher and pupils.

A more official schedule relating to successful lessons is provided by Ofsted. In any school inspection theirs is the responsibility to evaluate the:

> standards of work in [each] subject, particularly the standards achieved by the oldest pupils in each Key Stage, highlighting what pupils do well and could do better … how well pupils are taught, highlighting effective and ineffective teaching in the subject and relating the demands made by teachers to pupils' learning and the progress they have made.
>
> (Ofsted 2000: 48)

These elements, pupils' learning and the degree of effectiveness of those responsible for teaching them, are assessed separately but also in terms of the interplay between teaching and learning. Much has been made of the flat language used in Ofsted reports in presenting their views for purposes of comparisons between schools. Nevertheless, these reports can at times be seen to break out of these self-imposed constraints where excellence of teaching and learning have been seen (and clearly enjoyed) by the evaluators as well as the participants. The report on the science department in a secondary school in the north of England in Reading 6.1 makes the point.

Reading 6.1 Ofsted Inspection Report Ref. No. 118075, September 1999

Science

101   Teaching is very good and has clearly contributed to the recent rise in standards of attainment. In the lessons observed, no teaching was unsatisfactory, in three quarters it was good or better and in over half it was very good or excellent. The basis of this very good teaching lies in meticulous planning, resulting in lessons that are interesting, demanding, often exciting and often fun. Particular care is taken to ensure that pupils are not faced with work that they cannot do. A Year 7 class containing all levels of ability, in their very first science class, thoroughly enjoyed a lesson involving the observation of burning. Pupils were individually encouraged to extend their work so that each pupil reached an appropriate level. The practical skills involved were nicely judged to challenge the children, but not overawe or frighten them. They left the lesson believing that science is wonderful and that they could do it.

102   Most teachers manage their classes very well and enjoy excellent relationships with their pupils. The personal attention which teachers give to individual pupils' progress and any difficulties, whether with learning or personal problems, is evident in their lessons. Pupils respond with trust, respect and affection. A Year 8 class of lower attainment was put into sensitively arranged groups, provided with a wide range of short sections of work of varying difficulty and all pupils were given personal encouragement and attention. Every child in the class gave of his or her best and all

showed great pride in their work. Their reluctance to stop work at the end of the lesson was evident. This aspect of teaching is particularly evident in helping the many pupils who have the emotional and behavioural difficulties that often arise from problems faced out of school. Many boys who lack maturity find settling to school work very difficult. The skill and sensitivity with which almost all the science teachers approach these pupils have been a major factor in raising the attainment of boys.

103   Teachers have very high expectations of their pupils, do not accept the pupils' often low self-image and never give up on them. This feature is best illustrated by the introduction and teaching of the 'Science Plus' option in Year 10. Low-attaining pupils can choose to follow a certificate of achievement course that is carefully tailored to their interests and minimises the effects of their weaknesses. This course has been so successful in raising motivation that in 2000 all 15 pupils in the course passed, 14 gained a distinction and the remaining candidate gained a merit. In addition, 12 of these pupils also gained pass grades in the GCSE.

104   A weakness in the teaching occurs when teachers fail to establish good relationships with pupils. A slightly abrasive and hectoring approach adopted in one lesson resulted in pupils not being motivated and therefore not as productive as they might have been. A basically well-planned lesson was not fully realised and resulted in satisfactory rather than good learning.

105   The contribution made by science teachers to the improvement of pupils' basic skills varies. They are acutely aware of the difficulties which many pupils have with literacy and are unusually skilled in dealing with these problems. The whole-school approach to numeracy is less well-developed, but the science curriculum is carefully designed to ensure that aspects such as measurement and the drawing of graphs are given sufficient attention. The contribution to pupils' learning of information and computer technology is seriously limited by lack of access to equipment.

106   The quality of learning of many pupils is limited by lack of confidence and low aspirations. Tackling these problems is at the heart of the philosophy underlying the work of the science department. By establishing a positive and happy atmosphere in almost all lessons, teachers are gradually helping pupils to become more confident learners. The success that pupils experience in lessons is motivating them to ever greater effort and to setting their sights higher … .

107   Management of the department is excellent … . A great deal of successful attention has been given to the performance of boys. The particular needs of gifted and talented pupils are being actively addressed by the school piloting CASE (Cognitive Acceleration in Science Education) and by the full involvement of the department in the whole-school policy, designed to meet the needs of such pupils. The assessment of pupils' work

and progress is now outstanding. The department is able to analyse the performance of individuals and groups, monitor the effectiveness of teaching and provide pupils with sensible and detailed information on what they need to do to improve.

108   The number of specialist science teachers is barely sufficient to cover the demands of the curriculum. Some of the sets, particularly at A level, are too large. The support staff are well qualified, very dedicated and are making a significant contribution to the raising of standards. However, there are not enough technician hours to do all the work.

109   Since the last inspection, every aspect that was criticised has been radically improved.

Comment

In the extract in Reading 6.1, what emerges is the crucial relationship between the methods planned and taken by science staff to raise attainment in the subject and the mediation of these to pupils. Teaching strategies here blend successfully with focused planning, assessment for future teaching and learning plans, and a house-management style that clearly convinces children that they can learn and they can succeed.

Essential learning purposes: meeting pupils' needs

Fitness for purpose

The *Framework for the Inspection of Schools* (2000) sets out the factors which are considered in the evaluation of departments and schools such as the one set out in Reading 6.1. In determining their judgements, Ofsted considers the extent to which pupils:

- behave well in lessons and around the school and are courteous, trust-worthy and show respect for property
- form constructive relationships with one another and other adults
- work in an atmosphere free from oppressive behaviour such as bullying, sexism and racism
- reflect on what they do, and understand its impact on others
- respect other people's differences, particularly their feelings, values and beliefs
- show initiative and take responsibility

(Ofsted 2000: 41)

These factors describe both the conditions necessary for successful working of planning for classroom strategies, and the school and department ethos which determine the extent to which planning for teaching and learning can be realized. They are, then, fundamentally important.

This established, how can teachers address some of the criteria set by Ofsted (OHMCI in Wales; DENI in Northern Ireland) in planning and implementing their lessons? One important aspect of planning is to consider whether the tasks set for the pupils are appropriate for the learning purposes of the lesson or unit of work. A teacher's decision to set a particular task or use a particular teaching strategy should relate to the overall learning purpose of the lesson in question. For example, a clear explanation from the teacher can be an effective teaching strategy if the learning purpose is to impart specific knowledge. But this same strategy is inappropriate if the learning purpose is co-operative work in order to make a discovery or to establish a set of key, moderating points in order to address a problem or issue. In planning approaches, teachers need to consider whether they have set varied learning tasks and used a range of teaching strategies across a unit of work to address all of the key planned learning purposes. Moreover, a class teacher will need to strike a balance here between routine (sufficient similarity about the way in which lessons are approached so that the pupils feel confident) and variation (sufficient difference so that the pupils are motivated, engaged and developing their language skills in all the areas of speaking, listening, reading, writing and thinking).

It is also of importance in terms of 'fitness for purpose' to consider the balance of stirring and settling activities in any lesson. For instance, a thought-collection process with a whole class might be considered a 'stirring' activity, while asking pupils to work independently to read a passage and answer questions might be considered a 'settling' activity. If it is known that a scheduled class is coming from a PE lesson, it is likely that members of it will either be tired or highly stimulated. An appropriate activity can be either be 'settle' or 'stir', as appropriate. Experienced, expert teachers also give consideration to the balance of 'stirring' and 'settling' activities which they introduce into their lessons across a range of classes in any one day. Teaching is emotionally and physically demanding and therefore a wise beginning teacher will note this and guard against whole days and lessons consisting predominantly of 'stirring' activities, for example. These matters were explored in detail in Chapter 5.

Matching pupils' needs

Another critical aspect in planning for effective teaching and learning is to match activities to the needs and attainment levels of individual pupils. This also was raised in Chapter 5 in terms of additional questions at the planning stage. For example:

- How are tasks to be set that are appropriate for the range of attainment levels within a class?
- How does the teacher acknowledge the fact that different children have preferred learning strategies and respond differently to particular teaching strategies?

Raising these questions is not to suggest that teachers attempt to teach in thirty different ways to suit thirty different individuals within the framework of every lesson. This would be an impossible situation and both Simon (1994) and Wood (1988) have counselled against it. But it does mean that the issue of matching work to the needs of individuals should be given proper attention in planning lessons and that, across a unit of work, teachers should use a variety of approaches that can begin to address a range of needs. This point made, the reader is referred to Chapter 8 for a focus upon groupings in relation to class management issues.

Both 'fitness for purpose' and 'matching to individual needs' lie at the heart of the Ofsted guidelines for reporting on the quality of teaching as can be seen in the references made to them in the previous section of this chapter.

Teaching strategies and learning activities

In the previous section, 'fitness for purpose' was noted as key to the selection of teaching strategies. The common teaching strategies and learning activities are itemized below and each is useful only perhaps insofar as a teacher considers its appropriate use and the degree to which it is likely to engender the learning gains planned.

Input from adults other than teachers (AOTs)	Visiting speakers such as fire fighters, community workers, senior citizens
Ideas generation	All ideas accepted from the class and written up usually for the class to share as a joint resource
Computer-assisted learning	Word-processing, databases, Internet access, modelling, spreadsheets, desk-top publishing, literature searches
Demonstrations	Class teacher shows how to do something or shows what happens when …
Discussion/talk	A forum for sharing views, for whole class or small groups. May be focused on questions set or may be a formal debate
Drama activities	Role play to explore an idea or a character; simulations requiring more elaborate role play and supportive materials and detailed preparations by participants, eg a town-planning enquiry
Teacher exposition	To explain concepts, to question at an appropriate level, story-telling, to summarize finding/learning of a class when appropriate
Problem-solving/ analysing/predicting	Activities designed to allow pupils to recognize, analyse and solve problems – to illustrate concepts and to develop skills
Games	Individual, pair, group and whole-class options. Cross-curricular applications and valuable for pace/time considerations in a lesson
Self-supported study	Pupils working individually with individual support provided by teacher or another pupil at a later stage
Practical work	Designed to illustrate concepts, develop skills, apply understanding in new contexts

Surveys/investigative work	As part of development of understanding of how to produce and organize data
Visits and fieldwork	Extending the resources of the classroom and methods of enquiry
Video/DVD use; audio and video recording	Multi-media use for information retrieval and creative and communication use

(Adapted from A. Shelton Mayes (1995)
Appendix 2)

Making decisions about the setting up of one activity in preference to another requires a clear rationale, which in turn means looking at the learning demands that a particular activity places on pupils. The following key questions can usefully inform the teacher's decision about methods to be used at this stage:

- What are the concepts, skills, attitudes and values the beginning teacher wants the pupils to explore understand learn?
- What activities, groupings, resources, teaching strategy will best support these learning purposes?

Contained within each question are others which draw out a more precise shaping of pupil activity in the lesson or task. Making a decision about the type of learning demand required will usually suggest an appropriate teaching strategy. Additional questions that might be considered would include:

- Are pupils expected to listen or to contribute?
- Will this require exposition from the teacher or a question-and-answer session?
- Will pupils interact with the teacher or with other pupils?
- Will this entail a whole-class discussion chaired by the teacher or small-group or paired discussion?

Comment

The details outlined above illustrate how teaching strategies and learning activities can be analysed to assess the ways in which they relate to particular learning purposes. Variety of learning activity is important, of course, but appropriate, integrated use is most valuable. The project described in Reading 6.3 later in this chapter is an illustration of this.

Teaching skills for teaching strategies

Reading 6.2 outlines what have been presented (Perrott 1982) and confirmed (Cohen *et al.* 1999) as key teaching skills. Whatever the choice of topic for a class, the nature of its introduction is centrally important (Perrott 1982). Five teaching skills are seen by her to be essential for a well-structured and presented lesson or activity. Reading 6.2 is an extract of a more detailed examination of teaching skills (Shelton Mayes 1995) and begins with a reference to Perrott's work.

Reading 6.2 Five essential teaching skills

Five essential teaching skills

- Set induction (introductions)
- Closure (summing up)
- Stimulus variation
- Clarity of explanation
- Use of examples

Set induction (introductions)

This refers to the teaching activities that precede the learning task and have an impact on the outcome of the task: for example, beginning a new unit of work, preparing for a practical session, or preparing to view a video. In such situations the teacher could:

- focus the pupils' attention on the task by gaining their interest, for example with a visual stimulus associated with the task ahead
- use examples to give meaning to the new concept (this is especially useful when dealing with abstract concepts)
- use question-and-answer to move the pupils from past work or current knowledge towards the next task
- provide an organising framework for the task ahead. Making explicit both the aims and objectives for the lesson, and the stages of the lesson, will allow pupils to play a more active role in their learning.

Closure (summing up)

This occurs when the teacher draws attention to the important points of the activity and reinforces what has been learned. This is also a time to use praise and encouragement to create a sense of achievement.

Stimulus variation

The teacher has a responsibility to make tasks interesting for children; assuming content to be intrinsically interesting is not sufficient. Perrott lists a number of ways in which teachers' voice patterns, gestures and movements around the class can either focus attention or distract. These include:

- moving around the classroom
- scanning the room to engage pupils' attention
- maintaining eye contact with the whole class
- smiling, frowning or nodding to encourage or discourage particular pupils' behaviour
- expressiveness, tone, rate of speech
- planned silences and pauses.

She also includes changing the group structures within the class and varying the use of sensory input since 'research studies indicate that pupils' ability to process information can be significantly increased by appealing to sight and sound alternately'.

Clarity of explanation

Perrott identifies the most important aspects of effective explanations as continuity, simplicity and explicitness. Points to consider include:

- Does the teacher make the explanation explicit?
- When information is given to pupils is there an explanation linked to it.?

Clarity of explanation depends on the skilful use of both logic and language.

Logic

Teachers should consider the following questions regarding the coherence of their explanations.

- Is the explanation sequenced clearly?
- Are the connections between the various points obvious?
- If the teacher diverges from the main point of the exposition, is the relationship between the divergence and the main topic made explicit?

Language

Teachers should be aware of their own use of language and monitor the quality of their explanations by asking themselves questions such as the following:

- Am I articulate?
- Do I use grammatically straightforward sentences?
- Do I explain specialist or technical terms?
- Do I use language familiar to the pupils?

The most successful teachers make greater use of a variety of different types of explaining:

- interpretative which explains the meaning of terms – a 'what is' explanation
- descriptive which describes a process or structure – a 'how does' or 'how is' explanation
- reason-giving which offers reasons or causes – a 'why is' explanation

Use of examples

Teachers can generally provide a relatively concrete example to connect with pupils' current knowledge and experience and move them towards an understanding of new and relatively abstract ideas. To be effective the relationship between the example and the concept being taught needs to

> be made explicit. There are two approaches to using examples, these being:
>
> - to provide some examples and then infer or generalise from them (the inductive approach)
> - to give the generalisation first and then relate it to a number of examples (the deductive approach)
>
> Both approaches appear to be equally effective (Perrott 1982), the important point being to keep the examples simple and within the pupils' experience.
>
> Perrott's categorisation provides a useful set of guidelines for improving a teacher's use of any particular teaching strategy, since whatever approach is chosen will require introducing, explaining and summing up.

Source: Shelton Mayes (1995).

Effective questioning

Points raised in this chapter about the choice of methods available to teachers to help pupils secure the planned learning gains of a lesson, or sequence of them, have referred to the importance of asking questions. Indeed, researchers have identified that this activity may well occupy 30 per cent of a teacher's time in a lesson (Brown and Edmondson 1984).

The clear advantages of using questioning as a classroom method (Petty 1993) have been found to be that it:

- encourages understanding rather than rote learning
- provides instant feedback
- helps to modulate the pace of a lesson
- reveals flawed learning and allows 'unlearning' to occur
- can motivate pupils by allowing them to demonstrate their learning and reinforce it through teacher response
- can provide a practice opportunity for pupils to use recently-acquired ideas, vocabulary and subject 'logic'
- allows the teacher in one-to-one questioning to diagnose the difficulties of a pupil
- can be used to discipline a student
- can encourage the development of high-level thinking skills.

Moreover, Ofsted has maintained that questioning is the most important factor in pupils' learning achievements in cases where questions are used to elicit and assess their knowledge and to challenge their thinking (Ofsted 1994).

The disadvantages may be that it:

- can be time-consuming
- may not engage all pupils
- is a teaching strategy which requires skill and careful planning.

Questions may be 'open' or 'closed' (Brown and Edmondson 1984). The latter have one correct answer usually whilst open questions enable a range of responses to be made, including personal and value-laden ones. Barnes also uses a third category, the 'pseudo-question', which the teacher phrases as an open question even though he or she is looking for a particular reply (Barnes 1969). Brown and Edmondson, however, urge caution in the use of any classification system; for example, a question may change type depending on the context in which it is used or on the teacher's underlying intention in asking it. It may be a genuine question or it may be a managing device.

Common questioning errors by teachers may relate to:

- the structure and/or vocabulary of questions being too complex
- the level of questions pitched inaccurately, so being too easy or too difficult
- the type of questions chosen being perceived as too inconsequential
- targeting questions predominantly to a particular group
- failure to place questions within the context of the lesson and prior learning
- providing too little thinking time for pupils to respond to challenging questions
- class management difficulties; all pupils need to listen and follow the rules associated with questioning sessions
- poor presentation of questions in terms of volume, clarity or insufficient engagement with pupils through eye contact or movement around the room when appropriate.

Planning for overall balance for questioning, as with so many elements of teaching strategy, is important here. In relation to his research in this area, Wood (1998) takes the view that:

> Frequent, specific questions tend to generate relatively silent children and to inhibit any discussion between them. Telling children things, giving an opinion, view, speculation or idea, stimulates more talk, questions and ideas from pupils and generates discussion between them.

(Wood 1998: 175)

Two points remain. First, teaching methods and the learning activities highlighted in this chapter require management. A review of possible groupings relating to gaining feedback from pupils was provided in Chapter 4, Language and Learning. Further consideration of the forms this might take, in groupings arranged by a subject teacher and working with groupings of pupils designated within the school context, is taken up in Chapter 8. Second, an accent on presentation and the skilful mediation of methods chosen by a subject teacher or form tutor produces a need to take care of the voice and to develop its range of capacities as one would a musical instrument. Listening to colleagues and taking from them ideas about voice use for impact, interest, attractiveness and management for different purposes, is yet one more challenge for the beginning teacher, and one which may contribute in large measure to the success of the methods outlined here.

Methods in action: an example

In this final section, it is appropriate to have a look at a sequence of lessons, organized by a PGCE student, which demonstrates the multi-faceted learning gains possible when a range of teaching methods and learning activities, appropriate to learning context and purpose, is successful. Reading 6.3 outlines the planned learning purposes and some of the activities within a project sequence with a Year 8 group of 29 pupils (17 girls and 12 boys; attainment range of Levels 4– to 6–).

Reading 6.3 Oxted Millennium Project

Subject: English

Focus: Teaching and learning in Key Stage 3 (incorporating ICT and numeracy)

Learning purposes

To provide opportunities for pupils to develop their public presentational skills, both oral and written, with a focus on persuasion. The framework of the project is designed to develop organizational and planning skills, negotiating within small groups, with a considered use of library resources and ICT.

[Planned learning gains relating to National Curriculum Programmes of Study follow here.]

Oxted Millennium Project

We are delighted to inform you that the Lottery Council has awarded OMP 1 million pounds to create a new facility for the local community.

The Chairperson of the County Council (your teacher) invites groups to submit their proposals. All groups will be given the opportunity to present their ideas to the Members of the Council (the rest of the class) who will select the winning proposal. The winning group will be awarded the contract and group members will receive a certificate.

What to do

Groups   You need to work in a 'project group' of 5 people, including a chairperson, a scribe, designer and anyone else your group might need. Don't forget – roles can be shared!

Facility   What do you think the money should be spent on? Would it be of interest to the whole community or would you focus on one group? Generate your ideas, discuss them and choose the best ones.

Survey   Think of 10 questions that you could ask to find out what local people think about your ideas, including the interviewee's age, sex, hobbies; whether there should be an entrance fee, etc. Write your questions in your project note book and ask your family and friends for their views.

Chart   Using Excel, produce a chart (e.g. bar or pie) to show your findings from the survey. Transfer this to Word and add an explanation of the information it contains. You could use this to support your proposal to the Council.

Details   Once you have chosen your project, discuss the details and make a list of them, such as location, transport, entrance fee (if any), facilities, etc.

Plan   Draw up the plans for your project, showing where it will be on the Oxted map and what it will look like (an artist's impression or sketch would be useful). Don't forget to label all the necessary details.

Submission   Write a description of your project, explaining why it is such a good idea. Be persuasive!

Presentation   Present your project to the members of the Council for them to vote on.

Good Luck!

Use the IT lessons to produce your charts, final submission and any letters to the Council.

Use the library lessons to research your ideas, look at artists' impressions, maps and plans and anything else that might be helpful.

Use your imagination!

Lesson record/evaluation form

Class 8a3 Thursday 25 February 1999 Oxted Millennium Project

General impression

- In library – independent sustained reading – took a while to settle.
- In classroom, good atmosphere – children interested in task but noisy and excited. Got into groups as instructed (I had decided these previously). Lesson to set up and launch task. Seemed successful – children engaged and interested.

Pupil learning

- Reading – independent reading skills, including book selection

- Project – getting into groups, how to negotiate tasks and direction and reach consensus
- Early days.

Teaching and learning strategies

- Silent reading – own choice of books
- Move to different classroom
- Teacher talk
- Mixed-ability/behaviour groups selected by teacher
- Groups told who they were and where to sit
- Worksheets handed out – teacher read questions
- Last 10 minutes – think about ideas for survey – recorded on board
- Set out homework on board.

Resources

- Library/own choice of books
- Classroom – worksheets – 1 per child; maps – 1 per group
- Board.

Classroom management

This is always a noisy, lively group. Very enthusiastic about task – repeated need for waiting/asking for quiet.

Assessment

Explained purpose/focus of assessment:

1 Speaking and listening – how individuals perform in group work
2 Speaking and listening – how individuals perform in presentation
3 Writing – assessment of individual progress logs
4 Writing – assessment of final group submission

Cross-curricular issues

Working in groups – negotiating consensus; taking responsibility; organization of self; civic issues – needs of community

Key skills: numeracy

Creating and conducting surveys to incorporate into submissions

Key skills: ICT

Using Excel to create charts/tables. Pasting into Word for explanation and presentation. Choice of range of packages as pupils deem appropriate for their group's needs

Project evaluation

At class level, the framework of the project gave all pupils the opportunity to develop their 'public' presentational skills by giving them a 'real' project which they could develop and present to a 'real' audience. Devising their own surveys and canvassing their friends and family gave the project an authentic air and most pupils were involved and interested, as evidenced by the quality of the final presentations. The maturity with which the pupils listened to their peers' presentations and the fairness of the voting was extremely pleasing.

Working in groups, with each member fulfilling their choice of task, engendered a sense of responsibility and ownership of the project and the group members divided the work in a largely fair and equal manner. Pupils negotiated roles according to their different talents but were all expected to take part in the final presentations. The notes researched in the library sessions demonstrated a growing ability to evaluate and to adapt non-fiction information while the quality of charts and texts produced in the computer sessions was impressive.

At an individual level, the contribution of each child to the final presentation, including some very quiet class members, demonstrated a general understanding of the different facets of public presentation and some children revealed significant persuasive skills. There were, however, one or two pupils who avoided work and another time I would endeavour to ensure their full participation by setting them individual targets. However, the strategy of keeping an individual log of each child's progress was a valuable tool in keeping the majority on task. If teaching the sequence in the same context again, I would try to allow more time for the class to question the presenting group, thereby developing both the listening skills of the audience and the responsive skills of the presenters. I was, however, delighted with this sequence and would use it again.

Source: H.Burr, PGCE student 1999.

Conclusion

Throughout their professional careers, teachers learn. The beginning teacher here has planned for all pupils to develop the range of their presentational skills and to learn more about devising and interpreting data. The 'real' audiences built into the project and the authenticity striven for in relation to research and the tabulation and presentation of findings, provided momentum and a clear schedule of learning activities. Opportunities to evaluate the process, skills involved, the presentations given, and what pupils themselves made of the learning gained, clearly illustrate a key point made at the beginning of this chapter: teaching methods are not mere applications upon a lesson or lesson sequence; they propel and are embedded in a symbiotic teaching–learning relationship.

The beginning teacher here, although 'delighted with this sequence' learns, from it and is prepared to make adjustments to the methods used in any future re-working of it, notably in relation to questioning pupils. The careful planning for an appropriate integration of ICT resources and strategies in this project to enhance and extend learning is clear, and it is this aspect of teaching and learning which is the subject of Chapter 7.

References

Barnes, D. (1969) *Language, the Learner and the School*, London: Penguin.

Brown, G.A. and Edmondson, R. (1984) 'Asking questions' in E.C. Wragg (ed.) *Classroom Teaching Skills*, Beckenham: Croom Helm.

Cattell, R.B. (1931) 'The assessment of teaching ability' *British Journal of Educational Psychology* 1: 473–89.

Cohen, L., Manion, L. and Morrison, K. (1999) *A Guide to Teaching Practice*, London: Routledge.

DfEE (1999) *Teachers; Meeting the Challenge of Change. Technical Consultation Document on Pay and Performance Management*, London: DfEE Publications.

Gannaway, H. (1976) 'Making sense of school' in M. Stubbs and S. Delamont (eds) *Explorations in Classroom Observation*, London: John Wiley.

Kyriacou, C. (1997) *Effective Teaching in Schools: Theory and Practice*, Cheltenham: Stanley Thornes.

Hay McBer Report (2000) *Research into Teacher Effectiveness*, London: DfEE Publications.

Office for Standards in Education (Ofsted) (1994) *Primary Matters: A Discussion on Teaching and Learning in Primary Schools*, London: Office for Standards in Education.

—— (2000) *Framework for the Inspection of Schools*, London: Office for Standards in Education.

Perrott, E. (1982) *Effective Teaching*, Harlow: Longman.

Petty, G. (1993) *Teaching Today* (2nd edition) Cheltenham: Stanley Thornes.

Saunders, M. (1979) *Class Control and Behaviour Problems: A Guide for Teachers*, Maidenhead: McGraw-Hill.

Shelton Mayes, A. (1995) *Teaching and Learning, Secondary Document 5*, OU PGCE student resources.

Simon, B. (1994) 'Why no pedagogy in England?', in B. Moon and A. Shelton Mayes (eds) *Teaching, Learning and the Curriculum in Secondary Schools: A Reader*, London: RoutledgeFalmer.

Wood, D. (1988) *How Children Think and Learn*, Oxford: Basil Blackwell.

7 ICT
A creative support for teaching and learning

Introduction

There is no doubt that there has been little short of what might be termed an ICT revolution in education. This revolution constitutes a major support for teaching and learning processes in schools. Hesitations in relation to a statement containing the words 'revolution' and 'ICT in schools' might be answered by reference to the (still) large numbers of teachers-in-post who can recall that pre-photocopier banda machines were once the sole means available to them of reproducing text and graphic materials for their pupils. Experienced colleagues in English departments may remember, too, that a visit to the cinema with pupils was the necessary option to provide access to a high-quality celluloid version of a Shakespeare play. Digital anything was still a fiction and the subject teacher's own collection of photographic slides or a cine-film version of an event or subject-area activity were the usual practical ways to supplement the resource banks of schools.

Today's technological resources and routes to mediating meaning and understanding in lessons are many: video tapes, digital cameras, all-purpose CD/radio/tape players, Powerpoint presentations, electronic Smartboards, computer power, Internet access and school websites, are all available to support teaching and learning. For leadership and management purposes in education, telephone and video conferencing, scanners, laptops and a teachers' virtual college offer further opportunities to share and shape communication, professional development and achievement in the classroom.

The opportunities and gains available to teaching and learning have been well-rehearsed (HMI 1989; Watson and Tinsley 1995; Marx *et al.* 1998) and relate to progress, extension of skills' range and preparation for and successful participation in the world of work. These matters form the substance of this chapter. The first section, the largest, focuses on the claims for ICT-use in the school curriculum and practical representations of it. The second section broaches five key areas raised by the British Educational Technology and Training (BETT) organization's national debate on ICT in schools; and the final section raises the issue of investment in technology and training in our schools and for our teachers.

ICT as a creative support

Information and communications technology (ICT) has been compulsory for all pupils aged 5–16 since the introduction of the National Curriculum in 1988; it originally formed part of the National Curriculum Technology Order. Today, pupils are given opportunities both to pursue discrete ICT skills as well as to enhance learning within different subject domains. The New Opportunities Fund (NOF) provided a launch-pad for significant investment in hardware, in particular. It provided the impetus, too, for schemes such as, for example, the Learning Schools Programme (LSP) which had rapidly attracted (by 2001) over 140,000 of the UK's 400,000 teachers to on-line learning attached to their own specialist areas.

ICT is about access to information systems as well as to varieties of communication. This dual capacity affords it a huge array of potential uses. Certainly its different capacities for strengthening subject study and response, broached in Chapter 2, have been characterized as enhancing, extending and transforming.

Examples for each might be:

- enhancing a subject area
  - the use of spreadsheets
  - other graphical representation of word text
  - use of audio or videotape material
  - use of photographic equipment or material

- extending a subject area
  - use of the web to access other sources and varieties of information
  - use of CD-Rom resources

- transforming a subject area
  - conversations with other practitioners using video or audio conferencing or electronic conferencing
  - email exchange of opinion and documents.

These are convenient and helpful characterizations to consider in terms of subject and teaching and learning processes. The example in Reading 7.1 refers to what can actually happen to re-define teaching and learning. Claims made only a few years ago find their substance here. Relationships between teachers and learners are re-shaped since the learners involved will have greatly increased access to vast amounts of information. In this situation, teachers will need to become partners in the learning, and leaders of learning, too, pointing to 'future possibilities and new identities' (Leach 2001).

The variety of composition modes available is graphically visible. So, word-processors make it possible to alter the ways pupils compose texts, allowing them to concentrate on content and creative possiblities. Set alongside this, email communication equates to a sound-bite response and is often attractive to pupils who traditionally have failed to produce the dominant required mode of extended, handwritten responses. Such pupils have also been taught to use spell-checker functions so as to release them to concentrate on the content and organization of their responses when this takes priority over the secretarial skills of a task. As ICT-use continues to develop:

> Teachers who are at present the major source of, or controllers of, the information needed for learning will find that they have become ... tutors, guides, counsellors, sources of judgement and experience rather than providers. They will

still be of vital importance, because they will be the people with whom ideas are discussed and tested, from whom encouragement and discipline are obtained, and above all who assess and aid progress. They will be the ones who teach the students to learn.

(OECD 1992)

These observations carry weight practically a decade after they were made. The processes indicated by them will also continue to require negotiation and adjustment by teachers and pupils (McCormick 1992).

The National Grid for Learning

Several sources of support for teachers have been noted above. The National Grid for Learning (NGfL) is another. Launched in 1998, this site, at www.ngfl.gov.uk, had the declared intention to be 'the UK's main educational gateway to the information superhighway', to 'enable people to take advantage of the new information age' and particularly to support schools and all other educational institutions 'both in their daily work and their continuing professional development'. This in turn was seen as nurturing a 'connected society, improving the quality and availability of educational materials, and increasing and widening access to learning for all' (BECTa 2000) and contributing to the planned modernizing process outlined in Chapter 1. Meanwhile, funding for sustained support for ICT in schools was being maintained; between the time period 1998 and 2004 an investment of 1.8 billion pounds was allocated – through the NGfL and the New Opportunities Fund (NOF) teacher training programmes.

At the 2001 BETT Show, an exhibition conference-showcase for technology hardware, software, training programmes, and expositions of achievements and intent by interested parties, the Minister of Learning and Technology reaffirmed government commitment to training, development and funding, announcing the start of a debate about what constituted effective and good practice in ICT both for the teacher and the learner. The website of the British Educational Communications and Technology Agency (BECTa) was nominated to host the on-line national debate (at www.becta.org.uk). The scope of this debate was designed by BECTa, QCA (Qualifications and Assessment Authority), Ofsted and NAACE to elicit response about five core features of the debate about ICT. These were described as *control*, *quality*, *capability*, *creativity* and *scope*. For each of these features, respondents were asked to comment about the effective teaching practices which might best describe each of these features. In addition, the questions were posed: how might ICT assist the teacher in achieving them? Further, what kinds of things would pupils be doing when these features were in evidence? These are intriguing questions to ponder and are addressed in more detail in a later section of this chapter.

Meanwhile, two major goals in relation to ICT-use were prominently showcased at the BETT Show 2001. These were outlined as:

1   ensuring that every pupil leaves school fully capable of using the new technologies since 90 per cent of jobs in the UK now involve some sort of interaction with IT

2   using ICT to drive up standards of achievement in schools; anecdotal and research evidence points to ICT as a potent tool for teachers. More systematic analysis of gains, based on large samples, was recommended.

ICT achievements cited by BETT included these facts:

- In 1996, one in twenty primary schools had Internet access; by 2000, nine out of ten primaries and virtually all secondary schools were connected.
- In terms of access, in 1996, there was one computer for every 19 pupils in primary schools; in 2000, this had improved to one for every 13 pupils.
- The development of an on-line TeacherNet site, an adjunct of the DfEE website, to provide materials and direct links to information and targeted support for teaching and learning in National Curriculum subjects.
- As a development of TeacherNet, the launch of a pilot in March 2001 of at least 1,000 lesson plans and linked resource agencies.
- The continued development of the NGfL portal – the largest in Europe.
- The commissioning of pilots and materials for what are counted now as minority and specialist subjects such as Latin and Japanese.
- The launch of GridClub, for children aged 7–11, designed to enable them to make sense of the net, through participation in interest-focused clubs, such as animals or sports.

There remained challenges to be negotiated, however. Set alongside these notable achievements, for example, was the issue of consistency and quality of use. The set of gains, indicated above, had not been distributed evenly. Any tour of a school's ICT provision-in-use rapidly underscores how in-school budget allocation decisions over a number of years have left their mark happily or with rough consequences upon schools. Moreover, initial national allocations of money for hardware provision were not as soundly matched by widespread and thorough support and training. It is fair to state, however, that the imbalances created have increasingly been leavened and, it appears, will continue to be so. Meanwhile, issues such as ethical aspects of Internet use, health and safety dimensions, levels of ownership of computers by teachers themselves, regular access to computers in schools, and how to assess individual inputs of pupils to collaboratively laden activities, have remained some among very varied concerns in relation to effective teaching and learning to which teachers have sought answers in schools.

And indeed, by 2001, over 200,000 teachers had registered for their ICT training entitlement and 28,000 more teachers owned a computer as a direct result of the assistance-to-buy scheme which then provided £500 of the outlay cost. The eligibility criteria for this subsidy continued to be positioned to take account of government initiatives. In 2001/02 Key Stage 3 maths teachers were targeted for the scheme, in order to firm up the gains of the designated Year of Maths strategies of 2000. This strategic targeting clearly had a logic attached to it: resources are not limitless, and phased, focused subsidy appeared sensible from this pespective. From another view, however, that of the teacher of geography, for example, fired up to enhance, extend, even to transform practice, this might have appeared frustratingly unhelpful.

Yet more positively, all of the achievements listed by BETT and described above have been designed to facilitate 'best practice' in subject-area teaching. It is to these gains that the beginning teacher is directed. Identifying the stretch and detail of this concept is one of the desired ends of the great debate alluded to earlier.

The perceived potential for ICT-use is in no doubt, then, and the practical examples given in this section as well as indications of the resource supports for teachers and learners in this area, have underlined a continually developing future for learning and teaching methods in schools using ICT. A look at some of the detail in relation to the ICT National Curriculum itself is useful here. The main themes apparent in the curriculum are described as:

- finding things out
- developing ideas and making things happen
- exchanging and sharing information
- reviewing, modifying and evaluating work as it progresses

with a *breadth of study* requirement.

The expectations required of pupils for ICT at Key Stages 3 and 4 as outlined in the National Curriculum are listed below.

At **Key Stage** 3 pupils are:

> increasingly independent users of ICT tools and information sources. **They have a better understanding of how ICT can help their work in other subjects and develop their ability to judge how and when to use ICT and where it has its limitations.** They think about the quality and reliability of information, and access and combine increasing amounts of information. They become more focused, efficient and rigorous in their use of ICT, and carry out a range of increasingly complex tasks.

At **Key Stage 4** pupils are:

> more responsible for choosing and using ICT tools and information sources. They use a wide range of ICT applications confidently and effectively, and are able to work independently much of the time. They choose and design ICT systems to suit particular needs and may design and implement systems for other people to use. They work with others to carry out and evaluate their work.

The decision-making, problem-solving, collaborative and organizational implications of these outcomes, along with the specific ICT skills of handling information, modelling, controlling and measuring, clearly have potentially telling impacts for learning across the curriculum.

In terms of the classroom context, and for beginning practitioners, the 'ten golden rules' suggested by Nicholls as ones to follow to enhance pupils' learning using ICT can be usefully considered, tried and reassessed for any subject area in terms of contexts and pupils' needs. They are outlined in Figure 7.1 and are taken up again later in the chapter.

1   Identify the learning aims and objectives for the pupils that can be enhanced by the use of ICT

2   Select appropriate ICT resources to meet the learning aims

3   Ensure that the pupils have enough ICT skills to be able to carry out the activity

4   Plan the timing of the activity to include non-ICT tasks such as question and answers, group work, pupils' discussions

5   Plan enough lessons to enable the activity to be completed

6   Decide on the groupings of the pupils – they do not always have to work alone

7   Introduce the lesson to all the pupils before working on any ICT

8   Intersperse the ICT activity with whole-class guidance and direction

9   Allow enough time for the pupils to reflect on and evaluate their achievements at the end of the lesson

10   Allocate homework or other assessed work in which the pupils extend their thinking about the activity, and through which you can find out what they have learned.

Figure 7.1 Ten 'golden rules' for ICT-use to enhance pupils' learning

Source: Nicolls (1999: 81).

Such a firm practical sense as demonstrated in the 'golden rules' above (and supplementary others generated by particular classroom and school contexts) need to be harnessed judiciously to the polemic of ICT potential. Careful planning, organization and alert use of opportunity and local knowledge about pupils in a teaching group all have to be pronounced parts of a lesson in which ICT features. Where resources have to be shared and turn-taking exercised, protocols and routines are not negligible elements of a lesson. In Reading 7.1 (opposite) an experienced teacher relates a not-to-be-forgotten lesson where ICT-use featured and was observed by adult visitors. The class is a challenging one in which pupils are often unpredictable and wear their emotions at surface level. The school is a pre-secondary phase one but the details and application are clearly accessible to any teacher.

Many of the 'golden rules' for ICT-use, referred to in Figure 7.1, are in evidence in this case. The lesson has been well-planned and organized; the ICT resources are prepared, appropriate and integrated with the lesson sequences; the support assistant has participated in lesson planning and preparation; the lesson's issues are introduced before the individual ICT activity and using a form of collaborative technology, the Smartboard; the lesson itself is interactive and varied and the ICT activity is interspersed with other events of the lesson; the mathematical language used by the children is viewed as an enhancement and, for many of them, an extension of knowledge and application of skills; a plenary session clarifies and confirms processes and learning, allowing the opportunity to reflect on and to evaluate what has been seen and done in the lesson. What is apparent, too, beyond these achievements, is the sense that the overall sum of these parts is far greater in its impact: these

Reading 7. 1 An average ICT lesson in the life of a teacher of emotionally and behaviourally disturbed (EBD) pupils

At the morning briefing I'm informed that the Maths Adviser will be observing my Maths lesson with the school Maths co-ordinator! Despair hits me and it's only Tuesday morning. Do a quick check … and then look out of the window to see just how windy it is. Okay so far.

The planned lesson is on number patterns and I've included use of our new interactive Smartboard in my planning booklet. It's only the second time I've used the Smartboard but I'm well planned and prepared, so here goes.

I have a mixed class of MLD (Mild Learning Difficulties) and EBD (Emotionally and Behaviourally Disturbed) pupils – mainly EBD. Lessons therefore have to be differentiated and well planned. The lesson follows the morning break and the SUN IS SHINING. A good start to any EBD class lesson. The first part of the lesson, the mental maths, goes well in the classroom. The appearance of two strangers watching doesn't make things any different, yet. Ten minutes later we all head for the computer room for our interactive main lesson. The pupils file through chattering excitedly. The support assistant has set up the room already (essential part to remember) and the pupils sit in the chairs in front of the Smartboard. We discuss the previous day's lesson looking at patterns in number. So far so good. Suddenly I realise that all the pupils are sitting to attention, arms crossed and looking at the board. This is unusual, even I admit this (but it does look good with advisors in). Suddenly, I realise the pupils have remembered the last interactive lesson when I chose those pupils who sat well to come to the front of the class and move the objects on the board. Who was it who said that some pupils don't learn as quickly as others? All pupils seemed to remember this and to have the whole class concentrating on what I was saying was brilliant.

The main lesson went very well. We used the number square from 'My World' and the pupils took it in turns to come to the front and look for the next number in the pattern and circled it. With such a large number square pupils were having quite a high degree of success. All the pupils were involved and each had a turn at coming out to the front and circling a number. The less able pupils circled the lower numbers and the more able circled the higher. One of the best parts of the lesson was the extensive mathematical language used. It was remarkable. Describing the patterns and using complicated terms of position was a great achievement for some of these pupils.

The next part of the lesson was independent work. The pupils each went to a computer and worked on individual number squares according to ability. When they had completed their square they had to discuss it with an adult and then they printed it out. With two extra adults in the classroom this was great and the pupils showed off and explained their work to whoever was nearest. The only blip in the lesson was when C and M both went over to the printer to see if their work had printed out and they began arguing over whose work would come out first. A swift support assistant intervened before things got out of hand.

At the end of the main lesson all the computers were switched off and we went back to the classroom for the plenary. All pupils had something to show for their morning's work. A computer printout is physical evidence and the pupils described their individual patterns in great detail to the rest of the class. At the end of the lesson the adviser told me to sit down and have a rest. She was worn out watching me and complimented me on the lesson. It was the first time she had seen the Smartboard being used. However, I have to admit that the introduction of the interactive lesson is a great bonus. As I have become more confident using it the pupils have benefited. Lessons are FUN, and varied ... .

Advice

1   To avoid arguing when at the computers I now ask all the pupils to copy their work onto their disk first and then make sure that an adult is near the printer when work begins to get printed.
2   Each pupil has an individual disk to record work onto which is used instead of a workbook. Pupils also enjoy looking at the different work that they have completed.
3   Always have the Smartboard set up before you go into the computer room. This avoids a lot of unrest, potential outbursts and arguing, since you can't give all your attention to the pupils when attending to it.
4   Experiment.

Source: www.ngfl.gov.uk, copyright BECTa 2002.

variable children were clearly engrossed and making progress. One of the learning gains claimed for appropriate and successful ICT activity in Figure 7.2, that of improved motivation and attitudes to learning, finds a vivid expression in this teaching and learning context. The pleasure, pride and enjoyment of the class teacher, too, is tangible. The rhetoric of potential in relation to similar contexts using ICT does not seem inappropriate in this particular context.

The point made once again here and throughout this book is that teaching and learning are a dynamic process: the gains outlined above cannot be successfully achieved without teacher competence and confidence, and efficient and creative planning and management, as well as the appropriate application of ICT functions, to effect desired learning outcomes in specific subject areas and across the curriculum. It is no small point that an indiscriminate use of ICT to a task which is better approached by some other means may well be unproductive beyond the lesson in question.

Figure 7.2 outlines a span of learning gains which can potentially be achieved through ICT-use in teaching and learning across the curriculum.

Area of learning benefit	Type of ICT activity		
	Electronic communication: email, on-line chat, video conferencing	Access to resources held elsewhere: WWW, CD-Rom, interactive TV	Creating information for access by others: web-sites, CD-Rom, multimedia
Improved motivation and attitudes to learning	Provides a real respondent, actual context and purpose Encourages peer review of spelling, syntax, etc.	Encourages motivation by using an interactive and interrogative medium Makes accessible high-quality, multimedia resources Enables pupils to find unique, topical items of information	Creates opportunities for creativity, 'real-life' contexts and teamwork Enables pupils to contribute to a 'global encyclopaedia'
Improved subject and vocational learning	Gives first-hand access to local unpublished information Provides personalized answers to pupils' own questions Gives pupils time to work out email or fax replies at their own pace Involves learners actively by requiring an immediate response to video conferencing and chat	Provides on-line learning materials Makes international, up-to-date information available Develops literacy and extends vocabulary Enables access to otherwise unpublished information Provides pupils with choices of learning modes	Develops writing and authoring skills Provides an opportunity to demonstrate grasp of a subject Encourages learning through making hypertext links within and between sites
Development of network literacy	Enables pupils to extend traditional skills of reading, writing, speaking and listening Gives opportunities to access and transfer files	Encourages development of navigation skills Provides opportunities to locate and adapt material for use in assignments	Facilitates awareness of electronic publishing standards, issues and processes

(continued on next page)

Development of independent learning and research skills	Enables pupils to pursue their own enquiries Provides unmediated access to experts and native speakers	Helps learners develop search strategies and scan, sift, compare, evaluate and use information Prompts cross-curricular and cross-topic connections Encourages lateral thinking and stimulates reflection on thinking and learning skills	Develops editing skills and selection of content
Social development	Enables direct interaction with others across boundaries of ability, gender, culture, age, status and nationality In the case of video conferencing, develops conversational skills and awareness of turn-taking	Encourages collaboration and mutual support Increases pupils' confidence and self-esteem	Develops sense of audience Encourages teamwork, e.g. seeing other points of view Encourages pupils to write to attract and keep people's attention

Figure 7.2 Some of the possible learning gains of ICT-use

Source: 'Connecting Schools, Networking People', copyright BECTa 1998.

Learning gains and ICT activity

Figure 7.2 conveniently indicates a range of learning gains and the types of ICT activity which could be employed to help to produce them. These gains are described as:

1   improved motivation and attitudes to learning
2   improved subject and vocational learning
3   the development of network literacy
4   the development of independent learning and research skills
5   social development.

Learning gain (1) is well represented in the account given in Reading 7.1. Here, ICT is a support to plans and activities, constitutes an organizing principle of the lesson, and provides interest and skills' enhancement in relation both to mathematical concepts and ICT knowledge, understanding and application. And, linking to learning gain (5), it certainly provides opportunities for creative contexts for learning as well as fostering team work and participation. The use of video conferencing has a clear set of gains attached to it when considering the social development gains proposed by the matrix in Figure 7.2. Conversational skills, turn-taking, the development of effective listening and of a sense of audience and interacting beyond and between boundaries of gender, ability and of nationality, are all encouraged by such creative ICT supports for learning.

Learning gain (2) refers to improved subject and vocational learning. The infinite array of resources available to expand learning and types of learning is apparent to any regular user of the worldwide web. The immediacy of synchronous conversation through video conferencing or of considered, asynchronous communication through email or fax has its own uses and learning gains for different pupils in varying contexts. The choice of learning modes here is a real expansion of learning opportunity for pupils in that choice can be provided and the exercise of choice itself produces an experience and a learning gain.

Vocational learning is provided by the encouragement of learning through hypertext links between sites, although the distinctions between vocational and non-vocational learning can be seen fruitfully to be blurred.

ICT activity can also be seen to contribute to learning gain (3), the development of network literacy. A competence in literacies of increasing numbers is being required of pupils and the adults they will become in this century. The demonstration of competence in reading, writing, speaking, listening and thinking is written into the National Curriculum syllabuses. The term *literacy* has itself come to represent a shorthand term for 'competence in'. So we need, for example, our pupils to be literate and also 'literate in' numeracy, media comprehension and citizenship. 'Network literacy' here relates to the development of navigation skills and the growth in computer housekeeping expertise that come with accessing and transferring files within the pupil's own data-keeping system.

The development of independent learning and research skills, learning gain (4) of ICT activity, has long been a desired learning outcome of teachers when planning schemes of work for classes. Here the range and type of activity indicated provide a clearly visible means to its growth. What a teacher is able to do quite quickly is to assess the degree to which a pupil has made down-loaded information, for example, her or his own. Skills of editing, summary, selection of important illustrative detail, and a command of issues and of intended audience and purpose of the pupil's writing using the web source material, are all amenable to assessment. The simple action of requesting that the original web material accompanies the new piece of writing which was drawn from it facilitates appropriate assessment in most cases.

Social development, learning gain (5), dovetails back into learning gain (1): improved motivation and attitudes to learning. The 'direct interaction with others across boundaries', the encouragement of team work and the increase in self-esteem and confidence are all outcomes of improved motivation and attitudes to learning and also contribute to them.

There is no doubt that there currently exist multiple sources of support for beginning and experienced teachers wishing to widen their own subject resource banks. Detailed overleaf is a small selection, with the notes introducing them, from the vast array of choice on the NGfL website's Virtual Teacher Centre. The kinds of learning gains possible, reviewed above, can clearly be further enhanced by subject-specific resources available to teachers on the worldwide web, adapted to source and shape planned learning outcomes for classes.

Virtual Teacher Centre's subject-area resources

Old maps

Main content by Key Stage study unit or topic History KS1/KS2 Local history, Victorian Britain Teacher resource KS3 Britain 1750–1900 Teacher resource KS4 Britain 1750–1900, Local history, …

The essential guide to rocks

Main content by Key Stage study unit or topic KS1/KS2 teacher resource KS3 Geomorphological processes, Tectonic processes, teacher resource KS4+ Geomorphological processes, Tectonic processes, teacher resource General …

Organizations for Science

Here you will find links to subject associations, national projects and other science-related bodies.

Music wing

Author/organization responsible for site: Andy Murray Suitability of resources to age/purpose and UK curriculum: KS2 (immediately useable), KS3 (immediately useable), KS4 (immediately usable), Teacher …

ICT in Geography: a pupil's entitlement to ICT

There is a huge potential for ICT to enhance the teaching and learning of geography. As part of a project …

The economy

There is a huge potential for ICT to enhance the teaching and learning of geography. As part of a project …

Challenging poetry for Key Stage 3

Context: challenging poems to stimulate and extend the thinking of Year 9 pupils. ICT is used as an essential tool …

Wired for health

Health information for young people and their teachers, from the Department of Health and the Department for Education and Employment …

The Web Gallery of Art

Author/organization responsible for site: The Web Gallery of Art General comments: The Web Gallery of Art is a virtual museum …

Subject resources for Mathematics

This area contains links to web sites that have been approved as having useful curriculum content as well as the …

(www.ngfl.gov.uk, copyright BECTa 2002)

There are currently multiple requirements of teachers-in-training using ICT in schools and the TTA (1998) publication, *The Use of ICT in Subject Teaching*, outlines these. Behind and beyond the detail lie the key considerations for any subject teacher; the challenge of integration of ICT approaches within the planning, doing and evaluating of teaching and learning over a school year is a key one. And, as stressed earlier, it is the appropriate use of such means which is often a key to effective teaching and learning. The following example illustrates this. Listed on opposite is a selection of subject-area websites at www.ngfl.gov.uk. A teacher of geography might well view what is available and decide that, having accessed 'Old Maps', the first edition Ordnance Survey maps for the local area indicated they will provide a rich resource for study of the ways in which economic growth and development occur. The details below indicate what is on offer here.

Old Maps

Main content by Key Stage study unit or topic

History

KS1 N/A

KS2 Local history, Victorian Britain, teacher resource

KS3 Britain 1750–1900, teacher resource

KS4 Britain 1750–1900, Local history, teacher resource

Geography

K1–4 Context and scales, Places, teacher resource

General comment

Refers to issues such as: source/author; intended audience and purpose of site; value over other media for studying particular topics; potential to engage pupils; obvious potential for pupil or teacher activities.

A useful resource for a wide range of enquiries and activities. The Ordnance Survey and Landmark Information Group have worked together to produce an on-line database of the first edition OS maps. This provides free access to first edition historical maps of Great Britain dated between 1846 and 1899. This site allows you to view historical maps simply by entering a place name, an address or a grid reference; alternatively it is possible to use a county gazetteer.

The persuasive pull of social and economic geography may well be a strong one to an individual teacher, presented with the details of this resource. If, though, the main requirement in syllabus terms was connected, say, with map reading, then vast amounts of class time cannot be allocated to other intriguing issues and activities indicated on the site. Any competent teacher of course uses class and homework time to follow up connections and routes beyond an official syllabus, but the time constraints and considerations of balance have to be weighed too. In addition, an irresistible question will have to be posed: is the particular tool being considered, the ICT tool, the best one possible?

Reading 7.1 outlined the learning and social gains visible in a classroom of emotionally and behaviourally disturbed pupils. The point was made that the 'golden rules' of any ICT-infused lesson were in evidence (and more besides as a further perusal of Figure 7.2 and the learning gains of ICT-use will confirm). So, to what actually might all these routes and possibilities lead in the secondary school classroom, lab, or technology block where classes come and go for set portions of time and tight syllabus coverage seems to dominate department practice (despite, say, a declared collegiate wish to educate widely in scientific, mathematical or historical terms)? Appropriate ICT-use is potentially able to provide a notably supportive element in any framework of teaching and learning. The following example illustrates this.

BECTa Best Practice Awards

The 2001 BECTa Best Practice Awards, to promote and reward exemplary ICT practice among teachers, and to attempt to disseminate it, can provide an illumination of what is possible in action. BECTa declared that 'We are looking for practice that is replicable … above all, we are looking for practice that will make the experience of school even more relevant to students.' Part of the slide presentation relating to the 'best practice' of the winner of the secondary subject category (here, science) is outlined in Figure 7.3. The four slides shown below, adapted from the presentation,

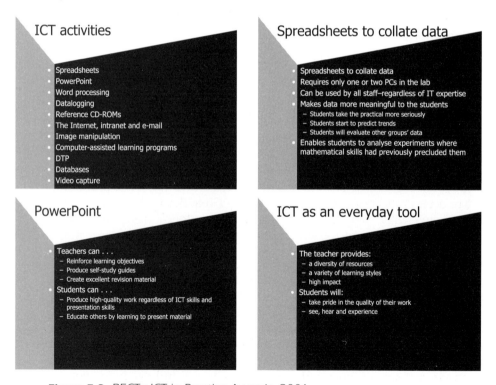

Figure 7.3 BECTa ICT in Practice Awards, 2001

Source: www.ngfl.gov.uk, copyright BECTa 2002.

indicate something about the range of activities engaged in by the subject department and the peceived teaching and learning potential of ICT here and in other curriculum areas.

This is one notable example of forward thinking and effective use of ICT by teachers and pupils, of the kinds indicated in Figure 7.2. The specific ICT requirements for subject areas can be seen to be adaptable across other curriculum areas – and this is the case, of course, with other subject-cited ICT requirements. The National Curriculum ICT elements for English, for example, of applications, communicating, information modelling, handling data, control and measurement, can be applied elsewhere. The range of activities and subject-based activities and focuses using these is shown below.

Art and Design

Applications	Commercial art
Communication	Multimedia for students' portfolios
Modelling	Spreadsheet to model design specs
Handling data	Surveys
Control	Embroidery

Business and Commercial Studies

Applications	Commercial packages, administrative systems
Communication	Business letters, email, Internet
Modelling	Business modelling
Handling data	Pay packages, databases

Drama, Dance and Music

Applications	Ticket booking, lighting control, recording studios
Modelling	Lighting sequences
Control	Lighting sequences, MIDI interfaces

English

Applications	Publishing, news services, advertising
Communicating	Word-processing, multimedia, email, Internet
Handling data	Class surveys, database of books/reading

Humanities (Geography, History, RE)

Applications	Weather stations, archiving, museums
Communication	Multimedia, word-processing, posters, projects related to culture and beliefs
Modelling	Spreadsheet modelling, building design packages, simulations
Handling data	Surveys, database, Internet
Measurement	Weather, wind speed, rainfall

Maths

Applications	Space programme
Communication	Multimedia, email projects
Modelling	Number patterns, algebra
Handling data	Class database, graph work
Control	Programming language
Measurement	Accurate short/long period measurements

Modern Foreign Languages

Applications	Internet, teletext, translation services
Communication	Multimedia, DTP, word-processing, email
Modelling	Café bills
Handling data	Class surveys, topic database

Physical Education

Applications	Recording, timing
Communication	Events, leaflets, posters
Handling data	Personal/group performance database/spreadsheet
Measurement	Accurate timing, recording

Technology

Applications	Industrial production, engineering, electronics
Communication	Health and safety posters, design (logos, packaging)
Modelling	Building design
Control	Lathes, textiles/embroidery

Science

Applications	Nuclear power stations
Communication	Safety posters, word-lists
Modelling	Experiment modelling
Handling data	Graph work, data logging
Control	Experiment control
Measurement	Accurate short/long period measurements

(Capel et al. 1999: 40)

The best practices possible and the potential for progress suggested by them are empowering, particularly in a well-provisioned school. In a less well-equipped school, there remains the challenge to provide what is, after all, a National Curriculum requirement for pupils' skill development and confident command by teachers of what is on offer in the ICT domain. Nevertheless, research evidence of the 1990s (NCET 1994) provides compelling reasons for using ICT in schools. These are that:

- children who use computers at home are more confident when using one at school
- IT can provide a safe, non-threatening environment for learning
- it has the flexibility to cater for individual use and need
- difficult ideas can be made accessible by IT presentation
- immediate access to rich resources of materials is quickly provided
- pupils can take risks with their learning
- reflection upon and re-working of work are encouraged
- computer simulations can stimulate analytical and creative thinking.

The detail contained in, for example, *The Use of ICT in Subject Teaching*, will undoubtedly change but the principles will remain constant. Behind and beyond the 1998 detail lie the key considerations for any subject teacher; the challenge of integration of ICT approaches within the planning, doing and evaluating of teaching and learning over a school year is a key one. And, as stressed throughout this chapter, it is the appropriate use of such means which is often a key to effective teaching and learning.

It is this question relating to appropriateness which beginning teachers will need to have at the forefront of their planning. Often, they realize the potential of and are excited and energized about it. They are aware, too, of their relatively privileged position in departments as competent practitioners of ICT and the of capacity ICT-use to contribute positively and with skill to their subject areas. Reading 7.2 provides some extracts of thoughts and evaluations about ICT-in-practice.

Reading 7.2 ICT-in-practice

Beginning teacher 1

Information Technology

I was able to provide individual support in this lesson.

The class teacher was trying to make sure that all members of the group had up-to-date classwork and homework and was finding it difficult to do both this task and deal with all the questions from individual pupils. Due to the nature of the lesson it was impossible for the teacher to stop the lesson and deal with the queries on the board.

As I have a working knowledge of information technology I offered to walk around the room and assist the pupils with their work.

I was able to offer advice and help to sort out problems with mail merge and letter layout.

As this was only my second day in the school I found the experience enjoyable and exciting. I found that I was able to explain the order of tasks well to the group and that they understood my explanations. My experience as an NVQ information technology trainee came in useful in the context of this lesson.

Beginning teacher 2

ICT has played a role throughout this scheme of work. Initially, I carried out a lesson using ICT to compile surveys for an information-finding exercise. The use of word-processing packages and clip art allowed pupils to compile questionnaires which were taken home and completed for homework. I chose to complete this exercise using ICT as it lent itself well to the format of a survey. I also felt that pupils would gain a more realistic insight into the part layout plays in developing a survey if they had to complete it in a realistic environment. Pupils soon became aware of the need to make sure questions were short and to the point rather than long-winded. Pupils were also quickly aware that they had to make their work stand out from the others in the group and so began to introduce tick boxes. …

Pupils were working in pairs on the task so that they could share ideas and good practice with one another. I introduced the rule that the work had to be checked … before printing. Pupil learning was facilitated in that they were able to use ICT skills (gained in subject-specific lessons) in a realistic situation. Differentiation was planned for in a number of ways including:

- by outcome: all pupils were given the same remit but were left to work out presentation on their own
- by support: all pupils were offered support during the lesson but some required it more than others
- by task: all pupils were given the same task but opted to complete it in different ways
- by resource: pupils were given access to computers as a realistic way of completing the piece of work
- classroom management was not problematic as the school has a set routine for behaviour within ICT rooms and all pupils are aware of this.

Beginning teacher 3

[The local context has impacted upon the force of ICT-use in this beginning teacher's school.]

Computers have a wider role to play. As I discussed earlier … the economic background of my partner school is undergoing a shift from traditional manufacturing to administrative and tertiary sector jobs. Without fail, all the major employers in the area now operate via computer database systems and experience of computers is a distinct advantage in the job market. At X school the change in the job market has influenced a change in school subjects with business studies being one of the most rapidly developing subjects on the school timetable.

Source: Beginning teachers, OU PGCE course, 2000.

Comment

Different aspects of ICT-in-use are evident here. Beginning teacher 1 is excited at the immediacy of her impact in a new context and role. Her skills are used and are filtered to aid pupils' technical and learning gains. Beginning teacher 2 is planning for the different needs of her pupils within a scheme of work. ICT-use here is appropriate and integrated. The third beginning teacher is working within a school context which has already responded to the changed local work situation beyond the school, in order to equip pupils to operate effectively within it. These are all examples of ICT-use in schools which embed best practice of different varieties.

The national debate about ICT: five core areas

In an earlier section of this chapter, reference was made to the terms of a national debate about ICT-use in teaching and learning. This BECTa-, QCA-, Ofsted- and NAACE-generated activity in 2001 sought to elicit responses relating to five core areas of teaching and learning processes. These are set out below as: *control, quality capability, creativity* and *scope*.

Control   Teaching empowers pupils to take control of their own learning, engaging interactively with the technology, thus enabling them to work independently at the most effective pace and at the most appropriate level.

Quality   Teaching encourages pupils to use ICT to develop and improve their work and enhance its presentation.

Capability   Teaching supports pupils in developing the capability to use the new technologies both effectively and to their full potential.

Creativity   Teaching involves ICT-use to inspire pupils' creativity, allowing them to explore the possibilities of any or all of the multi-media tools available.

Scope   Enabling pupils to employ ICT to provide access to experience, information or resources in ways that are not possible with other media, and to carry out work that would otherwise be too difficult or impossible.

For each of these areas contributors were invited to answer such questions as:

- What would the effective teaching practice that results in these persuasive processes and outcomes look like?
- What might ICT do to assist the teacher in achieving these processes and outcomes?
- What might the pupils be doing as a result of practice incorporating these features?

It is worth pursuing some of the practical ramifications in learning terms of the five areas raised for debate, above, which, although separated as strands of a debate, are clearly interrelated. In this chapter the term *pupil autonomy* might represent what is described in relation to the area of *control*. ICT can empower pupils and their teachers to take control of different things. Here an appropriate level of work, suitably paced, is presented as a potential learning (and teaching) gain. ICT-use does not automatically, of course, confer a happy fit between ability, pace and level of work undertaken. Pupil and teacher negotiation about this, based on evidence, cannot cease to be part of the teaching–learning process. Effective teaching practice, then, raised as one of the three key questions impacting upon the debate, would refer to issues such as empowering students, following negotiation of the kind described above, increasingly to make soundly based decisions (confirmed by the subject teacher) about pace and level of classwork tackled using ICT.

The *quality* dimension of the debate relates to supporting pupils to 'develop and organize their work and enhance its presentation'. This is not a negligible element, given the BETT figure cited at the beginning of the chapter that, even currently, 90 per cent of jobs now involve some IT interaction and knowledge of functions-use that come with this. It is not an issue to be dismissed as overly functional or as 'out there', since preparation for adult – and work – life is an educational responsibililty of schools. Moreover, a knowledge and understanding of the mutual interplay of content and presenting such content to best effect in a wide range of curriculum subjects is other aspects of learning to be gained by a conscious consideration of it. To the question of how ICT might assist the teacher in achieving more in the five areas outlined, then, clearly, group and class discussion of the issue, using ICT-generated exemplar materials and an introduction to basic software packages which illustrate and enable quality presentation, are starting points.

The *capability* feature which 'supports pupils in developing … the new technologies both effectively and to their full potential' is closely meshed with both control and autonomy. Again, exposure to software programs, appropriately gauged to ability, interest and planned outcomes of learning, is core here. Constructing a personal web page, a common-enough feature in the adult world of ICT-use, might be one practical translation of this; the capability to use Powerpoint to aid presentations by pupils, as touched upon in the 'best practice' example cited in Figure 7.3, would be another. The *scope* issue of the debate, that which enables pupils to have access to experience, information and resources 'in ways that are not possible with other media, and to carry out work that would otherwise be too difficult', represents a strong claim for ICT-use in schools. Storing and interrogating information accessed by different means and producing a report using desktop publishing would demonstrate one part of this feature. What exposure to the information and communication capacities of technology does most quickly, arguably, is to present this feature convincingly to pupils. To the question which asks what pupils might be doing as a result of practice incorporating these features, we can look at the *creativity* dimension of the debate as an indicator of this.

This area relates to ICT-use 'to inspire pupils' creativity, allowing them to explore the posssibilities of any or all of the multi-media tools available'. Again, this relates to all of the other features. The notion of creativity itself is used in different ways in varying contexts. Here it is used as a resulting condition inspired by flexible and exciting ICT exploration. Elsewhere, it is commonly associated with 'flair', an elusive capacity which one has or has not: a happen-chance affair. In *All Our Futures* (DfEE/NACCCE 1999), a report from the National Advisory Committee on Creative and Cultural Education, it was seen as able to be taught and developed – and in the domains of the sciences, mathematics and technology as well as in the more traditionally associated creative arts of music, drama, dance, literature and art. The arguments pressed were that:

- 'the essence of creativity is in making new connections' (1999: 72), going beyond subject boundaries;
- subject organization in school has itself contributed to the stymying of creativity (ibid: 74). Dissolving divisions has created new areas (biophysics and biochemistry; narrative techniques in social sciences; the use of qualitative research methods to complement and frame quantitative sources for research in the social sciences);
- nearly 2 million adults now work in the 'creative industries' of advertising, architecture, design, leisure software and computer services – the replacement work world for the manufacturing base of the UK;
- it is stressed as a must-have dimension of a changing world and the economic, technological, social and personal challenges contained within it (ibid: 54–62).

In schools, the problem-solving capacities of pupils and the development of their thinking skills as part of the systematized approach to enhancing creativity was argued for strongly in this publication. In terms of key issues of the 2001 national debate which provided a focus for discussion in this section, the report argued the imperative of enabling 'young people to make their way with confidence in a world that is being shaped by technologies which are evolving more quickly than at any time in history' (ibid: 54). Tellingly, the report made the point that 'creative processes are purposeful and ... they involve growing control over tools and materials'. The national debate and debates that followed have appeared to point to what is argued here: 'In future, new technologies may create divisions between those who can use them and those who cannot. This argues for systematic programmes of IT education in schools' (ibid: 21).

Second-stage achievement using ICT

Chapter 1 of this book pointed to the challenges inherent when speed of change, and an inventory of ambitious targets relating to teaching and learning and linked to a standards agenda, jostle with the largely uniform organizational structures that schools have to be in a national framework offering a recognizably consistent service. In this chapter another variable has been added to the challenge: ICT used flexibly and creatively to enhance teaching and learning and in the context of an entitlement IT curriculum. Rather unneven provision and access in UK schools initially provided some brakes to what was possible and this was accentuated in cases where pupils and teachers did not possess a home computer which might temper such school-based differences. Ownership or access by themselves do not, of course, deliver competence or creativity; and training and development issues also impacted upon first-stage achievement and progress.

Many factors, then, shape what is offered and how it is offered in the classroom. What is apparent is that the professional development obligation placed upon teachers and reviewed in Chapter 14 needs to take into account the scope and challenge of ICT competence and confidence of all teachers. The point is made there and is again worth raising: newly qualified teachers will undoubtedly be better equipped than large numbers of long-serving colleagues to address the ICT agenda and to interpret it creatively and systematically. They may well find, too, that they are rapidly the new leaders in schools in this area of their responsibilities. So, how might beginning teachers, entering new schools and confident in their ICT skills, be guided in working with more experienced colleagues who are less certain of their capacities to enhance teaching and learning? Reports about such situations from newly qualified teachers have been very positive, as Reading 7.2 indicated. They have often quickly assumed a key position in a department because of their skills but more often, possibly, because they have been willing to mediate these to other colleagues in a sensitive, practical and non-judgemental manner.

This, then, is a staged process. In 2001, the first-ever Minister of Technology and Learning made the point, indirectly, that all revolutions have stages attached to them:

> The first stage – which has lasted from 1997 till now – was focused on securing the investment to bring schools up from a situation where many were struggling to fund even the most elementary ICT provision to a situation where teachers were able to start making effective use of ICT in the classroom. There was considerable urgency about this. There had been considerable under investment for a number of years. The revolution taking place outside the classroom was gathering pace and our schools were in real danger of getting left behind. In the process of this rapid change over the last two years or so, we have achieved a great deal .... And I believe we are now ready to move to this second stage where effective use of ICT can be made, systematically, to help drive up standards.
> (Speech by Minister of Learning and Technology at BETT, 10 January 2001)

Core needs have already been indicated: further investment for in-school resources; training for teachers with a less targeted allocation of subsidy for home computers; newer teachers with ICT competence rewarded for developing their colleagues, are some. Software design is another facet of the equation which commands attention. If, as argued, there are teachers who are not confident technology users, then learning how to use a new piece of software can be a confusing and certainly time-consuming process. Tailoring software programs to different levels of user competence could be one way forward. Scaffolding is important, too. As teachers use multimedia programs, for example, prompts could profitably remind them of background information relating to what they are viewing. Efforts to manage the technology successfully can of course undercut the reflective processes of teachers in the same way as this can affect the performance of pupils. An 'Issues to Consider' field that asks teachers to think about aspects of a video clip viewed on screen, for example, will go some way to redress this (Marx et al. 2000). The extended and desired conversations of chat groups and forums-on-line are also less likely to be well trawled by teachers unless they also have a route to well-sourced materials relevant to work in schools. These same materials, moreover, may only represent for teachers a convenient alternative source to texts available – or not – to them. They will have little to do, for example, with profound professional development. As Marx *et al.* observe: 'If lesson plans published on a site are sketchy and lack the elaborations to scaffold teacher learning, it is less likely that the plans will help teachers teach differently than in the past' (ibid: 289).

The thrust of this chapter has indicated many gains and some variation of success in relation to ICT-use in schools. Descriptions and evidence of excellent teaching and learning using ICT are legion; yet practical experience of some secondary schools also reveals circumscribed tools, restricted and partial teacher training, and the power of ICT undercut by computer-use of a pedestrian or inappropriate kind. Certainly, that a revolution has taken place in terms of thinking and talking about ICT-use in subject areas to enhance teaching and learning is not in doubt. A contextual, cultural change has occurred, as was pointed out at the beginnning of this chapter and we are undoubtedly experiencing a catch-up period in the UK in relation to teacher ownership of computers. Another complexity presents itself, however, here: in 2001, home access to the Internet by children of school age had reached 60 per cent; and the access rate to a home computer was even higher, at 82 per cent (Office of National Statistics 2001). So, for many, school is not a primary source for the regular use of this premium facility. This raises an equality issue relating to non-ownership and non-access, out of school hours, by children and teachers, which itself can be compounded by irregular provision and access inside school.

But catch-up in relation to describing anything reminds us that this is a staged process. The in-evidence variation of ICT provision in schools invites a debate about greater ICT investment as part of a national plan to relocate priorities and returns on such investment in a societal and global frame. These areas, after all, are often centrally placed in arguments pressing innovation and change in education, and considerations which restrict debate to an analysis of provision at school level, neglect the links.

Moving on

Global competitiveness is commonly cited as a core reason for innovation and change in many areas of social and work life. Yet even the number of training days for employees across the UK had fallen – from five in 1996 to three in 1999 – a total loss of 50 million training days (Puttnam 2000). The five training days teachers are allocated and the general feeling by teachers themselves that these are inadequate when set against their professional development duties and personal development targets make this an interesting figure to consider. And in the information technology sector itself, the UK was projected as having a shortfall of over 300,000 skilled workers by the end of 2003. The Basic Skills Agency, moreover, describes another pull on targeted resources, calculating that 24 per cent of the population are, in different ways, 'functionally illiterate' and that the same number are functionally innumerate. This then is a society of astoundingly variegated needs; and it is at a societal level, perhaps, that solutions might profitably be sought.

This certainly was the argument put by the chairman of the General Teaching Council in 2000 (Puttnam 2000: 5). Canada was cited as an illustrative example of how massive financial investment in education (including technology), and strategically undertaken to have wider economic and social impacts, literally pays off. Put another way: the economic and social costs to a nation of low literacy – and ICT skills – are enormous. Key details of the example are set out overleaf.

During the 1990s, the Conference Board of Canada calculated that Canada would lose more than $4 billion in present-value terms across the working lifetimes of 14,000 youths who dropped out of secondary school instead of finishing their studies.

By their estimation, each male 'drop-out' would lose some $130,000 over [a] working lifetime. The level of human waste was of course utterly unquantifiable.

The Canadians calculated that as an investment vehicle, education has a higher rate of return than almost any alternative investment project you can think of. The rate of return to society of investment in secondary school education is 19% for males and 18% for females (women still receiving lower rates of pay across the board.)

The Canadian Government came to the conclusion that, were they to reduce the drop-out rate of 34% to 10% over a ten year period, they could save $25 billion in hard cash alone.

(Puttnam 2000: 5)

Putting aside variables which might undercut like-for-like national comparisons, it is not a negligible point that the larger social and education implications of investment – or not – are relevant to the concerns of this chapter. Whether the issue is one of low levels of literacy or restricted IT skills, social or global imperatives require that financial considerations of costs must count those that go beyond the school gates. Just as subject department budget allocations (and subject-focused concerns) in schools have not always been for the greater good of education in schools, so too the regular vying of different ministries in Whitehall for government budget allocations might be seen to have had a similar effect in national terms.

A more systematic and literal opening-up of schools and their (much-expanded) resources to wider communities would begin to spread impacts and potentially place budget decisions within a wider frame, it is argued (ibid: 5). A GDP (Gross Domestic Product) expenditure higher than the current allocation of 5.2 per cent and nearer to 7 per cent by 2005 was suggested as more realistic in terms of enabling the ambitious plans of a second phase of development to occur. The 'world-class' education system espoused by government is about 'strengthening the links between schools and the rest of the community' (ibid: 6) as well as improving teachers and standards (ibid). Moreover, the return-on-investment factor is by no means the central one (though it might be politically persuasive), for 'It's also an opportunity to … put schools at the heart of the communities they serve – and to connect them with all the members of those communities' (ibid: 9).

Some idea of the possibilities and practicalities of this community-placement process was outlined in Chapter 1, Reading 1.2. Resources in the school described there were increased and targeted to enhance community participation. A central idea guiding the process was that schools are not organizations to be sloughed off by individuals at the first available point (or dropped-out of) but are essential parts of living, developing communities of people who are at ease with entering them and benefiting from them. Arguably, then, the real ICT revolution, one that encompasses educational growth and aspirations with a national development strategy, is yet to come. But the caution is given: 'the next five years are absolutely critical' (ibid: 6). The digital divide in schools and in society is a national, not a local, concern.

These matters of school, community, national and international significance are notable, certainly, but the introduction in this chapter of issues related to them, though important for a beginning teacher to access and to form a view about them (not least because experienced colleagues will have a view), nevertheless ought not to undercut an appreciation of the tremendous gains in classrooms across the UK in terms of imaginative, technically competent and confident use of ICT in subject-specific teaching and learning in what, it is argued, has been a phased revolution.

Conclusion

One function of this chapter has been to describe the exciting potential of ICT-use in secondary subject areas and to provide some practical indications of 'best practice', developments and possibilities. Another declared purpose has been to raise appropriate questions in relation to what has been termed by many as the ICT revolution in schools and to weigh the extent of this. ICT has been pressed both as a key support to a changing view of teaching and learning and as a path to securing higher-order gains of competence and confidence. The prize of the autonomous learner, making progress in individual terms and as a social being, is within reach in many subject areas in schools. The chapter's third section raised the issue of social and global demands and invoked the prospect of expanded outcomes in relation to these as a result of less stringent, compartmentalized funding of different government departments and a more strategic and integrated approach to it. This, it was argued, would help to secure the root-and-branch gains needed for ICT in schools and the enhancements, extensions and transformations possible in subject areas and in personal terms. ICT provision and use can be viewed as a socially and economically pinned issue. For the beginning teacher, there now exists a cutting-edge opportunity to make imaginative and skilled inputs to teaching and learning in schools using ICT as a creative support.

References

BECTa (2000) *Making the Most of the NGfL: An Introduction to the National Grid for Learning for Secondary Teachers*, Coventry: BECTa.

—— (1998) *Connecting Schools, Networking People*, Coventry: BECTa.

Capel, S., Leask, M. and Turner, T. (1999), *Learning to Teach in the Secondary School*, (2nd edition) London: Routledge.

Cox, M. (1999) 'Using information and communication technologies (ICT) for pupils' learning' in G. Nicholls *Learning to Teach*, London: Kogan Page.

DfEE/NACCCE (1999) *All Our Futures: Creativity, Culture and Education*, London: HMSO.

DfEE/QCA (1999) *The National Curriculum: Handbook for Primary Teachers in England, Key Stages 1 and 2*, Norwich: HMSO.

—— (1999) *The National Curriculum: Handbook for Secondary Teachers in England, Key Stages 3 and 4*, Norwich: HMSO.

HMI (1989) *Information Technology from 5–16*, London: HMSO.

Leach, J. (2001) 'ICT, creativity and the classroom' in B. Moon, A. Shelton Mayes and S. Hutchinson (eds) (2002) *Teaching, Learning and the Curriculum in Secondary Schools: A Reader*, London: RoutledgeFalmer.

Marx, R.W., Blumenfeld, P.C., Krajcik, J.S. and Soloway, E. (1998) 'New technologies for teacher professional development' in R. Moon, J. Butcher and E. Bird (eds) (2000) *Leading Professional Development in Education*, London: RoutledgeFalmer.

McCormick, R. (1992) 'Curriculum development and new information technology' in R. Moon and P. Murphy (eds) (1999) *Curriculum in Context*, London: Paul Chapman/OU.

Nicholls, G. (1999) *Learning to Teach*, London: Kogan Page.

OECD (1992) 'New technology and its impact on classrooms' in B. Moon and A. Shelton Mayes (eds) (1995) *Teaching and Learning in the Secondary School*, London: Routledge/OU.

Puttnam, D. (2000) 'The revolution to come: teachers, teaching and ICT', Geoffrey Hubbard Memorial Lecture, Royal Society of Arts, 14 December 2000.

TTA (1998) *The Use of Information and Communications Technology in Subject Teaching*, Annex B of DfEE Circular 4/98, London.

Watson, D. and Tinsley, D. (eds) (1995) *Integrating Information Technology into Education*, London: Chapman and Hall.

8 Classroom management

Classroom management in practice cannot be isolated from all the other issues that contribute to good teaching and good schools. The most efficiently managed class will learn little if the material presented to pupils is dated, irrelevant or dull, and likewise, the most interesting of material, if taught in a badly organized or lacklustre way, is of little value. The management of classes cannot occur in a vacuum. The attitudes and values that frame the process are as significant as the skills and expertise displayed. A school's ethos is of critical importance in promoting effective classroom management and effective learning.

These points established, competent classroom management features as a prime concern for the beginning teacher. Without this in place, little learning may occur; and its absence, often referred to as a lack of classroom control, represents a real fear for all teachers that experience may largely temper but never deliver as a certainty in all situations. However, effective classroom management can be much more than this. At its best it is about organizing pupils and resources imaginatively for learning to occur, about pupils taking on some responsibility for their learning and talking about it, and it is about teachers who lead as well as manage and encourage these personal and social dimensions in the pupils they teach. This last point is central. A teacher's relationship with a class propels management and leadership issues and determines what is possible.

Clearly, effective communication, key teaching skills, successful lesson components, detailed and appropriate planning for differentiation, assessment opportunities and learning development, highlighted in Chapters 5 and 6, remain core requisites. Added to these, and impacting measurably upon consistently effective class management, are other issues, too. These are:

- time and timings
- the physical environment of the teaching space
- class and group arrangements
- tackling problems of management.

Time and timings

Planning for effective lessons requires that use of time and the timings attached to learning activities are centrally placed. Making decisions about the relative importance of activities and the time allocations to be tagged to them is an important skill for the beginning teacher to develop. Misjudgements can make plans falter; yet at the same time the capacity to tap into the energy and ideas of a class, about how to organize a project, for example, as well as to ideas about lesson content, is also needful.

One of the most crucial organizing tasks in terms of classroom management is associated with the beginnings and endings of lessons and the way pupils transfer from one activity to another during the lesson.

Beginnings of lessons

Beginnings can take many forms. The problems that some teachers can experience at this point often relate to a poor opening or unclear exposition of what is to come. Making reference to the learning activities of the previous lesson is an important way of making connections and generating progression. Certainly it is essential to establish with pupils the purposes behind the work upon which they are about to embark and to make clear the ways in which the lesson will be organized. Experienced teachers frequently offer these points of advice to a beginning teacher about the start of lessons:

Beginning well

- Try to arrive before the class.
- Always ensure that the class is quiet, with bags put away and coats off before beginning the lesson.
- Have some stimulus as well as yourself to set the class going – a prompt on the board, an OHP or a chart, for example. A prompt allows the teacher to become more mobile in the class and avoid being rooted behind the teacher's desk or at the front.
- Scan the whole class regularly and make eye contact with as many individuals as possible; use pleasant, firm and friendly smiles!
- Keep the introduction short and, if you need to impart an extended amount of information, use a resource in addition to talking.
- Make the first pupil activities clear and straightforward; avoid being overwhelmed early in a lesson by a multitude of questions about how something is to be done.
- Be clear about the sequence of activities, the 'what happens next'.
- Be aware that latecomers may interrupt an introduction; have a form of words that tells them to sit down and wait and that you will clarify what has to be done once the lesson is underway.

Some teachers develop a way of working that allows them to begin a lesson a little way into the allotted time. A classroom routine or procedure may include, for example, an element of reading or written work that all pupils attend to on an individual basis as soon as they enter the room. The teacher then chooses a moment when everyone is present and the class is settled to introduce the topic of the day. There are some areas of the school curriculum where individual or group openings to a lesson may be the norm. For example, project work in Design and Technology may not require teacher input to direct an activity. However, it is important for beginning teachers to establish themselves and their presence in the minds of the pupils. Reiterating what the pupils are to do or reinforcing some aspect of classroom practice helps to establish teacher presence and identity.

Endings of lessons

The endings of lessons also present organizational challenges. There will, again, be school routines depending on the class and the time of day. If it is the end of the school day, chairs may be put on desks to help cleaners in their task. There will be routines relating to the checking and putting away of equipment. Pupils may keep their books and files or they may be retained in the classroom. Schools and departments within a school differ in their practices and these routines need to be learned. Consistency on these issues will be as important as the openings of lessons. The ending of a lesson is one of those areas of practice that experienced teachers make look easy. Advice about this offered by experienced teachers to beginning colleagues has regularly referred to the points illustrated below.

Ending well

- Find ways in which some of the 'ending tasks' can begin well in advance of the end of the class; books and equipment can be collected by the teacher as s/he goes around talking to pupils.
- Ensure that the ending of the lesson is not too overcrowded; it is unwise to try to summarize the lesson, collect equipment, set homework and leave the room tidy, all in the space of two or three minutes.
- Revise the lesson plan if the time pupils take over certain activities is longer than projected; it will not be productive to rush through important concepts in five minutes simply to ensure that the specifications of a lesson plan have (nominally) been met.
- In most circumstances a moment of quiet before the class leaves, and a word of commendation in the context of thinking about what they've achieved, creates a pattern and routine that is helpful and pleasurable.

Transitions within lessons

Much of what has been raised so far about beginnings and endings of lessons applies to transitions (movements) from one activity to another during lessons, whether as a whole class or in terms of groups changing activities. It is crucial to think ahead to make these as smooth as possible and ensure they occupy the minimum amount of lesson time.

Key points for consideration here relate to the need for:

- The preparation of resources for a transition; valuable teaching time can be lost if the class teacher or pupils disappear into a store cupboard! (If a video is to be used, it is clearly sensible to have set it at the right place before the lesson.)
- Pupils to be warned in advance that a change of activity is impending. A plan for late finishers to catch up as part of homework, for example, can be useful.
- Smooth transitions. Ones that change the atmosphere of the class too abruptly can be unsettling and create difficulties for a beginning teacher. The majority of experienced colleagues will be able to handle this, even using it purposefully as a teaching technique for a planned learning purpose.
- Noting that if transitions are to be individual or group-based rather than class-based, then the ground rules or procedures for making a change must be clearly set out, particularly if teacher presence is necessary to check work before the change can be made.

These are all organizational tasks that can soon become part of the management repertoire of the practising professional.

The physical environment of the teaching space

Room arrangement is an extremely important aspect of classroom management. This will vary according to purpose, and some rooms (laboratories and workshops, for example) will have fixed furniture. A new teacher will usually have to work to the pattern established by another subject teacher so it is important to think about alternative patterns of organization. 'Fitness for purpose', the term examined in Chapter 6, can once more be used here. Group discussion work, for example, will involve a particular form of table organization. The need for all pupils to have a clear line of sight to the chalkboard or video monitor may create other requirements. Whatever the layout, however, these points of advice are valid:

- Room layout may need adjustment to ensure that it is easily circulated, if necessary, by teacher and pupils.
- If furniture layout will need to be changed during the lesson, how this will be managed will need careful planning.
- Sensitivity to the usual teacher's rules about who sits where is required by the beginning teacher in placement. Many teachers insist on pupils occupying the same position (and this certainly helps in the initial process of learning names). Certainly it is part of the subject teacher's responsibility to decide which pupils sit where and for what reasons, so that effective learning can occur.

The physical environment of the classroom involves more than furniture layout. The accessibility and layout of resources form important management tasks that need to be factored into planning. The quality of display in the room is another matter for consideration. The quality of the physical environment conveys a very important message about the value given to teaching and learning in the room. Rooms with shelves stacked with outdated, unused, grimy and disintegrating textbooks, with fading and torn wall displays, or with yellowing periodic tables pinned up years before, are not only unhelpful spaces; they are counterproductive to learning. By the same token, a well-cared-for and imaginatively arranged room will support and extend the work of pupils and statements about serious learning endeavours made by a class teacher.

Class and group arrangements

The ability to plan for productive groupings within a class as well as for whole-class learning is an essential teaching skill. Chapter 5 on planning raised issues relating to the need to differentiate by resource, support, activity and outcome so that progression for individuals as well as for whole classes can occur. Chapter 6 on classroom methods highlighted some key teaching skills to develop and learning activities to encourage. This section focuses on elements of class groupings and the ways in which they can shape the nature and outcomes of learning. First, the issues of managing inappropriate behaviour by pupils in mainstream classes are addressed, but it is a clear assumption of this chapter that the beginning teacher has high expectations of what each pupil can achieve and so plans and manages classroom learning accordingly. The strategies described in relation to dealing with poor pupil behaviour are offered in order to stress that the subject department, the pastoral care system of the school, and senior management support, are all resources available to underwrite classroom approaches towards those pupils who do not wish to learn, disrupt a class and affect the learning experience and achievements of others.

E.C. Wragg wrote that 'teachers need considerable skill to select topics, activities and ways of working from the vast array of possibilities' (Wragg 1984: 2). This is so and experienced colleagues will confirm that:

> Good teaching is not just a matter of being efficient, developing competence, mastering technique and possessing the right kind of knowledge. Good teaching also involves emotional work. It is infused with desire, pleasure, mission, creativity, challenge and joy. Good teaching is a profoundly emotional activity.
>
> (Hargreaves 1995)

The appropriate balancing of these two major aspects: focused, planned-for organization of the learning purposes of individual pupils and classes, and an emotional investment in it, provide the challenge which constantly requires attention and assessment.

Ability groupings

Yet, of course, in any class described as setted by ability, the beginning teacher will find a great range of difference in capacities and motivation, requiring differentiated approaches, sufficient to challenge. Pre-planned groupings of different kinds for appropriate learning purposes within such classes will be found needful and productive. This is an area requiring greater attention than can be allocated in this text and the reader is referred to the detailed debates in Moon *et al.* (2002), Ireson *et al.* (1999) and Benn and Chitty (1996).

Group work

Most teachers consider group work an important part of their repertoire of strategies, especially useful as a vehicle for addressing some of those learning purposes relating to pupils' social development, such as co-operative work. Peer interaction is also cited as an important method of learning, because children are often more relaxed with each other than they are with teachers, and opportunities for language work and conceptual understanding may be increased (Wood 1998; Wood and O'Malley 1996).

Bennett and Dunne argued that 'co-operative groupwork is not a panacea for children's social and cognitive development, it is one option or approach in the teacher's repertoire which must sit alongside other approaches such as individual and whole-class work' (Bennett and Dunne 1992: 190). Nevertheless, they present a careful argument for using co-operative group work in problem solving and applications work where abstract talk should predominate. They recommend that all group-work tasks should be dependent on an element of 'problem solving' (which in their opinion always involves decision making) and that a useful distinction can be drawn between 'discussion' tasks and 'production' tasks. 'Discussion, not having an end-product, leads to abstract talk, whereas production tasks promote talk relating to the action necessary to achieve the end-product' (ibid: p. 72). A parallel distinction is drawn by Barnes and Todd when they describe teachers' use of the terms 'tight' and 'loose' tasks to explain group activities requiring correct or fixed responses on the one hand, and those that can be more free-ranging on the other. The tasks tend to be associated with different types of talk by pupils (Barnes and Todd 1977).

Bennett and Dunne set out three models of co-operative group work which emphasize the social aspects of setting tasks:

- Pupils work individually on identical tasks for individual products, but are asked to talk to each other about their work, to help each other, thereby establishing co-operative endeavour.
- Pupils work individually on 'jigsaw' elements of a task, so that a certain amount of co-operation is built into the task, especially in terms of planning and organization. (See Chapter 4 on Feedback strategies.)
- Pupils work jointly on one task for a joint outcome, so that co-operation is of paramount importance.

(Bennett and Dunne 1992: 91)

Reading 6.3, 'The Oxted Millennium Project' in Chapter 6, shows some of these facets in action and also the beginning teacher's evaluation of the learning gains achieved through them.

Of course, the pointers given above in relation to group work have to be managed in action: that is, relating to individuals, differentiating their needs and routes to learning and achievement, whilst being alert to the classroom climate and the proportion of pupils on task, and mindful of how pupils in the class might be learning. This is a multi-faceted 'management' concern. Reading 8.1 contains extracts from a PGCE student's evaluative review of a Year 7 sequence of lessons on advertising. The subject is English but its general application for any subject teacher is clear. The complex nature of the endeavour is apparent, even in this abridged extract.

Reading 8.1 Year 7 advertising project: extract from a review-evaluation

Learning and teaching strategies in English

… The following learning strategies can foster a 'deep approach' to English teaching: clear explication of aims and objectives; group work; appropriate differentiation; acknowledgement of pupils' learning styles; effective use of language and communication; equality of opportunity; encouragement of autonomous learning; pupil motivation; appropriate classroom management; and finally, varied use of resources, including ICT. The examples below directly demonstrate how my professional development through English teaching has contributed to effective pupil learning and school improvement.

Year 7 advertising project

In my classroom teaching I have made the learning aims and objectives explicit to each class. During a Year 7 lesson on advertising, I introduced a complex, differentiated scheme about advertising. This took a four-lesson sequence to complete – from questionnaire, through collation of information, analysis of results and summation of findings, to conclusion. In these sessions I was careful to structure the process explicitly, indicating aims and objectives before moving on. The sequence began with a focal, whole-class questionnaire session and ended with an 'evaluation of findings'. The pace of the lessons was clearly delineated at each stage and I maintained a brisk working atmosphere, a strategy which ensured that I was able to keep the lesson 'in the air'; the pupils were engaged throughout and were excited about the potential end result.

This example demonstrates how my PGCE lesson plans have sought to transpose the initiative of the exercises away from the teacher and to the pupils, making the process both social and active; it is during the dynamics of the group work and individual activity sections of the lesson that the pupil learning takes place, and as Vygotsky (1978) argued, prompts a mix of internal development processes that are able to operate only when the child is interacting with peers in their shared environment and in co-operation.

The major part of the work of the advertising sequence was done in pupil groups which were differentiated by levels of potential attainment. The higher attainers were given the most complex element of the analysis process; the lower attainers were able to collate the questionnaire information and the summary of their findings directly contributed to the project summary. This was a productive learning strategy.

Classroom management

Crucial to the success of this exercise was the classroom organization and management. This Year 7 group was lively and excitable. It was, therefore, important that direct guidelines were laid down at the beginning of the sequence. I emphasized throughout the importance of coming to order on command, of not talking when I was giving instruction and of keeping the general noise down to an acceptable level. On reflection, I felt that my classroom management technique was not always successful and in the future I would make sure that the ground rules were clearly identified from day one and reinforced frequently; clearly stating standards of behaviour is an opportunity to act in a position of authority. ... During the sequence of four lessons I only had recourse to use of direct discipline procedures a couple of times and these were never stronger than a verbal reprimand.

Source: S. Bridges, PGCE student, 1999.

Comment

One gains here the impression of an alert, enquiring beginning teacher, directing attention to how all the many requirements for teaching and learning might best be facilitated. The reflective practitioner is here, too, able to review what has happened and plan to act differently in a similar context so that professional growth and more profound learning can occur.

And professional growth *does* happen. This is illustrated below where recorded differences between experienced and beginning teachers in connection with classroom management are set out.

Experienced teachers

- Were usually very clear about their classroom rules
- Did not hesitate to describe what they thought was 'right' and 'proper'
- Were conscious of the massive effort needed to establish relationships with a new class
- Used their eyes a great deal to scan the class or look at individuals
- Were quick to deal publicly with infraction of their rules
- Were more formal than usual
- Were especially brisk and businesslike
- Established their presence in the corridor before the class even entered the room
- Introduced themselves formally.

Beginning teachers

- Were not so clear about classroom rules, either their own or those of other teachers in the school
- Did not use terms such as 'right' and 'proper' when talking about rules
- Were unaware of the massive collective effort the school and individual teachers had to put into starting the school year
- Made less use of eye contact and were very conscious of themselves being looked at
- Often neglected early infringements of classroom rules which then escalated into larger problems
- Concentrated in their preparation on lesson content rather than rules and relationships.

(Wragg 1984)

The beginning teacher whose work is set out in Reading 8.1 can be recognized in the description above in terms of feeling that the ground rules had not perhaps been sufficiently outlined or stressed to his Year 7 class, but his reference to 'coming to order on command' and the way he 'emphasized throughout' the importance of this indicates several of the traits of more experienced colleagues, outlined above. In addition, his capacity to move beyond what he has done and resolve to change practice in this area marks a stage of professional growth, through experience and reflection.

More about rules and routines

These need to be relevant and appropriate to the age-group. Rules need to be small in number and so memorable. Mawer (1995) and Siedentrop (1991) make the point that most rules in school tend to relate to the key areas of:

- respect for others, pupils and teacher
- respect for the learning environment
- support for the teaching and learning, planned and in progress
- safety.

Routines, those everyday school activities such as register-taking in tutorial groups or at the beginning of lessons, are many. These have been categorized as *preliminary* (entering/leaving classrooms; answering questions); *transitional* (pupil dispersal in lessons); *instructional* (gathering together for demonstrations; defining boundaries for work areas); *housekeeping* (record-keeping; collecting valuables) and *closure* (finishing an activity; leaving the learning space) (Fink and Siedentop 1989). These routines and rules together support teaching and learning. It is the mediation of them by teachers and the acceptance or rejection of them by pupils that help to realize or rupture learning. It is this latter scenario that is the focus of the next section.

Tackling class management problems

There is no doubt that class management difficulties feature as a prime concern among beginning teachers. Without 'control' in evidence, little in learning terms can be achieved and it is the loss of control which is feared. Haggarty (1997) cites unprompted, early concerns about this subject made by mathematics students on a teacher Internship Scheme:

- I aim in the long term for complete silence when I am talking … I expect children to talk quietly to each other about a problem and about nothing else.
- To be able to keep order in the classroom it is essential to be strict.
- It is important to assert … dominance from the start … [and] establish the fact that the classroom is [his own] territory into which pupils can come.

(Haggarty in McIntyre 1997: 66)

The increased pressure upon schools in the late 1990s to keep down the rate of pupil exclusions for misbehaviour and to reduce unauthorized absences put support structures within schools, and teachers in classrooms, under strain at a time when the crusade for increased standards of achievement at all Key Stages was also being publicly aired by government.

Teachers, then, with the support of colleagues, are required to be able to deal with emotional and behavioural difficulties in their pupils as well as small-scale acts of misbehaviour which can (often) be anticipated and redirected more positively.

Emotional and behavioural difficulties in mainstream schools

The DfEE-commissioned research paper, *Emotional and Behavioural Difficulties in Mainstream Schools* (Daniels *et al.* 1999), reports on a study of mainstream schools' responses to pupils whose special educational needs result from emotional and behavioural difficulties (EBD). Its central aim was to identify how mainstream schools achieved effective practice in provision (and evaluation of provision) for pupils with EBD. Few, if any of the findings are novel:

- good teaching: characteristics required of a good teacher of pupils with EBD are the same as those for good teaching generally
- an appropriate curriculum: this must be challenging
- an effective behaviour policy: the approaches taken with pupils with EBD are an extension of behaviour policy for all pupils
- effective leadership: from senior management
- a core of dedicated staff: who share in developing, and actively promoting for pupils, the values, ethos and aspirations espoused by the leadership team
- staff who are able to learn from their actions: who put their positive beliefs into practice

- key members of staff who understand the nature of emotional and behavioural difficulties: who are able to distinguish these difficulties from general naughtiness.

These findings, though, are important and stress the point that such pupils are the shared concern of all teaching staff.

Avoiding and managing pupil misbehaviour

All teachers, whatever the calibre of their practice and the length of their experience, will have to deal with misbehaviour from some pupils. Research studies such as those by Munn *et al.* (1992) stress the importance of 'reading' situations and anticipating problems. The guidance provided by beginning teachers' professional associations points, as this text has done, to the importance of:

- planning and preparing thoroughly for lessons
- nurturing teacher–pupil relationships
- developing a repertoire of teaching skills
- avoiding confrontations
- distinguishing minor infringements from more major incidents
- following school policy and practice for punishments given
- identifying and using the support structures available in school.

Most misbehaviour is minor in nature (Munn *et al.* 1992; Wragg 1984, 1993), usually comprising non-task-related talking, being out of an allocated place, or inattention. Deliberate disobedience, and oral and physical aggression is far less common and, as Kyriacou (1997) maintains, 'Most pupil misbehaviour falls much nearer the non-compliance end of the continuum than the disruptive end' (ibid: 121).

The Elton Report (1989) outlined the strategies and sanctions commonly used by teachers to manage difficult individuals and classes. They were rated in terms of their perceived effectiveness. In rank order, the most effective were judged to be:

1 reasoning with the pupil(s) outside the classroom setting
2 reasoning with the pupils(s) in the classroom setting
3 keeping back in detention a pupil or pupils
4 sending a pupil direct to the head, deputy or other senior teacher in the school
5 requesting a pupil to leave the room temporarily
6 requesting suspension of a pupil
7 holding a discussion with the whole class about why there are behaviour difficulties
8 setting 'extra work' as a response to misbehaviour
9 referring a pupil or pupils to another teacher
10 removing privileges
11 deliberately ignoring minor disruptions or infringements.

These findings provide interesting material for discussion among beginning teachers. Balance and contextual factors are important, of course. Ignored minor disruptions have often been experienced as leading to an escalation of misbehaviour. At the same time, it may well be counter-productive to note every item of minor disruption and risk confrontation, so that the first strategy, reasoning outside the classroom setting (or inside it) at the end of the lesson, may be appropriate and productive on occasions as an option to try.

For their part, pupils themselves have cited qualities they wish to see demonstrated by teachers tackling behaviour infringements (Lewis and Lovegrove 1984). These have been shown to be: teachers remaining calm when reprimanding pupils; the presence of clear and reasonable rules; the avoidance of extreme sanctions; fair warnings given of possible sanctions; and teachers taking responsibility for the maintenance of the learning climate in the classroom. These elements can be seen as central in avoiding confrontation with pupils.

The rights and responsibilities of teachers and learners

Much pupil behaviour modification work relates to the idea of the class working as a community which requires rules and routines to operate effectively and happily. For this to occur and to be sustained, the rights and responsibilities of teachers, their classes and the individuals within them need clarification and reinforcement.

As was stated earlier in this chapter, good class management is not about a reactive, sterile control that creates passive pupils and a teacher who 'delivers' a syllabus. Class management needs to be a positive endeavour since its planned-for purposes are too. These purposes are: to establish high expectations; improve pupils' performance; ensure that pupils can achieve their agreed targets; create opportunities to monitor attainment; enable a teacher to identify areas for improvement; motivate pupils through advice, encouragement, feedback and reinforcement; and to keep pupils on task. These multi-faceted and ambitious happenings require a mutual respect and a set of agreements: a code of conduct. Below is the attempt of one Year 11 class to formulate what the properties of this might be.

All members of the class have a right to:

1   equal opportunities
2   stimulating lessons
3   speak and be heard without interruption
4   work without interference
5   a healthy and safe working environment
6   their own privacy and property
7   respect
8   ask questions
9   make mistakes without being ridiculed
10 be themselves
11 support to enable them to learn to the best of their ability
12 freedom from racial, sexual or social harassment.

(Produced by Year 11 pupils at Kelvin Hall High School,
Kingston upon Hull)

The same twelve items outlined above would, of course, apply to the subject teacher with the additions of: the right to be able to teach and manage a lesson so that effective learning for all can occur; the right to change course in a lesson if professional judgement argues a strong case; and the right to make (occasionally) a poor joke!

And it is humour, appropriately and wisely used, for common enjoyment and never for sarcastic and denigrating effect, which can smooth the awkward moments and small setbacks of a lesson. When pupils refer to a teacher having 'a good personality', and are then probed to unpack the meaning of this term, it is the possession of a non-threatening sense of humour that often forms a large part of this definition.

Finally, Reading 8.2 contains a beginning teacher's comments on what has been learned through the interplay of practice and reflection about the technical aspects of these matters. The evaluation extract presented here naturally relates to a range of teaching and learning aspects; those connected with management issues raised so far and later in this chapter are highlighted.

Reading 8.2 A PGCE student's lesson evaluation-review sheet

General impressions

As the class (Year 8 mixed ability) had been slow to settle on occasions, I decided to meet them at the door and request that pupils line up, enter the room in single file and stand behind their desks until silent. This tactic worked very quickly. Pupils had brought in newspaper stories as requested and were keen to begin work. Pupils quickly grasped their first task – identifying differences in layout of national and local pages. Pupils also presented a local news story which they were to make into a national front page. We talked through using different colours to highlight different areas of text and also about how they would need to expand their story to include pictures and quotations ...

Pupil learning

Pupils were able to employ knowledge of headlines and layout to the national papers and were also able to comment on such things as headline size, use of photographs and emotive language. Pupils began to re-edit stories and I was pleased to see that some of them had chosen stories relating to their culture. Pupils will continue ...

Teaching and learning strategies

I began the lesson with a very strong teacher presence in order to establish a firm, sensible atmosphere for the rest of the lesson – this tactic worked and I will use it again if necessary. I try to incorporate a number of strategies within all lessons for this group and this included a teacher-led session at the beginning and at key points throughout the lesson. Pupils tasked in pairs to begin with and compared stories from different newspapers. This was then fed back to the class who were able to add any information they had missed. Pupils then listened to a teacher-led session explaining the re-editing process – this was highlighted by being written on the board. Pupils then tasked individually but were allowed to talk as I felt that 'two heads are better than one' when thinking of headlines, etc. Pupils remained on task well and I moved around the room to offer help as required. I also felt the need to monitor the work output of a small number of boys in the room and this I did by sitting at their table and talking about their stories with them. In doing this I was hoping to offer necessary support without appearing to be singling the group out from the rest of the class. I also felt that this approach would also give the group a chance to speak to me on a more personal one-to-one basis. I found that the approach worked and that the boys began to respond in a more positive manner.

Resources

Resources included newspaper front pages brought in by pupils and some spares brought in by myself. I had to ensure that all unwanted papers were cleared away at the end of the lesson and that stories were stored safely for next time. I also used the whiteboard for making notes and writing general instructions.

Classroom management

Behaviour management in this lesson was much easier. The group was quieter and I feel that this was due to the structured start of the lesson. The boys in the room were more responsive and compliant and worked well. I did have a minor problem with Dale who threw his pencil case at another child. I spoke to Dale at the end of the lesson and was told that he had not intended me to see the incident. I spoke to Dale about his attitude and also told him that he is not to sit next to any of his group of friends for lessons the following week. I adopted the strategy of speaking to Dale at the end of the lesson as, when spoken to in front of others, he puts on a façade of insolence and says that he is being picked on. To avoid [this] … I spoke to him as his friends were waiting outside. I also spoke to the KS4 coordinator as I feel that an underlying problem with Dale's attitude is the fact that he struggles with the work of set 1. It transpired that Dale has been moved into set 2 or 3 for most other subjects. I have been asked to monitor his progress during this half term and to give feedback at a later date as it may be necessary to move Dale into a set where he is more able to cope with the work …

Cross-curricular issues

The discussion of the content and presentation of national news stories led to a discussion about murder and terrorism. A small group within the class was also keen to talk about the need to understand and respect the views of others even if we do not agree with them ourselves – this was in the context of a story about terrorism. Looking at specific cultural newspapers (from the Sikh community) led to a discussion about the importance of strong religious beliefs in people's lives.

Source: E. Hadley, PGCE student 1999.

Comment

What is interesting in this account, above, is that so much of it can be highlighted as having a bearing on 'class management'. The classroom management category of the review appropriately considers individual and group responses, an ongoing concern about Dale and strategies used to tackle this concern, not least using the knowledge and support of other colleagues, here the Key Stage 3 co-ordinator. What is also apparent is that the other elements of the lesson, resource collection and storage, the more formal addresses at key points of the lesson, the monitoring of work output, and the varied organization of tasks, all enabled lesson purposes to be sustained and learning outcomes to be achieved within the context of a sequence of lessons.

Conclusion

There is much advice, then, born of research studies and experience, that can be offered to beginning teachers about pathways to successful classroom management. Clearly, contexts impact upon the degree of detailed advice that can be taken up wholesale, but the general principles outlined in this chapter will remain reliable. One emerging implication of the material presented is that teacher-as-manager is an insufficient role for the ambitious catalogue of learning outcomes outlined to occur. A teacher-professional is a trusted adult for the vast majority of pupils, and the expectations they have of their teacher beyond a command of their subject, for consummate fairness, unfailing common sense, and the ability to divine what has not been said, are huge ones. The role, then, patently contains very much more than a management function. The Hay McBer model of teacher effectiveness, referred to in Chapters 1 and 6, voices an expectation that successful teachers have the distinct role of teacher-as-leader, creating trust, having respect for others and making a difference. This 'leading cluster' (Hay McBer 2000: 8) comprises the characteristics of managing people, having a passion for learning, showing a high degree of flexibility and holding people accountable, both pupils and those with whom a teacher works in a school.

This requirement and these characteristics can be both challenging and realized in school life, not least in relation to issues of inclusivity, the focus of Chapters 10 and 11 of this book.

References

Barnes, D. and Todd, F. (1977) *Communication and Learning in Small Groups*, London: Routledge and Kegan Paul.

Benn, C. and Chitty, C. (1996) *Thirty Years On: Is Comprehensive Education Alive and Well or Struggling to Survive?* London: David Fulton.

Bennett, N. and Dunne, E. (1992) *Managing Classroom Groups*, Hemel Hempstead: Simon and Schuster Education.

Elton Report (1989) *Discipline in Schools*, London: HMSO.

Fink, J. and Siedentop, D. (1989) 'The development of routines, rules and expectations at the start of the school year' *Journal of Teaching in Physical Education* 8(3): 198–212.

Haggarty, L. (1997) 'Readiness among student teachers for learning about classroom management issues' in D. McIntyre *Teacher Education Research in a New Context: The Oxford Internship Scheme*, London: Paul Chapman Publishing.

Hargreaves, A. (1995) *Changing Teachers, Changing Times*, London, Cassell.

Hay McBer Report (2000) *Research into Teacher Effectiveness*, London: DfEE Publications.

Ireson, J., Hallam, S., Mortimore, P., Hack, S., Clark, H. and Plewis, I. (1999) 'Ability groupings in the secondary school: the effects of academic achievement and pupils' self-esteem', paper presented at the British Educational Research Association Annual Conference, University of Sussex, Brighton, 2–5 Sept 1999.

Kyriacou, C. (1997) *Effective Teaching in Schools: Theory and Practice* (2nd edition) Cheltenham: Stanley Thornes.

Lewis, R. and Lovegrove, M.N. (1984) 'Teachers classroom control procedures: are students' preferences being met?' *Journal of Education for Teaching*, 10: 97–105.

Mawer, M. (1995) *The Effective Teaching of Physical Education*, Harlow: Longman.

Moon, B., Shelton Mayes, A. and Hutchinson, S. (eds) (2001) *Teaching, Learning and Professionalism in Secondary Schools*, London: RoutledgeFalmer.

Munn, P., Johnstone, M. and Chalmers, V. (1992) *Effective Discipline in Secondary Schools and Classrooms*, London: Paul Chapman.

Siedentrop, D. (1991) *Developing Skills in Physical Education*, 3rd edition, CA: Mayfield Press.

Vygotsky, L. (1978) *Mind in Society: The Development of Higher Psychological Processes* (ed. M. Cole), Cambridge, MA: Harvard University Press.

Wood, D. (1998). *How Children Think and Learn*, (2nd edition) Oxford: Blackwell.

Wood, D.J. and O'Malley, C. (1996) 'Collaborative learning between peers: an overview' *Educational Psychology in Practice* 11(4): 4–9.

Wragg, E.C. (ed.) (1984) *Classroom Teaching Skills*, Beckenham: Croom Helm.

—— (1993) *Primary Teaching Skills*, London: Routledge.

9 Assessment

Assessment in education is the process of gathering, interpreting, recording and using information about pupils' responses to an educational task. At one end of a dimension of formality, the teacher reading a pupil's work or listening to what he or she has to say. At the other end of the dimension, the task may be a written, timed examination which is read and marked according to certain rules and regulations. Thus assessment encompasses responses to regular work as well as to specially devised tasks.

(British Educational Research Association 1992: 2)

Introduction

Teachers have always used assessment in a variety of ways. The very language of teaching is the language of assessment: 'Well done', 'You've really grasped that idea', for example. Pupil–teacher communication at that level is the very essence of teaching and learning. It is these exchanges that enable understanding to be forged. It follows, therefore, that teachers have begun to give more explicit consideration to classroom processes and procedures of assessment. And these are often a far cry from the sort of school report illustrated in Figure 9.1 (overleaf).

This report represents a 'gathering and recording of information' of a sort, without any interpretation of that evidence, or any indication of how it might be used to develop the next stages of the pupil's learning. Reports traditionally were arranged in a fairly standard format, with subjects arranged along the left-hand side, term marks, examination marks and class positions indicated next, followed by teachers' comments fitted into the remaining one line of space. The comments, as Mary James's report shows, were usually no more than a brief 'Well done', or 'Good. Works well'. The form teacher's and headteacher's comments were a few lines summing up their perceptions of the 'message' of the report. Pupils were not its intended primary audience, and certainly not participants in its writing. Nor was the information designed to inform either curriculum change or to negotiate new ways of working for the pupils. Mary James's '23rd. Disappointing' for French stands as a judgement, with no indication of why it was disappointing, or what could be done about it. Many adults have similar reports stored away in a cupboard somewhere, or in their minds.

Assessment practices then, as can be seen, do not stand still. Nor do they exist in a social, cultural or educational vacuum, but are a product of a particular historical

EWELL COUNTY SECONDARY SCHOOL

NAME: JAMES _____

FORM: 3G.
NO. IN FORM: 36
POSITION IN FORM: 7th

TERM ENDING: 26th July 1961
AGE: 15 Yrs. 4 Months
AVERAGE AGE OF FORM: 15-1.

SUBJECT	Term % Marks	Term Position	Examination % Marks	Examination Position	Progress	REMARKS
RELIGIOUS INSTRUCTION	72	3rd	73	6	B+	Very good work
ENGLISH — ESSAY			65	5		
LANG	75	28	84	2	A.	Well done.
LIT.	80	1	65	11		
FRENCH	47	19	31	25	D+	23rd. Disappointing.
MATHEMATICS	63	11	58	16	C+	Solid sound work during term. Somewhat below expectation in exam.
HISTORY } SOCIAL	64	23rd =	59	14th	B	Good
GEOGRAPHY } STUDIES	74	25	91	2	B+	Excellent exam result.
SCIENCE						
BIOLOGY	74	3	65	4	B	High standard of work maintained.
CHEMISTRY	79	1/30	43	13/30	B-	Very good work. Must work harder in exam. Satisfactory.
MUSIC						
ART	60	2	-	-	A	A good year's work
LIGHT CRAFT						
NEEDLECRAFT	70	1			B+	good work
HANDICRAFT						
TECHNICAL DRAWING						
HOUSECRAFT						
COMMERCE						
PHYSICAL EDUCATION						B	Good. Works well
GENERAL KNOWLEDGE						

ATTENDANCE :— _____ out of _____

FORM TEACHER'S COMMENTS: _____ has continued to work conscientiously throughout the term. She should, however, attempt to work more quickly during the examinations. She tends to be somewhat too methodical & slow on these occasions.

HEADMASTER'S COMMENTS: One or two disappointing exam results but good progress generally over the past year.

Signature _____

A—Very Good D—Only Fair
B—Good E—Not Satisfactory
C—Moderate

Parent's Signature: Robert H James

Figure 9.1 A sample school report

Source: The Open University 1990: 14.

and social context. As such, they can never be value-free or politically and philosophically neutral. This partly explains the fierce debate about the nature and form of assessment, radically changed by the 1988 Education Reform Act. In 1988 maintained schools in England and Wales became subject to the requirements of a National Curriculum and national testing. Northern Ireland adopted a parallel statutory framework shortly afterwards. A new assessment structure emerged. This was designed to test what pupils had learned of what was pledged as an 'entitlement curriculum' for all and shaped to provide what pupils could reasonably be expected to know, understand and be able to do at age-related Key Stages and at different levels of accomplishment.

This was far from unproblematic. The rather static descriptions contained within the attainment levels appeared to be at odds with the learning theories, such as constructivism, which were beginning to have an impact on the classroom. The model of pupils' learning embedded in the National Curriculum levels of attainment – linear, with levels of difficulty somehow objectively evident – did not match classroom experience nor the kinds of research work available for consultation. The reality of uneven and recursive development of learning was grossly simplified in these levels descriptions. It was a less expensive model of assessment, however, than others, such as teacher assessment, which required in the early days of National Curriculum implementation what seemed very costly agreement trials. Summative tests became the dominant mode and publication of the results of each school reinforced their importance and this mode of assessment.

Over the past ten years or so, teachers have attempted to bridge the gap between in-class interactive methods of teaching and learning with an assessment activity that validates and measures such an activity. At the same time educational research, most notably the work of Paul Black (1998a) and Dylan Wiliam (1998b), and research and development work in schools which has focused on assessment, has demonstrated how the day-to-day use of assessment in the classroom is a key factor in raising pupils' standards of achievement. It is against this background that the sections of this chapter are set. The chapter considers:

- changes in assessment practice and teachers' obligations in relation to assessment, recording and reporting
- assessment for learning: formative assessment
- assessment of learning: summative assessment
- assessment issues: debates and considerations.

Changes in assessment practice

Changes in assessment practice across the whole age-range have followed in the wake of developments in assessment at examination level. These in turn have changed as the result of economic and social developments and the opening up of access to higher education. The GCSE examination, first introduced in 1988, replaced the General Certificate of Education (GCE) O level and the Certificate of Secondary Education (CSE). The growth of the comprehensive system fuelled arguments for a single unifying assessment system: 'a comprehensive examination for the comprehensive school'. This shift is important in that it introduced an examination system based on *differentiation* and *grade-related criteria*. The purpose was to facilitate the GCSE's assessment of pupils over a wider range of attainment.

Over the last two decades of the twentieth century, influenced by these developments in examination criteria, there have been significant changes in the way assessment is approached in schools, most notably by an increased emphasis on:

Formative assessment (TA)	Summative assessment (TA)	KS3 NC tests and KS4 qualifications
Assessment for learning	Assessment of learning	Assessment of learning
happens all the time in the classroom. It is rooted in self-referencing; a pupil needs to know where s/he is and understand not only where s/he wants to be but also how to 'fill the gap'.	is carried out at the end of a unit or year or Key Stage or when a pupil is leaving the school, in order to make judgements about pupils' performance in relation to national standards. TA is rooted in level descriptions/grade criteria.	provides a standard 'snapshot' of attainment at the end of Key Stages.
This involves both the teacher and the pupil in a process of continual reflection and review about progress.	Teachers find standardization and moderation meetings important quality-assurance opportunities.	A pupil's performance is described in relation to the national standards – measured in levels or grades.
When teachers and peers provide quality feedback, pupils are empowered to take the appropriate action.	TA is a valuable part of the data held and used for management purposes.	The optional tests for Years 7 and 8 also provide summative assessment information for schools to use to monitor their school's performance.
Teachers adjust their plans in response to formative assessment.	Teachers often use information about pupils' performance in summative tests/exams and their Teacher Assessments formatively.	

Figure 9.2 Teachers' perceptions of formative assessment

Source: QCA Report on Teachers' Perception of Formative Assessment, April 2000, Appendix 4.

- the move to criterion referencing, i.e. assessing pupils' achievement against specific curriculum criteria rather than using an assessment system which was designed to indicate how well a pupil has achieved in relation to others in the class;
- assessing achievement across the full range of the pupil's work and activities in school. Pupils are given feedback on a wide range of skills and activities, such as their wider contribution to their development through activities such as work experience and personal and social education, in addition to feedback on their examined subjects;
- assessing pupils' progress against their previous attainment (ipsative/self-referencing), and setting targets for the next stage;

- making assessment an integral part of the teaching/learning process. This approach included involving pupils in self-assessment;
- the use of normative referencing to assess pupils' attainment against national standards.

This has led to the increased accountability of schools and the education system as a whole through the publication and comparison of results.

Brown (2001) has usefully summarized the new approaches to assessment practice. She writes that 'traditional' assessment came to be questioned on four major grounds: *reliability, validity, fairness* and *purpose*. She describes how a more constructive role for assessment in supporting teaching and learning entered the debate, and how *criterion-referenced assessment* (providing information about what the individual pupil has achieved) has come to be seen as complementing *norm-referenced assessment* (marks or grades which allow comparisons between pupils to be made). Further, the 'who assesses' question has widened from teachers/examiners to include peer-group or self-assessment; 'when to assess' means not end-of-term exam halls but at 'the site where learning takes place'; 'how to assess' moves away from exams and tests; and 'what to assess' includes criterion-referenced approaches which allow descriptions of what has been achieved. The 'why assess' question has shifted to admit the idea of 'information gathering' as contributing to the improvement of educational practice. The distinction Brown makes is between *formative assessment*, 'that is the use of information gathered to improve the current educational process', and *summative assessment,* 'that is a report at the end of a course … which purports to predict future performance'.

Linked to formative assessment is *diagnostic assessment*. This approach to assessment is one which focuses particularly on the difficulties pupils are experiencing so that advice and support can be given to the pupil, and the appropriate teaching strategies used. Finally, an approach to assessment which has changed the practice of assessment over the past decade is the emphasis given to *evaluation*. This is where the classroom teacher uses assessment to discover how effective teaching has been. This form of assessment is also used to make judgements about the effectiveness of a school or LEA, for example to generate school league tables based on GCSE results.

A QCA report (QCA 2000) sets out the different types of assessment, each serving a distinct purpose, as seen in Figure 9.2. Teachers use all these approaches to assessment. When talking to parents about a pupil's work, teachers describe a pupil's performance in relation to level descriptions or grade criteria (*criterion referencing*), how he or she compares with national standards (*normative referencing*) and how much progress (*self referencing*) he or she has made. The pupil may not be performing at the nationally expected level but he or she may have made excellent progress since the beginning of the academic year in September.

Accompanying this shift in terms of the purposes of assessment has been a significant change to the statutory requirements for teachers' main duties in relation to assessment and recording achievement. These statutory requirements are summarized overleaf.

Teachers in secondary schools have to monitor pupil progress through formative assessment and respond to formal external summative assessment requirements

Statutory requirements for teachers in relation to assessment and recording

- Keep individual educational records and then up-date annually: DES Circular 17/89
- Provide written report to Parents at least once a year: DfEE & QCA KS3 ARA Booklet
- Carry out end of KS3 Teacher Assessments and National Curriculum Tests and report results to parents: DfEE & QCA KS3 ARA Booklet
- Provide comparative information of School Performance in Governors' Annual Report to parents and in the School's Prospectus: DfEE Circular 8/99
- Set school's targets for the public examinations at KS4: DfEE Circular 11/98
- Complete the common transfer form when a pupil transfers to another school: DfEE Circular 15/00.

(national tests, examinations at 16, 17, and 18). They may also use internal school developed summative tests. External summative assessment has always provoked controversy. Finding reliable and valid forms of summative assessment has proved difficult. The issues surrounding national tests and examinations are explored later in the chapter. First, however, a look at formative assessment.

Assessment for learning – formative assessment

It is only recently that the importance of making formative assessment processes more explicit has been recognized. Following the introduction of the National Curriculum, assessment arrangements and the requirements to test pupils at the ages of 7, 11, 14 and 16, assessment practices in schools were dominated by summative assessments, an approach which emphasized the procedures and products of assessment, rather than the process. Black and Wiliam's (1998b) research into assessment pointed out that learning is driven by what teachers and pupils do in classrooms. This in turn depends on the quality of *feedback* and the use of *formative assessment* to adapt teaching to meet the needs of pupils. This research shows that the emphasis given to summative assessments in schools may have been unintentionally counter-productive for pupils, and made it harder for teachers to raise standards. They point out that the dominance of short, summative, external testing takes teachers away from formative work, or assessment for learning, and that the extensive use of tests encourages rote and superficial learning. They also make the point that none of the many policy initiatives over several decades has offered teachers any help with the task of formative assessment, although advisory services and subject associations have attempted to emphasize its importance. These research findings were reinforced by the Qualifications and Curriculum Council's own evaluation of teachers' perceptions of assessment (Neesom 2000). This found that confusion exists about the different types of assessment in use. The confusion may well be the result of the over-emphasis, nationally, on summative tests.

Two of the 'best' definitions of formative assessment come from very different sources:

> Assessment is to be seen as a moment of learning, and students have to be active in their own assessment and to picture their own learning in the light of an understanding of what it means to get better.
>
> (Black and Wiliam 1998b: 30)

> Clues to the effectiveness of formative assessment are how well teachers listen and respond to pupils, encourage and, where appropriate, praise then recognize and handle misconceptions, build on their responses and steer them towards clearer understanding. Effective teachers encourage pupils to judge the success of their own work and set targets for improvement. They will take full account of the targets set out in individual education plans for pupils with special educational needs.
>
> (Ofsted Handbook 2000: 61)

The publication of *Inside the Black Box* (Black and Wiliam 1998b) began the shift of emphasis from raising standards through testing to raising standards through classroom assessment. Black and Wiliam conducted an extensive survey of research literature. They found a clear and incontrovertible message that initiatives designed to enhance effectiveness of the way assessment is used in the classroom to promote learning can raise pupil achievement. The scale of the effect would be to improve performance of pupils in GCSE by between one and two grades, with lower-attaining pupils likely to gain more substantially.

A year later, *Assessment for Learning: Beyond the Black Box*, published by the Assessment Reform Group, set out to advance the work of Black and Wiliam and to make proposals for future policy developments. The Group maintained that 'There is no evidence that increasing the amount of testing will enhance learning. Instead the focus needs to be on helping teachers use assessment, as part of teaching and learning, in ways that will raise pupils' achievement' (Assessment Reform Group 1999: 2, para. 1). It is worth remembering this point when the national agenda seems to suggest that standards are raised solely through the use of tests. Some schools, and particularly those deemed by Ofsted to be under 'special measures' or to have 'serious weaknesses', feel under particular pressure to resort to tests to prove that they have action plans that guarantee that their pupils will make progress.

Such is the strength of this evidence for the value of formative assessment, or assessment for learning as it is beginning to be known, that government agencies like the Qualification and Assessment Council (QCA) have started to give a much greater emphasis to it. They, and teachers' professional bodies, like the GTCe, provide support for teachers to develop their assessment for learning skills through providing advice, case studies and research summaries on their websites.

Approaches to formative assessment

Research, such as that carried out by Black and Wiliam, or by projects such as that carried out by Suffolk Advisory Service (2001) into feedback and marking, indicates that improving learning through formative assessment depends on the following five, deceptively simple, key factors. These are:

- modelling quality: showing pupils the learning strategies and goals
- dialogue and the provision of effective feedback to pupils
- a recognition of the profound influence assessment has on the motivation and self-esteem of pupils, both of which are crucial influences on learning
- the active involvement of pupils in their own learning
- the need for pupils to be able to assess themselves and understand how to improve.

Modelling quality

When pupils are clear about why they are *learning*, they will be more successful. This means communicating clearly what the pupils will be learning and how they can recognize their success. Teachers need to be careful to keep instructions about the organization of the lesson separate from information about the learning.

> The teacher tells us what the lesson is about and what the activities are for. At the end of the lesson, he gives us a summary. I like that because it tells me what we have learned.
>
> (Pupil in a middle school, Suffolk LEA, 2001)

Learning intentions can be shared with pupils through 'modelling': showing pupils pieces of anonymous work that meet and do not meet the learning objective. A pupil's response can be used in the classroom to show how he or she responded to the question and how the response compares to the mark-scheme. Encouraging pupils to review anonymous work against assessment criteria helps them to recognize expectations and they can suggest the next steps to meeting the criteria.

Teachers need to demonstrate what the standards they are expecting might look like, to show pupils how to employ the learning objective. The processes and skills can be modelled too. If the reason for the learning task is to develop evaluative skills, then teachers can 'model' the 'evaluative thinking' by demonstrating the reflective questioning about whether an end-product satisfies the original specification.

Dialogue and effective feedback

A key aspect of formative assessment is providing pupils with feedback that gives them specific guidance on how to improve their work and how to get the help and support to do this. A recent report into pupils' perceptions of the criteria for 'good work' found the most frequently mentioned were effort, presentation and accuracy.

> Most of my teachers say I could improve on my presentation. It's not very helpful because they've said it so many times. (Y9)

Usually I know if it's good by how much time I've spent on it. (Y10)

We did a story and Miss said it was very good – my punctuation and paragraphs. (YI0)

(QCA 1999: 7)

One of the most important ways teachers communicate with pupils about their work is through their marking of completed tasks. However, marking

> often fails to offer guidance on how work can be improved. In a significant minority of cases, marking reinforces under-achievement and under-expectation by being too generous or unfocused. Information about pupil performance received by the teacher is insufficiently used to inform subsequent work.
>
> (Ofsted 1996: 40)

The word 'marking' itself displays some of the older types of assessment. It is, however, a word that in use has a very broad meaning. Most, if not all, pupils look keenly at the comments and corrections teachers make. They often share with each other the outcome of a marked piece of work and good marks or approving comments may be reported at home. Work that goes unmarked is a source of disappointment to pupils and can result in critical comments made by them about teachers.

Most teachers develop routines and procedures for marking. Marking targets need to be realistic in terms of time and energy. Certain types of pupil work may require less detailed attention than others. Some teachers also choose, in marking the work of the class, to give a few pupils more detailed attention than others and keep a record of this in a mark book. The Suffolk LEA survey (2001) emphasized, that whatever strategy is relevant, it is important, above all else, to value pupils' work. They suggest the use of post-its and comments in the margins as an alternative to defacing work by writing all over it.

Many schools have policies about marking and these should be studied carefully. Here are a few guidelines. Good marking:

- offers the opportunity to open up a dialogue with each pupil; comments will refer back to previous advice and look forward to setting new targets
- is sustained over time; comments towards the end of a book or file, and therefore term or year, are as detailed and as fresh as at the beginning
- is focused around the work in hand and goes beyond general comments of a 'good' or 'could do better' nature
- is selective in making clear the important areas for approval or criticism independently of the more detailed corrections that may be necessary
- is legible and shows up clearly in the text.

Motivation and self-esteem

It is also important for teachers to appreciate how comments and feedback to pupils can create a positive or a negative culture. Comparisons with other pupils should be avoided. Classroom cultures which emphasize 'gold stars' or a 'place in the class' encourage pupils to concentrate on the ways to obtain best marks, rather than focus on their learning. Pupils, particularly low-attaining pupils, avoid putting themselves in situations where they might fail, and avoid challenges. Motivation and commitment improve if pupils know that their work is regularly and consistently looked at and appraised in a way that relates to the task attempted and the learning planned and explained. James (1998) provides valuable advice for teachers about giving feedback and gives warning that bad feedback is worse than no feedback.

Active involvement in learning and assessment

Evidence from the Black and Wiliam review showed that teachers need to build in opportunities for pupils to express their understanding. The authors argue that the dialogue between teachers and pupils should give all pupils the chance to think and express their ideas. There is no clear line between instruction and formative assessment. Pupils benefit from opportunities for formal feedback through group and plenary sessions. This provides opportunities for pupils to explain themselves, helping them to clarify their knowledge and understanding and to articulate their thinking. Where this works well, there is a shift from teachers telling pupils what they have done wrong to pupils seeing for themselves what they need to do to improve. Therefore, giving feedback involves making time to talk to pupils and to teach them to be reflective about both the learning objectives and their work/responses.

Self-assessment and understanding how to improve

There are some activities where pupils can mark the work themselves, and other points in the course when it is useful for pupils to review progress in a self-assessment activity. Pupils not only become clearer about what they are trying to achieve, they also gain training in self-assessment strategies. This has been at the core of much of the work on Records of Achievement (see Chapter 12). This is an under-developed area of assessment. A very interesting study carried out for the QCA (QCA 2000) revealed some of the problems of pupil self-assessment. Based on interviews of over 200 pupils aged from 3 to 13 years, the study was designed to gain insights into their perceptions of assessment (see Figure 9.3). The study found that there was little evidence of systematic self-assessment and few pupils reported having the opportunity to develop their knowledge and understanding of this skill.

The study showed that pupils lacked confidence in judging their performance and were given few opportunities to practise self-assessment skills. Higher attainers knew what was required, and adapted better to varying assessment practice. 'For formative assessment to be productive, students should be trained in self-assessment so that they can understand the main purposes of their learning and thereby grasp what they need to do to achieve' (Black and Wiliam 1998b: 10). In order to make self-assessment effective then, pupils have to be 'let into the secrets' of teachers' professional practice (Sutton 1991). Review and reflection opportunities are essential for learning and time must be built into lessons and schemes of work for these to occur.

Self-assessment

There was little evidence of self-assessment being used as a strategy to support learning or of it being widely used before GCSE. The types of self-assessment reported were usually little more than a mechanical marking process.

Primary (Y3 and Y6) and Secondary (Y9)	14–19 (GCSE, A level and GNVQ)
In Years 3, 6 and 9 students referred to marking their own and peers' work: 'In my head. Once in maths I ticked my own work. It's not good to mark your own work because you don't know if it's right or wrong' (Y3).	Less than 25 per cent of GCSE, A level and GNVQ students had opportunities to assess their own work. 'Sometimes I feel I've done a really good piece of work and I'd like to say so.'
There were rare mentions of some peer- and self-assessment, in English: 'Sometimes we think about how we could have done better and how we could have improved it' (Y9).	Types of self-assessment reported were limited in scope (using Maths answers at back of books, marking tests). Exceptions included peer assessment of drafts of work in A level English with the comments being used to rework the essay.
Students did, despite this, show some degree of skill at self-assessment at all levels. Year 3 and 6 students were able to evaluate their own work, often by comparison with previous pieces of work and always with reference to teacher validation of their views: 'We don't know what we've got until she shows us' (Y9).	Male students were more confident that they knew the quality of their work. Over 90 per cent of students compared their performance with others with typical comments being 'All the time – competitive between friends' (male) and 'All the time – make myself feel bad' (female).

Figure 9.3 'The LEARN Project: Phase 2' Guidance for Schools on Assessment for Learning

Source: QCA 2000.

Formative assessment, assessment for learning, is about using professional judgements. As a beginning teacher's experience grows, so will the ability to home in quickly on significant aspects of pupils' work, for praise, for criticism and to provide a structure from which the next stage of learning can develop. Such judgements, however, are not absolute. In-school discussion and moderation procedures (usually at a department or faculty level) are, therefore, valuable in exploring areas where the criteria for assessment are open to interpretation.

Assessment for learning involves the use of classroom assessment to improve learning. It differs from the assessment of learning, which measures what learners know or can do. This aspect of assessment, summative assessment, is the focus of the next section of this chapter.

Assessment of learning: summative assessment

Preparing pupils for external examinations and assessment has been an increasingly important part of the secondary teacher's role. The introduction of the GCSE in the 1980s, the much higher participation rates in A level, AS level and vocational or vocationally related courses post-16, and most recently the introduction of national tests, have significantly extended the range and type of externally accredited courses. Tests and examinations are often the source of educational controversy. Are they a fair measure of any candidate's ability? Are the uses to which they are put appropriate? How accurate are the marking and grading systems used? Are there any gender or cultural biases in the assessment techniques used? External agencies, including the major examining boards, go to a great deal of trouble and considerable expense to ensure the reliability and validity of the techniques they use.

The purpose behind national external assessments has been clearly formulated:

- to identify individual achievements, strengths and weaknesses in detail, in order to help them in the next stages of their learning
- to enable parents to put their child's attainment in context
- to assist parents and the public by making available, at local and national level, information about attainment in schools
- to help schools in evaluating their own teaching.

The difficulty, however, is less with the purpose than with the means by which it should be achieved. In particular:

1   whether all the purposes set out above require standardized external assessment rather than school-based teacher judgement;
2   the extent to which the same external standardized assessment techniques and tasks could provide valid and reliable judgements to meet the range of purposes;
3   the problem of reconciling the need to give plentiful assessment information to cover all aspects of curriculum attainment comprehensively with the equally important need to report the outcomes in a relatively straightforward way to parents and to the pupils themselves.

Currently external summative assessments fall into two categories, namely national tests and qualifications. National tests, for example at the end of Key Stage 3 in core subjects, are not a qualification and no certificate is issued.

Qualifications fall into three categories:

1   General qualifications, such as GCSEs and A levels.

2   Vocationally related qualifications, such as vocational A levels.
3   Occupational qualifications, such as National Vocational Qualifications, that test skills and knowledge to do a specific job.

These qualifications are arranged in a national framework accepted in England, Wales and Northern Ireland. This is set out in five levels showing the development through GCSE, A level, degree and postgraduate professional qualifications and takes in the NVQ levels 1–5. The publications and web resources of the different national agencies provide up-to-date information about the specific arrangements for any one year. This has been an area of considerable flux, although the attempt to introduce national frameworks is intended to provide some stability. Debates about assessment, whether the post-16 assessment framework, GCSE, SATs, teacher summative assessment or assessment for learning, share a number of key issues and controversies about external summative inspection of particular arrangements and contexts. The next section of this chapter points to some of these.

Assessment issues: debates and considerations

What should be the weight given to teacher assessment?

In the UK there are more externally marked assessments than in any other country in Europe. A feature of the reforms since the end of the 1980s has been a shift to external verification of teachers' work. At the same time, there have been increases in the amount of summative assessment teachers are required to do. At the end of Key Stage 3, teachers are required to finalize their summative assessment judgements and submit them to the national data collection agency. Some argue that this has gone too far and diverts resources away from the core task of teaching and learning. What importance, for example, should be attached to school-based and assessed coursework?

Summative teacher assessment is described by the QCA to be:

> ... an essential part of the national curriculum assessment arrangements ... tests provide a 'snapshot' of attainment at the end of the key stage, while teacher assessment ... covers the full range and scope of the programmes of study and takes account of evidence of achievement in a range of contexts, including that gained through discussion and observation. In the non-core subjects, and for pupils working below level 3 in mathematics and science and below level 4 in English, teacher assessment provides the sole means of statutory assessment.
>
> (DfEE/QCA 2001: 8)

Teachers need explicit and shared understanding of the national standards to make summative judgements about pupils' performance. Opportunities for teachers to meet to discuss the standard of their pupils' performance and how it compares to the national standards are vitally important. There are three prime reasons for this:

1 Pressure is taken off the individual teacher's decision-making and assigning the standard judgements has the 'quality assurance' of the subject department.
2 Time is needed to standardize work before moderation can happen.
3 This professional development opportunity raises teachers' expectations.

The elements below clearly need to be included in schools' assessment policies:

- Standardization – assigning the best-fit level descriptions/grade criteria to the pupil's performance;
- Moderation – assuring that the teachers' judgements are in line with the national standards.

There is some debate about the differences which emerge between teacher assessment judgements and test results. It is not unusual for there to be a one-level difference between the test and the summative teacher assessment, with teacher assessment generally coming out higher. This is not at all surprising; they are arrived at in very different ways. The tests do not and cannot assess all the Programmes of Study, or the course specifications, whilst teacher assessment is the product of judgements made over time and over the full range of contexts and the full Key Stage 3 and 4 curriculum.

Is the division between academic and vocational assessments divisive?

Repeated attempts have been made to give some equality of esteem to academic and vocational qualifications. The linking of NVQ levels with GCSE and A levels within a national framework is one example. The relative esteem of the academic and the vocational in contemporary society still, however, raises concerns as to whether any equality can be achieved. This is particularly an issue at post-16 where the establishment of vocational courses in schools has, in the past, been difficult as the result of several factors:

- The General National Vocational Qualifications (GNVQ) offered in FE colleges were mediated by staff who have more experience than colleagues in comprehensive schools of teaching vocational education requiring new skills and assessment methods.
- A relatively limited number of vocational alternatives were available in most schools. Few selective schools were interested on broadening their sixth forms in a vocational direction.
- In theory it was possible for pupils to mix and match GNVQs with other qualifications, but, in practice, a form of educational apartheid operated in school sixth forms, with the high-attaining pupils still attracted (and propelled) towards A levels traditionally valued by universities.
- Less academically successful pupils were encouraged to remain on roll (securing valuable income for the school).

- Traditional A level courses were retained in schools mindful of the publication of their A level results, university entrance rates and status as 'effective' schools.

Ball (1991) recognized the tension:

> So long as most of the able and highly motivated fast-learners choose an academic A level route at 16, while the slower learners, late developers and the unmotivated are offered vocational courses, parity of esteem is neither likely nor appropriate.
>
> (Ball 1991: 41)

The national qualifications framework aims to avoid this division and to maximize participation, achievement and progression in order to meet the needs of employers and higher education looking for students with a broader-based curriculum and a wider range of skills. The academic/vocational tensions within the school curriculum continue to be the source of debate.

Should tests and examinations be age related?

In practice most tests and examinations are age-specific, whether Key Stage tests or GCSE and A levels. Indeed, newspapers often report the achievements of those taking examinations at an earlier age than expected. There is increasing pressure, however, that questions these linkages. How a school and a school curriculum could respond to decoupling ages and courses is, however, problematic.

Can standards of national assessments be guaranteed over time?

This is a major area of dispute. Some argue that the much higher number of entrants for A level or degree examinations must lead to a dilution of standards. Others say that we are becoming a better educated society and the evidence is there in the increasing numbers gaining higher grades. This subject makes its appearance in the popular press each year in August with the appearance of the GCSE and A level results, when it is always possible to find an ex-examiner prepared to provide controversial copy by saying that standards are declining! However, there are complex technical difficulties in measuring performance over time, not least because the knowledge, understanding and skills being assessed by examinations change over time. This controversy is likely to continue for some time. The introduction of the new post-16 framework raises new issues about guaranteeing national standards and raises the questions as to whether post-16 pupils are more likely to take on demanding programmes than previously.

Can external assessment data be used to judge schools?

This is another question that has dominated the education reform process. Evidence from external assessments is being used to judge schools, and tables of school results have been published for some time now. There are arguments, however, that suggest these may not take into consideration the socio-economic context of the school, and, indeed, the first results and schools league tables published in 1992 did not. The raw data of examination results brought no surprises, with those schools at the 'top' being located in socially advantaged areas, generally with a selective intake (see Chapter 13). SATs and examination results are now 'benchmarked' in a joint DfEE/Ofsted/QCA publication known as the *Autumn Package* (DfEE 2000b). The first benchmark shows the distribution of performance for schools nationally, so enabling schools to benchmark their results against national results. Prior attainment benchmarks show performance distributions for groups of similar schools, categorized by the relevant KS2 prior attainment. 'Free School Meal' benchmarks show performance distributions for groups of similar schools, categorized by the percentage of free school meals. (The proportion of pupils eligible for free school meals is taken from annual school census information.) There is still a great deal of controversy, however, surrounding the use of examination results and, indeed, in 2001 the Welsh Assembly decided to stop publishing such tables although they continue in England and Northern Ireland.

Should the formal moment of assessment be at the end of a course?

Traditionally, examinations were held at the end of a course. In GCSE and post-16 an increasing number of courses are based on modules or units of work. These are assessed and the result aggregated into a final grade. Some see this as a fairer representation of achievement, others see it as creating too much pressure or as a distraction from the rigour that comes with an exam.

How should results be transmitted?

In the past simple grades were given. The national tests adopted a similar approach with numerical level scores. The difficulty is that by making a result easily comprehensible (Grade B or Level 4, for example) you mask the actual achievement. Bringing together the scores in writing and reading, for example, might obscure what the achievement of each is. On the other hand, attempts to provide more qualitative information have suffered from a complexity, and even a presence of jargon, that have limited the usefulness of the process.

Should the government set targets for examination passes?

The government has proposed that by 2007, 85 per cent of 14-year-olds at KS3 should have achieved Level 5 and above in English, mathematics and ICT. For science the target is 80 per cent. Intermediate targets have also been proposed for 2004 with each local education authority being required to aim for 65 per cent in English and mathematics and at least 60 per cent in science at Key Stage 3. Whilst this policy is aimed at raising standards and setting high expectations, there are those who argue that year-on-year improvement in pupils' external assessments results in the school curriculum being driven by summative examinations and distracts teachers from developing assessment for learning. Too much focus on summative assessment, rather than assessment for learning, could, in the end, be self-defeating.

How do UK external assessment results compare with elsewhere in the world?

This is another question which attracts a lot of interest but which is technically diffi-cult to answer. Finding common curriculum areas across which comparisons can be made is problematic. Some countries appear to do well in basic numerical, computa-tional activities, for example, but score poorly where more open-ended investigative activities are assessed.

How many tests and examinations should there be?

The UK is unique in Europe in having an extensive examination system at 16 and at 18. Many argue that given the high staying-on ratio the notion of a 'leaving examina-tion', the GCSE, is an anachronism and more attention should be focused on devel-oping a unified 14–19 curriculum.

Is the emphasis on single-subject examinations appropriate?

Most examining at GCSE and A level is based around subjects. Many have argued that achievement across a group of subjects is more important than single subjects. The French Baccalaureate, for example, or the International Baccalaureate, has attracted a great deal of interest from those who seek to broaden the post-16 curriculum.

Externally, the main attempt to broaden the post-16 curriculum came from the International Baccalaureate, first presented in 1971 as an international pre-university entry qualification operating in three languages: English, Spanish and French. Pupils take six subjects (three or four at the higher level) in two languages, a science, mathe-matics and one of the humanities, together with an option. The IB is offered in some British schools, but has made more impact in some countries than others, partly due to its fearsome academic reputation. It does not embrace vocational possibilities.

A British Baccalaureate (Finegold 1990) was proposed a decade ago as a radical, modular, single, cross-ability range replacement for the divided pathways of the academic and the vocational British education post-16. The Dearing Report (1996) rejected the British Baccalaureate, but it did inform his committee's thinking in the creation of more coherent routes of progression in the post-16 curriculum. Sugges-tions to broaden the curriculum, particularly at post-16, often come into conflict with those who wish to retain what is often called 'the gold standard' of A level. Over the past decade, however, the post-16 curriculum has been subject to review and moves to provide a broader base to the course followed after GCSE examinations (also see Chapter 2).

This key issue is one that continues to inform policy decisions and to create a tension underpinning the post-16 curriculum. These tensions persist despite the emergence of a comprehensive post-16 education which is presented within a framework of a national education system. This brings some coherence to the prolif-eration of post-16 courses and qualifications. However, the tenacity with which the underpinning principles have been so strongly adhered to is of particular significance in understanding the present context.

Conclusion

In the coming years there are likely to be significant changes in policy and practice towards assessment. As the curriculum evolves so assessment has to adapt. Currently, for example, an enormous investment is being made in developing Information and Communication Technologies (ICT) in schools. This is beginning to have an impact, not only on the process of assessment but also on the purpose and focus of assessment. ICT, for example, may be one way in which the well-established linkage between assessment levels and age is loosened. How employers respond to the new structure of national qualifications may also impact on assessment systems. The extent to which teachers can be trusted to assess accurately may also change. Assessment is likely to be a key area for continuing professional development within which some of the controversies and dilemmas raised above can be explored more fully.

Assessment is not easy and there is no purchasable blue-print for it. This chapter provides a range of perspectives for teachers to reflect upon when they consider what strategies to employ to raise achievement. The overwhelming evidence is that formative assessment raises standards and the central, effective way to raise standards is, indeed, to use formative assessment and to *make it count* in the classroom. This is not to say that summative assessment does not have a place, of course; but the nature and importance of this remains in contention. The terrain of 16+ curriculums and assessment will continue, too, to be the source of debate and subject to seizure by the key organizing participants. But it will be the classroom practice of teachers, working with their pupils, that will result in raising standards. Their voices and views, too, will need to be heard and integrated into any further re-formulations for this to occur in a sustained and creditable way.

References

Assessment Reform Group (1999) *Assessment for Learning: Beyond the Black Box*, Cambridge: University of Cambridge School of Education.

Ball, C. (1991) 'Learning pays: the role of post-compulsory education and training', interim report, London: RSA.

Black, P. and Wiliam, D. (1998a) 'Assessment and classroom learning' *Assessment in Education* 5(1): 7–74.

—— (1998b) *Inside the Black Box: Raising Standards through Classroom Assessment*, London: King's College.

British Educational Research Association (BERA) (1992) *'Dialogue: Policy Issues in National Assessment'*, Policy Task Group on Assessment, Avon Multilingual Matters.

Brown, S. (2001) 'Assessment: a changing practice', in B. Moon, A. Shelton Mayes and S. Hutchinson (eds) *Teaching, Learning and Curriculum in Secondary Schools: A Reader*, London: RoutledgeFalmer.

DfEE (2000) *Autumn Package Key Stage 3*, DfEE Pupil Performance Team, London: HMSO.

DfEE and QCA (2001) *KS3 Assessment and Reporting Arrangements*.

Finegold, D. *et al.* (1990) *A British Baccalaureate: Ending the Division Between Education and Training*, London: IPPR.

James, M. (1998) *Using Assessment for School Improvement*, London, Heinemann.

Neesom, A. (2000) *Report on Teachers' Perception of Formative Assessment*, London, QCA.

Ofsted (1996) *General Report on Secondary Schools*, London: HMSO.

—— (2000) *Handbook for Inspecting Secondary Schools*, London: HMSO.

Open University (1990) *E271 Curriculum and Learning, Block C Part 1*, Milton Keynes: The Open University.

QCA (1999) *The LEARN Project: Phase 1*, CLIO Centre for Assessment Studies, University of Bristol, London: QCA.

—— (2000) *The LEARN Project: Phase 2*, CLIO Centre for Assessment Studies, University of Bristol, London: QCA.

Sutton, R. (1995) *Assessment for Learning*, RS Publications.

10 Inclusive education
Gender and ethnicity

Introduction

Of the many factors that affect pupils' experience of school, gender and 'race'[1] are among the most important. This is reflected in a significant level of national and international research, together with the legislation which frames practice in schools. In many countries legislation for equal opportunities which impinges directly on school policies and practice has been enacted as a result of public pressure. The Sex Discrimination Act (1975), the Race Relations Act (1976) and the Disability Discrimination Act (1995) laid the legal foundations for sex, 'race' and disability equality in schools in the UK. Since the mid-1970s, teachers, schools and local authorities have been developing equal opportunities policies and practice aimed at supporting the achievements of all pupils, whether male, female, black or white.

During the same period there has been a range of legislatory and regulatory intervention by government to provide for and safeguard the interests of children who have special educational needs. The Warnock Report in 1978, the 1981 and 1996 Education Acts, and the Special Education Needs Act (2000) set in motion and subsequently strengthened a move towards the integration into mainstream schools of children who experience difficulties in learning or who have disabilities.

Awareness of these concerns, and their implications for inclusivity, is now well developed and features regularly in official and semi-official pronouncements on the state of the education system. It is these matters that make up the subject matter of this chapter and the next.

This chapter looks specifically at the issues of gender and ethnicity in the context of inclusive education. It explores a number of areas:

- The development in thinking around equity and social justice and the 'phases' of national concern about gender and 'race'.
- A review of the ways in which pupils' gender or ethnicity (collectively referred to as equal opportunities in relation to school policies) influence their experience of school.
- The centrality of an overarching concern for inclusion as an education value which underpins improving educational standards.
- Approaches to achieving inclusion and maximizing pupil opportunities through pedagogy and the formal and informal curriculum.

Beginning teachers need to think through the policies and practices they observe in particular schools. For example:

- Is there an explicit recognition of the statutory framework surrounding equal opportunities/social inclusion issues?
- Have equal opportunities policies been formulated and approved by governors?
- Are the practical manifestations of these policies debated amongst teachers?

Understanding equal opportunities and inclusive education is an important aspect of a teacher's professional knowledge. It is also an area about which most adults have formed views and values. Unlike, for example, lesson planning, it is an area in which beginning teachers will possibly have had some experience before they entered teacher education. It is an area that can call into question personal values and so challenge an individual's identity. As such it can be seen as threatening. Here are some beginning teachers' views of developing their understanding of equal opportunities:

> My natural reaction at first to EO is a groan ... I mean we know it's important, but surely it's been done to death!! It seems to crop up everywhere and be overplayed ... but on following the PGCE course I have begun to realise how fundamental EO policies are to the successful running of a school. I only had a general notion about what was involved before – now I see the complexity of some of these issues, often ridiculed as being 'politically correct'.
>
> (OU PGCE student, 1996)

> At a classroom level in preparing my lessons and thinking about classroom management, I was made aware of the need to consider equal opportunities and was able to go back to the course materials after some practical experience and analyse how the various approaches had worked and how they could be improved.
>
> (OU PGCE student, 1996)

Beginning teachers need to consider the sources of inequality, racism and sexism and approaches adopted in schools to counter these negative influences. This necessarily involves an examination of personal knowledge and assumptions about gender and ethnicity, as well as looking at the ways in which racial discrimination, sexism and privilege shape all our lives.

From equal opportunities to social inclusion

Throughout three decades following the passing of the Sex Discrimination Act (1975) and the Race Relations Act (1976), schools, supported by initiatives from their LEAs, developed equal opportunities policies. These policies were extended to include disability in the 1980s. Initially, this work was viewed with some scepticism as being more about the agenda of feminism and anti-racist groups than the about pupils' attainment and experience. However, classroom- and school-focused research and monitoring revealed significant differences in the experiences of pupils depending on their gender or ethnicity. This research, together with the intervention it prompted, also reflects the different 'phases' of concern about gender and ethnicity. Whilst they are roughly chronological, these 'phases' are by no means mutually exclusive and linear. Aspects of the work carried out in the different phases can still be of relevance to schools and pupils' experiences today.

Equal opportunities phase   This is marked by a concern about the low aspirations and limited educational experiences of girls within male-dominated structures – in society in general and in relation to school knowledge, aspects of school organization, the gendered images of subjects and the hidden curriculum.

Equity and social justice phase   This is marked by a realization that individual children have multiple identities relating to their sex, social class, ethnicity, family culture, etc., all of which need to be addressed if social inequality is to be reduced or eliminated. Sex and 'race' inequalities interact in a highly complex way. For example, expectations of gender roles are not always the same, but vary between social classes and ethnic groups.

Achievement-orientated phase   This is marked by the emphasis given to school effectiveness and quality through the close monitoring of pupils' attainment in SATs and public examinations. The question of boys' underachievement has been linked to a perceived wider crisis in masculinity:

> Throughout the 1990s, boys' performance in school took a nosedive … . From the end of the 1980s onwards, it was men in the eye of the storm not women. First came evidence that the job market was beginning to discriminate against men. More men than women were losing their jobs and 'male' industries were closing down while areas of women's work were expanding. The new patterns of work – part-time and flexible – seemed geared to women not men. There was also evidence that men were finding the changes more difficult than women; some perceived shifts in the family as entirely to their disadvantage, and were, in some communities, seriously disaffected.
>
> (Coward 1999: 9)

Ethnicity – pupils' experiences of school: the research evidence

Policies on equal opportunities related to ethnicity found in schools today are the product of a long and problematic history. Part of this history was the struggle by ethnic minority groups to bring to the fore an awareness of institutional racism. Initially, the underachievement of black[2] pupils was seen as being the 'problem' in school. Policy to counter this was based on the assumption that black pupils, rather than school systems and assessments, were the problem. In Reading 10.1 Mary Fuller charts the background which provides the historical context for today's policies on ethnicity.

Underachievement and schools

The underachievement of black pupils in schools has been a recurring theme of educational reports. This underachievement, particularly of Caribbean-heritage British pupils, especially boys, and their disproportionate exclusion from schools,

Reading 10.1 The historical context for today's policies on ethnicity

Education and minority ethnic groups

Since the early 1960s when black pupils began to appear in significant numbers in British schools, their education has been a cause for concern. Initially these concerns focused on the concerns of some white parents that the very presence of black children in schools would depress educational standards. The response from the Department of Education and Science was the issuing of a circular (7/65) which sanctioned the dispersal of 'immigrant' children to ensure that they were not concentrated in particular schools. The following Reading summarizes the research findings into black pupils' experience of schools in the 1970s and 80s.

During the 1960s and early 1970s, the DES's main concern and its main educational policy was to meet the language needs of immigrant and black pupils – essentially seen as teaching English to Asian pupils. During this time there was governmental concern at the relatively low attainment of black pupils but it was thought that the problem was temporary and as black pupils received all their education in the British system they would begin to reach the same level of attainment as their white counterparts.

Studies of underachievement rely on one of two main types of evidence: either individual psychometric tests to measure ability or group tests to measure performance. Group tests include verbal reasoning, reading skills, teacher assessment of children's school performance and achievement in public examinations. The Inner London Education Authority (ILEA), who were responsible for the single largest proportion of schools serving black pupils, began systematic studies of pupil attainment in the 1960s. These demonstrated that 'immigrants' in primary school performed poorly in English, maths and verbal reasoning as compared with the white children and that Afro-Caribbean children were showing particularly low levels of attainment. Subsequent research in ILEA and elsewhere appeared to confirm these findings (see Tomlinson 1983, for a review of this literature).

From early on, black parents and teachers had been concerned that their children weren't doing as well as hoped in school and had themselves marshalled evidence to put pressure on LEAs to take action. Probably the most famous of these reports was written by a black teacher, Bernard Coard (1971), who highlighted the large number of Afro-Caribbean children in special (ESN) schools, that is schools for children who were diagnosed as being 'educationally subnormal'. (Closer analysis of the data shows that it was Afro-Caribbean boys rather than girls or Asian pupils of either sex who were over-represented.) Community groups in Redbridge investigated the performance of Afro-Caribbean pupils in this outer London borough (Redbridge CRC 1978), concluding that black pupils were still performing poorly when compared with white pupils.

Twice during the 1970s, the select committee on race relations and immigration investigated education. In its second report it noted black parents' continued frustration at the lack of action about their children's education in mainstream and ESN schools. The government responded by setting up a committee of inquiry, initially chaired by Anthony Rampton and subsequently by Lord Swann (DES 1985).

Both reports have had a significant impact in confirming the under-performance of Afro-Caribbean pupils and for helping to perpetuate that agenda in discussions about the education of ethnic minority pupils.

Let's now look at more recent research. In their review of 1980s' research, Drew and Gray (1991) referred to studies of examination results, concluding that not much had changed since Rampton. Even where figures were corrected for social class there was still an element of underachievement. So minority ethnic underachievement can't be wholly explained (or explained away) by social class position. ILEAs continued monitoring of pupils' examination results indicated that, at the end of the decade, levels of achievement among pupils of Bangladeshi, Turkish and Caribbean background were lower than in other groups. So differences between groups continued to exist, but this doesn't mean that whites are top of the table of achievement.

Moving into the 1990s, there is national testing at each Key Stage in a child's education and results are made public. The Inspectorate/Ofsted make annual returns about standards achieved in state schools. Official guidance materials since the 1992 Education Act require those inspecting state schools to include standards of achievement of individuals and groups and the guidance also includes a section on equal opportunities. Results of testing 7-year-olds (Key Stage 1) in 1990 suggest that young children from minority ethnic groups were not doing as well as white children (Consortium for Assessment and Testing in Primary Schools 1991). Monitoring of older pupils at Key Stage 3 (age 14) and at GCSE indicated that in 1990/91 male and female pupils of Bangladeshi origin and boys of Afro-Caribbean origin were substantially underachieving in comparison with pupils from other ethnic groups (DES 1992).

Racism in schools is proposed as an alternative reason for underachievement (Redbridge CRC 1978; DES 1981, 1985; Commission for Racial Equality 1988; Mac and Ghaill 1988; Troyna and Carrington 1990; Gillborn 1990; Mirza 1992). Teacher attitudes and behaviour (low expectations of black pupils, prejudice, individual racism); hostility and prejudice between pupils; a Eurocentric curriculum; inappropriate assessment, and selection and pastoral procedures (institutional racism) are the most frequently cited issues. Whatever the relative importance of teacher racism (Foster et al. 1996) it is the factor that teachers and others involved in education should keep uppermost in mind because it is the one for which they have most direct responsibility and could do most about. Cronin (1984) suggests that educational research should focus on what happens in schools, to show how pupils underachieve rather than simply repeat that they do. Such research would also uncover school processes by which some pupils become high achievers.

Concern with racism as a cause of educational underachievement led to solutions being sought within the practices of education itself. A case can be made for not framing discussions in terms of the underachievement of minority ethnic group pupils, but in terms of black pupils being disadvantaged by the education system as it currently stands.

Source: Prepared for the Open University by Mary Fuller. Extracts on Education and 'Race', course materials from 'Exploring Educational Issues – Block 5, Equality and Education'. (This reading has been edited.)

was starkly presented in an Ofsted Report 'Recent research on the achievements of ethnic minority pupils' (Gillborn and Gipps 1996). The report found:

- that in the last decade there had been improvement in the levels of attainment among ethnic minority groups in many areas of the country;
- dramatic increases in examination performance in certain minority groups experiencing economic disadvantage, such as Bangladeshi pupils in the Borough of Tower Hamlets;
- in higher education people of ethnic minority background are generally well represented among those continuing education to degree level, although there were significantly different university admissions rates between the ethnic groups.

This work raises the question as to whether a focus on 'underachievement' is an appropriate way to conceptualize pupils' experience. This focus can obfuscate the causes of underachievement and lead to simplistic interpretations. Some minority ethnic groups in schools outperform white pupils, and achievement is further influenced by the factors of social class and gender.

The impact of racism on pupils' attainment has been identified by a wide range of surveys and reports (DES 1981; CRE 1988; Gilborn 1990; Mirza 1992). The 1988 survey carried out by the Commission for Racial Equality (CRE), drawing on evidence from LEAs, individuals and local Community Relations Councils, found that racial harassment was widespread in schools. The survey concluded:

The problem of racial harassment extends right through the educational system from nursery and infant schools to colleges and universities and affects pupils, students, parents and staff. Incidents of harassment do not occur in isolation; they spill over between the school, the street, the housing estate and the football terrace. Abuse, graffiti and violence as both threat and actuality serve as a constant reminder of the intolerance in white society and the vulnerability of ethnic minority people.

(CRE 1988: 16)

Here are two examples of the racial harassment pupils experience in schools and the ways in which it affects their achievement:

> A young Sikh published his own account of the regular verbal and physical harassment that he had experienced in the seven years he had spent at schools in the South. Much of that harassment was directed at his hair and his turban, both regarded as sacred symbols. Sometimes teachers would join in or even initiate jokes. The main effect, he said, was to erode his self-confidence and capacity to concentrate on learning.
>
> A seven-year-old girl at school in the North West was subjected to persistent name-calling by a white child of the same age, whose older sister also beat her up. The abuse escalated and the families became involved. The mother went to the school to discuss the problem when she saw that her child was becoming increasingly disturbed, to the point of bed-wetting and attempting to bleach her skin. The child's reports to the teacher had no effect.
>
> (CRE 1988: 11)

Teacher attitudes and behaviour, and above all, their expectations of pupils, can have a negative impact on pupils' self-esteem and attainment. Cecile Wright's work (1987a, 1987b) illustrates how teachers construct stereotypical views of Asian and Afro-Caribbean pupils. The stereotypes can, in part, be a product of the interaction between teacher and pupils in the classroom. She draws the following conclusions about the experience of primary school for pupils of Afro-Caribbean and Asian origin which result from teacher expectations and teacher–pupil interaction:

- Both groups of pupils faced negative responses from some teachers in the classroom. This occurred when children were seen as being a threat to classroom management or to teacher effectiveness.
- Some teachers perceived Asian pupils as being a problem because of their supposed limited cognitive skills, poor English language and poor social skills. However, teachers also had positive images of pupils of Asian origin, expecting them to be highly motivated, courteous and industrious.
- Afro-Caribbean pupils, especially boys, were amongst the most criticized and controlled groups in the classroom. Furthermore, in contrast to the Asian pupils, some teachers' images of Afro-Caribbean children were negative.

Black pupils of Afro-Caribbean and Asian origin, therefore, experience school in similar but also in different ways. In all cases, pupils' ethnicity influences their inter-action with the teacher and with teachers' expectations of those pupils.

This work on the racism found in schools and the racial harassment pupils were subjected to has led to solutions being sought within educational practice itself. This approach identifies the education system as it currently stands, not the underachievement of minority ethnic group pupils, as being the focus of change and the frame for discussion. However, progress in adopting these strategies in a concerted way in terms of affecting and changing practice in school has been slow.

The Ofsted R   ising attainment of minority ethnic pupils – school and
LEA responses' (C   99) found:

- Whilst most schools have equal opportunities policies, few have clear procedures to implement these policies and their impact on practice is limited.
- Fewer than a quarter of 25 LEAs visited have a clear strategy for raising the
  attainment of minority ethnic groups.

Much of the work on black underachievement and its causes has focused primarily
on ethnicity. More recent work increasingly takes an approach of considering the
combined effects of education inequalities in relation to 'race', class and gender. In
their comprehensive study of this, Gillborn and Mirza (2000) conclude:

- ethnic inequalities of attainment vary from one area to another but, despite
  the variability, distinct patterns of inequality are consistently visible;
- inequalities of attainment in GCSE examinations place African-Caribbean,
  Pakistani and Bangladeshi pupils in a disadvantaged position in the youth
  education, labour and training markets, and increase the likelihood of social
  and economic exclusion later in life;
- social class and gender differences are also associated with differences in
  attainment but neither can account for persistent underlying ethnic inequalities: comparing like with like, Afro-Caribbean, Pakistani and Bangladeshi
  pupils do not enjoy equal opportunities;
- ethnic inequalities are not new, but neither are they static. Evidence shows
  that in, some cases, the inequalities have increased in recent years. African-
  Caribbean and Pakistani pupils, for example, have not shared equally in the
  rising levels of GCSE attainment.

Later in the chapter, we discuss the ways in which schools have responded to these
debates about the underachievement of minority ethnic pupils and what constitutes
effective practice in relation to anti-racism in schools. At this point, the effects of
gender on the schooling experience of boys and girls are considered.

Gender – pupils' experience of school: the research evidence

Over the past two decades, women and girls have succeeded in winning more equal
access to education. In Reading 10.2 Janet Holland charts the main developments
affecting gender equality in schools. In 1996 a research project, commissioned by the
EOC, was set up to assess whether the educational changes of the late 1980s and 1990s
strengthened or interrupted the trends of the 1980s, or whether they generated new
trends towards greater gender equality. The main findings of the project were that
there was improved examination entry and performance patterns of girls due to the
introduction the General Certificate of Secondary Education (GCSE), a new, broader-
based examination for 16-year-olds. Largely because of this, girls had caught up with
boys in Mathematics and Science at GCSE and there had been an increased entry and a
closing gender performance gap in most subjects apart from Chemistry and Economics

Reading 10.2 The main developments affecting gender equality in schools

Writing in 1989 and quoting a host of studies, Deem (1989: 21–2) has usefully summarized the main findings of a decade of research into classroom interaction, which employed observation, participant observation, ethnography and other intensive methods and covered a wide variety of educational establishments.

- Boys in mixed classes tend to be more dominant and disruptive than girls.
- Boys tend to occupy more teacher time than girls; they answer and ask more questions, and are more likely to call for help.
- Boys, whatever the level of achievement, tend to be confident and as a result often overestimate their own abilities and underestimate those of girls. The reverse is true for girls: they tend to lack confidence, particularly in areas of the curriculum which they see as male, to underestimate their own capabilities and to overestimate those of boys.
- Boys frequently use girls as a negative reference group. (A positive reference group is one with which a group or an individual wishes to identify; a negative reference group is one from which separation and disassociation is desired.)
- Teachers tend to have different expectations of girls and boys. Different standards of behaviour are considered appropriate and acceptable/unacceptable. Boys' work is often expected to be more untidy. Girls who are considered to be behaving in a disruptive way may simply be behaving like most boys. Definitions of creativity tend to differ along gender lines.
- In mixed secondary schools, sexual harassment is a major aspect of male/female interaction, although its existence is often denied, or its importance underplayed.
- In lessons where equipment is used (for example, science, computing, mixed gym lessons) boys tend to monopolize the equipment, so that girls have little opportunity to use it unless they are in single-sex groups.

Source: Prepared for the Open University by Janet Holland. Extracts from course materials from 'Exploring educational issues – Block 5, Equality and Education' (1999). (This reading has been edited.)

which were still largely taken by boys, and social sciences, largely taken by girls. Male students achieved relatively less well in English and the arts, humanities, Modern Foreign Languages and Technology. Also, single sex girls' schools continued to be particularly successful in examination performance (reported in Ofsted/EOC 1996).

At the age of 18, stereotyped choice re-emerged. There was higher male entry into Advanced Level (A level) sciences (Physics, Technology, Computer Studies, Geography, Chemistry, Mathematics) and an increasing male entry into English and Modern

Foreign Languages. There was a higher female entry for the arts and humanities though, overall, males gain higher A level grades in nearly all subjects, especially Mathematics, Chemistry, Technology, History, English and Modern Foreign Languages. However, this male grade superiority was gradually being eroded with a marked improvement in female performance at A level, particularly in Biology, Social Sciences, Art and Design.

Conventional stereotyped entry and performance patterns also re-emerged post-16 for those students seeking vocational rather than academic qualifications. Here, young men had a slight (7 per cent) advantage over young women in numbers gaining vocational qualifications and were also more likely to gain higher awards. Young women and men also chose different subjects, courses and levels of award, related to the labour market sector to which they aspired, many of which are conventionally confined to one or other sex.

Additionally, students' perceptions of gender issues, across a range of ages and social groups and localities, were viewed as more open and more sensitive to changing cultural expectations and/or changes in the labour market than previously. Thus, girls and young women appeared more confident and positive about their future working lives and opportunities, and boys and young men also seemed aware of gender debates about women's working lives. Nevertheless, occupational choices for both sexes remained generally conventional and stereotyped.

In the mid-1980s, research moved away from a preoccupation with the underachievement of girls. Results of GCSEs show that at 16+ girls, in fact, do better than boys.

The evidence from examination results, particularly from GCSE results, does indicate that changes in examinations and assessment over the past few years, together with a developing awareness of gender issues in the classroom, can affect pupils' attainment in school. It is also encouraging as a teacher to realize that work done on equal opportunities in school and in the classroom does have a beneficial effect on pupils. However, in the past few years, national concern has focused on the underachievement of boys. The 1993 HMI/Ofsted report *Boys and English* brought to light boys' poor performance in literary skills. The report suggested that the gap between girls and boys in language-based subjects can be explained by the fact that girls' attainment has improved. The underachievement of boys in public examinations at GCSE level has been linked to the perceived wider crisis in masculinity. Throughout the 1990s, boys' performance in school took a nosedive. This prompted a renewed focus on boys' attainment. A summary of the data for gender achievement at Key Stage 3, Key Stage 4 (GCSE) and at A level in 1999 is below.

Gender achievement

Key Stage 3

At Key Stage 3 the overall proportion of pupils reaching the expected Level (5+) is lower than at earlier Key Stages.

The gap between boys and girls achieving the expected Level in English has increased to 18 per cent.

In mathematics and science boys and girls' achievements are broadly similar.

This picture has remained relatively unchanged for several years.

Teacher-assessed results for non-core subjects at Key Stage 3

In all subjects (except for IT and PE) 10 per cent more girls than boys achieved the expected Level. Note that in the core tested subjects, girls outperformed boys in the teacher assessments even when the test results were the same (i.e. in English and maths). This should be recalled when looking at the gender gap in the teacher-assessed subjects.

Key Stage 4 (GCSE)

In 1999, 10 per cent more girls than boys achieved 5 A*–C grades at GCSE.

Girls are still performing markedly better in English. Performance in mathematics is broadly similar. Girls do slightly better in double science but when boys' performance in the three separate sciences is taken into account the picture is again broadly similar.

Girls do better in all other subjects displayed (i.e. history, geography, IT, modern languages and art and design). The gap between girls and boys is greatest in Modern Foreign Languages and Art and Design.

Additional data

More boys than girls achieved no A*–G passes.

The vast majority of pupils who were permanently excluded from school in 1997/8 were boys.

In 1998 two out of three pupils in special schools were boys.

A level

The take-up of subjects varies greatly by gender. English is particularly popular with female students, while mathematics and physics are dominated by males.

The gender gaps in these subjects are generally small. Looking at students getting A or B at A level, the only gap larger than 4 per cent is in geography, which is 7 per cent in favour of females.

A preponderance of one gender entering a subject does not generally result in a gender gap in favour of that sex. For example, males do better in English and females do better in physics.

DfEE Standards website www.standards.dfes.gov.uk

There are many ways in which statistics can be interpreted. Overall, and particularly at A level, proportionately more girls qualify in arts subjects and more boys in science subjects. At A level the vast majority of passes in mathematics, physics, computer studies and economics go to boys. Assessment is, however, about more than outcomes. The whole process, and in particular the ways in which tasks are set, are influenced by gender considerations.

There is a considerable body of research into the area of gender and assessment. Murphy (1994) points out that particular modes of assessment have a gender bias. Multiple-choice questions, for example, have been shown to advantage boys, while the introduction of coursework as a major component of the GCSE examination has been shown to improve girls' performance. There is also some evidence to suggest that the image of the subject – for example, the 'masculine' image of science – may influence pupils' motivation to succeed. Murphy's main argument focuses on the role of language in assessment tasks, and the assumption that pupils have the same sets of shared contexts and assumptions as the assessor. In discussing the implications of this research for practice, Murphy argues that bias in assessment tasks is not about 'unfairness', since 'neutral tasks' which suit most pupils are impossible to set, but rather about understanding how the different experience of pupils, both in and outside school, affects how they may or may not construct meaning in their assessment tasks.

Work done on boys' underachievement in GCSEs is increasingly pointing to the effect that peer-group pressure has on boys' attainment. The peer-group pressure that boys are subjected to at school has a detrimental effect on their attainment. The culture of adolescent boys rejects diligence. It is not acceptable among their peers for boys to show themselves to be diligent, to read for pleasure, to do their homework conscientiously, to revise for examinations, or to be seen as 'the teacher's pet' by answering questions and working hard in class. At the same time, boys are more likely to be put in detention for bad behaviour than are girls, girls have a higher level of participation in school events (such as school councils) than boys and they generally gain more merit marks than do boys.

> … it seems that a dominant construction of femininity as sensible, and masculinity as silly and selfish, continues from the primary school right up to the late secondary school years … . The sensible/silly opposition was reconstructed in terms of maturity and immaturity, or as the boys might have put the latter, 'having a laugh'. Indeed, I have shown how this construction of masculinity as 'having a laugh', and the successful utilisation of this construction in the classroom, bore considerable status and power. Boys' construction of masculinity as selfish appeared to overlap strongly with the construction of masculinity as competitive, but was still very much in evidence, and could be used by boys to dominate other students and the classroom space. … In terms of the impact of these gender constructions on learning, an immediate assumption might be that girls' sensible constructions fit better with the school ethos and with learning orientation than do boys' silly-selfish ones.
>
> (Francis 1999)

These are the main findings of research into the different experiences of school for pupils from different ethnic groups and girls and boys. How did schools respond to these research findings and what effect did these responses have? We now turn to consider school policy and practice.

Equal opportunities: gender – school policy and practice

By the 1980s, a range of local authority and school-based strategies had developed to counter these inequalities. The focus on equality of opportunity was a focus on helping all children to fulfil their potential. Teachers became increasingly aware that educational outcomes could be influenced by factors outside the school's control such as a pupil's sex or social, cultural or linguistic background. Under the Ofsted Inspection Framework for School Inspections, schools' arrangements for equality of opportunity were evaluated according to the extent to which the particular needs of individual pupils and groups of pupils arising from gender, ability, ethnicity and social circumstances, were met within the teaching and the life of the school.

'Equal opportunities' in schools throughout the 1980s and 1990s embraced the following:

- developing an understanding and awareness of how cultural diversity and racism affect pupils' learning and can lead to inequalities
- developing an understanding and awareness of how the curriculum syllabus and content can exclude the experience of women, black and disabled people as well as the experiences of a variety of social groups
- acknowledging and meeting different learning needs while recognizing that those needs are influenced and informed by a pupil's gender or 'race'
- developing an ethos in school where pupils and staff have self-respect and respect for others
- reappraising the school structures and practices to see if these are discriminatory in effect.

These aspects are still current. Along with a concern about performance, value-added policies, school improvement and standards, and the broader-based and more inclusive concepts of entitlement and effective citizenship, these issues have become part of the mainstream culture of schools.

Is social class still the real divide?

With the focus on boys' underachievement, it is all too easy to overlook the fact that attainment in school is affected by a complex interplay of race and social background as well as sex. The focus on the underachievement of boys is likewise affected by society's wider concerns over 'the crisis in masculinity'. Schools also appear to be in the middle of having to resolve different interpretations of data. The monitoring of school examinations by gender has produced a 'standard crisis' account which has boys failing, with a growing gap between the attainment of boys and girls which worsens with the age of the pupils.

In addition to patterns of differential attainment by gender, other studies have focused on differences in examination performance by social class:

> While, overall, girls do out-perform boys at GCSE – working-class girls do marginally better than working-class boys in public examinations – the difference is not significant enough to reduce class inequalities within gender (or racial groups). Analysis of external examination results at all ages show working-class under-achievement is the real issue. The gap is particularly noticeable post-16.
>
> (Plummer 1998)

At the same time, there are those who claim that the 'crisis' presented by the achievement gap is the result of research methodology:

> … using the most popular method of comparing groups over time there appears to be a crisis in British education. Differences between social groups, in terms of examination results expressed in percentage points are increasing over time and so education is becoming increasingly polarised by gender, class, ethnicity, and income. Using the second method, when these differences are considered in proposition to the figures on which they are based, the opposite trend emerges. Achievement gaps between groups of students defined by gender, ethnicity, class and income actually appear to be declining.
>
> (Gorard *et al.* 1999)

Where does this debate over the interpretation of statistics leave schools? The answer to this lies in the importance of schools monitoring their own examination data for patterns and trends of underachievement. But it also highlights the fact that equality of opportunity is about more than outcome data. It is about pupils' attainment, but it is also about their values, attitudes and ambitions. Schools need to analyse and be aware of the impact they have on pupils of different race, gender and social class background and to focus on those who are in danger of underachieving. This involves the monitoring not only of examination results, but also patterns of pupil grouping, pupils with special educational needs, pupils' option choices, work experiences, destinations, exclusions and staffing. This in turn requires teachers to become their own researchers and points up the value of school-based action research projects in changes in school practice aimed at improving the educational attainment of all pupils.

Gender: changing school practice

Closing any gender gap which exists in pupils' attainment, or in other areas of schooling such as long-term aspirations, careers advice, post-16 experience, etc., depends on schools' awareness, expectations and attitudes to the issue. In determining their judgement on a school's results and achievements, Ofsted inspections consider

Here are some of the strategies schools have used to support pupil achievement and to implement equality of opportunity:

- Single-sex grouping in co-educational schools. This move has resulted from monitoring of classroom behaviour and option choice which has indicated that mixed sex groupings disadvantage either girls or boys. Its aim is to provide a learning environment where pupils feel comfortable, … for example, girls in single sex maths and science groups and boys in those subjects where they are doing less well, for example in English.
- Single-sex grouping also provides the opportunity to explore the social construction of gendered behaviour.
- Role modelling aimed at challenging male and female role stereotyping. This involves inviting people who have successfully

challenged gendered employment stereotypes into school from the locality.

- Mentoring strategies aimed at supporting particular groups who are in danger of underachieving. Schools have successfully drawn mentors from their locality to support pupils in Years 10 and 11, but this is increasingly being targeted at younger pupils.
- Whole-school strategies. The visibility of practice aimed at closing the gender gap on school development plans and in the school documentation is an important aspect of keeping this issue high priority at a time of competing demands.
- School-based research. Work on closing the gender gap is closely linked to work on raising the attainment of underattaining pupils. Schools can only carry out this work effectively if all aspects of school life, not just the results of SATs and examinations, are carefully monitored and inform staff discussion on the school culture, teaching strategies, staff recruitment and roles, resources, etc.
- School-based research has raised the following suggestions:
  - Teachers need to be aware of, and adapt their teaching styles specifically to, boys' literacy levels and learning needs.
  - Boys defined learning as performing a skill, not practising or refining a skill. This leads to demotivation.
- To improve the motivation of boys, teachers should consider:
  - taking time to listen to the boys in order to build relationships which show that they are valued and respected as both learners and individuals;
  - recognizing that some boys are 'under pressure' and require pastoral support;
  - helping develop and clarify the boys' career ambitions;
  - tabulating routines to help the boys work consistently over time;
  - developing tasks that require thinking rather than copying;
  - using examples to which boys can relate;
  - using humour.

Source: DfEE Standards website

the extent to which pupils work in an atmosphere free from oppressive behaviour such as bullying, sexism and racism. Schools have developed their equal opportunities gender policies to match their particular pupil intake and circumstances.

Ethnicity and cultural diversity: changing school practice

As a result of the Gillborn and Gipps report (1996), Ofsted was asked to report on the effectiveness of initiatives to raise the attainment of minority ethnic pupils and to identify what could be done to tackle problems of racial tension and harassment in schools. The following list of good practice in raising attainment in pupils' from minority ethnic groups is based on this survey.

- The importance of monitoring the implementation of equal opportunities policies. Whilst schools generally had equal opportunities policies, few monitored their implementation. The message conveyed here is that equal opportunities policies need to result in action and change.

  > In the school which has been most effective in bringing together greater equality for all its students, the senior management team have concentrated on developing an ethos which values learning and all pupils equally. This has been achieved by a tightly focused system of monitoring to raise attendance and achievement levels, giving additional support where needed and the careful preparation of pupils for examinations.
  >
  > (Gillborn and Gipps 1996)

- The use of attainment data. Schools need to analyse attainment data by ethnic group and use this to target support. Teachers' impressions of pupil attainment rather than accurate data can serve to reinforce commonly held stereotypes.

  > The school analyses GCSE results by ethnicity and gender and produces results for each ethnic group. Departmental heads are asked to compare results with previous years, overall performance, national averages and estimated grades and to identify the significant differences in performance by ability, gender, teaching groups and ethnic groups. Departments are asked to identify factors contributing to these outcomes and to suggest both department and whole-school strategies which might further raise achievement.
  >
  > (ibid.: 1996)

- Research carried out by Ofsted, the DfEE, the CRE and academic researchers (Blair *et al.* 1998; Ofsted 1999; Weeks and Wright 1999) has identified certain school practices which are significant in terms of developing inclusive education. These practices can be summarized as:
  - The LEA and the headteacher are significant in terms of providing leadership on equal opportunities and social justice. Where headteachers show strong, committed leadership, school practice develops.
  - There is no one 'correct' way to respond to ethnic diversity in schools.
  - The most effective schools are the 'listening schools' which take time to talk to parents and pupils and take their views seriously. As a result of listening, schools reapprais and chang their practices to develop a more inclusive curriculum.
  - Schools have clear procedures, which they implement, for recording and acting on racist incidents.
  - The school ethos enables pupils to discuss 'race' issues and share concerns.
  - The school has high expectations of pupils. Underachievement is not acceptable.
  - Schools, as a routine part of self-evaluation, use ethnic monitoring.

Conclusion

In developing these practices, schools should be aware and be influenced by the Macpherson Report (1999) into the murder of the black teenager, Stephen Lawrence. This report made four major requirements of education and of the communities in which schools function. It recommended the amendment of the National Curriculum to value social diversity; referred to the duty of LEAs and school governors to develop strategies to prevent and address racism in schools; required Ofsted to examine and implement these strategies; and called for community and local initiatives to provide cultural diversity and prevent racism. Responding positively to these recommendations and to the implications raised in this chapter in relation to gender and 'race' equality is the challenge facing all schools. Dissolving barriers to learning, and seeking out ways to include all pupils, are at the heart of equality of opportunity – of access, achievement and recognition of excellence.

Notes

1   Throughout this chapter, the word 'race' is in inverted commas because we accept the arguments against the notion that there exist distinct 'races'.
2   Throughout this chapter, the term 'black' refers to Caribbean heritage British pupils, and pupils of Asian origin.

References

Arnot, M., David, M. and Weiner, G. (1996) *Education Reforms and Gender Equality in Schools*, EOC, Manchester.

Blair, M., and Bourne, J. with Coffin, C., Creese, A. and Kenner, C. (1998) *Making the Difference: Teaching and Learning Strategies in Successful Multi Ethnic Schools*, London: DES.

Coard, B. (1971) *How the West Indian Child is Made Educationally Sub-Normal in the British School System*, London: New Beacon Books.

Commission for Racial Equality (CRE) (1988) *Learning in Terror: A Survey of Racial Harassment in Schools and Colleges*, London: CRE.

Coward, R. (1999) *Sacred Cows: Is Feminism Relevant to the New Millennium?* London: HarperCollins.

Cronin, A. (1984) 'Supplementary schools: their role in culture maintenance, identify and underachievement' *New Community* 11(3): 12–14.

Deem, R. (1989) 'Exploring educational issues' (the 208 Course Team) Block 5, *Equality and Education*, Milton Keynes: The Open University.

Department of Education and Science (DES) (1981) 'West Indian children in our schools', Cmnd. 8273, London: HMSO (the Rampton Report).

—— (1985) 'Education for all: the report of the Committee of Inquiry into the education of children from ethnic minority groups', Cmnd. 9453, London, HMSO (the Swann Report).

Drew, D. and Gray, J. (1991) 'The Black-White gap in examination results: a statistical critique of a decade's research' *New Community* 17(2).

Foster, P., Gomm, R. and Hammersley, M. (1996) *Constructing Educational Inequality*, London: Falmer Press.

Francis, B. (1999) 'Sensible selflessness and silly selfishness revisited: constructions of gender and status in the secondary school', paper presented at the British Educational Research Association annual conference, University of Sussex, Brighton, 2–5 Sept 1999.

Fuller, M. (1997) 'Education and Race' (EU 208 Course), Block 5, Unit 4, *Exploring Educational Issues*, Milton Keynes: The Open University.

Gilborn, D. (1990) *Racism and Antiracism in Real Schools*, Buckingham: Open University Press.

Gilborn, D. and Gipps, C. (1996), *Recent Research on the Achievement of Ethnic Minority Pupils*, Ofsted, London: HMSO.

Gilborn, D. and Mirza, H.S. (2000) *Education Inequalities. Mapping Race, Class and Gender*, Ofsted, London: HMSO.

Gorard, S., Slaisbury, J. and Rees, G. (1999) 'Revisiting the apparent underachievement of boys; reflections on the implications for educational research', paper presented to the British Educational Research Association annual conference.

HMI/Ofsted (1993) *Boys and English*, London, HMSO.

Holland, J. (1997) 'Exploring educational issues – equality and education', (Course EU208) Unit 3, *The Gender Agenda in Education*, Milton Keynes: The Open University.

Mac an Ghaill, M. (1988) *Young, Gifted and Black*, Milton Keynes: Open University Press.

Macpherson, W. (1999) *The Stephen Lawrence Inquiry*, CM 4262–1, London: The Stationery Office.

Mirza, H.S. (1992) *Young, Female and Black*, London: Routledge.

Murphy, P. (1994) 'Assessment and gender' in B. Moon, A. Shelton Mayes and S. Hutchinson (2001) (eds) *Teaching, Learning and the Curriculum in Secondary Schools: A Reader*, London: RoutledgeFalmer.

Ofsted (1999) *Raising Attainment of Minority Ethnic Pupils – School and LEA Responses*, London: The Stationery Office.

Open University (1999) *Exploring Educational Issues* (EU208), Milton Keynes: The Open University.

Plummer, G. (1998) 'Forget gender, class is the real divide' *TES* 23 January 1998.

Redbridge Community Relations Council (1978) *Cause for Concern: West Indian Pupils in Redbridge*, Redbridge: Redbridge CRC and Black Parents Progressive Association.

Tomlinson, S. (1983), *Ethnic Minorities in British Schools: A Review of the Literature 1960–1982*, London: Heinemann.

Troyna, B. and Carrington, B. (1999) *Education, Racism and Reform*, London: Routledge.

Weekes, D. and Wright, C. (1999) *Improving Practice: A Whole school Approach to Raising the Achievement of African Caribbean Youth*, London: Runnymede Trust in association with Nottingham Trent University.

Wright, C. (1987a) 'The relations between teachers and Afro-Caribbean pupils: observing multicultural classrooms' in M. Arnot. and G. Weiner (eds) *Gender under Scrutiny*, London: Hutchinson.

—— (1987b) 'Black students – white teachers' in B. Troyna (ed.) *Racial Inequality in Education*, London: Tavistock.

11 Inclusive education
Special educational needs

Introduction

The introduction to Chapter 10 outlined details of the legislation for equal opportunities which has impacted directly on school policies and practice and which was enacted as a result of public and political pressure. This legislation laid the legal foundations for equality in society, and, as one refraction of this, in schools in the UK. The Disability Discrimination Act (1995) was cited in relation to this, this legislation following that of two decades earlier which was directed to other issues of inclusivity in society: issues of sex equality, (the Sex Discrimination Act 1975), and ethnic equality, (the Race Relations Act 1976).

It was noted in Chapter 10 that during the same period government put into place a range of regulatory intervention measures to protect the interests of children who have special educational needs. The Warnock Report in 1978, the 1981 and 1996 Education Acts, and the Special Education Needs Act (2000) set up and subsequently reinforced a move towards the integration into mainstream schools of children who experience difficulties in learning or who have disabilities.

Implications for the practical ramifications of inclusivity for those pupils who have special educational needs provide the central aspect of this chapter. It focuses on the ways in which schools and the curriculum can be responsive to the disabilities of some pupils or to the difficulties in learning that some pupils experience. It considers the following related issues:

- integration and the inclusive curriculum
- special educational needs and the National Curriculum
- who experiences difficulties in learning?
- teaching and learning strategies for special educational needs.

Integration and inclusive education

In looking at learning difficulties and the disabilities of some pupils, we are addressing attitudes, concepts and assumptions that are deeply ingrained in public mythology. The issue is a fascinating one, and there have now been many studies that show how social understanding of pupils such as Paula portrayed in the case study in Reading 11.1 has changed over time. Categorizations, and even stigmatisation, of children with disabilities, for example, were, and unfortunately still are, part of our culture. Attitudes have changed significantly over the last few decades and there is now a range of legislative and regulatory interventions by government to provide and safeguard the interests of pupils like Paula.

This chapter can only provide an introduction for beginning teachers to the issues involved in special educational needs (and puristically the definition would also include the special needs of the most gifted and talented children in school; for the purposes of this book this is focused upon in Chapter 4). During their induction, and later as their careers progress, such teachers will be able to explore and experience policies and practices, make their own contribution to changing ideas and attitudes, and develop their own practice.

Reading 11.1 Case study: guidance on SEN thresholds

The level of difficulty

Paula is a wheelchair user in Year 10 in a large secondary school. She has severe mobility problems and only limited hand movements. Although assessed as having average ability Paula's attainments are below average, possibly reflecting difficulties in finding appropriate ICT equipment when she was younger. She has good social skills, is outgoing and friendly but her access to the curriculum is limited both by her physical and learning difficulties.

The response

Paula has a statement of special educational needs. The school buildings are fully wheelchair-accessible and her statement provides 20 hours of LSA (Learning Support Assistant) time to support her access to the curriculum and to facilitate her use of ICT. Since this does not cover all of the school week, Paula has been encouraged to develop independence in certain lessons, at the beginning and end of the school day and during lunchtimes. She has access to the SEN base at lunchtimes where she can do her homework or socialize. Flexibility within the curriculum provides a 'support' option that gives her supervised time to catch up on work where she has fallen behind. Apart from these provisions, she participates fully in school life alongside her peers.

Source: DfEE 2000

Commentary

The action taken to meet Paula's needs is typical of what might be expected for a pupil with significant physical disabilities and operating at a below average level. Additional provision extends across much of her timetable.

There is a clear focus in the action taken on enabling Paula to access the mainstream curriculum and achieve at a high level. The accessible nature of the buildings, the inclusion of Paula in as many school activities as possible and the availability of 'catch-up' time are all, therefore, important parts of this action.

Paula's case is just one example of how schools take action to include pupils with special educational needs. The integration of pupils like Paula into mainstream schools has been the result of shifting attitudes to disability and special educational needs.

One document that heralded a new perspective on special educational needs – the Warnock Report – was published in 1978. This report was significant in terms of shifting the clear boundaries which existed in 1978 between special and mainstream schools. It resulted in an increase in the integration of pupils identified as having special educational needs within the mainstream.

The Warnock Report is interesting in providing a historical overview of special needs provision since 1970. Most significantly, it recommended:

- the abolition of statutory forms of categoriz ation:

  Categorisation perpetuates the sharp distinction between two groups of children – the handicapped and the non-handicapped – and it is this distinc-tion which we are determined, as far as possible, to eliminate.

  (DES 1978: para. 3.24)

- the widening of the understanding of the term *special education:*

  … to elaborate the references to children who suffer from disabilities in such a way as to establish that they include those with significant difficulties in learning, or with emotional or behavioural disorders, as well as those with disabilities of mind or body …

  (DES 1978: para. 3.41)

- the development of a formal assessment procedure involving parents:

  We recommend that whoever refers the child for multi-professional assess-ment should inform the parents as soon as the [assessment] procedure has been initiated and should give them a form on which to make their own statement about their child's needs.

  (DES 1978: para. 4.60)

In terms of overall impact, the Warnock Report set in motion a series of moves, nationally through the 1981 Education Act, and locally through reviews of LEA provision, that have seen mainstream schools taking on an increased responsibility for children who experience difficulties in learning or who have disabilities. The 1981 Education Act recognized a continuum of special educational need, from children with severe and complex problems, thought to constitute about 2 per cent of the school population, to a much larger group of about 18 per cent who at some time in their school career may experience difficulty with learning for a variety of reasons.

This continuum embraces a very wide range of need, from minor and sometimes temporary learning difficulties, to physical or sensory impairment, emotional and behavioural disorders, and profound and multiple problems.

The 1981 Act emphasized the right of children with special needs to be educated with their peers in ordinary schools. Importantly, it also recognized that special needs should not necessarily be seen as a deficit in the child, but instead as an interaction between the needs of the child and conditions in the school, such as problems of access to buildings, a curriculum which is pitched at the wrong level, or inflexible teaching methods.

For children in considerable need who require additional or different provision from that which is generally made (the 2 per cent group), the Act introduced a formal process of assessment culminating in the issuing of a statement describing a child's needs and the provision which should be made.

The term 'special educational needs' or 'special needs' is now used widely in schools where it is used in a broad sense to cover aspects of teaching and learning that relate to learning difficulties. The phrase has now entered into the everyday language of teachers. There is, however, a statutory definition of SEN. Since the passing of the 1981 Act, further legislation has strengthened the principle of universal access to education and inclusion of all pupils in mainstream schools wherever possible. There has been a gradual trend towards greater integration of children with special needs into ordinary schools, instead of segregating them in special schools. In 2000, 1.29 per cent of the school population aged 5–16 in England went to special schools, compared with 1.65 per cent in 1987 and 1.72 per cent in 1982. Links have been established between special schools and ordinary schools, enabling joint lessons and other activities for children and teachers to take place. LEAs have developed SEN support services for ordinary schools.

One of the most significant changes in special educational needs provision has been the introduction of the Code of Practice (1994) for the education of 'children with special educational needs', new procedures for assessing 'needs' and specifying resources in 'statements of special educational needs'. This Code of Practice is now contained in the 1996 Act that consolidated all educational legislation passed since 1944. This Act does not apply to Scotland or Northern Ireland. In Northern Ireland a new Code of Practice came into effect in September 1998.

The 1996 Act defined special educational needs as follows:

A child has special educational needs if s/he has a learning difficulty which calls for special education provision to be made for them.

A child has a learning difficulty if s/he:

(a) has a significantly greater difficulty in learning than the majority of children of the same age; or
(b) has a disability which prevents or hinders the child from making use of educational facilities of a kind generally provided for children of the same age in schools within the area of the local education authority;
(c) is under five and falls within the definition at a) or b) above or would so do if special educational provision was not made for the child.

A child must not be regarded as having a learning difficulty solely because the language or medium of communication of the home is different from the language in which he or she is or will be taught.

Special educational provision means:

> (a) for a child of two or over, educational provision which is additional to, or otherwise different from, the educational provision made generally for children of the child's age in maintained schools, other than special schools, in the area.
>
> (b) for a child under two, educational provision of any kind.
>
> (Education Act 1996, Section 312)

A Special Educational Needs and Disability Bill was introduced in parliament in December 2000. Part 1 of the Bill makes changes to the Education Act of 1996. It:

- strengthened the right of children with SEN to be educated in mainstream schools
- requires Local Education Authorities to arrange for parents of children with SEN to be provided with advice and information about SEN matters and a means of resolving disputes with schools and LEAs
- requires schools to tell parents where they are making special educational provision for their child and allow schools to request a statutory assessment of a pupil's SEN.

The question of how best to provide for the integration of pupils with special educational needs into mainstream schools, and debates about the means through which this can be achieved, is one which will dominate educational policy for some time. 'Inclusivity' is a radical departure from the 'segregation' of pupils which typified educational provision for most of the twentieth century. It requires specialist training for staff and close liaison with social services and other support agencies. Here, important principles in terms of providing equal opportunities, and a clear definition of inclusivity, have been established. LEAs and schools are now legally bound to accept the duty not to treat disabled pupils less favourably, without justification, than non-disabled pupils. Schools are also now required to make progress in increasing physical accessibility to school premises and the curriculum. The Code of Practice which was a result of the 1996 Act introduced a clear statement of the rights of pupils deemed to have special educational needs, and clear procedures which had to be followed. The 1996 Code of Practice, quite rightly, will no doubt be amended as a result of evaluations of its initial years of implementation, but clear principles can be identified as providing the basis for SEN policy, no matter what the detail.

The Code of Practice

The Code of Practice introduced the following:

- A detailed five-stage model of identification and assessment of 'pupils with special educational needs', the first two stages of which are entirely dependent on the resources of the mainstream school.
- A recommendation that the 'special education needs co-ordinator' should help to devise 'individual education plans' for children identified as having special needs.

- A recommendation that students should be consulted about education decisions concerning them.
- A suggestion that formal assessments assign students to categories of 'learning difficulty', 'specific learning difficulty' (or 'dyslexia'), 'emotional and behavioural difficulty', 'physical disability', 'hearing difficulty', 'visual difficulty', 'speech and language difficulty', and 'medical conditions'.
- Detailed guidance on the formal assessment process and the following additions to the requirements of the law and guidelines:
  - a named person should be available, probably from a relevant voluntary society, to help parents
  - if the LEAs decide not to issue a statement they should provide the conclusions of the assessment to teachers and parents as a 'note in lieu'
  - when making a statement, LEAs should respond appropriately to differences in 'linguistic and cultural background'.

The Code also sets out the following staged process within which schools now work:

Stage 1: class or subject teachers identify or register a child's special educational needs and, consulting the school's SEN co-ordinator, take initial action.

Stage 2: the school's SEN co-ordinator takes lead responsibility for gathering information and for co-ordinating the child's special educational provision, working with the child's teachers.

Stage 3: teachers and the SEN co-ordinator are supported by specialists from outside the school.

Stage 4: the LEA considers the need for a statutory assessment and, if appropriate, makes a multi-disciplinary assessment.

Stage 5: the LEA considers the need for a statement of special educational needs and, if appropriate, makes a statement and arranges, monitors and reviews provision.

(DfE 1994: 3)

The Northern Ireland Code is a more succinct version of that in England and Wales. Understanding the Code and the processes and procedures associated with it is important. It sets out the legal framework within which schools and LEAs must work, including cases where a child is the subject of a formal statement of special educational needs. In 2000, 3 per cent of all pupils in schools had statements of SEN. A small number of schools identify more than half of their pupils as having SEN.

In all this, perspectives and assumptions need careful scrutiny. Dividing children into categories can lead to learning difficulties being seen as attributes of the pupils, rather than the result of the interaction between pupils and the learning environment:

> ... difficulties in learning [can be viewed as] indicating a lack of match between pupils ... and tasks. They are not something that pupils have irrespective of what they are learning. They indicate a breakdown in the relationship between students and curricula. This does not mean that some people aren't better at learning particular things than others, or that some people are not incompetent at many or most things. But it does direct us to finding ways of providing materials which are appropriate to the capacities and interests of pupils rather than towards the identification of failing pupils.
>
> (Open University 1992: 39)

The way in which teachers approach their classroom practice is related to the ideas they hold about how children learn. For pupils who experience learning difficulties it is most important that teachers adopt a view that looks at pupils' strengths as well as weaknesses. Beginning teachers need to understand the importance that they themselves, the teaching approach and the environment, can all make in either encouraging learning or presenting barriers. Teachers having high expectations of children, whatever their learning needs, is a key factor in pupils' achievements. As Paul Widlake has commented, '... we should avoid making the term special a euphemism for lesser; high expectations, backed by adequate resources and well-trained teachers, have changed lives' (Widlake 1990: ix). Adopting a notion of pupil diversity, where a continuum of learning needs is seen and it is acknowledged that these will change through time, is a useful framework in helping to find strategies for working in the classroom with a wide range of children.

Unusually, given the political controversies surrounding such educational legislation in the late 1980s and early 1990s, the publication of the Code was widely welcomed by all the main political parties. It sets out a series of tasks and responsibilities for schools and governing bodies and LEAs, as well as social service departments and health authorities. All schools have a copy of the Code and beginning teachers are recommended to look through it during their time in schools.

On the positive side the emphasis on individual need has been welcomed by some as providing a clear framework for the identification and assessment of particular pupils with 'special educational needs'. This has led to reports of 'greater quality of assessment and the planning of appropriate provisions' (House of Commons Education Committee 1996: vi, para. 6). Implicit in these discussions of the Code are issues of equality of opportunity in education, fairness in the allocation of resources and the question of whether individual learning programmes for pupils or a whole-school approach to learning support is more likely to encourage all learners to reach their potential. The effectiveness of the Code of Practice in meeting special educational need is the subject of monitoring and revision. The government's Action Programme for children with special educational needs, published in 1998, *Meeting Special Educational Needs: A Programme of Action* (DfEE 1998), referred to widespread agreement that the Code of Practice had led to improvements in teaching pupils with SEN, and that the Code should be revised in the light of experience since 1994, to build on good practice.

As a result of these developments, there has been a major investment in in-service training and education in this area, and all maintained and foundation schools are now required to develop policies, agreed by governors, for special educational needs provision.

Special educational needs and the National Curriculum

Increasingly, all teachers are involved in working with pupils with special educational needs. The National Curriculum handbook for secondary school teachers in England (DfEE/QCA 1999) incorporates a statement of curriculum entitlement 'Inclusion: providing effective learning opportunities for all children'. This provides guidance on developing a more inclusive curriculum, which is based on the principles of:

- setting suitable learning challenges
- responding to pupils' diverse learning needs
- overcoming potential barriers to learning.

This statement sets out the background to entitlement to the National Curriculum for all children, and examines some of the means by which pupils who experience learning difficulties can have access to it. It is important to realize that it is only as recently as 1988, with the Education Reform Act, that all children finally had the same statutory entitlement to a broad and balanced curriculum (including the National Curriculum). In fact, before 1970 about 30,000 children identified as having severe learning difficulties had no access to an education in school at all, as provision for their learning needs came within the National Health Service. Since that time there has been a transformation of attitudes towards the educational provision for all pupils. This transformation has been based on the following principles:

- All pupils are entitled to the same broad and balanced curriculum.
- Pupils should, wherever possible, be taught alongside their peers.
- There is a continuum of learning needs in classes.
- Learning difficulties arise when there is a mismatch between the pupils' learning needs and their learning context.
- Most special educational needs are of a mild and temporary kind.
- The teacher's professional role is to provide appropriate learning experiences for the full range of children.

These have had a significant impact on the teacher's role because all pupils, whatever their educational needs, have become part of the professional responsibility of classroom teachers in mainstream schools. Before this, when the school could decide the curriculum for pupils, those who experienced learning difficulties were often taught apart from their peers and offered a limited curriculum focusing on basic numeracy and literacy skills. Now these pupils are entitled to full involvement in all the subjects of the National Curriculum. In secondary schools specialist subject teachers have become teachers of all pupils, whatever their educational needs. This means that all teachers need to develop skills for supporting these pupils and appropriate teaching and learning strategies for dealing with a wide range of pupils in the classroom. A framework for this work is provided by the following questions:

- How are pupils identified and assessed?
- How is provision for pupils' special educational needs organized and managed?
- Who is the special needs co-ordinator and 'responsible person' and how does he/she approach his/her role?
- What resources are available for support, e.g. support staff, teacher expertise, materials, etc.?
- What is the range of pupils' difficulty, and which pupils have statements of special educational need?
- How are the National Curriculum requirements, in particular the reporting, recording and assessment, managed for pupils with special educational needs?
- What work do different departments do on special educational needs?

Who experiences difficulties in learning?

The Warnock Report (DES 1978) estimated that 20 per cent of all pupils fall into the special educational needs category at some point in their school life. Of these, very few would require long-term support, the majority requiring temporary support. The report also made clear that the majority of these pupils (that is, 18 per cent of all pupils) were in mainstream schools. However, because of the issue of context, placing a figure on numbers of pupils who have difficulties with learning is likely to be arbitrary. The following examples will help to make this clear:

- A child with impaired mobility who uses a wheelchair will certainly experience difficulties in a school with stairs, steps and narrow doorways; but these difficulties will not arise in a school with ramps and other access features.
- Using a classroom text which does not match the reading attainment of the pupils in the class will give rise to learning difficulties that would not arise with an appropriately chosen text.

A teaching approach that fails to appreciate that classes contain a wide range of children will give rise to learning difficulties. A classroom that has a range of resources adapted to meet particular learning needs will have fewer such pupils. An important point is that the full attainment range is involved here. Pupils who are capable of working at the highest Levels of the National Curriculum subjects may exhibit emotional and behavioural difficulties in class if they are given inappropriate learning tasks.

Leaving aside the issue of context, the range of pupils in mainstream schools is likely to include some pupils with physical or sensory impairments, and some who have intellectual or emotional difficulties in learning. The term 'special educational needs' then covers a wide range of circumstances:

Cognition and learning – general learning difficulties

General difficulties may show themselves in the low levels of attainment across the board in all forms of assessment, difficulty in acquiring skills (notably literacy and numeracy), difficulties in dealing with abstract ideas and generalizing from experience, a range of associated difficulties, notably in speech and language and in social and emotional development, for example.

Specific learning difficulty

Some difficulties affect only some aspects of pupils' learning, for example difficulties with motor control skills. Some pupils attain highly in some curriculum areas, or they may have higher attainment in one mode of presenting or recording their work, e.g. better oral than written work. Specific learning difficulties may manifest themselves through signs of frustration and low self-esteem, and in some cases behaviour difficulties.

Behavioural, emotional and social difficulties

This covers behaviour such as age-inappropriate behaviour, or socially inappropriate behaviour which interferes with the learning of pupils, signs of emotional turbulence and difficulties in forming and maintaining relationships.

Communication and interaction difficulties

This covers speech and language difficulties and autistic spectrum disorders (characterized by a triad of impairments of social relationships, social communication and imaginative thought).

Sensory and physical difficulties

This covers hearing impairment, visual impairment and physical and medical difficulties. Some children who experience physical or medical difficulties have no problems in accessing the curriculum and learning effectively. Having a medical diagnosis does not necessarily mean that a pupil has special educational needs.

Pupils who experience difficulties with text

Problems in using texts are among the most common reasons why pupils are said to have learning difficulties. 'Text' is used here to mean any material in the classroom from which pupils are expected to extract meaning – whether it contains pictures, words, or a mixture of both.

The teacher's role in developing pupils' attainment in reading is firmly embedded in the primary teacher's repertoire of skills. Secondary school teachers, however, 'have often not been shown how to develop their teaching repertoire in ways appropriate to their subject and to the development of reading within it' (McGowan and Turner 1991). Indeed, the same authors report that a common response to reading difficulties observed in secondary schools is for teachers to reduce the opportunities for those pupils to read, leading to a vicious circle of underachievement.

In identifying the range of special educational needs, the process itself produces categories of learning difficulty. This raises the danger of 'labelling' pupils according to this categorization. Whilst any learning difficulty needs describing and diagnosing in order to provide the pupil with the appropriate level of support, teachers need to see beyond the label and not make stereotyped assumptions about the capabilities of individual pupils. For example, pupils who have vision or hearing impairment or pupils with specific learning difficulties who experience severe problems with reading and writing may also show a clear grasp of concepts in discussion work.

Teaching and learning strategies for special educational needs

Some schools have units attached to them which provide specialized support for pupils with particular types of learning needs: for example, emotional and behavioural difficulties (EBD) units or hearing impaired units. But with the increased availability of educational support technology, many more children are able to work alongside their peers in mainstream classes.

The remainder of this chapter examines how teachers can help children who experience difficulties in learning to make progress.

Paul Widlake suggests that '… too often we refer to failing children when we should more properly be examining failing system' (Widlake 1990). How do teachers and schools create learning environments that support a wide range of pupils and what kinds of teaching and learning strategies are most effective? How do teachers build pupils' self-confidence and self-esteem, important dimensions in the development of successful learners? Part of the answer to these questions relates to whole-school organization and policies. For example, what is the whole-school policy on special educational needs, and how are external agencies used? But another part of the answer lies in work of the individual teacher – such as differentiated teaching and the use of learning support staff.

In considering each of these approaches, it is important to bear in mind that, by developing teaching strategies and learning activities that support pupils who experience difficulties, an improved learning environment is created for all pupils.

Differentiation

Differentiation is an important approach to teaching classes with a wide range of learning needs, including special educational needs. But differentiation is equally important in classes with a narrower range of attainment, as in setted classes. It involves teachers providing differentiated tasks for pupils working at different attainment levels, or with different background knowledge of the subject. Differentiation is based on the recognition that all classes are not heterogeneous. (For a more detailed discussion of differentiation, see Chapter 5.)

Inclusive pedagogy

Simply including pupils with special educational needs by admitting them into the school or classroom does not necessarily mean, of course, that their needs have been met. Approaches to teaching and learning, classroom methods and management need careful evaluation in terms of their effectiveness at achieving inclusion. Recent work which describes teaching and learning in inclusive schools and classrooms (Sebba and Sachdev 1997; Thomas *et al.* 1998; Tilstone *et al.* 1998) reveals a clear consensus on the teaching strategies which create more inclusive classrooms. These strategies are:

- co-operative peer learning
- peer-mediated instructional approaches
- multi-age grouping
- team teaching.

Pupil grouping

There is no single, clear-cut way of ensuring the quality of pupils' learning including pupils with learning difficulties and physical disabilities and non-English speakers in the classroom. Success will depend on factors such as the teacher's style, whole-school policies and SEN co-ordinator support for teachers to meet to discuss their concerns and to work out ideas for practice. In many schools, there has been debate around appropriate grouping arrangements. Research evidence (Hallam 1996) indicates that streaming of pupils by level of attainment tends to demoralize those placed in lower academic streams (also see Chapter 8).

The practice of withdrawing pupils from some lessons to focus on the teaching of specific skills is common in many schools. However, this method has drawbacks and limitations – normally the apparent gains made in small-group situations could not be sustained or generalized in different contexts, i.e. the classroom.

Pupils in this system lose the continuity of classroom activity when they are withdrawn. It was also found that pupil progress can be hindered by a possible conflict between the teaching methods used in the main class and those used in the withdrawal group. When the onus for supporting pupils fell to the support teacher working outside the class, there was less incentive or need for the class teacher to take an interest in examining how teaching for all pupils might be improved (Lewis 1995). There is an expectation in the Code of Practice that all teachers should take responsibility for the progress of all pupils, including those who experience difficulty in learning. So whilst there may be room for intensive specialist work in particular areas, strategies need to be adopted which maintain continuity for these pupils and also minimize the stigma attached to this form of additional learning.

The use of ICT

> All the power of the computer to motivate interest and enthuse, through the use of graphics, movement and sound can be used, in the same way as it is for children without special educational needs, but in many cases we need to find alternative ways in which children can interact with the computer ...
>
> (Learning Schools Programme, OU/RM 1999)

A useful starting point in the use of ICT in teaching pupils with special educational needs is to consider the types of areas which ICT can help. Three types of access have been identified (Day 1995) as being:

- physical
- cognitive
- supportive

Physical areas relate to the way in which ICT can be customized to meet a pupil's own particular need: for example, the use of screen magnification software for supporting pupils with visual impairments. Cognitive access applies to the development of our understanding of how pupils, all pupils, are using computers to enhance their teaching and learning. Supportive access refers to the way in which ICT can help pupils with particular activities. For example, pupils who have difficulties with spelling can use a spell-checker, or those who have difficulty communicating through handwriting can use a word processor. Speech software is now available that allows visually impaired pupils to talk to the computer. Not only words are understood, but also commands for navigating from place to place in a programme. There are also many ways in which Braille can be integrated into computer use. In addition to these particular approaches designed to create an inclusive classroom, in-class support is becoming increasingly widespread.

Teaching with in-class support

In-class support is where children who experience learning difficulties are taught within ordinary classes, with the learning support teacher working alongside the classroom teacher. Many schools, of course, use a mixture of withdrawal and in-class support. The use of specialist learning support teachers to help children within ordinary classes has grown since the early 1990s, and has become the most common way of working. Given this, it is important that beginning teachers are familiar with the role of specialist learning support staff and begin to explore how class teachers and learning support teachers can work together effectively, for the benefit of all children in the class.

Lovey (1995) concludes that probably the most important function of a support teacher is to develop a pupil's self-esteem by listening to stressed pupils, helping them complete work which otherwise would have added to the pile of unfinished bits, and often just by getting to know the pupils as individuals.

Much has been written about an ideal support model which encompasses regular liaison and joint planning of lessons between class and support teachers, a co-operative partnership of professionals of equal status in the classroom sharing the lead role (Bibby 1990). It is clear, however, that much support teaching in fact operates within an authoritarian, single-teacher-controlling, didactic framework (Lovey 1995). There are obvious contradictions and potential clashes inherent in a situation where, traditionally and conventionally, one professional has been seen to be alone in control, but suddenly a situation occurs where two professionals appear in the same place at the same time. One is obviously in charge and therefore has a legitimate role, and the other one can have nothing other than a subsidiary role. Bowers (1989) and Thomas (1992) highlighted sensitivity about the relative status of the class teacher and the learning support teacher as presenting problems in the move towards co-operative teaching. There is the important issue of who is in charge in the classroom. If the two teachers are not in close agreement, or do not get on, pupils will play one off against another. In the traditional, authoritarian, expert-teacher, apprentice-learner model of the classroom, one must be in charge, unless the support teacher is also an 'expert' in that subject area. Support teachers often lack status in the eyes of staff and pupils, lack authority and lack subject-specific knowledge. In this context, even the best qualified, most experienced teacher in the support role can be humiliated by lack of definition of role, being treated like one of the pupils, and not being able to act in the familiar capacity of authoritative adult.

As in so much of this area of work, implicit in these different aims, are contradictions. Arguably, if a support teacher's role is basically seen as managing the behaviour of 'difficult' pupils there is little incentive to consider change in pedagogy designed to include all pupils in the first place.

Despite these drawbacks, attaching individual support teachers to individual pupils is a form of provision which serves two very important purposes which have to be taken seriously when the beginner teacher is faced with the decision of how to organize this particular form of additional provision for pupils, since:

- it reduces the threat to the dominance and authority of the traditional role of the class teacher;
- it constitutes an easily identifiable arrangement and can be more readily justified as a discrete form of provision for pupils with statements if parents have recourse to the law.

In their discussion of forms of pedagogy which can respond to a range of differences in learning, attainment, aptitude and style, Clark *et al.* (1997) discuss the trend, in some schools, towards a much more flexible and creative use of support teaching. For example, individual teachers and/or groups or subject departments might be asked to put in a bid for in-class support for the purpose of developing differentiated strategies and schemes of work for all pupils. Alternatively, partnerships might be drawn up as formal arrangements, requiring class and support teachers to plan lessons together. Support teachers might also be regarded as full members of a department or year group, involved in any relevant planning.

Classroom activities

Following the moves to inclusive education has been a focus on classroom strategies to support the learning for pupils with special educational needs. Among many approaches these include:

- giving additional structure to pupils' tasks. This could take the form of breaking down the tasks into sections to build up sequences of ideas, providing pupils with writing frames to help them structure their work, building into the activity group discussion and opportunity to explore ideas through talk;
- narrowing the amount of material pupils have to work with;
- simplifying the language of instructions, textbooks. etc.;
- providing visuals for pupils to work with, rather than written descriptions;
- giving pupils first-hand experiences of things, such as visits to art galleries, a trip to France, science museums, the theatre or historical sites, etc.;
- using materials and resources so that pupils can experience and understand through sight, sound, smell and touch in addition to the written word;
- problems in using text, that is, any material in the classroom that pupils are expected to extract meaning from, whether it contains pictures or words or a mixture of both, require a range of activities designed to support reading and learning.

Materials, such as the QCA series (2001) *Planning, Teaching and Assessing the Curriculum for Pupils with Learning Difficulties,* have been produced to support teachers developing materials for use with pupils with special educational needs. Further guidance on inclusion strategies can be found at the National Curriculum inclusion website at www.nc.uk.net. A whole range of approaches to handling text for pupils of all attainments has been developed over the past years, strengthened by the work on literacy. (See Chapter 4 for further details relating to the KS3 strategy.)

Conclusion

The way teachers plan and implement strategies for the diversity of pupils' needs is a key expression of skill, knowledge and professional judgement. This chapter has considered strategies for working with a diverse range of pupils. The approaches described all require great skill in classroom management, and beginning teachers should not feel disheartened if at this initial stage they are not able to adopt such complex strategies. But teacher attitude has a major impact on those children who experience learning difficulties and it is here that issues of self-esteem and self-confidence can be more pronounced. Valuing the achievements of all pupils, together with a commitment to look critically at the learning planned and achieved, represents an important first step.

Teachers' individual approaches, the way their ideas are expressed in the minutiae of school life, provide a significant role model for all pupils and for the wider school community. Teachers, perhaps more than any other professional group, have a key role in responding to changes in social attitudes, but also of creating the impetus that initiates and accelerates such changes.

References

Bibby, G. (1990) 'An evaluation of in-class support in secondary school' *Support for Learning* 5(1): 37–42.

Bowers, T. (1989) *Managing Special Education,* Milton Keynes: Open University Press.

Clark, C., Dyson, A. and Millward, A. (1997) *Theorising Special Education*, London: Falmer Press.

DES (1978) *Special Educational Needs*, London: HMSO (The Warnock Report).

DfE (1994) *Code of Practice on the Identification and Assessment of Special Educational Needs*, London: HMSO.

DfEE (1998) *Meeting Special Educational Needs: A Programme of Action*, London: DfEE Publications.

—— (2000) *Guidance on SEN Thresholds,* London: DfEE Publications.

DfEE/QCA (1999) *The National Curriculum Handbook for Secondary Teachers in England*, www.nc.uk.net, London: HMSO.

Hallam, S. (1996) *Grouping Pupils by Ability: Selection, Streaming, Banding and Setting*, London: Institute of Education.

Lewis, A. (1995) *Special Needs Provision in Mainstream Primary Schools*, Stoke: Trentham.

Lovey, J. (1995) *Supporting Special Educational Needs in Secondary School Classrooms*, London: Fulton.

McGowan, P. and Turner, M. (1991) 'Raising reading attainment across the curriculum' *Multicultural Education Review* 12, summer, pp. 32–42.

Open University (1992) *Learning for All: (E242) Unit 1/2: Making Connections* (First edition), Milton Keynes: Open University.

QCA (2001) *Planning, Teaching and Assessing the Curriculum for Pupils with Learning Difficulties,* London: QCA. Subject specific guidelines which can be found on the National Curriculum inclusion website at www.nc.uk.net.

Sebba, J. and Sachdev, D. (1997) *What Works in Inclusive Education*, Ilford: Barnardos.

Thomas, G. (1992) *Effective Classroom Teamwork – Support or Intrusion?*, London: Falmer Press.

Thomas, G., Walker, D. and Webb, J. (1998) *The Making of the Inclusive School*, London: Routledge.

Tilstone, C., Florian, L. and Rose, R. (eds) (1998) *Promoting Inclusive Practice*, London: Routledge.

Widlake, P. (ed.) (1990) *Special Children Handbook*, Cheltenham: Stanley Thornes.

12 The teacher's wider role

Introduction

DfEE Circular 12/99 *School Teachers' Pay and Conditions of Employment* summarizes the statutory pay and conditions of employment of school teachers in maintained schools in England and Wales. This document refers to the requirement that teachers work under the 'reasonable direction of head teachers … (in relation to) … such particular duties as may reasonably be assigned' (para. 109). This broad-brush expression of what headteachers of schools deem to be 'reasonable' actually demands, in terms of everyday performance, an array of expectations, duties, levels of participation, areas of knowledge, skills and personal attributes which may seem nothing short of formidable to a beginning teacher. This chapter considers the practical dimensions and some of the clear rewards of what being 'professional' means through an exploration of the teacher's wider role in the school community.

The scope of the chapter

An outline of the interface between 'subject specialist' duties and 'wider role' requirements of the teacher forms the context for an exploration of the role of the form tutor and the opportunities inherent in working with a tutorial team and beyond it. The nature and scope of home–school partnerships are also broached in this chapter and the ways in which these are seen to act as a key tool in strengthening support networks for pupils. The final section sketches out the possibilities of beginning teachers making an individual contribution to whole-school activities and also focuses on the links between the school community and communities beyond. The much-expanded role that this implies for tutor-teachers indicates a need for multiple education and growth opportunities, planned and available as part of career-long professional development. Chapter 14 provides a more detailed examination of the issues and practical ramifications relating to continuing professional development within teaching. There are clear and wide-ranging professional duties placed upon teachers; these impact forcibly upon what is required of teachers and the way in which these duties are required to be demonstrated. These duties and requirements are outlined in the second section of this chapter. It is important first, however, to focus on the key elements it is safe to maintain that parents, pupils and outsider assessors of educational processes wish to see demonstrated every day in practical terms in a school community by tutor-teachers.

The social and personal care of pupils

The duty of care

The professional duties of teachers include that of safeguarding the safety and health of pupils whilst at school. This is commonly referred to in legal terms as 'the duty of care'. Teachers are expected to act *in loco parentis* – in the place of parents – providing the degree of care that could reasonably be expected from parents to their own children in similar circumstances and taking into account the degree of care that a teacher of a whole class can reasonably be expected to give whilst meeting this role. A set of expectations follows from this: teachers outline behaviour and response patterns required by pupils, they admonish and praise, they organize and pre-plan. As professionals they are expected to require the standards which a reasonably prudent, socially aware and careful parent would set.

All teachers, whether acting in a subject-specific role or as a form tutor, have to build this dimension into their work with pupils. Failure to do so could potentially result in situations damaging to the pupil and risk a charge of negligence of the *in loco parentis* role. This involves an ongoing assessment of risk. In considering a projected activity, the nature of the task planned, hazards which could reasonably be anticipated, the age and physical capabilities of the pupils and the environment in which the task will take place, need to be taken into account, as well as the school and LEA procedures which must be followed. Sometimes, even prudent planning reveals weaknesses or dangers and this undoubtedly results in further modifications to existing rules and procedures within the school community. What is clear is that every teacher acts in a pastoral role. So for a tutor, or someone such as a beginning teacher working to support a tutor, discrete tasks will emerge; but although tasks associated with a subject discipline may appear different in kind, in practice the two merge. One experienced secondary school teacher offered this view: 'We teach people not just subjects and almost every teacher in a secondary school also has to be a form tutor. Every one of us, anyway, is involved in pastoral care in our subject area; it is central, not a minor aspect of our role.' Established practice in the UK has stressed that the teacher's role extends to the social and personal care of pupils. The details of the wider professional role that this indicates are broached in the next section of this chapter. Schools commit heavily to this broad role and the sets of responsibilities attached to it. The Ofsted publication, *Inspecting Schools: The Framework* (2000), clearly recognizes this set of functions as an intrinsic factor contributing to effective schooling. The *Framework*'s evaluation schedule for short and long inspections highlights these questions:

- What sort of school is it?
- What can be inferred about pupils' attitudes, values and personal development?
- How good are the curricular and other opportunities offered to the pupils?
- How well does the school care for its pupils?
- How well does the school work in partnership with parents?

Tutors and tutor teams, working with processes and procedures which are designed to contribute concretely to school aims and positive assessments of the questions framed above form the heart of pastoral care systems in schools. Specifically, inspectors of schools evaluate and comment upon the attitudes of pupils to their school, their behaviour, including the incidence of exclusion, pupils' personal development and relationships, and the attendance rate of pupils on the school's roll. Judgements are made, too, about specific kinds of responses and abilities of pupils. In determining them, inspectors consider the quality of pupils' responses to their school and the quality of community life within the school, as shown below.

Quality of community life within a school

The degree to which pupils

- Are keen and eager to come to school
- Show interest in school life and are involved in the range of activities that the school provides
- Behave well in lessons and around the school and are courteous, trustworthy and show respect for property
- Form constructive relationships with one another, and with teachers and other adults
- Work in an atmosphere free from oppressive behaviour, such as bullying, sexism and racism
- Reflect on what they do, and understand their impact on others
- Respect other people's differences, particularly their feelings, values and beliefs
- Show initiative and are willing to take responsibility
- Have high levels of attendance.

In addition, a school will be evaluated in terms of how well it

- Cultivates pupils' personal – including spiritual, moral, social and cultural – development

Elements contributing to this are the extent to which a school

- Provides a broad range of worthwhile activities which meet the interests, aptitudes and particular needs of pupils
- Provides enrichment through its extra-curricular provision, including support for learning outside the school day
- Is socially inclusive by ensuring equality of access and opportunity for all pupils
- Provides pupils with knowledge and insights into values and beliefs … to develop their spiritual awareness and self-knowledge
- Promotes principles which distinguish right from wrong
- Encourages pupils to take responsibility, take initiative and develop an understanding of living in a community

- Teaches pupils to appreciate their own cultural traditions and the diversity and richness of other cultures
- Provides effectively for personal and social education, including health education, sex education and attention to drug misuse
- Provides for secondary-age pupils effective careers education and guidance, work experience and vocational education
- Has links with the community which contribute to pupils' learning
- Has constructive relationships with partner institutions such as other schools or settings.

(Ofsted 2000:37, 39)

Those aspects of personal, social, moral and cultural capacities required to be nurtured by the school and demonstrated by pupils may appear daunting to the beginning teacher when itemized. They simply provide, though, the detail of long-standing and familiar desired outcomes in the vast majority of schools. The specifics provided in *The Framework* ensure that at least an attempt at coverage of all of them is made by schools. What is useful is that the range and detail provided here, in effect, describe the heart of the form tutor's role and that of the tutorial team of which he or she is a part. It provides, too, a clear expectation of the school as the body responsible for the strategic planning that enables these processes and outcomes to occur.

Tutorial teams are organized in various ways by schools: by house, year group or some other vertical or horizontally arranged system, often reflecting their wider aims and particular ethos. The system chosen is usually managed by a deputy headteacher or assistant headteacher, and a group of heads of whatever pastoral units are adopted. All staff attached to them are particularly responsible for the well-being and progress of the pupils in their own unit. In daily terms, the range of responsibilities which will help to service the desired outcomes described in *The Framework* above is challengingly diverse. However, Ofsted has stated its view that:

> Where welfare and guidance are good, each pupil's needs and progress are identified and monitored by a member of staff who has the confidence of the pupil, and to whom there is ready and regular access. Pupils are able to maximise their opportunities; they feel secure and have high but realistic expectations based on a sound assessment of what they have achieved. Class teachers or tutors monitor pupils' progress and regularly discuss it with them and their parents. The school has clear, well-documented procedures for assuring pupils' well-being and health and safety when in the school's care. Governors, staff, parents and pupils are aware of these and observe them. A carefully structured and co-ordinated guidance programme, which includes health education and careers education and guidance, ensures that pupils are well-informed and are counselled wisely, particularly at points of transition. Teachers have skills appropriate to their responsibilities for guidance and have access to, and make use of, professional support both from within the school and from specialist services.

(Ofsted 2000: 73)

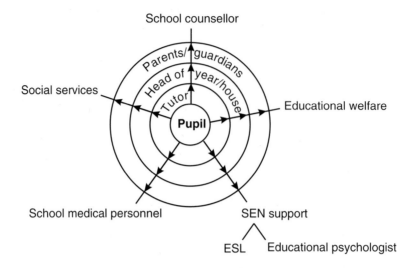

Figure 12.1 Pastoral support system for pupils

Source: 'OU E883 Study Guide' Stage 2, Block 5 Part C, Section 3, p. 235.

Care in action

The growing repertoire of skills a tutor develops and the influence generated from this, particularly with a tutorial form cared for during a period of four or five years, means that the different roles able to be played are extensive: as adviser, trouble-shooter, information-giver, counsellor, careers adviser, mediator, confidante or straight-talker. This list is by no means comprehensive, nor does any one role exclude others. The form tutor, of course, operates within networks of colleagues in different functions. One prime network is that set within the house or year system. What happens in the form room, and how, can be shaped to a large degree by decisions taken by senior colleagues about strategy, a point raised earlier. The pastoral support system which enables care in action to take place effectively might look something like Figure 12.1.

It may well be the case, given the particular roles taken by a form tutor and the proximity of access indicated in Figure 12.1, that she or he may be the member of staff who has the most information about a pupil in terms of school work, relationships with peers and with staff, personal concerns, and about his or her parents or guardians. Indeed, the tutor may well be the catalyst for a process of referral to be put in motion in cases, for example, of suspected child abuse, statementing, or medical or educational welfare concerns. Individual pupils may well look upon the tutor as the one person to trust or to arbitrate for them – with other members of staff, with other pupils, or with outside agencies. No form tutor should, however, be involved with outside agencies without the knowledge and support of the head of the tutorial unit or other senior staff and the parents or guardians. Such a wide set of responsibilities can be both onerous yet visibly rewarding. Everyday illustrations of care-in-action would be:

- A demonstration of knowledge of the individual child, his/her background and needs; familiarity with and up-dating of his/her school file and record, annual report on general progress.
- Seeking advice of and liaison with the head of house or year. Consulting about course options and careers.
- Notifying, initially to head of house or year, special difficulties encountered by the child. Appropriate follow-up to pupil's subject teachers.
- Fostering within tutees a school spirit and an attitude to school which allows maximum development of each individual within the group.
- Checking routinely, attendance, lateness, absence notes, uniform, standards of work and responses to others.
- Liaising with subject teachers and taking an active role in moderating the attitudes and behaviour of tutees proving difficult in subject lessons.
- Contributing to form, house or year activities, both social and academic.
- Attending and taking an active part in house or year assemblies.
- Participating in tutorial team meetings.
- Attending pupil case conferences.

Certainly, the different tasks encountered in any one school week will vary depending on the needs of pupils and how the tutorial management structure works. Some schools place a great deal of responsibility on form tutors for support and trouble-shooting. Others have a different support structure which may have been designed to take away some of the pressure from form tutors and put more responsibility upon heads of departments and heads of year.

The question might arise here: how have these descriptions of what care-in-action seems to mean come to be agreed and demonstrated in schools? The answer relates to the legal and professional duties which are placed upon teachers, and tutors, in their work. It meshes, too, with a UK educational culture of a commitment to a school ethos or corporate identity and the school-based commitments which accompany this. These important matters are addressed in the next section of the chapter.

Professional duties and school commitments

'Being professional'

Discussions of the term 'professional' in relation to teaching have been well-aired in recent years and particularly in terms of debates about what opportunities now exist for teachers to act autonomously and creatively in classrooms which have increasingly become subject to external regulation and monitoring. It is a view worth serious reflection by beginning teachers, during what has been a period of anxiety by their colleagues about over-regulation, that a set of national requirements has a proper place within a national public service sector. These requirements seek to guarantee nationally a group of basic standards of teaching within the teaching–learning process. It is a consideration to be weighed also that, in a new and fast-changing century, parents have been encouraged by government and its regulatory agencies to have high expectations of what education can and ought to produce for their children. Education is not alone in this respect; the health and police services have also experienced similar culture changes and expectations (see Chapter 1). It is a firm argument here that many opportunities *do* exist for creative and individually generated inputs to subject areas and to the wider professional role. It is to the practical implications of 'being professional' as a subject teacher at any level of experience and taking on one part of the wider professional role as a form tutor within the school community that this section is directed.

Circular 12/99, referred to in the opening paragraph of this chapter, goes on to outline those professional duties which are to be carried out 'in accordance with any directions which may reasonably be given to teachers' (ibid: para. 109). Placed beside this outline is the requirement upon headteachers to have 'an effective staff management system' in place which for 'many heads includes the practice of reporting to the governing body of the school about the professional development of all teachers' (ibid: para. 107).

'Professional development' has been a recurrent term in DfES documents in recent years and in schools, too. The descriptor 'professional' has traditionally been associated with a lengthy period of study-training; the presence of a self-regulating, publicly accountable professional body; a degree of autonomy; and an alignment with skills which are not commonly available. In the literature (and Chapter 1 refers to this) it has also been connected to a service dimension or certainly to a sense of moral purpose and responsibility. Setting aside here the fierce debates which have centred on teaching as a profession or otherwise, 'being professional' in teaching can be seen to arrange itself predominantly into two major areas: *professional duties* and *professional, school-based commitments*.

Professional duties

These duties relate to what a contractually obligated teacher is expected to perform under the 'reasonable direction' referred to above. They cover core, generic requirements of the role: teaching, assessing, reporting, being appraised, engaging in further training, covering for absent colleagues, and operating in an 'other duties'-wider role capacity. They include, too, personal and professional legal liabilities connected with race, gender, and health and safety issues. An indication of the wide reach of some of these categories of professional duty is given below.

Teaching duties

- Planning and preparing lessons and courses
- Teaching pupils in relation to their educational needs
- Assessing, recording and reporting on the attainment and progress of pupils.

Other duties

- Promoting the general progress and well-being of pupils and classes
- Providing guidance and advice to pupils on educational and social matters
- Completing records and reports on the personal and social needs of pupils and classes

- Communicating and consulting with pupils' parents
- Engaging in meetings arranged to carry out the above duties.

Assessment and reports

- Contributing in part to, or providing, oral and written assessments, reports and references relating to individual and groups of pupils.

Educational methods

- Participating in the preparation and development of teaching materials, methods of teaching, courses, assessment and pastoral arrangements.

Appraisals

- Participating in any agreed national framework for the appraisal of own performance or that of other teachers.

Review/further training and development

- Engaging in periodic review of methods of teaching and Programmes of Work
- Participating in schemes for further training and professional development.

Discipline, health and safety

- Sustaining good order and discipline; protecting pupils' health and safety on school premises and during external visits/activities.

Staff meetings

- Engaging in meetings connected with curriculum, administration or pastoral matters of the school.

Cover

- Supervising, and where possible teaching, pupils whose teacher is not present (usually no more than a three-day consecutive commitment in this matter is required by the staff of a school).

Public examinations

- Participating in arrangements for preparing pupils for public examinations and assessing pupils in relation to such examinations
- Recording and reporting such assessments
- Contributing to arrangements for pupils' presentation for these examinations
- Supervision duties during such examinations.

These professional duties are, of course, balanced by a set of rights owned by individual teachers. The right to a midday break means that a teacher cannot be *required* to supervise pupils in a subject-teacher or form-tutor capacity during this time. Moreover, statutory rights to leave for maternity, and for reasons of certificated sick-leave, are set out alongside the duties outlined.

Nevertheless, in practice, a great deal of individual (and extra) responsibility is implied in addition to the 1,265 hours per year stipulated as the maximum official number a teacher will be required to work. These 'directed' hours include class-teaching contact time, a 'pastoral' time input, a contribution to supervision duties, a schedule of subject, pastoral, whole-staff and other meetings judged 'reasonable', as well as pre-scheduled parents' meetings during the school year in support of the 'professional duties'. Crucially, they do not include, however, those activities which impact forcefully on fulfilling (or not) the stipulated professional duties. Further periods of time have to be allocated by a teacher in order to support school-based activities. So, the preparation of lessons, marking of pupils' work, formal assessment and report writing, the preparation and production of lesson and course resources of the subject teacher, compete for time slots with needful meetings with pupils and their parents of the same tutor-teacher. No indication of hours is given to teachers for these activities which are seen to relate in a powerful way to the vocational or moral purpose of professionalism: the day-to-day commitment and sets of responsibilities contained within a public-sector service role.

Professional school-based commitments

It is professional school-based commitments which contribute to effective teaching and learning just as forcibly as the formal responsibilities outlined on the previous page. Essentially, what might be called school-based commitments relate to the 'being professional' element of teaching. They mesh with the official set of professional requirements and, many would argue, they enable this formal set of duties to be met successfully. Certainly, the way in which they happen and the extent to which they occur equip teachers themselves to make judgements about the success of other colleagues in 'being professional'.

This range of school-based commitments can be seen to include:

- productive working relationships with a wide range of colleagues, personally and professionally
- an active appreciation of the ways in which an individual teacher can make a contribution to the social and cultural life of a school
- an appreciation of the importance of personal presentation of a teacher (speech, attitudes, conduct, cleanliness, dress)
- an understanding of how school policies on key issues will translate specifically into actions, attitudes, subject content and pedagogic matters within school
- an awareness of different audiences to the endeavours of school life: parents, governors, the headteacher, advisers, inspection teams; and the practical implications of this.

Both these sets of requirements are needed for any successful 'professional' response to a teaching job. Consider this advertisement for a Common Pay Spine (CPS) post for the factually-based post set out below:

Blaseney High School
For Children. For Learning. For the Future.

CPS Teacher of Science

Required for September 2002.

We are looking for a well-qualified, lively and enthusiastic Teacher of Science to join a well-resourced and hard-working department in new purpose-built accommodation within an improving school. The successful applicant will have an opportunity to teach the subject to GCSE level. This would be an exciting challenge for a recently qualified teacher but more experienced teachers would be welcome to apply.

The text makes it clear that qualities such as energy, commitment and tenacity will be required from applicants as part of a personal profile against which the expected range of professional duties and school-based commitments operate. It is an 'improving' school, and this gives the clue about an assumption that sustained efforts will be needed to support the improvement which has occurred and to better it. The heading: 'For Children. For Learning. For the Future.' indicates the mission area of the school. There is an expectation here that high activity levels, dedication and all the strands that 'being professional' involves will need to be constants.

These daily requirements, or constants, are fundamentally meshed with 'non-directed' activities and their impact on teaching and learning. Beginning teachers observe from their first days in school that a high-energy approach is not only desirable but essential. Taking each of the five school-based professional commitments areas outlined on p. 238, the following observations can be made about them:

Establishing effective working relationships with teaching and non-teaching colleagues

This is a central task and one which requires daily attention. Interactions of this kind relate to sharing common activities successfully, working in a variety of roles with the same and different colleagues; and establishing a sense of common cause and communal support.

An active appreciation of the kinds of contribution an individual can make to the social and cultural life of a school

This emerges through responding to tasks given by a head of department, a head of house or year, for example, and through a growing confidence in the beginning teacher about how to use experiences, skills and interests already possessed. Experience within the school itself and knowledge about its contextual factors help to shape a sense of what could be useful and productive in particular circumstances, and for whom.

The importance of personal presentation, in the ways indicated and in its widest sense

This has been much researched. The affirmation by pupils that teacher X 'has a good personality', when probed, arranges itself often into an appreciation by class pupils or by tutees of the personal attributes or skills of a teacher-tutor. A welcoming stance, a productive sense of humour, a revealed talent, a knowledge of things currently perceived as 'cool' by pupils and a clear and consistently applied sense of fairness relate to this dimension. 'Making a difference', the advertisers' incentive to potential entrants to teaching, is predicated upon this appeal. Marking, assessment, and other statutory duties form part of this frame but it is the ramifications of *impact* here – what is lasting and educationally meaningful in the widest terms – which mark out this area. Commonly seen newspaper columns about *My Best Teacher* are examples of the successful mesh between school duties and a school commitment which has been judged by 'consumers' as worthy of remark: remarkable, in fact.

An understanding of how school policies translate specifically into teaching and learning contexts

This requires, for example, that the successful applicant for the science teaching post, set out above, will manage to use chemicals, gases and equipment safely and teach pupils to do the same. It also implies that all teachers mediate their subject teaching within the context of whole-school policies. The teacher of English in the same school will be alert to integrating an appropriate amount of time for computer use, blending it with a range of other activities within lessons. It means too that their teacher of French will use strategies to involve all his pupils in oral as well as written responses. A further example might be that a mathematics teacher will be implementing the tutoring given at a staff meeting about how to enable a particular hearing-impaired pupil to participate in her class lessons. Such practices are often tangible expressions of school policy-making which in turn is itself often shaped by legislation and notions of 'fair play' for all within the school community. The Sex Discrimination Act (1975), The Race Relations Act (1976), specific sections of the Health and Safety at Work Act (1974) and of the Children's Act (1989) as well as the Disability Discrimination Act (1995) are examples of this. Other DfES circulars impact upon policy-making and processes too; Circular 10/95, for example, points to the responsibility of the education service in protecting children from abuse and of appropriate physical contact with children and the appropriate physical restraint of children. 'Professional school-based commitment', in this connection, then, can be seen as a multi-faceted outcome of expectations at different levels. It operates both in the macro-context of external bodies, such as the DfEE, Ofsted, the LEA and the local political situation, and within the micro-context of education, such as the school ethos, staffing levels in individual departments and shared or individual teaching rooms.

The attribute, an awareness of different audiences

This implies the need for appropriate responses to those, often external, agencies which impact upon teachers in the classroom. Generally, class teachers and form tutors without responsibility-promotion points only rarely interact with governors. In some schools, though, governors are routinely invited into classrooms and form rooms to share experiences and discuss key issues. Governors-as-mentors are not unknown in those schools which consciously encourage a dynamic interaction of their parts in order to enrich the sum of them. An Ofsted inspection framework will relate to the work of the whole school and assess its calibre as an embodiment of quality education processes, using resources well and setting high standards and expectations for all. It will also assess it as a community and against a set of expectations which include laudable values, expressed in positive attitudes (to learning, achievement, other people) and in its practices. A school will be expected to enable all pupils to make progress, and enjoy the wider life and opportunities on offer, safely and confidently. The classroom teacher will be expected to show an active affiliation to these opportunities and this wider life – in relation, for example, to extra-curricular activities – as a form tutor and subject department member. In these different capacities and demonstrations of them, professional duties and the school-based commitments and values of 'being professional' will merge and strengthen impact. Parents, too, will want to see indications of this – through consistent and encouraging responses to their children's class and homework tasks, reports written by staff and child-mediated reports, and opinions about class and tutorial happenings. Set alongside, and counterbalancing the need to meet the varied demands of external audiences, is a crucial point: pupils themselves represent the key, internal audience whose needs are mercurial and at the same time routinely core.

To sum up

Clearly, then, those teachers who are merely facilitators of learning or well-organized purveyors of curriculum content, and who view the tutor's role as predominantly an administrative function of their work, will not meet the demanding mix of professional attributes required in today's teaching posts, such as the one shown in this section. Michael Fullan's descriptions of nourished and continually developed school cultures, within which staff take an individual as well as collective responsibility in order to ratchet up internally identified new agendas and review processes (Fullan 1999), is near to a best-case description of the desired interplay of professional duties and 'being professional'. Having established the scope and interdependence of these terms for any teaching post, it is to other aspects the work life of the form tutor that we now turn in order to see the ways in which clearly stated requirements can be implemented in the classroom.

Care in everyday action: challenges

Confidentiality

Whatever the pastoral care system operating in a school, it is important to note that there are, and are required to be, boundaries beyond which a tutor is not obliged nor advised to pass. Managing to develop a close relationship with a form, while at the same time retaining professional distance, is part of the skill of tutoring and teaching. Finding the balance is part of the route to professional confidence and professional growth.

Students in schools, and beginning teachers, not infrequently find themselves the recipients of confidential information. If a tutee does request confidentiality, the tutor, in turn, must indicate that this is not a viable option. Advice can be given about whom to approach (a head of house or year, for example). If a confidential piece of information is given unsolicited, and if it appears to threaten the social and physical welfare of the child, a tutor, a subject teacher, or the form tutor is required as part of a 'professional duty' requirement to inform the head of house or year.

Listening and mediating

A form tutor is commonly called upon to listen to individual or groups of pupils, for example in discussions arising from a Personal and Social Education (PSE) lesson. Such a function requires that the tutor is:

- sensitive to both the verbal and non-verbal messages of the pupils
- responsive: demonstrating this, for example, by taking up a particular point
- probing, if need be, in order to help the pupils be more specific about what worries or angers them
- able to anticipate what might develop in order to avoid possible conflict.

In teaching, myriad situations and cases will present themselves for response by the form tutor. No two days will be alike.

Below are some typical situations which a beginning tutor might easily encounter:

- The class, unbeknown to you, has been planning a 'class trip'. One morning they present the proposals to you and ask you to help plan the visit.
- One pupil represents the class on the School Council. Two or three others from the class come to you and say that this pupil never attends and they want to propose someone else.
- Christmas is approaching and each class is asked to design and fill a Christmas hamper for distribution in the community.
- Television and newspapers are reporting a national fraud scandal. Where the blame lies is unclear, but a number of pupils ask if this could be discussed in class.

Most tutors would be pleased to see the growing cohesion of a tutorial group wanting to plan a visit, although they might intervene to ensure that, as the plans develop, specific development purposes are meshed into the plans. The problem of tutor-group representation could be used to explore further the nature and limits of pupil representation and the obligations it creates. Events such as Christmas activities draw people together, particularly when the planning involves the whole class, and a tutor would wish to foster this by attempting to engage all tutees, using their particular interests, strengths and resources. In the fourth situation, when a form group has good relationships and a good rapport they will often want to draw in the tutor's opinion on events of the day.

The precise response undoubtedly depends on the context and the tutor's experience. What is clear is that many similar (but differently arranged) situations will occur, providing an opportunity to develop dialogue and debate of depth as well as practical action on social and personal issues. Since schools have an important role to play in the social and moral development of pupils, these types of situations present powerful and enjoyable opportunities to further these aims.

Individual problems and difficulties of tutees also demand response. Whatever the particular outcomes may be, tutors are required to be possessors of an impressive and daunting list of personal characteristics and capacities. The beginning teacher rapidly learns that the tutor needs to be seen as, and actually to be, consistent, fair, firm, honest, reasonable and sensitive to the needs of pupils and colleagues.

Problems in the tutorial group

The situations which were described above are commonly found in a tutorial group. So are the kinds of problems cited below:

1 A pupil complains about being bullied and taunted by other pupils in the form.
2 A pupil known to the tutor as having difficulty making friends is found alone and in tears in the form room.
3 A teacher has asked a tutor to deal with a pupil who continually fails to hand in homework and with whom he or she has just had a confrontation. The teacher has declared that the pupil will not be allowed into class again 'until something is done'.
4 A tutor notices that a normally lively member of the form group has begun to arrive at school late, exhausted and irritable every day and has lost interest in other pupils.
5 On arrival at registration, the tutor is forced to interrupt a physical fight between two pupils. The rest of the class are inciting one or other of the pupils to continue.
6 A member of a form group informs the tutor that he or she has been offered drugs in school by an older pupil.

An experienced form tutor provided the following responses to these issues relating to individual tutees and their relationships with others:

> 1 A pupil complains about being bullied and taunted by other pupils in the form:
>
> > I'd reassure the pupil – find a safe haven (take the pupil seriously); inform the head of year; report the incident in writing. I'd never promise silence; problems must be shared.

2   A pupil known to the tutor as having difficulty making friends is found alone and in tears in the form room:

> I'd find time to talk through this issue (and probably other related issues) and be constructive in my advice. I'd find other pupils whom he or she feels can be trusted and explain the pupil's feelings to them. I'd try and provide active, positive support to allow future friendships to develop. I'd ask for regular feedback from the pupil.

3   A teacher has asked a tutor to deal with a pupil who continually fails to hand in homework and with whom he or she has just had a confrontation. The teacher has declared that the pupil will not be allowed into class again until something is done:

> I'd first find out from the pupil why the work has not been done, keeping calm and being careful not to provoke a 'no win' situation. I always try to develop strategies for making situations better, not worse! I'd explain why homework needs to be completed and maybe provide a classroom for the pupil's use, if space is a problem. With the pupil, I'd work out a regular timetable or routine to help and I'd ask for regular feedback from the pupil. I'd let the teacher know what I'd done.

4   A tutor notices that a normally lively member of the form group has begun to arrive at school late, exhausted and irritable every day and has lost interest in other pupils:

> I'd find time to talk to her/him, trying to gain trust and expressing my genuine concern for her/his welfare. I'd ask if there are issues which are worrying her/him, letting the pupil know what I'd observed. I'd try to help organize a useful routine, talking about sleeping patterns or home responsibilities, depending on what she/he says. I'd try to come up with practical solutions which she/he will be able to achieve. I'd always inform the head of year after such conversations.

5   On arrival at registration, the tutor is forced to interrupt a physical fight between two pupils. The rest of the class members are watching and inciting one or other of the pupils to continue:

> I'd attempt to stop the fight, but if this is not possible I'd send a pupil to get help immediately. Once they are separated I'd check for injury and get first aid if necessary. I'd isolate the two pupils, not letting them be left alone together. The head of year will help to get more information; you need help if there are lots of witnesses. The pupils' parents or guardians will probably need to be informed.

6 A member of a form group informs the tutor that he or she has been offered drugs in school by an older pupil:

> *I always believe the pupil; I never ignore such claims. I'd attempt to ascertain who the older pupil was and then inform the relevant head of year/house. This would be investigated by others in the school, and might involve outside agencies.*

It is crucial to remember that the kinds of responses indicated above will be based on experience as a tutor, through watching other teachers and by observing the school's responses across a range of situations. Issues of confidentiality may be involved and, importantly, there may be legal implications for actions taken. For that reason, particularly, beginning teachers need always to inform the form tutor to whom they are linked if any incidents occur.

Beginning teachers have to be especially alert to unexpected challenges. Pupils can, very occasionally, see a new or inexperienced teacher or tutor as a useful or welcoming person for sharing a worry or threatening situation. As indicated above, the tutor-teacher must tell the pupil that information must be shared with staff within the school. Advice and guidance must always be sought and taken from colleagues whenever challenges such as those outlined above arise, and in any phase of a teaching career.

High and low points

In 2001, another experienced teacher made the following observations about the highs and lows of a form tutor's work:

> My worst experience as a tutor? This was when one of my tutorial group, a boy I'd really worked hard with, was excluded. No one told me about this or consulted me. I can only imagine something confidential came up. I felt really let down, though …

> My best experience? Well, it's great that people who left in Year 11 last year – I'd had them for four years as a tutor – still email me and let me know what's happening … or ask me things. That's wonderful.

The tutor's role contains some of the same objectives and strategies as that of the effective classroom subject teacher. In essence, though, it is more wide-ranging, and arguably, ambitious.

The tutor and records of achievement

The National Record of Achievement

The processes connected with National Records of Achievement (NRA) are essentially those linked with formally recognizing pupils' achievements and experiences in order to present a more fully rounded record than subject-only achievements would reveal. The formal system currently existing was launched in 1991 and built on a range of other initiatives which had sought to motivate young people to learn and to make progress through processes of reviewing, recording and action planning.

Reporting documentation, though it varies from school to school, consists of more descriptive prose than used to be the case, embracing personal, as well as curricular, skills and achievements. Pupil involvement in this assessment has grown with the formal development in schools of pupils' self-assessment, target-setting and reviewing. The result has been a much fuller and more relevant picture of a pupil's progress to offer to parents, potential employers and other interested parties. In most secondary schools this record of personal achievement builds on records from the primary phase and follows through to a final summary document when a pupil leaves school. The National Record of Achievement constitutes a single, recognizable framework, so that individuals can transfer more smoothly within and between education, training and employment.

The form tutor has a key role in gathering and collating information about pupils. Where records of achievement are successful, they have become integral to the normal work and processes of the school. Tutors are often involved in one-to-one discussions with pupils in their tutor groups, agreeing the content of statements about progress and establishing appropriate targets for the future. In some respects, the process is similar to the style and purpose of the regular appraisal sessions that teachers themselves experience.

Records of achievement have the broad aim of helping pupils understand themselves better as well as celebrating their achievements. Tutors are given time to interview each pupil and to negotiate statements and targets with the aim of improving pupils' self-esteem and learning. This target setting is a positive way of encouraging the achievement of short- and long-term goals and of changing ways of working or behaving which might be standing in the way of a pupil's progress. It provides the opportunity for a one-to-one discussion of positive issues. The process is not, though, without its problems. Some reasons for this are that:

- Pupils' ability to express themselves varies enormously, and even the highest attainers in school need guidance in talking and writing about themselves even at a very basic level. 'I need to work harder' says very little of practical use! (See Chapter 9.)
- Ethnic, cultural, class and gender differences affect not only the language a pupil uses, but also the activities they choose to mention. For instance, pupils whose first language is not English may find tutorial (or subject) interviews very demanding linguistically; for others there may, for example, be problems attached to talking about activities occurring outside school.
- Pupils may not do themselves justice. They tend to focus on the easily remembered or surface features of improvement. Or they predominantly highlight things they have failed to achieve rather than more positive aspects of progress. There is now some research evidence that confirms the dangers of overly negative self-assessments. This is, in part, a reflection of an educational culture which has tended to be more explicit about failings than about successes.
- Pupils may interpret the process of reporting as an invasion of privacy and give responses which they consider the tutor wishes to hear and which have little or no relevance to them as individuals.

The Record of Achievement was conceived as a life-long process and in line with this provides the scheme free to all 16-year-olds and those on modern apprenticeships, national traineeships and other government-funded initiatives, as well as to secondary pupils in the compulsory school age span.

The DfES website at www.dfes.gov.uk has a link to details about the NRA scheme. What is made clear there is that an individual is expected to own, compile and up-date details contained within it. It is not an award in itself. It is designed to:

- encompass academic, vocational and personal achievements and experiences
- help plan learning and set targets for future achievement
- contain evidence of achievements, for example photographs and certificates
- motivate further achievement through acknowledging existing skills.

The expectation is that the NRA can help individuals to:

- prepare for an interview or a new job
- prepare for an appraisal interview
- adjust to promotion
- plan future training or qualifications.

During 2001, the NRA underwent a review prompted by Sir Ron Dearing's 1996 Review of Qualifications for 16–19-year-olds. The NRA Review Steering Group which followed made key recommendations for changes to the NRA system in order to extend the scheme more widely to 13-year-olds, and to provide better-quality support materials for the review, record and action-planning processes of the scheme. Closer alignment of the new materials, alongside employer standards such as Investors in People (IiP), is also an intention. Trials of the new materials were supervised by the DfEE under the name of *Progress File: Achievement Planner* (Figure 12.2). Evaluation of the trials (using a combination of in-depth questionnaire surveys, interviews and focus groups, as well as individual visits in order to talk to users and co-ordinators) found that, in general, users considered the materials to be an improvement on the current NRA. They particularly welcomed the shift of emphasis from the more static, presentational NRA document to the processes of setting targets, action planning, and reviewing and recording achievement.

'Progress File: Achievement Planner'

This is an interactive 'family' of materials, produced on paper and CD-Rom. Five guides: *Getting Started*; *Moving On*; *Widening Horizons*; *Widening Horizons for Trainees*; and *Broadening Horizons* are available and samples can be found through the NRA website link, indicated above.

What emerged from the trials and consultation period was the sense that the *Progress File* helped to develop an increased awareness of life-long learning, and was an incentive to focus on, developing and practising the skills of managing learning. It also was also cited as increasing development and awareness of key skills in users,

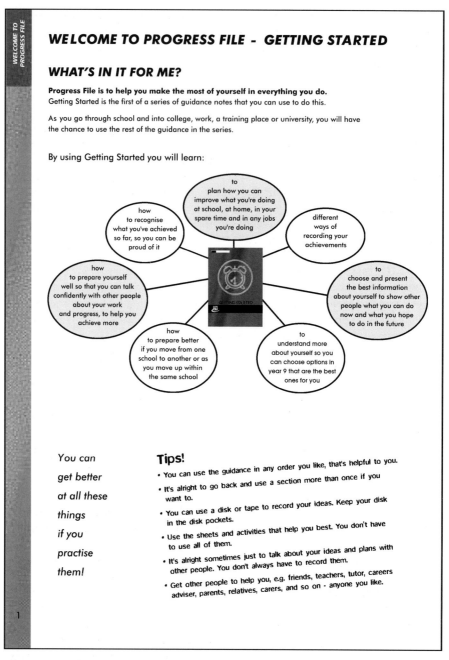

Figure 12.2 Progress File: what's in it for me?

eased target setting for individuals, and made a potential contribution to meeting whole-school/organizational targets. What emerged, too, was the view that these readjusted focuses and supports would foster a culture change by creating a holistic look at performance.

Clearly, any strengthening of the self-review, and joint target setting and review, processes will place even greater demands upon the form tutor in terms of time and of providing quality inputs to what is seen as a major tool in enlarging the skills' sets and widening the horizons of pupils.

The Personal and Social Education programme

The processual contributions of the beginning tutor into the personal and social education of pupils and in helping them to record and to respond to achievements of the widest kind for the National Record of Achievement scheme and developments of it have been detailed above. (Clearly, this same tutor, as subject teacher, will also contribute to pupils' academic achievement and social and personal gains demonstrated within a subject discipline.) By dint of access and the range of roles a tutor ideally can take, pupils can come to rely upon and be significantly influenced by such a tutor, whom they may be placed with for a considerable period of their secondary school life. In some schools the tutor may be asked to contribute to a whole-school Personal, Social and Health Education programme (PSHE) for pupils and be allocated a timetabled lesson to do so.

Such a programme will be widely based, encompassing sex and health education, careers education, study skills, and vocational, social, political and moral issues. Tutorial work will be planned and co-ordinated by a specialist senior member of staff and may involve extra-curricular work, exploring links with the community and the use of outside speakers.

In some schools, though, these themes are integrated into the conventional curriculum; so, for instance, sex education may be part of the science curriculum, health education part of the science and PE curriculum, and social and moral issues may permeate the whole curriculum.

In many schools there are elements of both of these approaches. Health and sex education, for example, often includes a tutorial dimension even when it is included in the conventional curriculum. Moral issues may be a part of religious education and corporate worship and be a part of the tutorial and guidance curriculum.

Tutorial work, whatever shape it takes, demands a great deal of the tutor. It requires skills in organizing group work and discussion; structuring situations so that pupils can express their thoughts to others but not feel threatened or sense that they are disclosing too much personal information; arranging activities to encourage peer-group interaction which is spontaneous but in control; and managing feedback sessions (see Chapter 4). Many of the strategies used by the tutor in her or his own subject teaching are applicable to tutorials and to personal and social education. The very strategies which distinguish an effective subject teacher help to define part of the role of an effective tutor. Clearly, careful planning, organization, evaluation and informed responses contribute to successful relations with a tutor group, just as they do with a subject-teaching group. Increased opportunities for contact with individuals and a more informed level of information about and from them, as well as an accepted, and indeed expected, greater flexibility of personal response to them, enable the tutor to react objectively and intuitively to the perceived needs of individuals and groups.

The school–carer partnership

Chapters 10 and 11 focused upon issues related to inclusivity in the classroom and the school community. It is worth stressing here that the same principles for inclusion operate, of course, in the tutorial setting. This is particularly so since it is here that problems and attitudes which threaten harmony will certainly surface at some point.

All of the valuable processes involved in such schemes as NRA, *Progress File* and the overt social and personal development programmes provided by schools will not have maximum impact unless there is a visible and effective home–school partnership in place. This involves a great deal more than parent–teacher associations or 'Friends of ...' bodies focused mainly on fund-raising, vital as these are. As Brighouse and Woods point out (1999), it must extend to communication about and involvement in the different ways the school has chosen to implement its statutory obligations relating to curriculum and care. Opportunities to support the work of the school at home and within school itself need to be described and put into action. These writers suggest that schools are not and cannot be self-sealed worlds. They:

> have become places where there are job opportunities for people with the right qualities but not necessarily with high-level qualifications, so jobs in the school meals service, in cleaning, as midday supervisors or classroom assistants have multiplied. Some head teachers have used the opportunity presented by these developments to recruit local parents to become support staff who themselves receive training on the job.
>
> (ibid: 39)

The implications here are interesting: school is a community, and an increasingly widening one, containing a whole range of adults belonging to the wider local community who may also be parents. There are rich implications of this, of course, for personal and social development work in school.

At a family–school level, it is the home–school agreement which impacts most forcefully. From September 1999, all state schools were required to enter into such an agreement with parents of pupils on roll. This has been seen essentially as a mechanism to include all parents (or carers) into the core work of the school as well as being a reminder to parents of their own responsibilities and rights as well as those of the pupil and of the school. It is also intended as a contract, to be signed by the parent, and, at secondary level particularly, by the pupil. The Secretary of State for School Standards gave the rationale for such agreements as:

> Even in the most difficult areas, schools can and do make a difference to the behaviour and attitudes of their pupils, especially when they are supported by other agencies. Good teaching, sound behaviour management, effective anti-bullying policies, clear rewards, consistently-applied sanctions and imaginative use of the curriculum all make a difference, and reinforce the message that all young people can achieve their potential (...).
>
>   ... We need to break the cycle of poor attendance, low educational achievement and damaged prospects in adult life (...)

Parents are a child's first teachers and it's an enduring relationship. They play a crucial role in helping a child learn. Children achieve more when schools and parents work together and parents can help more effectively if they know what a school is trying to achieve and how they can help.

(Smith 2000)

In describing the ethos of the school in the agreement, an outline of the different ways in which parents can become involved in the work of the school is given. These cover, for example, supporting homework study, asking questions about school life, attending parents' evenings and school functions as well as contributing special skills or interests to the school. Legal responsibilities of parents are outlined too, most notably those relating to pupil attendance and punctuality. The need for adherence to rules viewed as particularly important by the governing body of the school is stipulated in such agreements. Key regulations such as these, rooted in the declared ethos of a school, are put to parents in the original formulation of the agreement.

In the joint agreement, schools undertake to provide a high level of education provision and care for all pupils, and the internal review mechanisms of a school, as well as external inspection procedures, provide checks and balances upon this provision. Failure to comply with the signed agreement by the pupil will invoke the disciplinary procedures of the school, ranging from mild rebuke to permanent exclusion. This final sanction is not implemented lightly nor alone; the governing body of a school will be involved. Two key brakes operate here: an appeals system and the record a school has in relation to levels of permanent exclusion. Moreover, and before any permanent exclusion is considered, the school has a responsibility to invoke clear and recorded systems of support for pupils regularly failing to keep their agreements.

The tutor's role in relation to these processes, and the ones outlined in earlier sections of this chapter, is a vital one. It is the alert, active and involved tutor who can make a difference to what happens to individuals. A high-level skills-mix of negotiation, empathy, objectivity and humour, in an appropriately applied balance, can often rescue a tutee in danger of falling out of a synchronized balance with the school's activities and ethos.

Yet this is not the whole picture, of course. Issues of social class, minority ethnic groups, parents' own experiences in school when pupils themselves, media inputs to public perceptions, increased expectations of what schools can secure for pupils in terms of skills of the widest range, and of life expectations, have all produced undertows of different kinds. The central thread of the home–school agreement is that parents are co-educators and that it is at home that support of the best kind to the formal and informal educational processes provided by school can be given or denied.

Bastiani argues that a wider, more useful view of family–school relationships needs to include a detailed consideration of:

- the functions and key features of the two institutions
- the ways in which they relate to each other
- a realization of the dynamic and changing nature of the relationship

- the ways in which individuals who move between these worlds achieve (or fail to secure) an accommodation between the two
- any different political, social or philosophical differences between them

(Bastiani 1997: 6)

Certainly, a tension has arisen in recent decades relating to the identity of 'parents'. The politically driven push for parent input and parent power connected with the rhetoric of parent choice, along with such factors as the public airing of school examination results and league tables of school performance in this sphere, have created an image of 'parentocracy'. This was described by Brown as the 'third wave' in the development of universal public education, following basic elementary education for all, then 'meritocracy', an ideology based on age, aptitude and ability (Brown 1990).

This perceived and real emergence of parent power can provide a strong supportive feature of school life when volunteered in the spirit of the home–school agreement drive. Such power can appear threatening when support is withdrawn, leaving tutors and tutorial teams feeling vulnerable.

At its worst, the home–school relationship shows itself as one that is about suspicion and different values and modes of behaviour. At its best, and adapted for the secondary school context, there would be an all-encompassing web of interaction, such as illustrated in Figure 12.3.

In an era of rhetoric about partnerships, it is notable that partnership of a flexible, high-quality nature between home and school becomes and determines one of the most visible markers of a thriving school. Bailey described the process and product of such a partnership as most successfully depending upon and recognizing

the similarities and differences of each partner. There is overlap between the roles and expertise of teachers and parents, but there are distinct areas that are the prerogative of each. In short it is a means of establishing relationships in which both partners are respected and trusted, can communicate easily and clearly, and are working together towards the same end – a more effective and appropriate education for children.

(Bailey 1988: *Parents and the National Curriculum*, cited in Bastiani 1997: 15)

Tutors and teams: other contributions

The tutorial team

In secondary schools, tutors are subject specialists and operate most frequently as a team member of a subject department. Working with and for a head of house or head of year within a tutorial team is another distinct role to be taken on. It involves working with colleagues from other departments who themselves play clear roles as leaders or co-ordinators within them. These colleagues retain the status they have in their own subject units but are asked to take on a new role in this team which sets aside that status, yet uses the skills which reside in their subject role and which have generated such status in a different context. Any new status in the team arises from using honed skills in the new context. Successful teaching involves

Figure 12.3 Wheel of parent/carer involvement

Source: Bastiani 1997: 37.

collaborative team-working; successful tutoring requires the same. Each tutorial team seeks to implement effectively its school's policies but the ways in which this is done have distinct differences – shaped by the individuals who make up its membership. Creative solutions to challenges posed, and again these may be experienced differently by different teams in the same school, are sought here just as they are in subject teams. Such teams are differently balanced, too, and individuals often serve different functions, unwittingly or by design. Belbin (1981), for example, cites eight personality types that a productive, developing team should have. They are: *the chair* (a co-ordinating function); *the innovator*; *team leader*; *monitor-evaluator*; *company worker*; *team worker*; *completer*; and *resource investigator* (this last is the extrovert who promotes team spirit).

These roles are not meant to be mutually exclusive, and they certainly overlap, but a conscious consideration of them by the beginning teacher-tutor may well be helpful in terms of understanding the processes that occur in the tutorial team and seeking routes to make changes in one's own most regularly played role if this is judged as useful.

Contributing to whole-school initiatives

National Curriculum 2000 was much more explicit about how all subject teachers (who are predominantly also tutors) might contribute to pupils' ability to use language in different contexts. This aspect was explored in detail in Chapter 4.

Further, as occurred in primary schools, the requirements of the National Numeracy Strategy have called from September 2001 for a whole-school approach in the secondary sector. Citizenship, social inclusivity and ICT development are other pressing claims of the revised National Curriculum and increasing expectations of the education service. These cross-curricular claims may require the teacher-tutor to be a team member of yet other differently formulated groups. Teacher-tutors, then, working in a range of teams, serving different functions and using established and newly developing skills and roles, will be distinct marks of professional duties and school-based commitments of the twenty-first century.

Citizenship

From August 2002, Citizenship became a new National Curriculum subject at Key Stages 3 and 4, its Programmes of Study published in *The National Curriculum Handbook for Secondary Teachers in England* in 1999. These outlined the knowledge, understanding and skills judged as contributing to pupils' growth towards becoming informed and active citizens. Schools were encouraged to build upon existing provision and the *National Healthy School Standard* (DfEE 1999) was designed to support schools in encouraging a whole-school approach to citizenship, taking account of its local context.

Citizenship is described as having the potential, in conjunction with the framework for PSHE (Personal, Social and Health Education) at these same key stages, to enable pupils

> to play an effective role in society at local, national and international levels. It helps them to become informed, thoughtful and responsible citizens who are aware of their duties and rights. It promotes their spiritual, moral, social and cultural development, making them more self-confident and responsible both in and beyond the classroom. It encourages pupils to play a helpful part in the life of their schools, neighbourhoods, communities and the wider world. It teaches them about our economy and democratic institutions and values; encourages respect for different national, religious and ethnic identities; and develops pupils' ability to reflect on issues and take part in discussions.
>
> (QCA 2000a: 4)

The three strands of citizenship

This general statement of outcomes can be unpacked into three distinct strands. These are interrelated and are designed to be consistently present in education for citizenship:

- *Social and moral responsibilty* Pupils are encouraged to learn self-confident and 'socially and morally responsible behaviour', within and beyond the classroom, 'towards those in authority and to each other'.
- *Community involvement* Pupils are to learn about and to help in community projects in relation to their own localities.
- *Political literacy* Pupils will learn about the issues, institutions, practices and problems of democracy and the ways in which, as citizens, they can be effective in public life, in local and wider contexts, through skills and values as well as by knowledge acquisition. 'This can be termed political literacy, which encompasses more than political knowledge alone.'

(ibid)

The Programmes of Study for citizenship include the general teaching requirement on 'Inclusion: providing effective learning opportunities for all pupils', the three principles for inclusion being:

- setting appropriate learning challenges for pupils
- responding to pupils' diverse needs
- overcoming potential barriers to learning and assessment for individuals and groups of pupils.

Much of this entitlement dimension was broached in Chapters 10 and 11, and citizenship itself is both a confirmation of the principles outlined there and a widening of the knowledge, skills and understanding base which would both seek the translation of principles into action and strengthen the range of social and personal outcomes for pupils and, by implication, their communities.

And, as the logic of the planned outcomes implies, 'citizenship' is for everyone. Citizenship 'should be part of a school's celebration of the diversity of its population' and be part of the teaching and learning that supports inclusion, of gender, and of different social and ethnicity groups of a school. This social inclusion need is further underpinned by a strengthening of the Disability Discrimination Act (1995) to cover providers of education and the publication of an *Inclusion Index*, a mechanism for self-audit of progress made in relation to inclusion and produced by the Centre for Studies on Inclusive Education (CSIE) and other agencies. Specific ways in which citizenship can be visibly present in the values and ethos of a school include, in the QCA document *Citizenship at Key Stages 3 and 4: Initial Guidance for Schools* (2000a), examples such as: a shared mission statement; a welcoming atmosphere; codes of conduct for encouraging positive behaviour; challenging bullying or discriminatory behaviour; promoting courtesy and respect; raising and recognizing achievement; and valuing all members of the school's community.

Much of this is, of course, bedded deeply into the everyday life of many schools. Its required extension to all schools and its enhancement to include an accent upon the individual owning rights within, and owing responsibilities, to a community, as outlined above, marks a distinctive addition. It is, indeed, because schools have different levels of development in relation to PSHE and citizenship that schools are offered flexibility in the way they plan for and provide citizenship education. It is for this same reason, too, that the Programmes of Study do not contain a 'breadth of study' section. It is a requirement, however, that each school has a clear policy for citizenship, implements the citizenship order so as to teach the Programmes of Study and co-ordinates and manages successfully its implementation. Before planning occurs, the audit of a school's provision needs to provide answers to some central questions about citizenship-inclusion issues such as:

- What is currently provided?
- Where does it occur in the curriculum?
- Are the needs and entitlements of all pupils and communities within school being met?
- What are the outcomes?
- What is the evidence for claiming that these outcomes occur?
- Are citizenship links being fully developed at a local, national and global level?
- What are the local and national initiatives and opportunities available to a school?

Different forms of curriculum provision can be made for citizenship and this flexibility is designed to enable schools to take account of existing procedures and processes. So there exist the options of discrete curriculum time, of provision through different subjects, curriculum areas and courses, of citizenship events, activities or tutorial work or an appropriate combination of these options, as is the case with PSHE provision (QCA 2000b). To the first option, a caution is offered since the suffusion of the principles and practice of citizenship is a major aim which may well be undercut by its status as a 'subject'. Of the second option, taught and expressed within different curriculum subjects, examples might include:

- the role of the media in society and political and social issues in English and other literature
- political and other structures, such as the development of the franchise or party political system in history
- sustainable development and economic issues in geography
- diversity of cultures and religions in RE
- environmental issues in science
- economic and financial issues in mathematics or business studies
- issues of health policy and practice in PSHE and health and social care.

What, then, might this look like, interpreted imaginatively and with meaningful outcomes? Two examples are given below.

Citizenship in action

Pupils at Handsworth Grange School have set up a school radio station. The radio station aims to enhance the school's community action programme and to improve the school's communications with the surrounding community. Year 8 and Year 9 pupils make pre-recorded tapes to inform, educate and entertain listeners. The school has converted a music practice room into a radio and recording studio. The facility has also been made available to community groups. PSHE lessons are used to give time in the curriculum to the project and pupils are also encouraged to participate in the project through the extra-curriculum leisure programme. The project has particularly good links to the English curriculum and the development of key skills, as well as to the performing arts and to an expressive arts module of a youth award scheme. The project has been supported by the Rotherham Hospital and through the student enrichment programme at Sheffield College.

(ibid: 17)

Great Barr School has developed a range of activities to teach education for sustainable development (ESD). They have provided opportunities for pupils to become actively involved in initiatives such as creating duty teams for recycling paper and cans. It has allowed pupils to demonstrate that they can manage projects well and that they are able to articulate their opinions effectively through pupil representation or an action committee. Sixth–form students have worked with younger pupils. The school has consolidated electronic links with a partner school in Lyons and is exploring the feasibility of a joint environmental project. The school profile has been raised in the local community by working on a project with a McDonald's restaurant and further by students liaising with local press to gain media coverage. By giving pupils the responsibility for communicating information about ESD activities, their skills and confidence have greatly improved.

(ibid: 15)

Figure 12.4 outlines the key approaches. Assessment in citizenship 'offers pupils the opportunity to know how they are progressing; direct their efforts in areas of need; feel confident about their progress; gain credit for their participative activities' (ibid: 25). Form tutors and teachers record achievements and provide evidence of attainment. Award schemes and sources of support for teachers and schools are provided in an Appendix to guidance supplied to schools.

Controversial issues clearly enter this initiative for understanding and participation, and managing these successfully so that pupils have access to balanced information and ground rules for enquiry is part of a tutor-teacher's challenge in form-time, within subject areas, and actively in the school community and the linked communities beyond.

A concepts approach	A skills approach	An enquiry approach
• Democracy and autocracy • Co-operation and conflict • Equality and diversity • Fairness, justice and the rule of law • Freedom and order • Individual and community • Power and authority • Rights and responsibilities linking to aspects of knowledge and under-standing such as: • human rights (including anti-racism) • sustainable development • political and legal systems and processes • global citizenship • financial capability • respect and tolerance (including conflict resolution) • public, voluntary and community services.	• Skills of enquiry and communication will be used to explore contemporary issues, problems or events. • Such issues will be local, national and international. • Examination of media coverage of these issues will provide a useful basis for the development of skills of participation and understanding. This approach uses the development of the skills required (parts 2 and 3 of the Programme of Study) as the basis for promoting the knowledge and understanding of the Programme of Study (part 1).	The key concepts, knowledge, skills and understanding underpinning the Programmes of Study – promoted through questions. Typical Key Stage 3 enquiries might include: • Why is it important to be tolerant and to resolve conflict fairly? • How do individuals relate to their communities? • When we speak of global citizenship what do we mean? Typical Key Stage 4 enquiries might include: • How have the diverse national, regional, religious and ethnic identities in the UK emerged? • What is sustainable development? How viable is it at local, national and international levels? What happens if it is not? • In what ways do the law and human rights and responsibilities affect people's lives?

Figure 12.4 Three approaches to citizenship

School as a community and communities beyond

Any thriving school community is a widely based, open-looking one. Its pupils may ostensibly belong to a homogeneous group, by virtue, say, of restricted academic or geographical intake. Nevertheless, within such formal descriptions exists a great deal of difference in financial circumstances, in motivation, in family structure, and in relation to the physical, mental and personality differences that make up individuals. Adult constituents of the school community are similarly diverse in their attitudes, values, abilities and actions. They serve a wide range of functions too: as teachers, classroom assistants, welfare support workers, secretarial, cleaning and ICT staff, providers and supervisors of meals. There are others who visit to support the work of the school, among them careers and health advisers, police officers, providers of spiritual and cultural support, adjudicators, inspectors, local officials, and pupils and staff from other schools. This is an indicative rather than a comprehensive list. At its best, a school community integrates these differences, skills and functions harmoniously and uses them to develop itself and its capacities as a learning organization.

At the heart of this capacity for learning and renewal is the ability to be *inclusive of all* members of the school community. Chapters 10 and 11 focused on the details relating to this issue and to key referents of the issue, such as gender, social class, race and cultural diversity and special educational needs. The National Curriculum itself is predicated upon the principle that 'schools have a responsibility to provide a broad and balanced curriculum for all pupils' and one 'that meets the specific needs of individuals and groups of pupils'. Advice about detailed application of the three principles for inclusion: setting suitable learning challenges; responding to pupils' diverse learning needs; and overcoming potential barriers to learning and assessment for individuals and groups of pupils, is available from the National Curriculum website at www.nc.uk.net/general/general_inclusion/ All tutors will at times be placed at the sharp end of what these principles and practicalities entail.

Pupils who frequently change schools

Pupils who are notably mobile are often excluded from the opportunities available to the rooted majority of a school community. Children in this category often are characterized as living in poverty, unable to communicate well in the English language, and poorly housed. They may be travellers or 'looked-after' children in care. In the most recent figures available, relating to 1998, Ofsted estimated that there were 90,000–120,000 travellers in the UK and that 40,000 of these were children of school age. In addition, there were 50,000 'looked after' children in the care of local authorities in the UK (Henthorne and Dobson 2000). Schools near to bed-and-breakfast hotels are often a temporary base for different immigrant groups, some of whom have not received regular schooling or amongst whom the importance of girls' education is down-played.

There are pressures and opportunities for schools who experience such short-stayers in their community. An improving school wanting to sustain pleasing examination results may, unconsciously at least, regard this as yet another demand on already-stretched resources. An open, learning school will see the opportunities for education in the cultural diversity created and make these real for the mobile pupils as well as for the long-term pupils. Such situations require that inspectors of schools in which this is a feature need to be fully aware of the potential implications of mobility for school performance and other aspects of a school's life and weigh these factors appropriately.

Form tutors' expertise will undoubtedly be strengthened by such challenges and resource implications. If their schools' structures, ethos and the processes which support them are in place, the tasks involved are negotiable. Being part of a forward-looking learning community helps. Such an organization would have all or some of the following features: an agreed policy about the practice of teaching and learning; a teaching and learning staffroom; curriculum enrichment and extension; the celebration of teaching and learning; collaborative teaching, planning and assessment; an effective use of learning resources; collective review; professional development; action research; and community involvement in the learning school (Brighouse and Woods 1999).

Local and global communities

Any school, too, which implements central, cross-curricular questions such as the ones below, consistently and as part of a planned programme of intervention by all staff, to develop an awareness of detail, complexity and diversity, will be providing real support to the teacher-tutor responsible for care-in-action for all members of the tutor group.

Buck and Inman (1992: 16–17) identify a bank of questions to be addressed here, useful for a form tutor to pursue with a class, relating to power, control, influence and the balance of individual and co-operative living within communities.

These questions, and the processes and activities suggested by them, provide clear links between the school community, and local, national and international communities. Living with and learning about differences to enrich individual and corporate experience are their potential end-products. This can be so whether the school celebrates Divali, holds achievement assemblies, mounts an anti-bullying campaign, raises funds for European or other refugees, or implements a 'charity week' which supports the local hospice or drop-in centre. Many schools are currently living out many of the aspects outlined in the DfEE document, *Developing a Global Dimension in the School Curriculum* (2000).

The purpose of this publication is 'to show how a global dimension can be incorporated into both the curriculum and the wider life of the school. It means addressing issues such as sustainable development, interdependence and social justice at both the local and global level. It builds knowledge and understanding as well as developing key skills and attitudes'(ibid: 1). These relate, in turn, to citizenship, social justice, values and perceptions, diversity, conflict resolution and human rights.

One interpretation of this could be that, at Key Stages 3 and 4, a tutor may well be asked to contribute to a planned programme during which pupils learn about the effects of stereotyping and prejudice and how to challenge them assertively, whilst recognizing the importance of goodwill in relationships. By doing this pupils are encouraged to develop their own confidence and willingness to empathize with people very different from themselves. Clearly, if the same tutor also teaches English, further opportunities might offer themselves in texts such as Harper Lee's *To Kill a Mockingbird*, Mildred Taylor's *Roll of Thunder, Hear My Cry*, Robert Westhall's *Stone Cold* or Chinua Achebe's *Things Fall Apart*. If the tutor is a teacher of art and design, this work could be extended by asking pupils to explore the ways in which artists working in different cultures produce images, sounds, symbols and objects to convey meaning. The tutor who teaches PE may seek to enhance tutorial understandings by arranging for pupils to participate in sports played globally and to discuss similarities and differences and implications arising from this. The following examples, taken from the DfEE publication referred to above, indicate some possibilities for tutor contribution to a whole-school global awareness endeavour.

Example 1

Design and Technology

Pupils explore the effects of technology on the development of societies and the pupils' own lives. By doing this they can develop an understanding of social, environmental and sustainable development issues and explore ways in which the world can be improved. They can learn how the trading neighbourhood is the whole planet and that all communities, however remote, are potentially helped by global trade.

Example 2

Citizenship

Pupils learn about human rights, the media, the diverse nature of society in the United Kingdom and globally, and the need for mutual respect and understanding. They learn about the role and work of national and international organizations, and the importance of resolving conflict fairly, and develop the skills to discuss and debate topical issues. They learn to consider others' experiences.

By doing this they can become informed citizens and understand the world as a global community. They can learn about global governance and address such issues as international development and why it matters. They can develop their interest in topical, global issues and can become willing to take action and actively participate to improve the world.

Schools in the Manchester area participate regularly in an Earth Summit Day organized by the Development Education Project. They role play delegates discussing issues around development and the environment. In the schools' Earth Summit Day each class takes on roles representing the summit organizers, the international press, multinational corporations, development organizations and geographical regions. Discussions centre around questions such as 'How can international trade become fairer for all countries?' and 'How can we develop sustainable use of the world's resources?' Pupils gain an understanding of north–south inequalities and sustainable development as well as developing their skills of debating, presentation and co-operation.

[The document acknowledges that whole-school activities and initiatives in this context have been directly addressed to …]

show not only how a global dimension is incorporated across the curriculum but also how it has become part of the whole school ethos. This might include looking at how the school provides a basis for the spiritual, moral, social and cultural development of its pupils, and how understanding and respect are promoted.

These issues, as well as specific subject opportunities, can be expressed in mission statements and clearly incorporated within the school development plan. This helps to ensure that a global dimension features in all aspects of the school's work as well as being demonstrated through displays and exhibitions around the school, and being discussed in assemblies and collective worship.

(DfEE 2000: extracts from Key Stages 3 and 4)

One of the most exciting aspects of an enhanced global dimension is the opportunity it provides for whole-school activities. These can range from activities taking place in just one school, like an 'International Day', to a co-ordinated effort involving a number of different schools as well as the wider community. There are also opportunities to involve parents and local organizations by inviting them to contribute their knowledge and experience of the wider world in assemblies and as part of classroom discussions.

That activity, enhanced understanding and diversity are in evidence in multiple numbers of schools is not in doubt; that these facets can become part of the entitlement curriculum for all children in school is part of the thrust of the DfEE publication whose contents and strategies rest at *Recommended* status in relation to the National Curriculum.

Reducing administrative and other burdens: good practice examples

These are appropriately exciting possibilities for tutor-teachers and their different subject and tutorial groups and teams to appreciate and to venture upon in school communities which themselves operate within global contexts – or what is now routinely called a global village. Mindful of this, it is neither a deliberately prosaic nor unconsidered decision that the final section with which this chapter ends is focused on the reduction of administrative tasks for tutors. Few of the local, national or international community links will be made and nurtured if valuable time is swallowed by routine and copious administrative tasks. And it is the acknowledged burden of multiple clerical tasks which undercut, during busy work days, attempts to strengthen communities of any description. Only clear, imaginatively developed procedural systems can successfully release form tutors to spend time pursuing actively the goals and considering the kinds of debates and strategies indicated in this chapter, in order to secure quality relationships in strong communities.

The two 'good practice' examples in Reading 12.1 give some indications of the possibilities.

Reading 12.1 Exemplars from 'Cutting Burdens on Teachers'

Example 1

Hartsdown Technology College – collection of money from pupils

Hartsdown Technology College is a mixed 11–18 community school of about 1,100 students.

Problem

This school collects nearly £40,000 per annum in cash and cheques from pupils for a wide variety of activities such as school journeys, educational visits, sale of books and materials and charity collections.

Responsibility for the collection and safekeeping of these monies was, until three years ago, the responsibility of tutors. Money was handed to them in the 15-minute registration period at the beginning of the school day. This was considered to be unsatisfactory for the following reasons:

- the process was burdensome to tutors and made inroads into the small amount of time available for more important issues;
- accountability for money paid in was confused;
- formal recording and issuing of receipts to pupils was not practicable;
- teachers were unable to guarantee the security of cash left with them and regarded the task as an unreasonable responsibility.

Solution

The school has transferred all money collection, with the exception of three non-uniform days per year, to the school office. The system works as follows:

- the teacher responsible for the activity informs the office that money is to be collected, how much is due from each pupil and by when;
- pupils pay money (in whole or in instalments depending on circumstances) direct to the designated member of the office at the reception desk;
- pupils are encouraged to do this between 8.15 and 8.50 am (start of registration) but may do so at any time during the day;
- on payment the pupil is issued with a receipt which records the amount, the purpose and any amount still outstanding – the office retains a copy;
- each payment is recorded as it happens on a daily ledger by the member of the office staff, with daily totals for each fund recorded in the accounts.

The additional cost of the system is in the time of the member of the office staff responsible for collecting and recording payments (accounting and banking money collected was already done in the office under the old system of collection). The additional time is estimated to average 5 hours per week of a clerical officer's time across the school year, which equates to a cost of about £1,000 per year.

Benefits

The benefits of this system are threefold:

- greatly improved arrangements for collecting, recording and accounting for money, and for ensuring its security and the protection of staff;
- relief for teachers from a task which many find inappropriate, risky and burdensome;
- a saving of scarce tutorial time.

The teacher time saved is estimated to average three minutes per tutor per day throughout the year, or a total of about 315 teacher hours per year across the school.

Wider application

Hartsdown College believes this system can work in any secondary school. However, the following key features will aid success:

- a designated member of office staff who is on duty for at least 30 minutes before the start of school;
- access to back-up for that staff member at peak periods (mainly early July) or in the event of absence;
- an open reception area where there is room for pupils to queue and wait without disrupting the circulation of others.

Example 2

West Park Secondary School – monitoring pupil attendance and discipline

West Park School is a foundation 11–18 secondary school with 1,258 pupils.

Problem

The school monitors attendance by Optical Mark Reader sheets and the information is passed to the year tutors. Part of their role is to monitor pupil attendance and general discipline so that they have an overview of each pupil in these areas. The year tutors currently keep all their records on paper so that they are available to them as they ring or contact parents by letter or in interviews.

The school wanted these records to be available to other appropriate senior staff so that pupils can be tracked across both academic and pastoral fields.

The school intends to extend the role of these year tutors in order to make them responsible for the overview of each of their pupils academically as well as pastorally. This will require them to have access to the SIMS Assessment and Recording module.

It will also require the detailed pastoral records – often kept in narrative form in relation to particular incidents – to be kept electronically.

Solution

The school is using the SIMS MIDAS module together with the Assessment and Recording module. This enables staff to have ready access to up-to-date information on both academic and pastoral aspects of pupils.

As part of the implementation of this solution the school has purchased an additional five networked workstations at a cost of £5,000.

Benefits

The use of the two systems in concert allows the academic progress of pupils to be tracked alongside their pastoral development. This will allow more specific monitoring of individual pupils to compare academic and pastoral progress: for example, pupils with emotional and behavioural difficulties or underperforming pupils.

More immediate correction/praise and target setting is also possible as the data can be analysed electronically in ways which go beyond the current mental agility of a busy year tutor.

Information about pupil attendance and discipline, formerly kept on paper, is now available on computer. Checking for correlations in patterns of indiscipline, non-attendance, etc. is easier and, as training becomes more comprehensive, staff will become more creative in their use of the information.

It is anticipated that, over the year, 250 hours will be saved in form-filling.

Wider application

The system provides one model for any school wishing to adopt a comprehensive reporting and pupil monitoring system.

Source: www.dfee.gov.uk

What has become increasingly clear in recent years is that the sustained drive for higher standards in terms of examination grades and for high-quality professional pastoral care from tutor-teachers, indicated by such developments as the Progress File and home–school agreements, cannot sit easily with some of the traditional, time-consuming administrative tasks required of tutors. Awareness of this and of a declared commitment to reduce bureaucratic burdens on teachers was raised in Circular 2/98 with the rationale that 'Cutting unnecessary burdens on teachers helps us to raise standards in schools, and that is our top priority' (Secretary of State for Education and Employment 1998: para. 1), and, in the Green Paper *Teachers: Meeting the Challenge of Change* (DfEE 1998). Good practice guidance has been offered on the web by the DfES. A series of actual exemplars points to possible applications for schools and their senior managers weighing administrative necessity with the higher educational goals they wish to pursue.

These kinds of projects, and evaluations of them by practitioners, are useful points of reference for other school communities wishing to highlight and to develop quality tutor-tutee relationships. They potentially create more time, too, for valued outcomes of the kinds offered by *Progress File*, as well as for schools' own initiatives relating to the wider personal, cultural, social, moral and spiritual development of their pupils.

Conclusion

The scope of this chapter has necessarily been an expansive one. The wider role of the tutor encompasses the professional duties and school-based commitments outlined at the beginning of the chapter. The school community in which this wider professional role operates is a multi-faceted and demanding one. Working in tutorial and other teams, contributing skills and benefiting from the experience and strengths of other colleagues in these changing contexts, enables teachers to reach out to the communities beyond: local, national and international. The work of the form tutor, a substantial element of this wider role, ranges from myriad administrative tasks to potentially profound impacts upon the personal and social growth of individuals within the form group. At its best the duty of care becomes a great deal more. In order to support and nourish these ongoing and constantly widening requirements of the tutor-teacher's subject and wider, pastoral role, continuing professional development can be viewed as a necessity, an aspect which is considered in Part 3 of this book.

References

Bastiani, J. (1997) 'Linking home and school' *Exploring Educational Issues,* Unit 3, Milton Keynes: The Open University.

Belbin, R.M. (1981) *Management Teams: Why They Succeed or Fail,* London: Heinemann.

Brighouse, T. and Woods, D. (1999) *How to Improve your School,* London: Routledge.

Brown, P. (1990) 'The Third Wave: education and the idea of parentocracy' *British Journal of Sociology of Education* 11(1): 65–85.

Buck, M. and Inman, S. (1992) *Whole School Provision for Personal and Social Development: The Role of the Cross-curricular Elements,* Curriculum Guidance No.1, Centre for Cross Curricular Initiatives, London: Goldsmiths' College.

Dearing, R. (1997) *The New Qualifications Framework 16–19,* (revised version), London: HMSO.

DfEE (1998) *Teachers: Meeting the Challenge of Change,* London: DfEE publications.

—— (2000) *Developing a Global Dimension in the School Curriculum,* London: DfEE Publications.

Fullan, M.G. (1999) *The New Meaning of Educational Change,* London: Cassell.

Henthorne, H. and Dobson, J.M.(2000) 'Pupil mobility and social exclusion' *Education Review* 13(2).

Ofsted (2000) *Inspecting Schools: The Framework,* London: The Stationery Office.

Qualifications and Curriculum Authority (2000a) *Citizenship at Key Stages 3 and 4: Initial Guidance for Schools,* Suffolk: QCA Publications.

—— (2000b) *Personal, Social and Health Education at Key Stages 3 and 4: Initial Guidance for Schools,* Suffolk: QCA Publications.

Smith, J. (2000) 'Achievement, not exclusion must be our mission' *Education Review* 13(2): 15–19.

3 Developing as a professional

13 Effective and improving schools

Introduction

In the early stages of a career, teachers tend to focus on personal concerns. How well am I doing? What do more experienced people think about my progress? How am I getting on with my class or classes? Is everyone in the class learning in the way I intend? Will I be able to find the time to prepare for next week? For a newcomer to the teaching profession and to working in schools, much of the environment is unfamiliar. This can affect the physical perceptions of the school. The school playground, for example, often looks bigger on first sight than when it becomes familiar. Anyone with limited experience of schools would have difficulty making judgements about the school from his/her initial observations. Experienced teachers and school inspectors, however, often say that they can judge a school after just a few minutes in the reception area or a walk through the corridors. Such claims may need to be taken with equanimity. Schools can have bad days, and, if a problem arises, the reception area is not the best place upon which to make short-cut judgements. There is, however, some truth in the idea that experience of visiting many schools enables people to establish criteria to differentiate the more from the less successful schools. Consider these two scenarios:

School A

The bell rings. There is lively talk between pupils as they move purposefully to their lessons. A teacher is encouraging a group of loiterers who are hanging about. The atmosphere buzzes with energy and excitement, but both pupils and teacher are at ease and confident. The walls are bright with pupils' work and notices about after school clubs and other extra-curricular activities. Another pupil escorts an adult into the classroom. Mrs Akpenate is visiting to take part in a Year 10 oral history project.

School B

The classroom door is flung open seconds before the bell rings. Pupils rush out, not caring to notice or avoid the school dinner lady walking up the corridor. They leave behind their teacher who is collecting in the worksheets and books strewn across the tables and classroom floor. This is the teacher's second 'cover' lesson of the week. Staff illness is high. He can't wait until the end of the term when he moves to a new school. Six other colleagues are leaving too.

Down the corridor, pupils bang on the fire escape doors – this is a regular playground activity on a wet day. There are sounds of a skirmish and scuffle, so he decides to go the long way round to the staff room and avoid it. After all, he hasn't witnessed these events.

It is not difficult to pick out from these two sketches which is likely to be the successful and the unsuccessful school. Ofsted reports describe these differences in language which is more prosaic and which focuses mainly on educational standards and their contributory factors.

> Marking of students' work gives students too little guidance on how to improve. Unsatisfactory behaviour affects learning in a significant minority of lessons particularly in science, information technology, geography and physical education. The school gives insufficient information to parents about what is taught and their daughters' progress. Standards in literacy, numeracy and information technology capability are low. Teachers in most subjects give students insufficient support to develop these skills.
>
> (Ofsted report, inner-city girls' school, 1999)

> XXX is a good school with several outstanding features. GCSE results are improving faster than the national average. There is an outstanding range of extra-curricular activities. There is consistency in the good quality of teaching. Pupils are well supported by a dedicated and committed teaching and non-teaching staff. The school has outstanding leadership. Most pupils are well behaved and courteous. Relationships in the school are good … . Pupils enter the school with attainment levels below the national expectation and leave with levels of attainment that are in line with national figures … .
>
> (Ofsted report, girls school – in the same inner-city LEA, 1997)

These extracts clearly point to some of the features of successful and unsuccessful schools. Some of the features are obvious and would occur to any visitor. Others require a more detailed analysis of the school records. They both, however, raise the question as to why some schools succeed whilst others are less successful, and what developments are required in order for schools to improve. Part of the answer lies in the ways in which success is measured, but successful schools are not just about pupil attainment. They are also about the values they teach and the ethos and attitudes they foster.

The aim of this chapter is to introduce beginning teachers to the debates about what constitutes an effective/successful school and approaches to school improvement. It considers:

- an exploration of what is meant by effective and improving schools
- the impact of government policy on school improvement
- the research evidence for effective practice in school improvement.

Effective and improving schools

There has, of course, always been discussion about what makes schools successful. Research into school effectiveness over the past thirty years has produced a widespread acceptance of the conviction that schools do make a difference and that teachers can operate on the factors which matter. However, over the last decade or more there have been a number of developments, such as the publication of school league tables, which have given greater significance to the theme and provide the basis for considerable contemporary debate.

The debate, though, has been undercut at times, by a conflation of the two terms, *school effectiveness* and *school improvement*. Moreover, some findings of school effectiveness research have appeared to offer routes to school improvement. Certainly there has been strong support for the idea of identifying variables associated with effective schools and offering these as agenda items to support schools attempting to assess and improve their own performance. This performance would typically relate to a package of school characteristics such as strong educational leadership, an emphasis on basic skills, an orderly and safe environment, high expectations of pupil attainment and the frequent assessment of pupils' progress (SOED 1990). The implication offered was that factors associated with effective schools could be placed as a template upon the practices of ineffective schools and that action for improvement, through duplication, could then begin to occur. This approach was seen as providing a different but demonstrably proven structure for a school's pathway to improvement and so to effectiveness. The rationale for the effectiveness–improvement conflation is inherent in such prescriptions. It raises some key problems, however, in relation to easy transference.

Brown *et al.* (1995) offer a strong critique of a presumed link such as this. Their case focuses on structural and processual matters impacting upon the issue. These relate to management and organization issues, the different functions served by school effectiveness and school improvement studies, research findings, and social class issues. All these elements combine to undercut certainties relating to school effectiveness–school improvement connections.

Management and organization issues

School effectiveness research has focused predominantly upon factors associated with the success of schools. These are most commonly related to observable outcomes, the relatively stable characteristics of schools that are readily available for measurement, such as examination results, basic skills, attendance and exclusion rates, for example. In contrast, school improvement research and school improvement initiatives have largely focused upon context-specific needs and processes.

Brown *et al.* argue that the top-down model of change, operating nationally and within schools, places an emphasis upon formal organizational variables, assuming that teaching, learning, curriculum and social aspects will thereafter fall into place. Tibbit *et al.* (1994) stress the power for good or otherwise upon classroom teaching and learning that come with this organizational nesting, maintaining that:

> Conditions for effective teaching and learning (the classroom level) are constrained or facilitated by organizational conditions (school management and ethos) which, also, are influenced by environmental conditions external to the school in the overall social and policy context in which it has to operate.
>
> (Tibbit *et al.* 1994: 152)

It is at school level that much school effectiveness research and commentary are placed. Yet, Brown *et al.* (ibid: 9) make the point that accumulating evidence suggests that the greater part of the variance of pupils' achievements can be accounted for at classroom level (Fitzgibbon 1991; Harris *et al.* 1994). So it is to the insider teacher-practitioner level, they maintain, that innovation must be targeted and this in terms of school improvement and the processes of change (Brown and McIntyre 1993: 15–16).

School effectiveness and school improvement

Any systematic extrapolation about causes and effects in relation to school effectiveness and school improvement is made difficult by the flux of classroom life and the changing contexts of schools. It has been noted above that the relative certainties offered by statistics have provided material for school effectiveness researchers to sift and to construct conclusions apparently raised by the data. Particular sets of data have, however, sourced numerous contesting views and this situation has not been made simpler by studies which have appeared to generate different data and other meanings.

Essentially, however, it is the different functions served by the two strands of enquiry that distinguish them. School effectiveness research seeks to draw understandings based upon a norm-referenced system (that is, about one school in relation to other schools), commonly using large-scale quantitative methods, and to make statements that may be generally applied. School improvement work, in contrast, may be characterized as focusing upon an individual institution and its distinctive processes and multiple goals, and seeking greater success in a particular context.

Research findings and gaps in understanding

Some of the barriers to the general application of school effectiveness studies have been indicated above and school improvement initiatives and studies, it has been argued, do not realistically seek to generalize or apply specific strategies and findings to other schools in different contexts. Reynolds (1994) makes a case for more study of what are considered 'ineffective' schools or in relation to work that failed to turn round such schools. Grey and Wilcox (1995) take up a related idea and present the view that problems and barriers to change which are specific to ineffective schools might well be a productive focus of research. The simple division of schools into the two categories of 'effective' and 'ineffective' in the research literature is seen as limiting and inaccurate by Brown *et al.* (ibid). Hargreaves noted, though, a change of research emphasis:

faith in generalised and scientifically known principles of school effectiveness has begun to be superseded by commitments to more ongoing, provisional and contextually sensitive processes of school improvement.

(Hargreaves 1994: 15)

This trend continued (Hopkins and Reynolds 2001) along with an acknowledgement that definitions of 'effectiveness' and 'improvement' were, necessarily, contingent of time and place, and also that 'better theory' was required (Hargreaves 2001: 487).

In 2001, however, swift connections in public arenas were still being made between school effectiveness and school improvement; the implication was that 'effective' practices could be transferred from one school to another for 'improvement' to occur. It is not surprising that this has been the case, of course, given the public service agenda for uniformly higher national standards of achievement in education and in other public sector services (Davies *et al.* 2000). Using and building upon 'what works' and 'learning from success' became hallmarks of government strategy for better educational standards in Britain. The Standards and Effectiveness Unit (the SEU) of the DfES cited one of its central strategies for school improvement as 'evaluating and disseminating good practice to schools causing concern [including] … schools in special measures and with serious weaknesses' (i.e. ineffective schools) 'in order that all schools might achieve the pupil attainment rate of '20 per cent 5 GCSEs A*–C by 2001 and 25 per cent by 2006' (DfES SEU website accessed on 15 July 2001).

Social class and school effectiveness

School effectiveness studies have placed a key emphasis on achievement. Social class has been seen as one of the key determinants of achievement and often as a challenge for schools to moderate in terms of impacts upon achievement. By the same token, the case for value-added multilevel modelling approaches has accented the necessity for the socio-economic status (SES) of pupils to form part of the equation of measurement. In the Scottish research cited by Brown *et al.* it was this SES distinction rather than other 'effectiveness' elements which was cited as having most impact upon pupil achievement. They conclude that:

Reliance on generalised lists of characteristics and strategies for effective or improving schools, that are assumed to be invariant with SES, will not provide successful recipes.

Nevertheless, and this is the point of research endeavour and debate, contrary views do exist and the beginning teacher is advised to weigh up in practice and through experience the issues and arguments presented in this section and come to an individual view, since school improvement will always be part of a school's mission and school effectiveness debates will be aired regularly and with passion in public arenas.

Ofsted and school effectiveness

In 1994, Ofsted commissioned a team of researchers at the London Institute of Education to summarize all the key factors in school effectiveness. They identified eleven key areas, shown below.

1	Professional leadership	Firm and purposeful A participative approach The leading professional
2	Shared vision and goals	Unity of purpose Consistency of practice Collegiality and collaboration
3	A learning environment	An orderly atmosphere An attractive working environment
4	Concentration on teaching and learning	Maximising the learning time Academic emphasis Focus on achievement
5	Purposeful teaching	Efficient organization Clarity of purpose Structured lessons Adaptive practice
6	High expectations	High expectations all round Communicating expectations Providing intellectual challenge
7	Positive reinforcement	Clear and fair discipline Feedback
8	Monitoring progress	Monitoring pupil performance Evaluating school performance
9	Pupil rights and responsibilities	Raising pupil self-esteem Positions of responsibility Control of work
10	Home–school partnership	Parental involvement
11	A learning organization	School-based staff development

(Sammons et al. 1994)

Research, both in the UK and abroad, into the characteristics of effective schools has shown remarkable consistency in the issues identified as being key factors in creating school effectiveness. The Ofsted summary shown above reflects the move to monitoring and to schools' accountability that accompanied the educational reforms of the 1990s. The monitoring role and the evaluation of school performance are here presented as major contributory factors to schools' success.

Translating the factors of school effectiveness into school and classroom practice is, however, much more problematic. This is partly due to the fact that the issue of what makes a school effective is complex, and the relationship between cause and effect is not always straightforward. Leadership, for example, at both head and head of department level, is seen as being a key to success (Harris 2001). Yet analysing and measuring the impact and effect of leadership, or indeed any of the factors which contribute to effective schools, are problematic. Smith and Tomlinson indicate some of the problems of analysing leadership:

> … [there are]strong relationships between the style of management adopted by the head teacher and school effectiveness. This raises two related questions. One is about the direction of causation. It is not clear whether the head is able to adopt a given style of management (for example, ask teachers to provide records of children's work) because teachers are competent, relationships are good, and such requests can readily be met; or whether the standard of teaching and quality of relationships has been improved.
>
> The second related point is that schools, like other organizations, go through periods of relative stability followed by shortish periods of sudden change. The research will catch most schools in a period of relative stability. Let us suppose that the style of management by the head is, in fact, crucial in shaping the school. If the school is functioning badly there will be a style of management required to bring about a series of rapid changes, transforming the school into a good one. If the school is functioning well, there will be a style of management required to maintain stability. These two styles may well be entirely different. What research has tended to observe is the management styles associated with stable effective states. This says little about the styles required to transform a bad school into a good one, which would probably be entirely different. Assuming that what the head does is, in fact, critical in transforming a bad school, it is still quite possible that the head's style has little importance in maintaining an already good school, and that the causation in that case runs in the opposite direction.
>
> This point can be summarised by making a distinction between the conditions existing in an effective school, and the actions that have to be taken to transform an ineffective school into an effective one, or to maintain the performance of an already effective one. These two sets of actions may not be the same.
>
> Clearly, theories of how schools work need to be developed to take account of change and the maintenance of a stable state. These considerations suggest the need for a different kind of research, that studies schools as they change, and perhaps research that observes the results of taking specific actions.
>
> (Smith and Tomlinson 1990: 180–1)

More recently, work on school effectiveness and school improvement has attempted to study the links between educational outcomes with what happens in schools. The emphasis given to this research is that it needs to take into account the 'habits of everyday teachers' (Grey *et al.* 1999). The focus in the search for factors which contribute to school effectiveness has shifted from leadership *per se* to everyday classroom practice. Sammons *et al.* (1997) explored the extent to which practitioners' beliefs and perceptions about effectiveness are related to research findings about the key characteristics of effective schools. There is an increased awareness that, in the research into school effectiveness, more attention needs to be given to the teachers' perspective, since 'school effectiveness researchers have paid too little attention to the practitioners' perspectives and explanations of effectiveness' (Sammons *et al.* 1998).

In describing why teaching is an enjoyable career and in identifying what influences motivation, morale and job satisfaction, experienced teachers focus on the feelings of satisfaction they get from pupils' success and from the contribution they make to pupils' development. Despite the extensive demands made of the teacher-in-post, it is these same demands which contribute to successful and improving schools, and which contribute to teachers' job satisfaction, as the teacher referred to below explains.

Dave has taught in inner city comprehensive schools for the past eight years. He is now head of humanities in a large school which has recently been identified by Ofsted as an improving school. A few years ago, the GCSE results for this school were well below the national average, with only 19 per cent of pupils in Year 11 gaining an A–C pass in their GCSEs. This has now risen to over 40 per cent.

> When I first came to this school, it was way down the league table in terms of GCSE results. In the last few years, under the leadership of the new Head, things have really turned round. The leadership is important, but also the attitude and commitment of all the teachers in the schools is too. Pupil attainment has risen here because of their efforts, and their responses to the initiatives introduced by the management team. I think we all share similar outlooks on teaching. We get a great sense of achievement from seeing the pupils engage in the lessons. Successful and effective teaching has a lot to do with personal job satisfaction, with teachers' attitudes to the day-to-day routines and their enthusiasm for working with pupils. When I first started teaching, I couldn't wait to get started. I've changed over the past eight years and experience has now replaced some of that initial enthusiasm, but what I do – the success of the school and the pupil – still gives me great satisfaction.
>
> (Dave, head of humanities, 1999)

The research findings into school effectiveness resonate with the increasing expectations of what education can and ought to do for children. As such, this work has had an impact on government educational policy. The growing concern about educational standards has resulted in a wide variety of initiatives and interventions aimed at school improvement.

Government policy and school improvement

At the policy level, initiatives aimed at school improvement are based on:

- The measuring of school effectiveness in terms of pupils' attainment in examinations.
- Making schools accountable to the public for their 'effectiveness' through the publication of examination results and school league tables (in England and Scotland, though not in Wales [from 2001] and Northern Ireland).
- Regular school inspections and the publication of inspection reports.

- The requirement that schools' governing bodies set and publish targets and the actual performance against those targets in their annual report to parents for the percentage of pupils attaining five or more GCSEs or equivalent A★–C, the percentage of pupils attaining one or more GCSEs or equivalent A★–C, and the average point score for the school to be achieved in GCSE and vocational qualifications.
- A performance management system, which informs decisions about pay, designed to raise the standard of pupil achievement by establishing a clear link between pupil progress and teacher objectives. Under this system schools have to agree annual objectives for each teacher, including objectives relating to pupil progress and ways of developing and improving teachers' professional practice.
- The development of a systematic approach to schools' self-evaluation, based on a five-year cycle of review and target setting by schools aimed at raising pupils' attainment.

In addition to these requirements placed on schools, government initiatives aimed at improving pupils' attainment have focused on differentiated school provision and professional support. Some of these interventions are summarized below.

Government initiatives

The government has set the target that by 2004, there should be no secondary school anywhere with less than 20 per cent of its pupils achieving 5 GCSEs at Grades A*-C or GNVQ equivalents, and by 2006, none achieving less than 26 per cent. Some of the initiatives already taken to achieve this goal have been highlighted in different chapters of this book. They are put together here:

Education Action Zones (EAZs)

These allow local partnerships to develop new approaches to raising standards in disadvantaged rural and urban schools. Each EAZ includes a cluster of two to three secondary schools with their supporting primaries working in partnership with LEAs, parents, business and other representatives from the local community.

Generally, zone initiatives focus on four main themes:

- improving the quality of teaching and learning
- social inclusion
- family and pupil support
- working with business and other organizations.

Excellence in Cities

This is a three-year programme to improve the education of city children.

Beacon Schools

These are schools which have been identified by the DfEE as amongst the best performing in the country. The initiative is designed to raise standards through the dissemination of good practice.

Fresh Start

This has been a key element in the Government's strategy for raising standards in 'low performing' schools. It involves closing a failing school and opening a new one to replace it. This is a controversial strategy which has received a lot of media attention, largely due to the appointment of so-called 'super heads' and the resignation of heads appointed to take over Fresh Start schools. In some cases, the school has been closed, after the failure of Fresh Start to improve the school. At September 2000, 25 schools have been 'Fresh Started'. City Academies are a re-working of some of the essential ideas of Fresh Start.

Pilot partner initiatives for low attaining schools

All schools attaining less than 25 per cent 5 GCSEs at grades A*–C will be twinned with another school with a proven track record.

Teaching reforms

The government sees leadership as being crucial in the drive to raise standards in schools, and as such has introduced a series of measures aimed at supporting leadership of Heads (see also Chapter 1), Deputy heads, senior teachers and others across the school. These measures include the introduction of:

Advanced Skills Teachers (AST) These are teachers who are considered to be 'excellent' and who achieve the very highest standards of classroom practice and who are paid to share their experience with other teachers.

College for Headship This offers heads, deputies and other school leaders professional support. The College aims to be a provider and promoter of excellence, a major resource for schools, a catalyst for innovation, and a focus for national and international debate on leadership issues.

Raising the standard of new entrants into the profession The government is aiming to make initial teacher training more flexible and more rigorous in order to ensure that all newly qualified entrants to the profession have the relevant skills, knowledge and understanding.

Continuing professional development for all teachers One of the initiatives here is training for all teachers in the use of ICT. Learning and Teaching: A strategy for professional development (2001) underslines the need for a career-long, contractual obligation to professional development by teachers and accompanying duties by headteachers and LEAs to facilitate, assess provision and oversee outcomes (see also Chapter 14).

(Also see the DfES Standards website: www.dfes.gov.uk)

It is difficult to ascertain the impact of these government policies on school effectiveness and improvement. As mentioned above, a number of these initiatives have been viewed critically. Others have been given a lukewarm reception by the teaching profession. For example, with EAZs the DfEE claims that:

> Zones have shown that they can deliver improvement, as demonstrated by the summer 1999 exam results. At Key Stage 2, there was a 6 per cent average improvement in English and 12 per cent improvement in maths in EAZ schools, compared to national increases of 5 per cent and 10 per cent. There was a 2 per cent average improvement in the number of pupils gaining 1 GCSE A–G grade in EAZ schools compared to a national increase of 1 per cent.
>
> (DfEE 2000a)

However, studies by external organizations have indicated that the claims for the success of the EAZs have been inflated.

> The Government damaged the progress of its own initiative to tackle inner city underachievement, according to research conducted by Pricewaterhouse-Coopers.
>
> Ministers' emphasis on business involvement in Education Action Zones ensured that they started work in an atmosphere of hostility and suspicion with many teachers fearing their schools would be privatised … . Data from the DfEE showed that educational standards rose quicker than the average in zones, but it was difficult to attribute this to an 'EAZ effect' rather than to extra funding or other initiatives such as literacy and numeracy strategies.
>
> Teachers are divided on whether being part of the zone raised standards – more than half agreed it did while 40 per cent did not believe improvement could necessarily be attributed to the zone.
>
> (*TES* 24 November 2000)

It is premature to assess the impact of some government initiatives on school improvements. However, two government initiatives which have been in place for some time and so which can be evaluated in terms of their impact upon school effectiveness are:

- the focus on standards and examination results, and
- the impact of Ofsted inspections on school improvement.

The next section of this chapter explores the impact of these policies.

The debate on standards: defining terms and establishing criteria

Much of the debate about education over the past 20 years has been about whether schools are getting better or worse. Governments over this period have embarked on substantial programmes of reform aimed at developing more effective school systems and at raising pupil achievement and attainment. One of the most controversial government initiatives, first introduced in 1992, was the decision to release schools' examination results and tests into the public domain, as one important indicator of school effectiveness. For the government, the publication of schools' examination results was the logical culmination of several of its policies aimed at making schools more accountable to parents.

The publication of the raw data on schools' examination results is a crude and almost meaningless measure of a school's success. The first published results (1992) brought no surprises. Those schools at the 'top' were located in socially advantaged areas and generally selected their intake, whilst 'poorly performing' schools were from the inner city and socially disadvantaged areas. The data revealed little about what the schools had achieved with their particular intake (see Chapter 9).

Judgements made about schools on the basis of examination and test results have raised an important further issue in the standards debate. In particular, the questioning of the significance of raw data about schools has heightened educational and political interest in the 'value-added' approach to assessing school performance. Many argue that we should be more concerned with the progress pupils make during their time in a school than with their performance scores (however that is defined) at the time they leave. The latter, it is argued, is heavily influenced by socio-economic and other factors, while the former provides a more realistic measure of how well a school has done for any child.

McPherson's argument (1992), which states that no single indicator of school performance can serve all the normal needs of teachers, parents and the education system as a whole, still holds good. Schools serve a multitude of functions, not least the development of the range of pupils' abilities – the creative and aesthetic, as well as the scholastic. Inter-school comparisons of performance are difficult to establish, and probably impossible to represent in any adequate quantitative way. Judgements about successful schools have, therefore, to be based on more than public examination results.

The publication of examination data was, throughout the 1990s, refined to take into account factors such as the percentage of pupils with special educational needs, statemented pupils and levels of attendance. It is now widely recognized that schools with different intakes achieve widely differing results. At the same time it is accepted that there are sizeable differences in school effectiveness; pupils in some schools seem to achieve better results than similar pupils attending other schools. In terms of successful and improving schools, the publication of a school's examination data has served to focus the attention of each school on monitoring its own outcomes. Such an analysis enables schools to measure their success and identify areas for improvement. Benchmarking – the measuring of standards of actual performance in schools against those achieved by other pupils in schools with broadly similar characteristics – is now a feature of schools' annual planning cycles.

The publication by the DfEE of the 'Autumn Package' presents schools with benchmarking information which shows the range of performance of similar schools, grouped together on the basis of free school meals or pupils' prior attainment. This helps schools to compare their performance with similar schools and is seen as an essential step for schools in examining their performance and identifying areas where they can learn from others to raise pupils' attainment. The 'measure' of prior attainment, and the percentage of pupils on free school meals, are used because studies confirm that the former is the best predictor of pupils' subsequent performance, and the latter is an indicator which has been shown to be more strongly correlated with pupils' examination outcomes than other contextual variables – such as gender, ethnicity or urban/rural schools. This is the DfEE's rationale of the published data:

> To gain a full picture of a school's overall performance, you need to probe the reasons that may lie behind the numbers. This will help to identify priorities and strategies for school improvement. It can be useful to consider the attainment of different groups of pupils in the year group as well as the performance of the whole cohort. For example, to set challenging and realistic targets for all pupils it may be appropriate to consider separately the attainment of all pupils in the cohort who do not have special educational needs, and those who do.
>
> As no two schools are identical, the Department encourages schools to publish contextual information to explain their position in the benchmarked tables. For example, headteachers know which of their pupils joined during the course of a Key Stage, their performance relative to others in the cohort and the impact this had on the school's overall performance. This helps to contextualise the school's position in the benchmark tables. By looking at the performance of the school in this way, managers can get a more complete picture of the overall performance which will help with target setting.
>
> (DfEE 2000b)

These moves strengthen the scrutiny of results for accountability and diagnostic purposes at LEA, school and head of department levels.

Ofsted and school improvement

School examination results and performance indicators provide one way of measuring school effectiveness and improvement. School inspection is another. Historically, this has been the main instrument used to measure school improvement, but it was not until the 1990s, with the setting up of the Office for Standards in Education (Ofsted), that all schools were inspected on a regular basis.

According to current legislative requirements, schools must be inspected at least once within six years from the end of the school year in which they were last inspected. Ofsted decides the timing and type of inspection. There are two types of school inspection:

- a short inspection, which is designed for the most effective schools
- a full inspection, which applies to all other schools and to all pupil referral units.

(Ofsted 1999)

External inspection is seen as a main driving force in terms of evaluation and pupil attainment. One aim of school inspection is seen as providing:

> an independent, external view of the school and the standards it achieves. Inspectors tell the school what it does well, where it has weaknesses and why

they have come to their conclusions. They also look at how much the school has improved since the last inspection and where it needs further improvement.

(Ofsted 1999)

Note here the emphasis given to the inspectors telling the school what it does well and what it does badly. The facility to send in inspectors where a school is consistently failing is an important feature of the inspection process. Ofsted inspections identify features of 'failing' schools, that is, schools placed under 'special measures'. Research carried out by NfER (Scanlon 1999) has found that the majority of schools are placed under special measures for one of the following reasons:

- the quality of teaching was unsatisfactory
- poor exam results, underachievement
- lack of leadership/management problems
- behaviour and attendance problems
- failure to implement the National Curriculum.

Once identified as being placed under 'special measures', the school has to produce an action plan and progress is regularly monitored by HMI. Does this process lead to school improvement? NfER research which considered this question found:

Not surprisingly, the inspection process seemed to have had a more profound effect on special measures schools, compared with other schools. The two areas which improved most during special measures were 'quality of education' and, to a lesser extent, 'standards achieved by pupils'.

There were also some aspects of school life which seemed to have deteriorated substantially since inspection. This was most noticeable in relation to staff morale, as reported by teachers in both groups of schools. These findings are in line with previous research which suggests that schools generally can experience 'post-Ofsted blues' the year after inspection.

(Scanlon 1999)

The inspection process has been the subject of much criticism. These criticisms are generally based on the inspection methodology and the impact of inspection on schools' capacity to improve:

the intention is that the inspectors' reports will provide a 'clear view' of what action needs to be taken and, by virtue of being published, will put pressure upon school leaders to act, with 'action plans' following on soon afterwards. This assumes that inspections can get to the heart of complex matters in rather short periods of time. In practice, such research as we have on the processes of school improvement indicates that having a 'clear view' of the problems facing a school is only a small part of the change process .... Ofsted has committed itself to 'school improvement through inspection'. In the longer term, without substantial changes in the ways in which inspections are organized, Ofsted's role in ensuring that schools are held more accountable to their various constituencies is likely to outweigh its contribution to school improvement.

(Grey 1996)

Some years on then, from the first Ofsted inspections, there is a growing acceptance of the need for schools to be involved with their own self-evaluation in an attempt to link more closely the inspection process and school improvement. Many schools have regularly carried out systematic evaluations of aspects of their development, but this has generally been on an *ad hoc* basis, as a result of a particular LEA or school initiative, and the process has not necessarily fed into the areas Ofsted inspections consider. The processes and frameworks used currently as the basis for inspection have been modified in order to take into account a growing drive for school self-evaluation as well as the externally defined criteria against which judgements about a school's performance were made. The *Handbook for Inspecting Schools* (Ofsted 2000) states:

> Ofsted is committed to promoting self-evaluation as a key aspect of the work of schools.
>
> It is advantageous to base school self-evaluation on the same criteria as those used in all school by inspectors. A common language has developed about the work of schools, expressed through the criteria. Teachers and governors know that the criteria reflect the things that matter.
>
> (Ofsted 2000: 138)

The development of a 'common language' is undoubtedly a key feature of school self-evaluation and enables comparison to be made across a range of processes which brings together information on school effectiveness and school improvement. However:

> From a policy perspective, self-evaluation is viewed as a mechanism for empowering schools themselves to improve the quality from within, helping them to monitor their progress and to report accurately to their external constituencies – parents and the wider public. It is seen as contributing to the democratic debate about what constitutes quality at school and classroom level, and complementing the work of the external agencies. From a school perspective, self-evaluation has a more immediate purpose. Dialogue is focused more on the internal stakeholders and their contribution to planning and improvement at classroom, school and community level.
>
> (MacBeath *et al.* 2000)

Self-evaluation can have a positive impact on school effectiveness and improvement, but only if the school has ownership of the process. The 'official' and 'unofficial', and 'internal' and 'external', aspects of self-evaluation can create tensions whereby the process is seen as being directed, not at the needs of the school, but at the needs of an Ofsted inspection. At the same time, school self-evaluation needs to be embedded within the culture of schools and not seen as something which is imposed on the school by its senior management. This has raised suspicions amongst staff that self-evaluation also has a hidden agenda of feeding into appraisal and performance-related pay.

School effectiveness and improvement – some further paradoxes and dichotomies

This review of the work done on school effectiveness and school improvement has identified the following issues:

- Definitions of effective/successful schools based on research carried out in the 1970s and 1980s.
- Policy initiatives which are aimed at measuring school effectiveness and improvement – performance indicators and school inspections. Figure 13.1 also indicates a wider range of initiatives aimed at raising pupil attainment in schools.
- The search for the cause of school improvement and effectiveness is the focus of a whole mass of educational research and government initiatives.

This work ranges across measures of effectiveness and improvement, and the in-school processes. It has also raised questions about the limits of current reform strategies. It is accepted, for example, that some initiatives have produced an impact on levels of student attainment – for example, the English National Literacy Strategy (Barber and Sebba 1999) – but recent analysis of trends in examination results in English secondary schools suggests only a modest year-on-year increase, even in schools which have been identified as 'improving rapidly' (Gray *et al.* 1999). There is a growing body of research (Hopkins and Levin 2000) which indicates that policy reforms focus on the wrong variables in school improvement and effectiveness. External inspection, teacher appraisal and organizational development do not necessarily have a direct impact on pupil learning. Improvement work of a school-initiated nature, such as 'Improving the Quality of Education for All' (IQEA), has generated a set of conditions (see Figure 13.1) which, it is argued, provide the key to facilitating effective teaching and high-quality outcomes at classroom and school level (Hopkins 2000). Is there then a place for current policy directives in school improvement initiatives? Important aspects of school improvement work are accurate diagnosis, feedback and planning. Policy initiatives such as target setting, developmental planning and self-evaluation therefore *do* provide the basis for the work on school improvement. However, school improvement needs to embrace all aspects of school life, and the focus of where to begin lies in the classroom – in pupil motivation, in effective teaching and learning styles, in providing effective feedback to pupils and in quickly picking up problems that militate against achievement.

School self-evaluation aims at gathering together accurate diagnosis, feedback and planning in order to improve pupils' achievements. The work carried out by the NfER and based on their research into effective and improving schools, *Raising attainment in Secondary Schools – a Handbook for School Self-evaluation,* has provided a rationale and framework for schools to draw from in developing their own approach to school self-evaluation. This is how they see the benefits to schools of self-evaluation. Their observations are based on working with schools to develop self-evaluation strategies. Self-evaluation in its various forms is a positive experience for headteachers and class teachers in a number of ways. The benefits to schools of self-evaluation, reported by headteachers and other members of staff, can be listed as follows:

Proposition 1

Schools will not improve unless teachers develop, individually and collectively. Whilst teachers can often develop their practice on an individual basis, if the whole school is to develop then there need to be many staff development opportunities for teachers to learn together.

Proposition 2

Successful schools seem to have ways of working that encourage feelings of involvement from a number of stake-holder groups, especially students.

Proposition 3

Schools that are successful at development establish a clear vision for themselves and regard leadership as a function to which many staff contribute, rather than a set of responsibilities vested in a single individual.

Proposition 4

The co-ordination of activities is an important way of keeping people involved, particularly when changes of policy are being introduced. Communication within the school is an important aspect of co-ordination, as are the informal interactions that arise between teachers.

Proposition 5

Schools which recognize that enquiry and reflection are important processes in school improvement find it easier to gain clarity and establish shared meanings around identified development priorities, and are better placed to monitor the extent to which policies actually deliver the intended outcomes for pupils.

Proposition 6

The process of planning for development allows the school to link its educational aspirations to identifiable priorities, sequence those priorities over time, and maintain a focus on classroom practice.

Figure 13.1 Creating the conditions for school improvement: some propositions

Source: Hopkins and West 1994: 192.

- School self-evaluation can contribute to bringing about a *change in the culture* of a school, helping to formalise and to extend existing processes of evaluating teaching and learning and data analysis. One headteacher outlined how he was using a whole-school evaluative approach which rested on the ability to change: 'I believe in a thinking, changing school and a thinking, changing teacher who will develop a thinking, changing child'. One aspect of changing school culture is an increased willingness to use methods of evaluation that have not necessarily been used previously, including, for example, the technique of classroom observation by peers.

- Teachers' *professional development* can benefit from a school's commitment to self-evaluation, particularly in an institution where staff are encouraged to share expertise with colleagues and to take up training opportunities. Some schools have adopted an explicit approach, using packages such as 'Investors in People'; while for others professional review took place within a more general framework such as an LEA supporting framework.

- For some headteachers, particularly those recently appointed, school self-evaluation provides a mechanism with which to learn about their school and to *organize change*. In other words, the processes and mechanisms provide school senior managers with a framework (and 'levers') for the management of change. One headteacher sees self-evaluation as an important part of a process of strategic planning: 'fundamental to where you are, what you are achieving and where to move forward. If you don't [self-evaluate], you stagnate'.

- Schools can *develop their own agendas* for self-evaluation, enabling teachers to focus on aspects of the school that they identify as areas for improvement. Furthermore, the internal agenda set within schools can also help promote *ownership* among teachers of their self-evaluation activity. While it is clear that much of the impetus for self-evaluation is being generated by headteachers, particularly in the early stages, many are keen to encourage teachers to become involved in these processes.

- Many school interviewees say that they have benefited from having the support of a *critical friend*, whether an LEA advisor, consultant or colleague from another school. A critical friend who is external to the school can help teachers identify areas for development, meet the demands of a timetable for implementing and evaluating activities and can 'ask difficult questions'.

- School self-evaluation can be used to encourage *community involvement*. Parents, pupils and governors can provide useful feedback, inform classroom practice and help to set the agenda for change. There is evidence that self-evaluation has afforded some schools the opportunity to involve pupils and parents in the process. Several school interviewees say that their planned 'next step' in the evaluation process is to seek the views of parents or pupils: 'children know what helps their learning and what doesn't'.

- Self-evaluation packages and programmes, whether developed 'in-house' by LEAs or 'bought in', can provide schools with a range of *tools* for implementing evaluation activities. These may take the form of questionnaires for parents and pupils, observation checklists, files for recording data, or some other format. 'Toolkits' for schools avoid the need for teachers to 're-invent the wheel' and can facilitate the sharing of information across institutions. This is exactly how this Handbook should be perceived and used.

(NfER 2000)

Figure 13.2 is an extract from an NfER schedule, designed to help teachers evaluate classroom learning. It identifies the focus for observation, discussion and evaluation and raises relevant questions about classroom learning.

1.1	**Opportunities for achievement and progression**	**Evidence**
1.1.1	In what ways is previous work being acknowledged and built on, for individual pupils and for the class as a whole?	Classroom observation
	(Look for phrases like: You remember talking about …, Does this remind you of something we've already looked at?, etc. Linking back may need to be made at several points in the lesson, not just at the beginning; and may need to refer back to concepts or issues tackled some time ago, not just in the previous lesson.)	
	Do all students appear to understand what links are made and why?	
	(Look for non-verbal signals as well as the questions being asked.)	
1.1.2	What specific tasks are set?	Classroom observation
	Are tasks common to all students or differentiated?	
	If differentiated, in what ways: e.g.	
	■ by setting variations on the core task(s), ■ by outcomes expected, ■ by the kind of learning activity involved in the task, ■ by varying the pace or the rate of the activity, or ■ by dialogue with individual students?	
	(Note that these strategies are not mutually exclusive, but decisions about the relative emphasis need to be based on what is relevant for each individual student.)	
1.1.3	How clear are the criteria for success in each task?	Classroom observation
	Is success related implicitly/explicitly to:	
	■ each student's previous performance, ■ the performance of the group, ■ a predetermined set of criteria, ■ some combination of these?	Discussion with teacher; Example of pupils' work
1.1.6	How is learning reinforced and built on?	O, W
	Is this done for all individuals in the group?	
	How is the next stage of learning (as distinct from content) introduced and made clear?	
	Is it the appropriate stage in each case, especially for students who have demonstrated difficulties?	

1.2   Promoting self-esteem

1.2.1   How are low achievers, in particular, encouraged to carry   O, W T
on learning despite their difficulties?

Are there any obvious obstacles to their learning?

1.2.2   What feedback does the teacher give individual students?   O

Do there appear to be any assumptions operating in the
teacher's mind about individual students' performance?

If so, what sort of assumptions do these appear to be?

1.2.3   What are the teacher's expectations of the group as a T, W
whole, compared with other groups in the same year or
past years?

And what are the teacher's expectations of individuals
within the group?

Do these expectations match those of colleagues in other
departments or of the form tutor(s)?

What evidence is there to support them?

1.2.4   Generally, are there sufficient challenges within the learning O, W
tasks set for the whole ability-range?

Is there sufficient range of support for the learning tasks
set, for example
- clarifying the purpose and basic concepts of the
task,
- pointing out relevant resources,
- extending the timescale for completing the task,
- bringing in learning support expertise?

Figure 13.2 B1 Classroom learning

Source: NfER 2000.

Note
O = observation; W = pupil work; T = discussion with teacher.

This approach to school improvement reinforces the view that part of teachers' professionalism is a knowledge and understanding of the evidence base and research to which their practice is symbiotically related. It also reinforces the view that it is classroom teachers who in the end, through their daily classroom interactions, their enthusiasms and idiosyncrasies, their evaluations of the reflections upon their successes and failures, make a difference to pupils' learning and achievement. Amidst all the policy initiatives and the widening of measures for school improvement, it is important not to forget the personal dimension of teachers. Here we need to return to Dave, whom we met earlier in this chapter, and remind ourselves that teacher motivation and job satisfaction form the bedrock on which school success and improvement are built.

At the beginning of a career in teaching, it is important to be aware that schools' performance data, 'standards' league tables and Ofsted inspections all affect schooling and teaching. Teachers need to understand something of their purpose and form. In relation to measures of school effectiveness, or the issue of standards generally, it is important to appreciate the importance and complexity of the debate. It is also important, however, to remember that individual enthusiasm, interest and creativity, the reasons for entering teaching in the first place and the thirst to understand teaching in all its complexity, provide the personal dimension through which policies and initiatives can be implemented, interpreted and developed. Teachers' professional knowledge, values, motivation and personal constructs are central to improving pupil attainment.

Conclusion

The ways in which we make judgements about schools and the audiences to which these judgements are directed are important aspects of the wider professional role of the teacher. Increasingly, teachers have had to move into the front line in explaining school policies and achievements to parents and to the wider community, and in being held accountable, too, for pupil attainment. This is more than public relations for its own sake. The evidence suggests that parents and parental understanding of schooling can be an important variable in school improvement. The dangers lie in ill-advised judgements rather than the judgements themselves, and teachers and schools have a central task in explaining to their wider communities the different measures of school effectiveness and school improvement, and their own contributions to this process.

References

Barber and Sebba (1999) 'Reflections on progress towards a world class education system', *Cambridge Journal of Education* 29(2): 183–93.

Brown, S. and McIntyre, D. (1993) *Making Sense of Teaching,* Milton Keynes: Open University Press.

Brown, S., Duffield, J. and Riddell, S., (1995) 'School effectiveness research: the policy makers' tool for school improvement?' *EERA Bulletin* 1(1) March: 6–15.

Davies, H.T.O., Nutley, S. and Smith, P.C. (2000) (eds) *What Works?: Evidence-based Policy and Practice in Public Services*, Bristol: The Policy Press.

DfEE (2000a) Standards website www.dfee.gov.uk.

—— (2000b) 'A-Z of School Leadership' website at www.dfee.gov.uk.

Fitzgibbon, C.T., (1991) 'Multilevel modelling in an indicator system' in S.W. Raudenbush and J.D. Wilims (eds) *Schools, Classrooms and Pupils: International Studies of Schooling from a Multilevel Perspective*, San Diego: Academic Press.

Grey, J. and Wilcox, B. (1994) 'The challenge of turning round ineffective schools', paper presented at ESRC Seminar Series on 'School Effectiveness and School Improvement', University of Newcastle upon Tyne, October.

Grey, J. (1996) 'School effectiveness and school improvement' (EU208), *Exploring Educational Issues*, course materials, Block 3, Unit 6, Milton Keynes: Open University Press.

Grey, J., Hopkins, D., Reynolds, D., Wilcox, B., Farrell, S. and Jesson, D. (1999) *Improving Schools: Performance and Potential*, Milton Keynes: Open University Press.

Hargreaves, A. (1994) *Changing Teachers, Changing Times*, London: Cassell.

—— (2001) 'A capital theory of school effectiveness and improvement' *British Educational Research Journal*, 27(4) Sept: 487–503.

Harris, A. (2001) 'Department improvement and school improvement' *British Educational Research Journal* 27(4) Sept: 477–86.

Harris, A., Jamieson, I. and Russ, J. (1994) 'A study of departments adding significant value in South Bristol schools', personal communication cited in Brown *et al.* (1995).

Hopkins, D. (2000) *Seeing School Improvement Whole*, London: Falmer Press.

Hopkins, D. and Levin, B. (2000) 'Government policy and school development' *School Leadership and Management* 20(1): 15–30.

Hopkins, D. and Reynolds, D. (2001) 'The past, present and future of school improvement: towards the Third Age' *British Educational Research Journal*, 27(4) Sept: 459–75.

MacBeath, J. with Schratz, M., Meuret, D. and Jakobsen, L. (2000) *Self-Evaluation in European Schools. A story of Change*, London and New York: RoutledgeFalmer.

McPherson, A. (1994) 'Measuring added value in schools' in B. Moon and A. Shelton Mayes (eds) *Teaching and Learning in the Secondary School*, London: Routledge.

NFER (2000) *Raising Attainment in Secondary Schools: A Handbook for School Self-evaluation*, Lesley Saunders, Bob Strading, Peter Rudd, Slough: NFER.

Ofsted reports, HMSO, www.ofsted.gov.uk.

Ofsted (1999) *Inspecting Schools – The Framework,* London: HMSO.

—— (2000) *Handbook for Inspecting (Primary Schools/Secondary Schools) with Guidance on Self-evaluation*, London: HMSO.

Reynolds, D. (1994) Inaugural lecture given on 19 October 1994 at the University of Newcastle upon Tyne (in mimeo).

Rudd, P. (2000) NFER conference paper 'Evaluating school self-evaluation', presented at the CLEA Conference, Creativity and Culture, at Warwick University, July 2000.

Sammons, P., Hillman, J. and Mortimore, P. (1994) *Key Characteristics of Effective Schools*, London: Institute of Education for Ofsted.

Scanlon, M. (1999) *The Impact of Ofsted Inspections*, London: NFFR.

Scottish Office Education Department (SOED) (1990) *The Role of School Development Planning in School Effectiveness*, Edinburgh: HMSO.

Tibbet, J., Spencer, E. and Hutchinson, C. (1994) 'Improving school effectiveness: policy and research in Scotland' *Scottish Educational Review* 26: 151–7.

Times Educational Supplement (*TES*) 24 November 2000.

Smith, D.J. and Tomlinson, J. (1990) 'Studying schools and their effects', in B. Moon with J. Isaac and J. Powney (eds) *Judging Standards and Effectiveness in Education*, London: Hodder and Stoughton.

14 Career-long professional development

A lone walker comes across someone in the woods feverishly sawing down a tree.
He asks: 'How long have you been at that?'
The exhausted worker says: 'Hours and hours, and it's really hard work.'
The walker says to him, 'Have you considered stopping to sharpen the saw?'
'Oh no, I'm far too busy sawing,' came the reply.

(Adapted from Covey 1999: 287)

Introduction

The rapid flow of directives, strategies, task forces and publications designed to underpin the 1997 *Excellence in Schools* (DfEE 1997) campaign resulted in a great deal of focused activity in schools, subject departments and at an individual level, both in the primary and secondary sectors. Chapter 1 highlighted the details of these changes relating to structures and processes which were sustained through the period 1997–2001. Throughout these changing times many teachers held firm to their view that worthwhile continuing professional development (CPD) was not just about responding to government directives; it was also regarded as an area which teachers recognized as being important in itself in order that they might be able to prioritize points of focus and to identify paths to realize them in the classroom and for known pupils. At its best it was also about enjoyment and enrichment of the teacher-as-professional. A key problem in pursuing considered priorities and preferences, however, frequently related to restricted resource allocation. It also related to resource allocation linked to development agendas owned by external (often funding) agencies.

In the third millennium, though, there have been clear indications that teachers will not be expected to continue to saw the educational equivalent of increasing numbers of trees, however industriously, without sharpened tools. Career-long professional development, aligned to pay and career prospects, has been pressed strongly by government as the appropriate tool to use to deal with the expanding challenges of teaching.

This development and the culture change, both outside as well as inside schools, which have been sought by government to sustain it, may well have profound effects upon the beginning teacher. The practical impacts of these changes are examined in this chapter. In addition, the following aspects, designed to support the proposed changes, are considered. These are:

- the concept of professional development designed to support teaching and learning
- the role of the General Teaching Council in continuing professional development
- professional development opportunities
- developing leadership potential in a broad swathe of teachers using CPD.

Professional development to support teaching and learning

In 1993 the National Commission on Education published a report entitled *Learning to Succeed*. It had the following to say about twenty-first-century teachers:

> In our vision, a teacher in the twenty-first century will be an authority and enthusiast in the knowledge, ideas, skills, understanding and values to be presented to pupils. The teacher will be an expert on effective learning with knowledge of a range of classroom methods that can be intelligently applied and an understanding of appropriate organizational and management styles, conditions and resources. The teacher will have the capacity to think deeply about educational aims and values, and thereby critically about educational programmes.
>
> (NCE 1993: 197)

We have now arrived in the twenty-first century. There is still much made in DfES documents and by education officials about 'vision' and 'mission'. It can be argued, however, that a great deal has changed. These changes relate to the introduction of procedural and structural frameworks designed to underpin the widening range of what is required of teachers and what they in turn can expect to have in terms of their own needs and development. These requirements have been broached in Chapter 1 and are taken up again briefly in the third section of this chapter. Here it is appropriate to look at the framework of professional development, and the rationale underpinning it, which has been designed to support a career-long interplay of learning and doing.

The rationale for career-long professional development

In 2001, serving teachers offered these views about the value of CPD in their work:

> Without it, teaching becomes stale, uninformed, routine.

> I'm a professional, and like other professionals I want investment in my development.

> Teaching takes so much out of you; regular re-fuelling is essential.

> After a really effective course, I go back to the classroom, energised and eager to try out new approaches and to evaluate them.

I just know that all my classes benefit enormously when I bring back new ideas and ways of working. I also feel so much more confident when my ideas and strategies are confirmed as strong by other practising teachers in my subject area.

(DfEE 2000)

The rationale for CPD provided in the consultation document, *Professional Development: Support for Teaching and Learning* (DfEE, 2000a), related to a wish to 'transform educational standards and raise achievement in every school'. In order to realize this:

All teachers need the continually updated knowledge, skills and commitment to improving learning that so many confident teaching professionals already demonstrate. We need teaching to become a learning profession. Continuing improvement requires a user-friendly relevant framework for teachers' professional development, allowing access to best practice in teaching and learning and providing opportunities for continuing learning on and off the job.

(DfEE 2000: 3)

The belief underpinning this mission statement is that good professional development requires:

- time to reflect and set objectives
- recognition and commitment
- opportunity, particularly for work-based learning
- a focus on schools and teachers; and
- high-quality provision.

These five core elements provided the structure of this highly important consultation document and, following the high approval rating of its suggestions (a 90 per cent agreement for its central ideas of the document), were consequently securely embedded in the ensuing national strategy, *Learning and Teaching* (DfEE 2001b), and further developments described in the 2001 Green Paper *Schools: Building on Success* (DfEE 2001c). They also related to emerging official views of what constituted 'effective' teachers. This description was attached to those who were seen to take an active role in identifying their own career-long professional development needs and to give these a high priority. They would be required to 'share responsibility for commitment for development' and would be supported by the government in so doing. Professional development itself was to be focused, centred on raising standards in the classroom and linked to pupil learning as well as wider-based professional skills. An extended range of development opportunities would in the near future be made available and equality of opportunity safeguarded. Teachers would be required to learn on the job from current best practice with sufficient resources for the many core initiatives undertaken. ICT was to play a central role in supporting opportunities in professional development; and any resources provided were to be of high quality. Teachers and schools were invited to be 'discerning customers' of any such provision. To support this, good planning and evaluation processes were seen as 'essential'.

At this time, the government's accent on the global pressures on education, not least the argued link between global competitiveness and a nation's educational achievements, outlined in earlier chapters, made it unsurprising that one source for these principles had been taken from development strategies operating outside the UK. *Professional Development* cites a Working Paper from the Washington Center for the Study of Teaching and Policy and its view that:

> research confirms that good professional development is generally school or classroom-based, relates directly to what teachers are doing in their schools or classrooms, is often teacher-directed, and focuses intensely on assisting teachers to understand the subject(s) they are teaching.
>
> (DfEE 2000a: 4)

As Chapter 1 indicated, key structural supports for these developments were to be provided through the General Teaching Councils for England and Wales (as well as the Teaching Council for Scotland, established in 1965). These organizations were to link with the National College for School Leadership, the DfEE and DENI, the Northern Ireland Education Department, to orchestrate a more strategic, and yet flexible and universally accessible, professional development programme for teachers. Such an entitlement had been judged as needing to be career-long in its duration and tailored for its appropriateness to career phases. The GTCs 'will be well placed to represent the profession in relation to professional development and to shape future policy' (para. 7) and the National College for School Leadership would provide the framework and opportunities for leadership development for heads and a widening leadership spine in schools. The support was to have a wide reach too, the needs of individuals, schools and national strategic priorities impacting upon emerging forms and processes of professional development.

Targeted support, then, was designed to be at the heart of the tranche of professional development opportunities to be made available. What was centrally placed was the idea of a career-long structured programme for individuals which would, in turn, nourish school development and progress national plans for improvements in teaching and learning. It was linked visibly with the national quest for improved standards in education and the component parts which were seen to constitute this.

Figure 14.1 outlines the nature and sources of support available to teachers in the years since the 1970s. It was essentially piecemeal. Figure 14.2 develops the final part of Figure 14.1, outlining what the years 2000–10 might hold in this area. The facets of professional development projected here were shaped significantly by the General Teaching Council for England's (GTCe) document, *Continuing Professional Development: Advice to Government* (December 2000). It was the result of consultation processes of its Professional Development Advisory Group. This group consulted 1,000 teachers, the Subject and Specialist Associations and the Teacher Associations. Its thinking was also influenced by professional development 'in other professions and by international comparison' (p. 1). The advice was proffered to any government in power keen to seek out effective and satisfying professional development for its teachers.

```
┌─────────────────────────────────────────────┐
│  1970s                                        │
│          School / LEA / HMI based training    │
├─────────────────────────────────────────────┤
│       Higher Education Institutions – Awards  │
├─────────────────────────────────────────────┤
│  1980s                                        │
│       GEST – Higher Education Institutions /  │
│          LEA / School 'Baker' Days            │
├─────────────────────────────────────────────┤
│  1990s                                        │
│                    INSET                      │
│                    GEST                       │
│                    HEIs                       │
│                                               │
│         Training and Enterprise Councils      │
│            Teacher Training Agency            │
├─────────────────────────────────────────────┤
│              Investors in People              │
│          National Standards for Teachers      │
│               The Standards Fund              │
└─────────────────────────────────────────────┘
```

Figure 14.1 The emergence of professional development for teachers

Notes

GEST = DfEE-funded grants for education support and training
HEIs = higher education institutions
INSET = in-service education for teachers.

```
┌─────────────────────────────────────────────┐
│  1990s                                        │
│                    INSET                      │
│                    GEST                       │
│                    HEIs                       │
│                                               │
│         Training and Enterprise Councils      │
│            Teacher Training Agency            │
│              Investors in People              │
│          National Standards for Teachers      │
│               The Standards Fund              │
├─────────────────────────────────────────────┤
│  2000–10                                      │
│     •  New National Framework for teaching    │
│        standards                              │
│     •  National and school strategic planning │
│     •  Context-dependent professional         │
│        development                            │
│     •  Collective professional development    │
│     •  EO entitlement and contractual         │
│        obligation to CPD                      │
│     •  Career-long and phase-linked           │
│        professional development               │
│     •  Sabbaticals: funded opportunities to   │
│        work beyond classroom and school       │
│     •  Short secondments to share expertise   │
│        of a school or individual              │
│     •  ICT-infused professional development   │
│     •  CPD on-line                            │
└─────────────────────────────────────────────┘
```

Figure 14.2 A potential professional development scenario for teachers 2000–10

Source: Developing Blandford 2000: 65.

In projected scenarios made during 2000–1, sources of support were seen by government as being available from outside the perimeters of the education world: business, industry, voluntary organizations, consultants and professional associations were all presented in the consultation and national strategy documents as equal partners in the projected education and training processes, alongside more expected higher education providers. This development produced lively debates from HE institutions, attempting to map out future roles in relation to this national strategy (Furlong 2000). One major implication of systematic and comprehensive professional development, to be offered to teachers within official working hours, a situation existing in other major employing organizations and long-demanded by teachers' professional associations, presented itself. This related to providing cover for colleagues undergoing education and training opportunities. Such provision inevitably involved disruption of various kinds. Teachers and schools were asked to devise 'innovative approaches' so that development could be 'grounded … [to] build upon what is working well at the moment' (DfEE 2000a: 5, para. 12). Revealed as a core idea in the framework was that professional development needed to begin during the induction period of newly qualified teachers and support them in a phased way throughout their working career. The hope was that 'this targeted support will help NQTs to give their best to pupils from the start and thus raise classroom standards' … since … 'our significant investment in the support and training of every new teacher also reflects our belief in the necessity of a firm foundation for longer term professional development' (ibid: 5, para. 9).

The argument offered in *Professional Development* (and taken up in the 2001 national strategy) was that strong professional growth requires a number of key elements in order to impact directly and positively upon improved teaching and learning in the classroom. These five elements were referred to earlier in this section. Two final points remain to be made here. In whatever ways the detail of the consultation document is refined and re-shaped in the implementation years of the national strategy (this latter document spoke of having 'continued the dialogue' (ibid: 1)), it appears likely that the core elements of the proposed rationale and framework will remain since they align so strongly with other key features of the educational agenda visible in the last decade of the twentieth century. It is notable, too, that the five core principles of the DfEE's *Professional Development* consultation document are congruent with the GTCe's advice relating to CPD issues to governments in power during the next decade and beyond.

Figure 14.3 (overleaf), taken from *Teachers: Meeting the Challenge of Change*, the original driver for the national strategy for professional development, sets out the kind of successful practical partnerships it is possible to secure when staff at all levels in a school work together in a common purpose: to raise achievement and to achieve other professional development gains at the same time.

This common purpose was further supported by a Code of Practice which was to be widely distributed, outlining issues relating to quality, to providers of development and training where schools felt in need of them (this was renamed *Good Value CPD* in its final form (DfEE 2001d)). Not acceptable were scatter-gun techniques of content and delivery. External providers, where employed by schools, would be expected to 'prepare effectively' and agree the success criteria of the developmental activity proposed. They were required to 'deliver good provision informed by recent

Clapton School gained Investors in People recognition in November 1996. The school, which caters for girls from diverse ethnic and religious backgrounds, decided to go for Investors in People to motivate all its staff to increase their professionalism and skills; consolidate and extend their staff development programme; help develop a corporate identity; and raise achievement. There was strong commitment from the headteacher and the Senior Management Team who believe that staff development equates to school development. The benefits include:

- performance reviews for support staff
- an identified budget share to enhance support staff training
- awareness of the need to set measurable targets
- awareness of the need to monitor and evaluate progress
- a willingness to improve
- an in-house Management Development Programme
- the development of a community of learners working with a common objective

In 1997, Clapton School came second in the Observer's national school league. Headteacher Cheryl Day said, 'The school has undoubtedly improved for staff and pupils alike since we became recognized as an Investor in People. Our in-house Management Development Programme has significantly improved the skills and professionalism of all staff. The children have reaped the benefits.'

Figure 14.3 Clapton School, East London

Source: DfEE1998: 57.

research' and by 'those with expertise, using high quality materials'. The Code went further: providers would evaluate achievements in improving pupil learning' (DfEE 2000a: 23, para. 68), in conjunction with the school and staff being developed (DfEE 2001d: para. 17). Innovative approaches, using ICT in its many forms, were welcomed. Central to all of these points about quality was that the dissemination of success and the means to effecting it were viewed as crucial and effective tools for the professional development of teachers and the progress of pupils in schools.

Defining high-quality provision

The 1980s' model of dissemination, too often a form of 'cascading', was, by common consent in the profession, only patchily successful. Not unusually, it involved one colleague attending an external course who then was nominated as responsible for disseminating the experience, outcomes and potential applications to colleagues and pupils, often in what was called a 'twilight' session at the end of a work day. This responsibility was placed upon the deputed colleague whether sufficiently skilled and motivated to do this or not, usually with a reduced range of equipment and diluted resources, and irrespective of the quality of the provided course. The 'cascading' method and its rationale (it was relatively inexpensive, functional and appeared potentially effective) clearly had very little in common with the rationale of the documents referred to in this chapter. In these more contemporary publications, in contrast, the views presented were that: professional development is crucial to pupil progress; this was important to all staff throughout their careers in order to nurture professional growth and common understandings and concerns with colleagues; and quality outcomes involve serious financial investment by schools, supported by increased and sustained government funding.

David Reynolds has sketched out his views about some of the major obstacles which have denied strong continuing professional development in the UK. They confirm some of the ideas and issues raised so far in this chapter and present additional ones. He maintains that:

- teachers' capacity to participate in CPD has depended partly on their school's ability to pay for them to attend courses, on the availability of provision within travelling distance of their homes/schools and on the particular definitions of local universities and colleges about what courses to offer;
- there has been no attempt to ensure that provision reflected any coherent definition of the behaviours, attributes and characteristics that were necessary for teachers to do their jobs at different stages of their professional life cycle or career, informed by an educational research community focusing on issues related to teacher effectiveness and the characteristics associated with it;
- provision historically has moved its focus from one major concern to another, with the conventional concentration upon upgrading of subject knowledge of the 1970s and 1980s replaced by a concentration upon school management, school administration and school effectiveness in the 1990s;
- whole areas of educational knowledge that would be on offer as CPD to teachers in other countries have remained absent in the UK, particularly important being the area of teacher effectiveness, what is called in the United States 'instructional effectiveness', which can generate high-quality professional development opportunities in the theory and practice of teaching and learning;

(Adapted from www. gtce.org.uk)

Professor Reynolds goes further and usefully outlines the 'foundations' UK teachers need to be aware of in order to make best use of professional development opportunities. He cites them as needing to include:

- the teaching behaviours that are important in generating effective classrooms, not simply in the limited area of the management of the class, but the behaviours involved in the teaching of the class that have been addressed much less frequently;
- the questioning ability of teachers in terms of the quantity, quality and appropriateness of their questions to individuals and groups;
- teachers' ability to manage learning time, since time is the most precious resource possessed in education, after competent teachers;

- teachers' ability to keep children 'on task' for a high proportion of lesson time;
- teachers' capacity to generate high-quality review and practice from their pupils through appropriate use of individual and group work;
- teachers' clarity of presentation;
- teachers' ability to involve pupils in their learning, through exemplifying a love of their subject and a commitment to achieving high standards in it for all their pupils.

(ibid)

These guidelines are important. They represent the clear interplay of teachers' professional development in tandem with and influenced by the classroom practice issues raised in Part 2 of this book. They point also to the symbiotic and syncopated relationship between research findings and implications for classroom action and pupil participation in planned processes for achievement in teaching and learning.

Professional development and the role of the General Teaching Council

The emergence of the General Teaching Council for England in 2000, a checkered and long-overdue event, was outlined in the first chapter of this book. It will be recalled that the prime aims of the GTC were presented by that body as seeking to raise the professional status and public standing of teachers; providing an independent and influential voice for teachers; and maintaining and guaranteeing high professional standards of teaching.

The focus here is directed to the key concerns of this chapter: the nature and possibilities of professional development for beginning and other teachers. Many stakeholders in education expressed high hopes for the GTC (whether for England, for Wales or for Scotland). The balance of influence and power it eventually wields will be crucial for professional development needs and a renewal of the notion of 'professional' when describing teachers' roles in education. Whether it matures finally as a notably regulatory body of teachers or predominantly as a nurturing, supportive input to their professional lives, and perceptions of these professional lives by parents, government and pupils, will not be known for some years. Its proponents argue that a balance of these two functions will be feasible as well as desirable.

So what 'Making a difference for teachers', promised by Carol Adams, its first Chief Executive on its own website, will eventually mean in specific terms will depend upon matters which impacted greatly in the late 1990s. Political will, electoral change or continuity, the economic climate, future developments in relation to Ofsted and the TTA, teachers' responses to changing professional and cultural domains, and revised definitions relating to new standards of 'effectiveness' gradually emerging in the early years of the twenty-first century, will all impact further upon it.

What is clearly visible is the view, held by teachers' employers, that any professional development will be personally enriching for the participant but that what must have premier weight in any consideration of funding of development proposals are the gains available for pupils and the progress and achievements they might secure in their learning as a result of it. Improved performance will be more possible, it is argued, where better rewards and better support for teachers' work are forthcoming. Further, the improved status ensuing from this will, in turn, it is maintained, benefit recruitment and retention and offer a sound career path to those graduates who often have rejected teaching for reasons of materially poorer rewards and perceptions about its declining social status in contrast to other career options available to them.

It was argued in an earlier chapter that 'professions' have usually owned a degree of autonomy, have been self-regulating, publicly accountable bodies and associated with long periods of study-training, ultimately demonstrating a set of skills and understandings not widely possessed. Recent decades of external regulation of teachers and regularly voiced criticisms from public, and at times, politically shaped quarters produced both the fear and the hope that the GTC would have a regulatory function. The fear related to the extension of politically determined opinions and agendas into the organization. The hope was that the independence of the GTC would emerge strongly so that beginning teachers, especially, can have a real prospect of the promises about rewards, status and support for teaching and learning that have been espoused so regularly in recent years. In short: that the challenge to turn rhetoric into reality, taken up as an issue itself by the government in the 1998 Green Paper and voiced in the election debates of 2001, will materialize.

The role of the GTC in professional development: regulation and support

The debates about professional development were set in a broader context by the GTC in relation to its wider roles of regulating and supporting teachers. It is interesting that its independent regulatory function was stressed since: 'Only with effective regulation can the high status profession be maintained' (GTC website). Indeed, 'high status' and 'profession' (the key terms) are congruent with a body representing teachers and protecting and sustaining its own quality assurance procedures. A GTC operating for teachers and not upon them in terms of self-regulation issues – to include professional competence and professional growth – may be one pathway to consistently achieved professional outcomes. On its own website (www.gtce.org.uk), accessed on 27 November 2000, the GTC proposed to ensure that:

- the high standards of the many are not jeopardized by the few
- the status of the teaching profession is maintained in the eyes of the public
- children continue to receive the best educational opportunity.

These, and other areas related to the regulatory function of the GTC, were reviewed in Chapter 1, as was the changing role of teachers' traditional professional associations. The focus here is on the support function of the GTC in relation to the professional growth and related status elements of teachers.

On this site, key questions were offered to support all teachers in thinking about the concept and practice of professional development. These were:

- What kinds of professional development activities have proved to be most useful to you in stimulating and changing how you think about your own and others' practice of teaching?
- Should teachers think more like researchers?
- Do you make effective use of current research in 'effective teaching' and, if so, how do you access what's useful to you?
- What is the right balance between 'local' solutions and 'international' solutions, based on 'what works' elsewhere?

It presented, too, the following statement and accompanying questions to teachers to prompt them further in their thinking about their professional lives and growth within it:

> Research on the outcomes of professional development indicates that the most effective provision, ie, that which leads to sustainable change and improved practice, mobilises the values teachers hold as well as addressing their skills and knowledge. Do you agree with this or not? What values impact on your own practice?

It went on to ask, 'What would a statement of entitlement to professional development need to contain?'

British teachers, accustomed in recent years to an increase in externally imposed strategies, initiatives and directed course content, as well as a pronounced accent on skills and knowledge, will note the mention of values and links with research findings and professional development. It was an interesting change of accent and, arguably, one increasingly finding a mirror in officially emerging standards of what 'teacher effectiveness' was deemed to encompass. This point is taken up again in the final section of this chapter.

Reading 14.1 is a case study offered by the GTC. The exemplar was espoused as containing many key facets of the kind of productive professional development operating within a flexible learning organization – here, Adderley Primary School in Birmingham. Suitably contextualized, for primary or secondary application, and clearly able to be so, it was designed to offer support to teachers moving incrementally, as individuals and as members of teams, towards their own answers to the questions posed above.

Comments

This account of continuing professional development-in-action is a revealing one. It could almost be taken as a model of the widely flanked considerations described in *Professional Development: Support for Teaching and Learning*. The professional development described at Adderley is organic, not piecemeal, and it involves pupils in an active role. Flexibility, the management of change, and routinely applied evaluations, inform future professional development at the school. The sharing of expertise and of responsibility is threaded through the chosen activities of the school and pupil progress is at the heart of everything important that happens there.

Reading 14.1 Working towards a model of individual and school ownership of professional development

(The school is in an area of social and economic deprivation. It serves a local community where pupils are mostly of Asian heritage. The school has on roll 460 pupils. Usha Devi also has responsibility at Adderley for professional development, ITT and induction.)

All teachers would agree that high quality continuing professional development (CPD) is the key to ensuring individuals are equipped to meet the varied demands made upon them. Effective professional development has an underlying philosophy that develops intellect and creates learning communities where teachers can share expertise. It raises the standard of teaching and learning by having a direct impact upon classroom practice. This broad definition of CPD teaches individuals how to learn and promotes a culture where CPD is not an event but a process that takes into account the complexity of teacher knowledge and how this can be further developed.

A process-based approach encourages teachers to reflect upon their practice and constantly learn and develop from their teaching experience. This approach also encourages schools to evaluate their professional development and ensure it evolves to meet the changing needs of all the individuals within the establishment.

I am fortunate to work in a school where this process-based approach is a reality. At Adderley Primary, CPD is recognized as a priority within the school and supported by employees at all levels. The School Development Plan is written under the headings of Birmingham's seven processes of school improvement, one of which is staff development. Individual curriculum action plans also follow the same principle and identify opportunities for training and support.

The school's governing body has a strong commitment to staff training and development. It approves the funding required to maintain high staffing and to enable staff to participate in professional development activities and focus on pupil performance and standards. All staff are released from class for one afternoon a week to engage in monitoring and professional development activities. These activities change on a regular basis based on the objectives of the School Development Plan and teachers' individual learning plans. In the past year activity has involved monitoring standards, individual conferences with pupils, team teaching, visiting other schools, monitoring pupil progress in specific subjects and teaching in a different key stage.

There is an emphasis upon developing and sharing expertise amongst the Adderley team through a range of internal and external activities. Ongoing professional development for all staff is provided through workshops, involvement in school improvement projects, meetings, school visits, team teaching, class observations and courses. All members of the school management team also have a responsibility for staff development and training and lead 'learning teams' where members can share and develop expertise in a particular area or subject.

A flexible and creative staffing structure within the school also encourages individuals to work in a variety of different ways and disseminate good practice. For instance, we have non-class based literacy and numeracy curriculum leaders who operate as consultants in the school. They demonstrate, coach, lead and monitor standards across the school and provide training that meets the individual needs of staff and the children. They give specific feedback to all staff on a regular basis. They also ensure everyone is kept up to date with current developments and research into new teaching and learning techniques through oral and written reports.

Ongoing evaluations are important aspects of CPD at Adderley. Evaluations ensure staff development and training remains relevant, effective and continues to contribute to the achievement of the school's aims and priorities. The School Management Team regularly reviews CPD during the SWOT (strengths, weaknesses, opportunities and threats) analysis of the school. The headteacher holds regular meetings with learning support assistants, lunchtime supervisors and administrative staff, and I hold regular meetings with new staff to the school. All staff complete a course pro forma and assess the new learning they have acquired and how this will have an impact on teaching and learning.

This broad definition of CPD however, does not appear to be common amongst all schools. If teachers had to define CPD, their response would depend upon where they teach and the priority their school places on staff development and training. This is not an ideal situation, it does not encourage teachers to take ownership of their development or engage in life-long learning.

A commitment to staff development from the governing body and the School Management team is the first step in creating effective CPD opportunities for all staff. Schools need to become creative and flexible organizations that give staff the confidence to use their initiative and share their skills and expertise.

There needs to be a cultural shift in schools and a move away from a narrow and restricted definition of CPD. Teaching is a highly skilled and demanding profession that requires a broader definition of professional development to ensure that individuals are not only able meet the needs of the learner but also their own developmental and learning needs. This broader definition would also encourage providers and schools to develop sophisticated mechanisms for delivering and sustaining a range of CPD opportunities.

Creative organizations within schools and between schools can provide a wide range of professional development opportunities that can meet individual, school and national priorities. Engaging in research, working in partnership with educational establishments, visiting other schools, team teaching, observing others, mentoring, inter-agency partnerships, leading a project and working in a team are just some of the ways that teachers can develop new skills and knowledge.

Adderley is a learning community for staff as well as pupils. The philosophy of learning and sharing expertise together is shared by all staff and forms the foundation for effective CPD. We value each other's skills, expertise and strengths and constantly reflect on the impact we have on children, the progress they make, and the standards they achieve.

As teachers, we have profound impacts every day on our pupils' emergent intellectual and emotional lives. We are only too aware of the responsibility we have to inspire. Access to high quality professional development is a prerequisite for remaining inspired and inspiring. The following quote summarizes the impact a teacher has on children and emphasizes the importance of high quality professional development that inspires high standards of teaching and learning, professional conduct and reflective practice. Using the words of Ginott (1972),

> it is a school where individuals have come to the frightening conclusion that: I am the decisive element in the classroom. It is my personal approach that creates the climate. It is my daily mood that makes the weather. As a teacher I possess tremendous power to make a child's life miserable or joyous. I can be a tool of torture or an instrument of inspiration. I can humiliate or torture, hurt or heal. In all situations it is my response that decides whether a crisis will be escalated or de-escalated, a child humanised or dehumanised.

Our children deserve highly skilled and talented professionals who are able to keep up to date with educational changes through high quality planned professional development.

Source: Usha Devi, GTC Council Member and Deputy Head Adderley Primary School, Birmingham.

A distinct sense of the formidable importance of a teacher's role during every school day is plain, in Ginott's words or those of teachers in this school: 'to hurt or heal' the individual and society.

Day (1999: 131) reminds us of both the distinction and the interplay of education and training, a relevant issue here.

The exemplar material on professional development supplied by the GTC, such as that above, is notable in terms both of vision and practicality. There was, though, a recognition too that many teachers as individuals and as members of teams would want to begin anew with their professional development planning. Basic questions might be best in such a context. The GTC's own Professional Development Advisory Group may well do the same. Typical core questions about professional development might emerge on similar lines as those shown below.

- What are the aims of continuing professional development?
- What constitutes effective professional development?
- Which models of continuing professional development and opportunities do you think all teachers should have access to?
- How can continuing professional development build the capacity of teachers and schools to deliver improvement for pupils and build learning organizations?
- How should continuing professional development best draw on other teachers' expertise?
- How can continuing professional development give every teacher access to a network of professionals, in and beyond their school, with whom they can engage in innovation, develop knowledge and extend teaching skills?
- How can an entitlement to high quality professional development contribute to recruitment and retention in the profession?
- How can the role of teachers in monitoring and assuring the quality of CPD provision best be developed?

(www.gtce.org.uk)

One could add to this set of starter questions, but it is interesting that even these eight range widely over the central areas of individual development, network development, recruitment and retention issues, as well as access issues, pupil achievement and the very nature and purposes of professional development itself.

Professional development opportunities

There has been no shortage of ideas about what kinds of professional development opportunities could be productive to teachers during their career. It is certain that the detail and the formats of these will change as they become subject to implementation, evaluation and modification processes. Nevertheless, though names and formats will change, the ideas at their core represent opportunities available to meet the kinds of teaching, learning, team-building and personal growth needs indicated in this chapter.

By 2001, for example, there were six DfEE-funded professional development opportunities for teachers to access, tied to time-cost reference points. They were:

- allocations of about £3,000 for a Best Practice Research Scholarship
- two-week study visits abroad through the Teachers' International Professional Development scheme to learn from good practice and assess potential for adaptation
- £500 professional bursaries, for a chosen professional development activity
- sabbaticals of up to six-week periods, initially for teachers with experience in challenging schools
- early professional development for teachers in their second and third years of teaching, building on the experience of the induction year

- Individual Learning Accounts giving discounts of up to £200 a year off courses and other learning opportunities.

A head of a MFL department in an upper school in Bedfordhire provides some detail to explain of what a 'Best Practice Research Scholarship' might entail:

> A lot of research has been done in maths, geography and science, in applying thinking skills to students and their learning but there hasn't been much work done on languages. I'm interested in seeing if improving thinking skills can help improve the cognitive and communicative ability of my students. I have found that what I have learnt is already starting to have some impact in the classroom.
>
> I have received £3,350 over a year to do this and have attended sessions on visible thinking and mind-mapping. I've been on day-long and weekend residential courses and have enjoyed them immensely. Leading academics in the field are also there to help out.
>
> It has been brilliant for my professional development .... It has been particularly good that I have been able to apply what I've learnt to the classroom and that I have been able to develop networks outside of my own school environment.
>
> (DfEE, 2001b: 8)

During the induction year into teaching, an NQT will receive guidance and tutoring in relation to teaching and learning, class and school life, and professional development provision aligned to targets agreed, with an experienced mentor. The opportunities outlined above are designed to mesh appropriately with career development and need.

In addition to the development opportunities suggested here are the training and education schedules required of schools in responding to national initiatives (for example, the Key Stage 3 strategy, described in Chapter 4) or those linked to school or LEA development plans, for which funding is additionally allocated. Headteachers are ultimately responsible for organizing these schedules, usually within the contractual five days' allocation per year for their staff, and for the training and development needs identified in, for example, appraisal procedures relating to their staff.

In 2001, the General Teaching Council made known its view about entitlement to professional development opportunities, stressing that teachers must have access to a full range of CPD activity within the working year. In addition, they must, too, have the opportunity:

- for building and sharing expertise
- to develop the deep knowledge and values of professionals, beyond technical competence
- of access to a full range of developmental activity within the working year, to include:
  - training for the implementation of new initiatives
  - courses, including those which are award-bearing
  - learning in teams and with a more experienced teacher

- in-depth peer exchange/review of knowledge and skills within and outside of school
- research, critical enquiry and investigation
- distance or 'virtual learning'
- specialist, pedagogical and subject knowledge enrichment opportunities.

Team-working as well as individual endeavour are clearly a part of these processes. As well as needing formal leaders, such teams require participants who are able and willing to develop their own leadership potential within them. There has, indeed, been a growing recognition that leadership potential must be accessed in the early years of a teacher's career. A more customary view of effective school leadership, represented by having one principal leader only, positioned at the apex of a hierarchical pyramid within a school, has been replaced by a felt need for a broader leadership structure and for team-working formats where it is the norm for many participants to take leadership roles at appropriate times, using skills and understandings to benefit the development activity of different groups. The need to make as well as to take professional development opportunities suggests in the future a much more active role for beginning teachers who might rapidly find that they are comfortable with leadership roles of a particular kind (not least in terms of ICT skills and interests, for example, as was suggested in Chapter 7).

CPD and leadership potential for a broader swathe of teachers

Blandford's outline of the scope of professional development for teachers in schools (Blandford 2000) confirms that this is both challenging and multi-faceted. Through its processes, colleagues will potentially be able to:

- develop and adapt their range of practice
- reflect on their experience, research and practice in order to meet pupil needs, collectively and individually
- contribute to the professional life of the school
- keep in touch with current educational thinking in order to maintain and develop good practice
- give critical consideration to educational policy, in particular on how to raise standards
- widen their understanding of society, in particular of information and communication technology (ICT).

(Blandford 2000: 5)

Cautionary notes

A warning note to a full-steam-ahead approach is, however, provided by Fullan (1991: 49) in *The New Meaning of Educational Change*. He argues that schools experience multiple innovations (and the drive for systematic professional development as one part of performance management might be seen from a particular perspective as one such), but that only at individual and team level can integrations be managed and made meaningful in terms of teaching and learning. In *Continuing Professional Development*, Craft adds a note of hesitation, too, in relation to commonly expressed purposes of professional development (Craft 2000: 197). Craft refers critically to other writers such as Joyce and Showers (1988) who use a 'competitive framework' argument for professional development and its role in supporting pupils to enter a demanding and volatile economic market. Craft argues that these writers' views might, ironically, be taken to be too circumscribed and unambitious. What is clear, however, is that competing expectations by multiple audiences in relation to the professional development of teachers, and the visible results of it in classrooms, will continue to make themselves felt.

Hay McBer's 'Model of Teacher Effectiveness'

The Hay McBer *Model of Teacher Effectiveness* (Hay McBer 2000), referred to in Part 1 of this book, described one such set of expectations. This report, generated through a government-funded research project, was designed to tease out the kinds of things that effective teachers actually do, the ways in which they do them, and the links between effective teaching skills, professional characteristics and the 'classroom climate' that were associated with them. Planned-for and targeted professional development was seen as a constituent part of what effective teachers need to do.

In this Phase II Report, confidence-building and the accumulative edging towards new professional development agendas and proven paths to securing them were promoted. Effective teachers were seen as a force for 'transformation', all having leadership potential. And teachers currently in leadership positions were reminded that they could 'very usefully reflect on how to deploy a repertoire of leadership styles when working with their colleagues' (ibid: 86). What was equally clear is the expectation that all teachers would do a great deal more than 'facilitate' enquiry: they would help to lead and appear visibly as leaders in the classroom (ibid: 28), demonstrating a passion for learning (ibid: 29). They would respond flexibly to new approaches, adapting them to the learning context (ibid) and be committed to holding people accountable (ibid). Continuing professional development was seen as being at the heart of such processes. The radical changes implied here took up the vision of teachers of the twenty-first century evoked in other sources with which this chapter began. 'Star teachers' would work together with the result that their practices would become the norm:

> The star teachers of the twenty-first century will be those who work together to infuse their ideas into standard practice. They will be teachers who collaborate to build a system that has the goal of improving pupils' learning in the 'average' classroom, who work for the continual improvement of classroom practice. In a true profession, the wisdom of the profession's members finds its way into the most common methods, the best that we know becomes the standard way of doing something. The star teachers of the twenty-first century will be teachers who work every day to improve teaching – not only their own but that of the whole profession.
>
> (Hay McBer 2000: 110)

These 'star teachers', reminiscent of the 1993 NCE vision of teachers who 'have the capacity to think deeply about educational aims and values', referred to at the beginning of this chapter, would be rewarded commensurately (as Advanced Skills Teachers, the leader-learners of the profession, or at the least as an acknowledged multi-skilled, flexible and experienced Threshold Teacher).

And arising out of this was the strongly expressed expectation that teachers would need to continue to learn while they teach, since:

> this reminds them of what it is like to be a learner, and helps them develop their own skills and characteristics. This helps them to empathise with pupils and models the importance of continuous lifelong learning. In this way the school becomes a genuine learning community with a vibrancy and liveliness about it.
>
> (ibid: 24)

Re-shapings of the findings and the views presented in this Report will no doubt occur in the first decade of this century. It is an argument, though, that the agenda of change and the cultural shifts voiced in the Green Papers of 1998 and 2001 and in many other locations, as well as the key official publications relating to professional development referred to in this chapter, will have far-reaching impacts on professional learning, professional growth and the appraisal processes connected with performance management in schools. There is no doubt that these issues and their practical re-workings in schools will impact dynamically upon the working lives and professional development of beginning teachers. A mapping-out of career and professional development is made more possible in today's educational context than ever before; the more limited and happen-chance development and career opportunities available are to be increasingly replaced by new structures and more flexible routeways.

Currently, leadership and learning (and the strong connection between the two is made by Fullan and the core documents examined in this chapter) might focus profitably on central teaching and learning issues such as: supporting pupils' transfer from primary to secondary education; maintaining and developing teachers' subject knowledge; monitoring and identifying effective components of subject department and whole-school meetings; assessing the impact of improving school community links, particularly with parents; investigating strategies for improving pupils' and teachers' ICT skills; improving school attendance; identifying and developing productive cross-curricular links and study-support strategies. These are merely a few of many possible school-based projects available to individuals working in teams. organizing such initiatives and supporting them through meaningful professional development activity will, of course, require focused strategic inputs from the more broadly based leadership teams to be found now in schools. Quite simply, it is envisaged that greater numbers of teachers will lead in these areas. In addition, one of the key functions of broader leadership teams (and payment spines) will be to mesh curriculum development, pedagogy and staff development with systematic management and evaluation procedures and processes. This is not to say, of course, that professional development programmes which are found not to be successful in terms of their primary participants (teachers) or their recipients at one remove (pupils) are not to be valued or tried in a different context, or tried again. Moon (2000) usefully reminds us of Bruner's point about identity and self-esteem:

> The management of (these) is never simple and never settled, and its state is powerfully affected by the availability of supports from outside. These supports are hardly mysterious or exotic. They include such homely resorts as a second chance, honour for a good if unsuccessful try, but above all a chance for discourse that permits one to find out why, or how things didn't work out as planned.
>
> (Bruner 1996: 37)

Conclusion

Many questions relating to plans for career-long professional development remain for teachers and providers; it is an unfolding story and one contingent upon political as well as educational factors. The GTC joined its voice to that of the government in seeing both regulation and support as important factors in the process of what might be termed the re-professionalizing of teachers. Professional development is one aspect of the strategic design and drive to a formal modernization agenda. Managing this agenda will challenge all the interested parties. The systematic application of the central threads of the 1998 and 2001 Green Papers, better leadership and rewards, better training and better support, will, its advocates suggest, produce a better-equipped and more highly regarded professional group. The clear argument is that an enlarged public regard will ensue from higher standards of formal achievement by pupils in schools. The 'new possibilities' of training and development are exciting ones. It remains to be seen the degree to which these can be secured within the competitive cut and thrust of the market economy. If the promises of rhetoric can be realized, the possession of sharpened rather than blunt tools by all teachers will undeniably represent an excellent point of progress. And beginning teachers must be actively encouraged to be confident participants in this unfolding process, using these tools with both precision and creativity.

References

Blandford, S. (2000) *Managing Professional Development in Schools,* London: Routledge.

Brighouse, T. and Woods, D, (1999) *How to Improve Your School,* London: Routledge.

Bruner, J. (1996) *The Culture of Education*, Cambridge, MA: Harvard University Press.

Covey, S.R. (1999) *The Seven Habits of Highly Effective People,* London: Simon and Schuster.

Craft, A. (2000, 2nd edition) *Continuing Professional Development: A Practical Guide for Teachers and Schools*, London: RoutledgeFalmer in association with The Open University.

Day, C. (1999) *Developing Teachers: The Challenges of Lifelong Learning*, London: Falmer.

DfEE (1997) *Excellence in Schools*, London: DfEE.

—— (1998) *Teachers: Meeting the Challenge of Change,* London: DfEE.

—— (1999) *Teachers Meeting the Challenge of Change: Technical Consultation Document on Pay and Performance Management*, London: DfEE.

—— (2000) Archive of responses to consultation document, *Professional Development: Support for Teaching and Learning (2000)*, London: DfEE.

—— (2000a) *Professional Development: Support for Teaching and Learning*, London: DfEE.

——(2001b) *Learning and Teaching: A Strategy for Professional Development*, London: DfEE.

—— (2001c) *Schools: Building on Success*, London: DfEE.

—— (2001d) *Good Value CPD: A Code of Practice for Providers of Professional Development for Teachers*, London: DfEE.

Fullan, M.G. (1991) *The New Meaning of Educational Change*, London: Cassell.

Furlong, J. (2000) *Teacher Education in Transition: Re-forming Professionalism?* Buckingham: Open University Press.

Hay McBer (2000) *Research into Teacher Effectiveness, Phase II Report*, June.

Joyce, B. and Showers, B. (1998) *Student Achievement through Staff Development*, New York: Longman.

Lave, J. and Wenger, E. (1991) *Situated Learning: Legitimate Peripheral Participation*, Cambridge: Cambridge University Press.

Moon, B. (2000) 'The changing agenda for professional development in education' in B. Moon, J. Butcher and E. Bird (2000) *Leading Professional Development in Education,* London: RoutledgeFalmer in association with The Open University.

National Commission on Education (1993) *Learning to Succeed: A Radical Look at Education Today*, London: Heinemann for the Paul Hamlyn Foundation.

Storey, A. (2000) 'A leap of faith? Performance pay for teachers' *Journal of Education Policy* 15(5): 509–23.

Teacher Training Agency (2000) *Deputy/headteachers' Views on Accessing and Using Research and Evidence – Results of a Pilot Survey*, London: TTA.

—— (2000) *Improving Standards: Research and Evidence Based Practice*, London: TTA.

Index